GREEN ROOFS
in Sustainable
Landscape Design

GREEN ROOFS
in Sustainable Landscape Design

STEVEN L. CANTOR

FOREWORD BY STEVEN PECK

W. W. NORTON & COMPANY
New York • London

NOTE: The projects presented in this book reflect the accumulated wisdom of professionals in many fields. Although it is hoped that the reader will be stimulated by the information to pursue a course of study that might result in the implementation of some innovative green roof designs, the material in this book is nonetheless only an introduction to a new field. Furthermore, each project is unique and responds to specific requirements of its program, site, and budget. Therefore, do not try to copy or adapt any of the designs herein without acquiring a thorough understanding of green roof technology and without consulting appropriate experts.

Page 1: The moss sedum green roof (Xero Flor Type XF300c) at Amsterdam's airport. The vegetation reaches a maximum height of only about 1.2 inches (30 mm). See Chapter Four for a discussion of this project. (Courtesy of Mostert De Winter BV, the Netherlands).

Pages 2–3: Perennials at the Lurie Garden, part of the intensive green roof at Millenium Park Chicago. The dark frame in the background supports hedge materials which will form the Shoulder Hedge, a strong edge to the garden. See Chapter Five for a discussion of this project. (Courtesy of Perrie Schad)

Page 3: Plants in various containers being laid out at the Minneapolis Library in preparation for planting on the extensive green roof. See Chapter Three for a discussion of this project. (Courtesy of the Kestrel Group Inc.)

Copyright © 2008 by Steven L. Cantor
Foreword copyright © 2008 by Steven Peck

All rights reserved
Printed in Singapore
First Edition

For information about permission to reproduce selections from this book, write to Permissions, W. W. Norton & Company, Inc., 500 Fifth Avenue, New York, NY 10110

Production Manager: Leeann Graham
Book design by Gilda Hannah
Manufacturing by Chroma Graphics/KHL Printing

Library of Congress Cataloging-in-Publication Data

Cantor, Steven L.
   Green roofs in sustainable landscape design / Steven L. Cantor;
foreword by Steven Peck.
      p. cm.
   Includes bibliographical references, appendices, and index.
   ISBN 978-0-393-73168-2 (hardcover)
      1. Green roofs (Gardening) 2. Green roofs (Gardening)—Design and
construction. I. Title.
   SB419.5.C36 2008
   635.9'671—dc22

W. W. Norton & Company, Inc.,
500 Fifth Avenue, New York, N.Y. 10110
www.wwnorton.com

W. W. Norton & Company Ltd.,
Castle House, 75/76 Wells St.,
London W1T 3QT

0 9 8 7 6 5 4 3 2 1

To the memory of my mother,

Betty Goldstein Cantor,

the first person I knew with a thumb so green

that a garden blossomed at her touch.

ACKNOWLEDGMENTS

I am particularly grateful to experts who reviewed sections of the book. These include Charlie Miller (Chapters 1, 2, and 3, and parts of Chapter 6), Stephan Brenneisen (Chapter 1), and Steven Peck (Chapters 1 and 2).

Some of the material in Chapter 2 was developed as a result of sharing a seminar on green roof design with Colin Cheney and Angie Durhman of Earthpledge, in which I was grateful to participate. I am most appreciative of the thorough review of the plant list for intensive green roofs by Mark Davies, horticulturalist, in Chapter 3, and the plant list for extensive green roofs by Ed Snodgrass, and their comments on the text on plant materials.

I thank Margaret Ryan for her copyediting and Nancy Green, Andrea Costella, Vani Kannan, and Kristen Holt-Browning at W. W. Norton for their patience, tireless energy, and dedication to this project.

I thank Shane Luitjens, graphic designer, for his skills in formatting many of the digital images, and Eric Farber of Duggal for his expert guidance in the preparation of many prints and digital scans.

I thank the following for their comments, suggestions, or assistance: Michael Alicia, Deborah and Tom Bauer, Christopher Bram, Karen Brown, Eva Chiamulera, Justin Crocker, John Freeman, Jessica Katz, Margaret O'Brien, Luke H. Sandford, Cedric Tolley, and Hope Wright.

I thank Richard Kula for his review comments on the LEED process.

I thank Anne Marie Edden, Sergey Chudin, Richard Garcia, Leslie Peoples, Edward Schnell, Gary Sorge, and Jon Stocker of Stantec Consulting, New York City.

I thank the Central Branch and Park Slope Branch of the Brooklyn Public Library and the Deborah, Jonathan F. P., Samuel Priest, and Adam R. Rose Main Reading Room at the New York Public Library.

Finally, I thank my two sisters, Sally and Diane, for their ongoing support and encouragement.

HOMAGE
by Margaret Ryan

Prairie grasses bow
in billion bladed unison
going with
earth's breath

Glory rings her bell . . .

Humble grasslands rise
to rooftops
growing *prana* in the sky

CONTENTS

FOREWORD

Roofs have been called "the fifth façade" and "the forgotten façade." Our barren rooftops have also been designated "the last urban frontier." This book clearly demonstrates that green roof technology provides an exciting and virtually endless palette of design opportunities for innovators, who can play a key role in the reinvention of miles of wasted roof space on our buildings. Malcolm Wells, a visionary architect who advocated earth sheltered buildings, green roofs, and green walls during the latter half of the twentieth century, wrote in *Recovering America: A More Gentle Way to Build* (1999), "We look at architecture the wrong way, sideways, so what we see is just a thin sliver of the reality around us. To see architecture fully, you must stand it on its edge. When you do you always see dead land on display."[1]

The emergence of the green roof industry is part of a broader transformation now underway—a move toward a new type of restorative "living architecture" that seamlessly integrates inorganic and lifeless building components with living, breathing, restorative systems. The ascendance of living architecture as the central paradigm in twenty-first-century design demands much of us beyond the recognition of rooftops as missed opportunities: for example, a more multi-disciplinary and holistic approach to building design and implementation is necessary. When designed for optimum benefit, green roofs require the shared effort and cooperation of architects, landscape architects, contractors, planners, horticulturalists, ecologists, engineers, and others. For example, the award-winning green roofs by Green Roofs for Healthy Cities are always the result of a shared, collaborative, interdisciplinary design effort.

The power to transform our cities from unhealthy, stressful, overheated environments to healthier, more sustainable communities is completely within our reach—and I believe this transformation can be achieved within a generation. The city of Chicago, with its 3 million square feet (and counting) of green roofs, and the crowning achievement of its Millennium Park, demonstrates what can be achieved in just a few short years. Green Roofs for Healthy Cities tracks the square footage of green roofs implemented annually in each city, and encourages governments to support green roof implementation through direct and indirect investment.

If we invest in the widespread establishment of green roof infrastructure over the next twenty years, the positive impact of the resulting transformation will be enormous. The greening of our rooftops brings a multitude of infrastructure benefits that can solve existing problems into which we already pour billions of public dollars each year, such as the need to reduce the pollution of lakes, estuaries and rivers by the stormwater that we discharge regularly into them. Washington D.C. and partners are currently investigating the amount of capital the city could divert from the construction and maintenance of giant end-of-pipe tunnels designed to hold stormwater, toward green roofs and urban forests, which will not only capture stormwater, but also help clean the air and cool and beautify the city. Widespread green roofs can also help address other pressing problems, such as how to generate and transport power into the hungry air conditioners that operate longer each year, as our summers become hotter and the urban heat island effect threatens to make our cities more unbearable. Green roofs can reduce energy consumption within a building itself by blocking heat gain; they also cool the surrounding buildings, acting like external air conditioners. Combined with other measures, such as street trees and reflective pavement, green roofs can help cool an entire city. Each 1.8 degree Fahrenheit reduction in summer temperatures can shave 4 percent off the peak demand for electricity, resulting in tens of millions of dollars in energy cost savings, as well as less smog and particulate matter in our air and lungs. A partial attempt to calculate the economic benefits of only 8% extensive green roof coverage by researchers at Ryerson University in Toronto found over $300 million in resulting capital savings, largely from energy efficiency and improved stormwater management, and almost $40 million annually (as an additional benefit, the beaches would stay open longer, freer from the negative impacts of stormwater).[2]

Each and every roof and wall within our cities has the potential to become a source of regeneration and healing. A central tenet of living architecture is that buildings should give back more than they take over the course of their useful lives, and green roofs are central to this assertion. Imagine our cities if each building cleansed the air and water, each and every day. Imagine if all new buildings generated a surplus of clean green energy; produced healthy, organic local food; provided passive and recreational activities; and gave back to nature a home for the many species of plants and animals that are rapidly disappearing with the construction of each new subdivision. All of this is achievable with green roof technology, which provides a greater range of benefits than any other building component.

The greening of rooftops addresses some of the central goals of the Low Impact Development and Smart Growth movements, both of which are concerned with how to design more compact and denser communities.[3] Green roofs may help reduce community opposition to infill development projects, by turning inhospitable black roofs into enjoyable community resources. Within the pages of this book you will find examples of children's playgrounds, school gardens, lawn bowling facilities, bird and butterfly sanctuaries, community gardens, and ever-changing works of living art that grace the tops of many buildings, providing invaluable use and enjoyment. Let's build our cities up instead of out, and preserve high standards of design by using every inch of space available to the fullest.

The transformation to a more sustainable and restorative approach to building architecture and infrastructure is well underway, and you are part of it. In this book, Steven L. Cantor provides a wonderful snapshot of the history of this transformation. He also shares a wide range of project examples and design lessons drawn from experts around the world. His work clearly demonstrates that we have the power to determine what kind of world we wish to pass on to our children, and the people within these pages are already exercising that power. Roofs are the great canvases of this century, awaiting those poised to make a lasting contribution in sustainable design. We hope you will join us.

STEVEN PECK
Founder and President
Green Roofs for Healthy Cities
Toronto, Canada

INTRODUCTION

Our modern world is beginning to embrace sustainable design for healthful communities. The purpose of this book is to provide basic information about green roofs—one potentially dramatic element of a sustainable landscape—to design professionals, practitioners, students, and interested people who want to understand this evolving technology. What are green roofs for and how do they function? How can they be incorporated into modern architecture, landscape architecture, and urban design projects? If a green roof is a goal of the program for a new building or newly acquired building, what is the process whereby a designer and client can achieve a successful installation?

The definitions and terms have been compiled from publications and experts in both North America and Europe. Just as there has never been total agreement on both sides of the Atlantic on issues in the arts, culture, design, and politics, so there is no unanimous opinion on all aspects of green roof design. I occasionally highlight some of the differences because green roof design began in Europe, but this book focuses primarily on projects in North America. As research continues and more projects are installed in North America, an evolution in the expertise of designers and practitioners on this side of the Atlantic will no doubt occur, as will a resolution of some of the fractious issues that arise among different groups of scientists, designers, and installers throughout the industry, regardless of the geographical home base.

My intent is to provide basic information so that you become conversant with the vocabulary and technology; you can then seek further education, professional expertise, and resources as needed. The organization of the book is straightforward. In Chapter One I discuss definitions of different types of green roofs and green roof systems and the major advantages of green roof installations. I briefly introduce the Leadership in Energy and Environmental Design (LEED) certification process and sustainable design.

In Chapter Two I describe the design process in detail, emphasizing those aspects unique to green roofs. This section divides the design process, from the initial decision to include a green roof to the maintenance of the complete project, into eleven steps, which can be conceived of as a continuous feedback loop. To facilitate informed participation in the design of a green roof, I focus on what questions to ask, what pitfalls to avoid, and what documents may be necessary. However, I do not describe a detailed design and construction method step by step, as that is beyond the scope of this book.

Chapter Three features a discussion of planting principles, materials, and techniques. Understanding some of the typical plant materials that are suitable for intensive and extensive green roofs is an essential first step in green roof design. A profile follows of one of the major suppliers of green roof plants in North America, Emory Knoll Farms in Street, Maryland. This chapter continues with a description of the basic methods of irrigation and concludes with a discussion of the types of specifications needed for green roofs.

Chapters Four and Five present case studies of green roofs in Europe and North America, respectively. The wide range of projects that have been implemented over many decades in Europe can provide insight into efforts to implement green roofs in North America. I provide a broad-brush tour of projects in Europe to suggest what could be accomplished in North America and other regions where the technology is just being introduced. In Chapter Five, I provide comprehensive case studies of diverse projects in North America. In some cases I examine several projects by the same designer or design team to give the reader a sense of the typical design approach and style of that designer, as well as to compare similar or contrasting projects.

Chapter Six explores and predicts the potential for green roofs in landscape design in North America. Selected examples—from historic underpinnings to modern constructions—demonstrate the ways in which innovation is already leading to exciting opportunities for designers, as well as an improved quality of life for those who live in such environments. The examples are diverse, and, as with the European examples, the degree of detail is more limited in order to cover a wide range of materials.

The appendices contain supplementary materials from other sources: profiles of green organizations; a contact list for each project which includes the names and addresses of the major contributors to the book; a list of green roof products and manufacturers; sample project specifications; excerpts from the European green roof guidelines; and a metric conversion table.

All photos and illustrations for which no credit is given are by the author.

CHAPTER ONE
Overview

1-0. An extensive green roof at the Multnomah County Building in Portland, Oregon, designed by Macdonald Environmental Planning, PC. Suggesting the wind moving over the prairie, the graceful fence separates a 3,000-square-foot (278.7 m²) terrace from the 11,893-square-foot (1,104.9 m²) green roof.

The following definitions and discussion set the scene for the projects that are presented in subsequent chapters. The goal is to give you a sense of the major vocabulary of green roofs and a basis for understanding the different types of green roofs, as well as the many diverse approaches to design and implementation.

Definitions: green roof; extensive vs. intensive, substrate, growing medium

Green roofs are simply roofs bearing vegetation that may take many different forms. Some are mats of uniform vegetation and thickness covering a large expanse of flat or sloping roof. Such installations may be inaccessible to pedestrians, either for design reasons or due to the accumulated weight. *Extensive* green roofs are usually inaccessible installations in which the growing medium is a thin layer (about 1–6 in.; 2.5–15.2 cm) of often inorganic material. This definition and others that follow come from the German publication, *Forschungsgesellschaft Landschaft-sent-wicklung Landschaftsbau e.v*, or FLL (*Guidelines for the Planning, Execution and Upkeep of Green-Roof Sites*).[1] Europeans have tested and established standards for just about every element of modern green roof designs, including types of roofing materials, waterproofing, growing media, plant materials, and so on. European standards and definitions for the different types of green roofs and green roof materials are contained in the FLL. These guidelines have been widely adapted throughout Europe.

The publication was translated into English for the first time in 1992, updated in 1995, and a new 2002 translation was recently released. Two tables from this invaluable document are contained in Appendix D of this book.[2]

It is appropriate to refer to the principal component of the growing medium as a *substrate*, rather than soil or topsoil, because it often consists of primarily *inorganic* materials, drawn from nearby regions, which will not decompose over time and therefore will not require replenishment. For the purposes of this book, substrate is used to refer to the primary raw materials, usually inorganic components, of the *growing medium*. A small percentage of organic materials, nutrients, and other materials may be incorporated into the substrate, according to a precise recipe, to create the final growing medium.

In the FLL, the growing medium is referred to as the *vegetation support course*. In some green roofs, a distinction is made between an upper layer or substrate, which is comparable to our working definition of growing medium, and a lower, entirely non-organic substrate, which may facilitate drainage. Therefore, in this book there are some projects in which the term substrate refers to two courses. "Substrate" or "substratum" refers both to layers beneath the surface as well as the base on which an organism lives or grows. As a result, for some of the European projects in this book, the term "substrate" will refer to the full depth between the green

1-1. An extensive green roof at the Water Quality Center, Beaverton, Oregon. The eco-roof covers 8,200 square feet (761.8 m²) on a northwards sloping roof with a pitch of 1 in 6 and a growing medium depth of 3 to 4 inches (7.6 to 10.2 cm). See Chapter Five for a discussion of this project.

roof superstructure and the surface. The context in the use of the term should clarify its meaning.

Additional layers may be installed beneath the growing medium to prevent fine particles from being washed out, and to absorb excess water and direct it either to the storm water system or to the storage system for reuse. Still other layers function as waterproofing, insulation, and roof protection. The bottom layer is the roof deck itself. In European countries with a established market (Germany, Switzerland, Austria) simple so-called one-layer green roof systems, with just a protection fabric between the substrate layer and the roof membrane, are often used. These systems have proven to be as efficient for vegetation growth and other ecological issues as multilayer systems if the total substrate thickness is adequate.[3]

The plant materials for extensive green roofs are perennials, usually of limited height, selected for their hardiness and adaptability to the climatic conditions and other requirements of the specific roof's environment or microclimate. The most durable extensive green roofs feature a diverse palette of plant materials that share an ability to survive in thin soils, under adverse and exposed conditions, with limited maintenance. In temperate regions the most typical plantings are sedum mixtures, but other herbaceous materials and grasses may also be included. Despite their toughness, these plants still require some maintenance, depending on the type of green roof, the palette of plant materials, and the goals of the design.

Green roofs may also consist of plantings at varied depths in the midst of a completely designed environment. *Intensive* green roofs are those in which the growing medium is considerably deeper than that on an extensive roof, that is, more than 6 inches (15.2 cm). This greater depth requires a stronger structure to support the additional weight of the substrate and growing medium and may accommodate people. Often the growing medium is a lightweight topsoil with a mixture of organic and inorganic elements. Plant materials are more diverse than those for an extensive green roof, because they can be of significant height and more deeply rooted. When there is adequate structural support, trees, planters, or other major elements such as water features, pergolas, or sculptures can be added. Such roof gardens

require a high level of maintenance. Traditional roof gardens, with their pavements and typical amenities such as benches, pergolas, and planters, are examples of intensive green roofs, but the benefits they provide—shade, insulation, water storage, if not their aesthetic effects—occur accidentally, unlike contemporary green roofs, which are built in layers with modern materials.

In Europe *Forschungsgesellschaft Landschaftsentwicklung Landschaftsbau* guidelines distinguish between two types of intensive green roofs.[4] The roof garden development just

1-2. This intensive green roof by Madison Cox Design in a New York City roof garden provides shaded, private space for outdoor living in the heart of an urban environment. (Courtesy of Robert Martin Designs)

		Table 1-1. CHARACTERISTICS OF GREEN ROOFS Extensive and Intensive		
Characteristic	Extensive	Semi-Intensive		Intensive
Depth of Material	6" (15.2 cm) or less	25% above or below 6" (15.2 cm)		More than 6" (15. 2 cm)
Accessibility	Often inaccessible	May be partially accessible		Usually accessible
Fully saturated weight	Low 10–35 lb/sq ft (48.8–170.9 kg/m²)	Varies 35–50 lb/sq ft (170.9–244.1 kg/m²)		High 50–300 lb/sq ft (244.1–1,464.7 kg/m²)
Plant diversity	Low	Greater		Greatest
Cost	Low	Varies		High
Maintenance	Minimal	Varies		Varies but is generally high

(Used with permission of Green Roofs for Healthy Cities)

described, in which the resulting design might be similar to an at-grade park or garden, is referred to as an *intensive green roof*. However, a green roof that is more expansive than an extensive green roof but does not have the complexity of design or the design intent to provide amenities for people, may be referred to as a *simple intensive green roof*. Like extensive green roofs, simple intensive green roofs feature highly adaptive plants. Whereas the depth of the growing medium for a simple intensive green roof is about 3 inches to more than 6 inches (7.6–15.2 cm), the comparable depths for intensive roof gardens are from 4 to 50 inches or more (10.2–12.7 cm). In North America, where the green roof industry is evolving, an intensive green roof has meaning. However, the fine-tuning implied in the definition of a simple intensive green roof is rarely used. Instead, the term *semi-intensive green roof* is used to describe a depth of growing medium in which 25 percent is *above* 6 inches. This new term is quite useful in describing green roofs that have some characteristics of both extensive and intensive designs but do not fit easily into either category because of the plant materials used or the thickness of the system.[5] See Table 1-1.

Despite the rigorous European standards, North Americans tend to test materials for themselves because there can be dramatically different climatic conditions in particular sites than would be encountered in Europe. The American Society for Testing Materials (ASTM) has released five methods, practices, and guidelines for green roofs and is working on additional standards. The ASTM methods are directed at (1) standardizing definitions, (2) developing reproducible tests for critical media properties

such as weight, permeability, and moisture retention, and (3) offering guidelines for designers. This work also offers a useful bridge between European and American researchers and designers.[6] Requirements for green roofs are being incorporated into the planning and zoning codes of many cities in North America. In Portland, Oregon, for example, the impetus for green roof requirements was the protection of salmon spawning in the Willamette River. Following heavy rains, large quantities of runoff—the combined overflows from city storm drainage and the sewage system—would pour into the river, depleting its oxygen and endangering the health of the fish. In Chicago, Mayor Daley became so enamored of green roofs in cities that he visited on a tour of Europe that he sought to establish requirements for green roofs in the city. Chicago is now the leading city for green roof policy and program development in North America, with about 3 million square feet (278,700 m²) complete.[7] Washington, D.C., Minneapolis, Toronto, Montreal, Vancouver, and Winnipeg are all in different stages of implementing policies that support green roof infrastructure implementation. In New York City guidelines are being developed for proposed green roof designs to simplify the arduous process of securing a building permit.

Definitions: green roof, ecoroof, bioroof, living roof, brown roof, green roof infrastructure, living walls

In some ways the term *green roof* is not accurate because the featured plant materials—whether in an intensive or extensive application, whether a mixture of sedums or a rich combination of perennials and diverse species—are not green

Table 1-2. COMPARISON OF ECOROOFS AND CONVENTIONAL ROOFS		
Subject	**Ecoroof**	**Conventional Roof**
Storm water		
Volume retention	10–35% during wet season, 65–100% during dry season	None
Peak flow mitigation	All storms reduced runoff peaks	None
Temperature mitigation	All storms	None
Improved water quality	Retains atmospheric deposition and retards roof material degradation Reduced volumes reduce pollutant loadings	No
Urban heat island	Prevents temperature increases	None
Air quality	Filters air, stores carbon, increases evapotranspiration	None
Energy conservation	Insulates buildings	None
Vegetation	Allows seasonal evapotranspiration; provides photosynthesis, oxygen, carbon, water balance	None
Green space	Replaces green space lost to building footprint, although not equal to a forest	None
Zoning floor area bonus	3 ft² (0.28 m²) added floor area ratio for each ecoroof ft² when building cover over 60% (in Portland)	None
City drainage fee reduction	To be determined, may be up to 35% (in Portland)	None
Approved as storm water management	For all current city requirements (in Portland)	No
Habitat	For insects and birds	None
Livability	Buffers noise, eliminates glare, alternative aesthetic, offers passive recreation	None
Costs	Highly variable from $5–$12 per square foot ($53.8–$129.12 m²) new construction and $7–$20 ft² ($75.32–$215.20 m²) retrofits	Highly variable from $2–$10 per square foot ($21.52–$107.6 per m²) new construction and $4–$15 per square foot ($43.04 m²–$161.40 per m²) retrofits
Cost offets	Reduced storm water facilities, energy savings, higher rental value, increased property values, reduced need for insulation materials, reduced waste to landfill, added jobs and industry	None
Durability	Waterproof membrane protected from solar and temperature exposure lasts more than 36 years; membrane protected from operations and maintenance staff damage	Little protection, exposure to elements, lasts less than 20 years

(Used with permission of Tom Liptan, Portland, Oregon Bureau of Environmental Services)

1-3. Boston ivy (*Parthenocissus tricuspidata*) has completely cloaked the façade of this hotel in Vancouver and created a living wall.

sion of this project).[9] Yet another term, *brown roof*, has been used to refer to a living roof that replicates the hardscrabble environment of brownfields. These are industrialized landscapes that are now being subjected to increased pressures for development, resulting in the destruction of habitat for some endangered plant and animal species uniquely suited to these settings. Finally, the term *green roof infrastructure* was coined by Steven Peck to acknowledge the many public infrastructure benefits that widespread green roof implementation may provide. Whichever term is used— green roof, ecoroof, living roof, or brown roof—the concept is the same: they all imply the creation of a dynamic, living environment of plant materials on top of the roof of a new or existing structure.

A correlation to green roofs—called *living walls* or *vertical gardens*—is also advancing in North America, in which green roof technology is applied to the façades or walls of buildings. Although there is a long tradition of growing and training hardy vines on buildings, only now are the environmental advantages—insulation against summer heat and winter cold, dust reduction, the concentration of pollutants in the foliage—being widely acknowledged, and specific methods of installation being sought to insure the best results.[10] Stainless steel, durable plastics, and other modern materials may be used for supports, trellises, and meshes on which vines can be trained and grown (wood has a limited life span, so it may well have to be replaced, with considerable difficulty, after plants have matured). Patrick Blanc, a French botanist, has developed a plant wall or vertical garden constructed of metal, polyvinyl chloride and nonbiodegradable felt.[11] In the same way that green roofs rely on inorganic materials for stability, so they do not decompose and do not need replenishment, living wall structures may also be permanent. Other systems are being developed that rely on pockets for small amounts of growing medium. Modular units, such as stacked, hollowed-out building blocks, are also used. For modern roof gardens, such techniques create a natural extension of greenery onto adjacent walls, adding considerably to the richness of the design.

There are two general types of green wall systems: façade greening and living walls.[12] Green

all year round. Therefore, other terms have been coined to suggest a more accurate description. *Ecoroof* (or sometimes *bioroof*), for example, is the term preferred in Portland, Oregon, in acknowledgment of the non-green conditions that may occur, and because of the diverse ecological functions of green roofs within at least some applications throughout the region. The prefix *eco* suggests many of the economic benefits of green roofs, such as increasing the life span of the roof, property values, and energy savings.[8] See Table 1-2. The term *living roof* was coined by Dusty Gedge; the organization that he helped to found, Living Roofs, developed alternate habitats for a species of bird, the black redstart, on the roofs of proposed high-rise developments (see Chapter Four for a discus-

façades are trellis systems or training structures on which climbing plants grow vertically without attaching to the surface of the building. The main difference between living walls and façade greening is that the living walls are part of a building envelope system where plants are actually planted and grown within a modular wall system. In Canada, Dr. Alan Darlinton invented the biofiltration wall ("bio-wall"), which improves indoor air quality by removing toxic volatile organic chemicals (VOCs) and carbon dioxide.

Most of the green wall systems installed in North America and Europe to date are green façades that feature training systems or elevated containers. Modular trellis panels and stainless steel cable systems hold climbing plants away from the surface of the building. The foliage of the climbing plants reduces solar heating, particularly on walls that face the sun. Clinging vines such as English ivy and other aggressive species attach directly to wall surfaces without support; however, they are not recommended for new developments because of potential surface damage and increased building maintenance.

Japan is an innovator in green wall systems. To mitigate the urban heat island effect, the federal government of Japan and various cities offer incentives for developers to install green façades, living walls and green roofs. Tokyo suffers from poor air quality and climate change. The average temperature is now 5° F (3° C) higher than it was 30 years ago. On tall buildings, the ratio of wall surface to roof area is much higher. The government of Japan funded the installation and research for the Bio Lung, a 500 x 40 foot (152.4 x 12.2 m) green wall complex. The Bio Lung demonstrates thirty different green wall systems supplied by eighteen different manufacturers in Japan. During the 1990s, Japanese municipalities and federal government agencies realized that concrete highrises are the dominant form of urban development, which is contributing to the urban heat island effect. Legislation enacted in April 2001 by the Tokyo Metropolitan Government (TMG) requires that all rooftops and wall surfaces be greened on new construction projects with a footprint greater than 10,764 square feet (1,000 m²) for private development or 2,961

1-4. The living wall of the Aquafest Learning Center at the Vancouver Aquarium comprises 508 modular green wall panels (G-Sky). (Courtesy of Randy Sharp)

square feet (275 m²) for public facilities. Until 2005 this initiative focused on new construction, with 134.6 acres (54.5 ha) of greened rooftops, but since then, the TMG has started implementing policies that deal with existing buildings. Living wall systems first developed in Japan are now being used in North America.

Living walls reduce the surface temperature of buildings by as much as 18° Fahrenheit (10° C) when covered with vegetation and a growing medium. Green wall energy calculations depend on wall orientation, sun angle, wind flow, and microclimate around the building. Multiple benefits also include improved air quality, acoustics, health and well-being, and reduction of building deterioration by ultraviolet (UV) rays. The

technology of vegetated building envelopes is applicable for acoustical control at airports, bio filtration of indoor air, graywater treatment, and urban agriculture and vertical gardening, especially where space is a consideration. The transformation of urban environments with green canopies and living walls will help cities become more livable, cooler, and quieter.

Types of Green Roof Systems

Complete component systems and modular or prefabricated units offer two general approaches to green roof design. Some companies offer the complete range of all of the layers involved in a green roof, including the waterproofing system applied to the roof deck; they also provide warranties against leakage if the entire system is used (Figs. 1-5 and 1-6). Often such companies have a line of choices for extensive green roof designs and another group of products for intensive designs, with each collection advertised under a private label. They provide guarantees for these products if they are installed as one system and also include complete specifications, as well as the services of LEED-trained staff and other specialists. Even so, no company as yet actually manufactures all the components and materials. Therefore, it is often desirable to "mix and match" various components from different manufacturers to create the best product possible. The downside to this approach is that it can be more difficult to secure guarantees and full warranties, because each manufacturer or

1-5. Illustrative section of Zinco green roof. (Courtesy of Zinco)

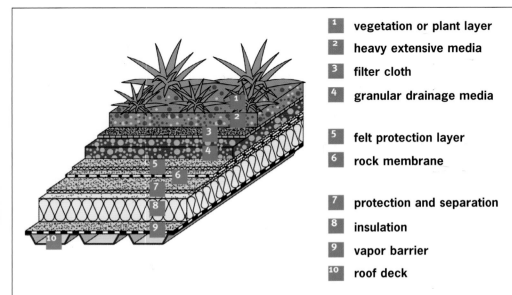

1. vegetation or plant layer
2. heavy extensive media
3. filter cloth
4. granular drainage media

5. felt protection layer
6. rock membrane

7. protection and separation
8. insulation
9. vapor barrier
10. roof deck

1-6. Illustrative section of Optigrün green roof. (Courtesy of Optigrün)

contractor might blame any problems that occur on someone else's product. It also may be difficult to perform testing to confirm how the system will perform, particularly the growing medium, with materials assembled from a number of sources. However, as the industry matures, these problems may disappear.

The other general approach is to use prefabricated or modular units that combine two or more green roof components, a strategy more popular in the United States and Canada than in Europe. There are several major manufacturers in America and Canada, and, as with the complete systems, solid warranties are often included. Modular systems have some advantages. The sizes start at a weight that one person can easily handle and then increase to dimensions and weights that require at least two strong workers who can handle all the components at once. Modular systems often work well where the area is relatively flat and has clear geometric edges, often rectilinear. Phased installations lend themselves to modular designs because each phase can be dovetailed to meet the next one, using the same modular components, which will fit snugly against the previous installations. Depending on the size of the module, it can be filled with the growing medium and sometimes even the plants themselves before installation in its final location.

Green Roof Layers or Components

A green roof system can be imagined as a thick sandwich of many layers, with top and bottom layers of vegetation and roof deck, respectively. From the top down, these layers include the vegetation, growing medium, filter fabric, drainage and water retention layers, root protection layer, insulation, waterproofing, and roof deck. In the material that follows, all of the layers are discussed, although some layers can be omitted and manufacturers may combine or mesh different layers to facilitate construction.

Vegetation

The vegetation for extensive roof systems in temperate climate zones in North America is

1-7, 1-8, 1-9. Steps in the installation of a modular system (Green Tech) at Silvercup Studios. See Chapter Five for a discussion of this project. (Courtesy of Balmori Design)

1-10. A diverse growth of sedums on the Copenhagen airport's green roof. (Courtesy of Ulrik Reeh, Veg Tech.)

1-11. A vigorous growth of sedum species on a green roof at the Autonomous University of Chapingo in Mexico City. See Chapter Five for a discussion of this project. (Courtesy of Tanya Muller)

usually a mixture of sedums that are well adapted to the thin layers of growing media and extreme conditions of drought, heat, cold, wind, and exposure. In North America the sedums are typically planted as plugs or cuttings. However, in Europe the use of pregrown vegetated mats (usually about 1 inch [2.54 cm] thick) is very common and affordable.[13] This technique was used for the first time in the United States at the Ford River Rouge facility, which is described in Chapter Five. For modular systems the plants are sometimes pregrown and planted in the modules at the nursery. The sedums are supplemented by other plants, often with a similar look but of different plant families. Such plants add contrasting color, texture, and bloom at different seasons. A variety of plant materials is a practical way to ensure diversity on the green roof, because at least some of the species selected for planting may not survive or may struggle, and the other species can take over and become well established. In addition, diversity gives some protection against infestations and diseases, in that some species will be resistant. Particularly for extensive green roofs, it is risky to try to specify, install, and maintain a rigid quantity of the various plant materials in set patterns, because in most cases some plants will adapt better than others—a process that should be encouraged. When aesthetic criteria are applied to extensive green roofs and the sight of clear forms from a distance is desirable, more maintenance will be required.

Extensive green roofs in Europe often include, instead of sedums, a mixture of herbs and grasses that is usually seeded rather than planted as plugs or cuttings. Earlier sedum extensive green roofs in Europe suffered from a lack of nutrients, because many building owners did not wish to fertilize to reduce costs. Also, restrictive environmental controls were implemented in some locations; in Switzerland, for example, it is illegal to fertilize green roofs because the storm water system may become polluted with high concentrations of nitrates and other fertilizer chemicals from the runoff. Over time, suitable palettes of plant materials that can withstand potentially low-nutrition conditions have been developed. In addition, most extensive green roofs in Europe are established from seed or cuttings because it has been found that many plug plants do not adapt well to difficult green roof conditions.[14] Plug plants are usually nursery grown under optimal conditions, so they do not always adapt to the harsh conditions on a green roof.

For intensive green roofs, as the thickness of the growing medium increases, the variety of potential plant materials increases dramatically. A wide range of plant materials, from sedums and perennial grasses to shrubs and small trees, both evergreen and deciduous, is suitable for intensive roof gardens with deep planters and irrigation systems. The plants must still be adaptable to extreme conditions. Semi-intensive green roofs, in which only a portion of the roof is an intensive installation, are sometimes recommended as a way to gain the diversity of plantings associated with an intensive installation with the lesser maintenance associated with extensive green roofs.

Growing Medium and Substrate

A well-drained sandy loam was typically used for the growing medium in traditional roof gardens, although it was usually referred to as the soil. In more modern roof gardens, as the soil manufacturing industry has developed, lightweight soil mixes that are still primarily topsoil (but with little or no clay-size content) and lightweight textural components have become typical. However, these soil recipes must be close enough to standard topsoils that plants can absorb adequate moisture and nutrients. A cubic foot of wet standard, well-drained sandy loam may weigh as much as 120 pounds (1922 kg/m^3), but a cubic foot of some of the lightweight mixes may weigh about two-thirds to one-half as much. Therefore, the savings in weight are substantial and essential for planters up to several feet deep and wide. But even on an extensive or intensive green roof spread over a large area at a much lower depth (thickness), it is usually an essential requirement to minimize the weight of the growing medium to save on the cost of structural support for the roof.

Soils with a high percentage of organic content may have disadvantages for green roofs, whether extensive or intensive. Over time, the organic components decompose and the surface level of the soil recedes. Of course, this is a natural process. In an at-grade garden, soil is replenished by the decomposition of leaves, thatch, and the carcasses of insects and animals so that equilibrium is reached, or the soil layer may actually increase over many years, as a permanent vegetative layer is established. The freeze–thaw cycle and other biological and natural processes contribute to small movements within the soil and the creation of new soil. In an at-grade garden, it is a routine operation to replenish topsoil, to add fertilizer, conditioners, and compost, and to spread mulch over time. By contrast, it is a difficult task on green roofs to replenish the growing medium without having to lift up some of the plant materials—a tedious process. It may also be a logistical challenge to haul additional substrate or growing medium to the roof via freight elevators, manual means, or crane. For these reasons a stable growing medium becomes a highly desirable component.

Other potential problems that high organic content may cause include excessive nutrient loss by the plants, and clogging of the filter fabric and the drainage layer. Plant materials may quickly exhaust the nutrients within the organic material and then suffer when these nutrients are not replenished. Some organic material may not mix that well with other ingredients in the soil and result in uneven drainage or clogged layers of the green roof system. Organic material such as humus has substantial weight and its periodic addition to extensive green roof installations pushes the load limits of the structural design. Organic soils are such a suitable growing medium that many weed species may seed themselves, and a high level of maintenance is required to keep the roof weed free. In some cases, organic soils retain a high level of moisture, but the plant materials or plant community that is being established prefers well-drained, even sere, soils. The cost should be evaluated carefully, both in terms of delivery to the site and hoisting to the roof. A sandy loam topsoil may not cost more than an engineered soil recipe consisting of a substrate plus additives, yet usually the excess weight of the loam soil is a sufficient reason not to use it. Finally, whereas many substrates or growing mixtures can be pumped to the roof, it is impossible to pump a high-quality loam topsoil to the roof; the particles adhere and the weight is too great.

The amount and types of organic materials and fertilizers to use, if at all, are debated within the industry as well as the extent of irrigation and the use of pesticides and herbicides. Maintenance varies drastically from one site to another, with some extensive green roofs requiring little or no fertilization, dethatching, spraying, and mulching whereas some intensive green roofs require a great deal. Maintenance practices sometimes require the removal of accumulated plant debris and thatch, because it might become combustible or unsightly. As previously noted, some cities, particularly in Europe, forbid the use of fertilizers or any chemicals because they are potential pollutants of storm water. Despite the degree to which irrigation during the first few years can ensure the survival and establishment of plant materials, in some cities no irrigation is permitted. Specific installations that are designed to replicate a particular habitat on a roof may not need any fertilization or irrigation and only very rare maintenance.

In general, inorganic substrates are preferred, with some additives to suit the specific conditions of each installation. Substrates that are locally or regionally available reduce transportation costs, although such availability is not always possible. When possible, local substrates are useful when the green roof design seeks to replicate a plant community that would be similar to what would grow in a similar site under natural conditions. The substrate selected predicts and limits the types of plant materials selected.

Typical substrates include crushed expanded shale, pumice, lava (scoria), terra cotta, calcined clay, expanded slate, or brick.[15] Experiments have been conducted with crushed, recycled concrete, but it tends to produce a pH that is much too high. Based on FLL guidelines, about 3–10 percent organic materials (mass, based on dry weight) can be added to provide initial nutrients to the newly planted green roof, but these additives are typically not replenished over time (although there may be periodic or occasional fertilizations). Some sedums, cacti, and similar plants thrive in what would be an inhospitable or impossible setting for other plant materials.

Whatever growing medium mixture is finally specified should be carefully tested to verify compliance with specifications, particularly regarding critical variables such as pH, weight, percentage of organic materials, the exact nature of the inorganic primary material, the drainage rate, the maximum density, and so on. This consideration applies for any medium being specified for an at-grade project. However, there is much less tolerance for error with green roof mixtures. Once installed, it is much more difficult to adjust the composition of a green roof growing medium than it is to incorporate additives into topsoil at grade.

Another factor to consider is the coarseness or fineness of the substrate and its ability to retain water, which may impact plant growth as well as potential habitat (the community of living organisms that may evolve under various hydrological conditions ranging from wet to dry). Coarse substrates tend to have a lot of porous spaces that allow aeration, but they cannot hold as much water as substrates with smaller pores. The ideal green roof substrate has enough spaces to expedite good drainage, while retaining sufficient moisture for the plants, so that their root systems can quickly absorb a high percentage of the rainfall that strikes the roof and allow the overflow to drain and collect in the lower layers of the green roof system. A conflict may arise between substrates and green roof systems that hold water, and therefore provide moisture for plants and other living organisms on the roof, and those that drain well but

1-12. Hoisting of the substrate to the roof at the Minneapolis Library. See Chapter Five for a discussion of this project. (Courtesy of the Kestrel Group)

result in too dry an environment for many plants, even hardy ones, to become established. In such circumstances, the design goals of the green roof can dictate which method to follow.

Slope can also affect moisture retention on the green roof. On a flat green roof there is a greater chance that moisture might build up within the growing medium and, over time, undermine the health of plants adapted to dry conditions. It is much more likely that plants adapted to dry conditions will thrive on a sloping green roof, because the excess water can run off. Based on the degree of slope, it may be necessary to adjust the moisture retention properties of the growing medium to create the best conditions for the selected plant materials.

A final consideration for the growing medium is whether some of the components should be sterile, or at least weed free. This decision may depend on the design intent: whether a set range of species is desired, without any weeds or invaders, or whether the designers prefer that whatever seeds might typically be associated with a particularly inorganic substrate or plant community be permitted to germinate. In general, we can distinguish between *sterile* and *sterilized* media. Well-composted organic material has essentially zero weed germination. It is typical to specify that composts be tested for weed

germination and oxygen respiration to ensure that they are stable.[16] Most other materials are often virgin. The typical factory-mixed substrate medium is sterile but not sterilized. The costs of certifying weed-free materials should be balanced against the potential increased maintenance costs if weeds are present. Unsterilized, the manure could harbor a huge number of weed seeds and those seedlings could easily outdistance, in growth and vigor, new sprigs, cuttings, or seeded areas.

Just as there is debate about the amount and extent of organic matter and the extent and cost of using sterile or sterilized materials, there is considerable discussion about what constitutes weeds. Some advocates of extensive green roofs prefer designs in which volunteer species, even if they are similar to what is planted or seeded on the roof, are not permitted (that is, they are weeded out). The extent to which the substrate is sterile and additives such as compost are sterilized will determine the advantage to those who maintain the green roof. However, other designers feel that an extensive green roof planting is a dynamic environment and that volunteer species are welcome, just as long as their roots do not penetrate the roof membrane or their cumulative height and weight do not exceed the limits of the structural design. Such sponta-

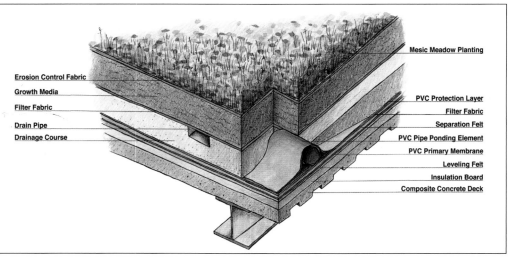

1-13. Most new green roof installations do not have surface drains, as all water is absorbed by the plantings and various layers, as shown in this cross section at Oaklyn Library. See Chapter Five for a discussion of this project. (Courtesy of Roofscapes, Inc.)

Erosion Control Fabric
Growth Media
Filter Fabric
Drain Pipe
Drainage Course

Mesic Meadow Planting

PVC Protection Layer
Filter Fabric
Separation Felt
PVC Pipe Ponding Element
PVC Primary Membrane
Leveling Felt
Insulation Board
Composite Concrete Deck

1-14. Where standard area drains are at the surface, they should be protected from clogging by a gravel layer.

neous vegetation may, in time, exceed what was originally planted, but if the green roof is functioning properly, this "takeover" is not perceived as a problem. A natural succession of plant materials is likely to occur over the life of the green roof. However, this variation is very difficult to predict. The depth and type of substrate, the climate, and moisture levels may all affect what vegetation becomes established. For such installations, weed seeds might be welcome, so it is not necessary to sterilize compost or other additives.

Filter Fabric

A layer of filter fabric separates the bottom of the growing medium from the drainage layer and the water retention system below it. The fil-

ter fabric, although minimal in thickness, is a critical element, because it prevents fine particles of the growing medium from clogging the drainage layers—which could prevent water from flowing or draining freely throughout the entire system. Water buildup can stress the structure of the roof and damage the plants.

Drainage and Water Retention Layers

Except for "one-layer" assemblies in which the medium also provides drainage, all green roof assemblies include some sort of specialized drainage layer. This layer may be synthetic or composed of a highly permeable granular mineral material, manufactured or contained in a sheet. The drainage layer collects any excess water not absorbed by the plants and the growing medium and directs it into a network of channels built into the system. Tests that measure the drainage capacity of both synthetic and mineral layers are available through the ASTM. The design of the drainage layer is critical to the success of any green roof assembly.[17]

Some assemblies also include a synthetic water retention layer that usually takes the form of plastic sheets with recesses or cups on the upper surface to capture and retain water. The drainage and water retention layers are sometimes combined by manufacturers into one element. The retention layer can augment the natural water-holding properties of the green roof. Most green roof media will retain 35–45 percent moisture, by volume. For comparison, most retention sheets hold about 0.25 inches of water per inch of thickness (0.64 cm/cm), with typical sheets retaining between 0.1 and 0.5 gallons per square foot (4.1 to 20.4 L/m^2) when properly installed.[18] All of the water stored within the individual reservoir cells of some retention layers is reabsorbed by the plant materials. Drainage layers may detain moisture long enough for most of it to be utilized by the plants, with the remainder released into the storm drainage system over time. Because the volume of runoff released during a storm is considerably reduced, the potential to overload the storm water system may also be reduced. The retention layer, with its numerous small reservoirs, or pockets, also may increase aeration and air flow into the green roof.[19]

In some green roof systems, excess storm water or rain water is collected and recycled. Sometimes gutters collect the rain water and direct it to cisterns at a lower level, even in the basement of the building. The water is pumped for irrigation or other usage, when needed.

Depending on the design and goals of the green roof system, the drainage layers will connect either to existing internal area drains or external drains on a roof, and thereby direct water to the existing storm drainage system. Area drains are surface drains on the roof that connect to storm pipes that extend into the building. External drains are gutters or scuppers that release water to the outside of the building or carry it through pipes affixed to the building. All area drains and scuppers require enclosures to protect them from clogging. These enclosures, often referred to as *inspection chambers*, should have lids that allow easy inspection of the drain or scupper.[20] The design of the pipe as it goes through the building should be as straightforward as possible, so that there is convenient access if repair or maintenance is required. A clogged pipe can cause myriad problems. The best designs minimize the potential for clogs, but also require routine maintenance practices.

Root Protection Layer

Some kind of protection layer or root barrier is needed to prevent roots from penetrating into the waterproofing and causing leaks. Root barriers are usually thermoplastic membranes, but copper foil and root-retardant chemicals have been used with some assemblies. Some building codes restrict the use of copper because it may react chemically with other elements, or a slight amount might leach into the water system.

Sometimes root barriers are integrated into other layers, such as waterproofing, that are part of the green roof system being installed. This method is more typically used in Europe, where there is considerable information about selecting plants and green roof layers that minimize the chance of root penetration.

Insulation

Depending on the climate, an additional layer of insulation may be installed underneath the root barrier to further limit heat gain and loss. The insulation must be lightweight but have great compressive strength, so that it is not crushed or squeezed out of shape by the weight of the materials (as well as people) above it. Depending on the green roof design principles and the properties of the waterproofing system, insulation may be installed either above or below the waterproofing layer. The most common materials for insulation are extruded polystyrene and polyisocyanurate. It is common practice among some manufacturers to install a layer of fiberboard on top of the insulation if it overlies the waterproofing membrane.[21]

Waterproofing

The waterproofing layer is, of course, essential, and many different materials are used. A very common roofing material is polymer modified bitumen. Some building codes prohibit certain materials. For example, mopped and liquid applied bitumen membranes typically emit undesirable fumes during the application process and may not be permitted. In some localities fire codes may prohibit the use of torch-applied membranes. This prohibition is more likely in dense urban areas where even a temporary bad odor or fire hazard can have a major effect on many people. Other common roof membranes used in conjunction with green roofs include (1) thermoplastics such as polyvinyl chloride (PVC) or thermal polyolefin (TPO), (2) EPDM rubber, and (3) liquid applied polyurethane. Some roof membranes double as a root barrier. Warranties for waterproofing typically cover ten to twenty years.

Roof Deck

Finally, there is the roof deck itself. The most common types of decks encountered in green roof projects are reinforced concrete, precast concrete planks, steel, and steel–concrete composites. However, many projects, particularly retrofit projects, may involve plywood or tongue-and-groove wood decks. Every deck must be investigated for its ability to bear the anticipated loads and its tendency for movement (especially at terminations and expansion joints). Frequently the type of deck dictates which method of waterproofing is optimal.[22] When greater loads are required, existing decks must be underbuilt with additional reinforcement—and, because of the cost, limited to only those locations where it is essential. In new buildings the deck must be built to conform with the load-bearing requirements of the planned green roofs. Sometimes a new roof deck is built uniformly, so that its minimum load-bearing capacity is greater than what is being planned for the entire green roof. This is an effective method for extensive green roofs. Semi-intensive green roofs may rely on load-bearing walls and structural columns where the deepest layers are installed, and then receive extensive treatment in locations where the loading is more limited. When intensive green roofs or intensive modern gardens are planned, it is more cost efficient to vary the structural detailing of the concrete deck where the most additional load-bearing capacity is required. However, if the budget permits, the greatest flexibility of design occurs when the roof deck can support substantial loads with ease, so that the design placed on it has a layout independent of the structural support.

In recent decades the United States and Canada have experienced a rapidly growing green roof industry in which European manufacturers have established subsidiaries across the Atlantic for supplying all the basic materials, such as roof membranes, waterproofing, and other components. More recently, North American firms have begun to develop unique green roof products.[23] Therefore, although the names and purposes of the various green roof layers will not change, how they are combined, assembled, and marketed will, no doubt, evolve.

Special Factors

The load or weight requirements and methods for detecting leaks take on particular significance in the design and maintenance of green roofs and roof gardens. Since green roofs are dynamic environments which evolve naturally or may be intentionally altered, such considerations must always be acknowledged and revisited as necessary.

Load requirements are divided between dead and live loads. The *dead load* of the roof refers to the actual weight of the materials used to construct it and those built elements that are permanently fixed in place. The *live load,* in contrast, is the weight added to the dead load as a result of the use of the space, such as people moving on and off the roof.[24] However, sometimes there are disagreements about such items as portable planters or other movable objects. Even with clear definitions, there can be room for different interpretations by building inspectors or reviewing personnel. Are they dead loads because they are fixed in place (at least for a certain time), or are they live loads because they can be moved from one area of the roof to another, or removed altogether? Similarly, the planting itself is usually defined in building codes as part of the dead load, but certain jurisdictions consider it live load, because it could be removed, and is therefore not permanent. The new ASTM standards specify uniform methods to predict the live and dead loads associated with green roof assemblies. Building codes usually specify a load requirement that is a combination of the dead and live loads. Other loads may come into play, such as the impact of winds, snow, or seismic action, so designers of a green roof or roof garden must allow for a safety factor. The total weight of all built components as a result of all loads should be less than the maximum load permitted. In the course of planning the design, it is often necessary to calculate concentrated loads, that is, the maximum load permitted at stress points—for example, where structural beams cross one another or meet columns. At such locations, it is often possible to support larger weights. This is a typical technique used for semi-intensive green roofs as well.

When the roof must be reinforced to support additional load, the construction changes typically start at the support for the roof deck itself. In most construction the majority of the weight is supported at the parapet walls and at points directly over the intersections of structural beams. Structural engineers are able to determine how much reinforcement is needed to support additional weight at different locations

Table 1-3. GENERAL ADVANTAGES OF DIFFERENT GREEN ROOF TYPES

EXTENSIVE	SEMI-INTENSIVE	INTENSIVE
Lightweight	Combines best features of extensive and intensive	Greater diversity of plants
Suitable for large areas	Utilizes areas with greater loading capacity	Best insulation properties and storm water management
Low maintenance costs and no irrigation required	Greater coverage at less cost than intensive	Greater range of design
May be suitable for retrofit projects	Average maintenance	Often accessible
Lower capital costs	Greater plant diversity than extensive	Greater variety of human uses
Easier to replace	Greater opportunities for aesthetic design than extensive	Greater biodiversity potential

(Used with permission of Green Roofs for Healthy Cities)

of either an existing roof or one being planned. The more efficient the design team can be in determining the purpose of the green roof, the type of green roof installation, and its various components, the easier it will be for the structural engineer to arrange for an increase in the load-bearing capabilities of different areas of the roof deck, as required.

One obvious concern with a green roof is how to detect and repair leaks as quickly as possible. After the waterproofing layer has been placed and sealed, verifying its watertightness can be accomplished by flooding the roof with water to a certain depth. With thermoplastic nonadhered single-ply assemblies, cuts are made at low points following the flooding to determine if moisture has entered below the membrane during the flood test. In the past locating small imperfections and leaks following a flood test could be very time consuming, because this method reveals only the approximate locations of leaks, and further investigation may be necessary. A newer, more advantageous method is becoming widely used: electric field vector mapping (EFVM).[25] With this method the waterproofing is installed over a conductive deck, such as steel or reinforced concrete. Points of water entry through the membrane appear as electrical grounds on the surface and can be mapped manually using a voltmeter and quickly isolated. EFVM is a method, not a product or system. However, in order to make green roofs consis-

tent with EFVM, the waterproofing membrane must be an electrical insulator, and the underlying deck must be integrally connected to building ground. Cast-in-place concrete decks satisfy this requirement, as do steel decks and steel-composite decks. Wood decks, pre-cast concrete plank decks, and decks that include supplemental vapor barriers are not compatible. In order to render these other deck types compatible with EFVM, a conductive layer can be installed under the membrane and connected to a building ground point (e.g., plumbing). This conductive layer can be a metal foil or a metal mesh. EFVM does not have an installation cost, other than the grounding foil or mesh associated with projects on non-compliant deck materials.

Other leak detection systems are also available that automatically pinpoint a leak. These so-called active systems rely on a mesh of cables with TDR transmitters installed at nodes beneath the waterproofing. The system pulses electricity through the network to detect electric properties associated with the moisture of the roof deck. Output showing the layout of the entire green roof can be directed to a computer monitor. By using such systems, repairs can be limited to the right spot, thus minimizing both replacement and maintenance costs. However, the equipment that must be installed during construction is quite expensive. This technology is rapidly evolving. An earlier method of detection involved the use of a crisscrossing grid of fine wires, but it is not as efficient and is much harder to install than the foil layer described above.

Advantages of Green Roofs

Green roofs offer many advantages over conventional roofs. The following discussion highlights the most significant advantages without attempting to determine their relative degree of importance, which might well depend on the goals of a particular green roof installation. See also Tables 1-2 and 1-3.

- *Aesthetics.* One obvious advantage is the addition to the environment of a visual amenity, a green space that is visible from many vantage points, instead of a typical asphaltic tar or other dreary roof. Some green roofs, as gardens, are also accessible to the public or private owners and add to the enjoyment of the property. In dense urban environments, the visual impact of even a few green spots cannot be overlooked, particularly if these gardens can be seen or used by many people.
- *Storm water management.* During and following heavy rains, the plant materials, growing medium, and the drainage layer (if it is designed for this purpose) in a green roof absorb significant quantities of rainfall and storm water runoff. This function reduces runoff volume and also reduces peaks for moderately sized storm events. Potentially, storm water systems can be sized smaller and the water quality of streams and rivers protected.[26] In major urban areas green roofs may eliminate or reduce incidents of combined sewage and storm water overflows that occur during or after heavy rains. By absorbing rainwater, a considerable number of well-designed green roof systems may allow the storm water system to operate without overflowing into the sewage system. Of course, storm water systems serve large urban areas. Even though the amount of water retained by a green roof is measurable, it would take the combined impact of a whole series of green roofs within the watershed of a storm drainage system to achieve a significant effect. This cumulative impact is being modeled in a number of cities, including Winnipeg, Toronto, and Washington, D.C.[27]

As green roof designs have become more sophisticated, not only do they retard the release of storm water during high-intensity rainfall, but they can also store excess water that can be used later for irrigation of the green roof plants.

- *Mitigation of the urban heat island.* Green roofs have promise as a collective design element to impact the urban heat island effect, well documented in major urban areas. The built environment, particularly dark-colored pavements and construction materials concentrated without intervening plantings, absorbs heat during the day and releases it slowly at night, so that most major cities are several degrees warmer than surrounding suburban or rural areas. The solar energy converts to heat, which hovers in the air around the building, so that air conditioning needs and costs greatly increase. Airborne particulates also contribute to the urban heat island. These contaminants absorb infrared radiation emitted at ground level at nightfall, when temperatures begin to drop, thereby reducing the amount of cooling. Other major factors associated with the urban heat island effect in large North American cities include an increase in smog formation and air pollution, greater energy consumption, health issues, and stress. Major airports, for example, with their vast areas of pavements uninterrupted by vegetative buffer, tend to be islands of heat within already overheated metropolitan environments. In contrast, the processes of evaporation from green roofs and transpiration by plants release water, and cool the ambient temperature of the building. If green roofs were installed on a large scale, such as on a series of warehouses or terminal buildings at an airport, they would have the potential to mitigate the heat island effect.
- *Acoustical and heat insulation.* Due to the thickness of the entire installation, from waterproofing to roof membrane, growing media and plant materials, green roofs act as acoustical barriers, reducing the volume of sound from traffic, airplanes, or other sources that penetrates the building. Similarly, because they have insulating properties (also due to their thickness) and some degree of resistance in energy transmission,

1-15. A photovoltaic installation atop a sedum green roof at Exhibition Hall #1 in Basel, Switzerland. The flat roof covers almost 4 acres (1.6 ha) and has an extensive sedum roof on volcanic substrate 2.75 inches (7 cm) deep in combination with 19,914 square feet (1,850 m²) of photovoltaic cells, which generate 215,000 kwh per year.

1-16. A diverse planting with some bare gravel areas encourages the use of the green roof by birds and insects at University Hospital, Basel, Switzerland. See Chapter Four for a discussion of this project.

1-17. An educational display at the Green Institute in Minneapolis provides context for visitors. See Chapter Five for a discussion of this project. (Courtesy of the Kestrel Group)

1-18. Plaques installed on the terrace explain the environmental benefits of this green roof, designed by Macdonald Environmental Planning, PC, at the Multnomah County Building in Portland, Oregon.

green roofs reduce air-conditioning requirements in the summer and lower heating needs in the winter. The cooler ambient temperatures that result from the installation of a green roof also improve the efficiency of air conditioning and lower its cost.

• *Filtering.* Another advantage of green roofs, similar to the impact of any significant planting or existing forest, is their ability to filter dust and soot particles from the air. Compared to a bare roof, which has no impact, the vegetation will trap many particulates that would otherwise contaminate the air or be inhaled by people or animals.

• *Reduction in carbon dioxide.* In this age of global warming, it cannot be overlooked that all plant materials, during the process of respiration, use carbon dioxide from the air to form starch and release oxygen. Given that carbon dioxide is the principal heat-trapping gas associated with global warming, the more that vegetative plantings can be increased, the greater the potential to reduce the amount of carbon dioxide in the air. The largest benefit of green roofs in reducing carbon dioxide emissions, however, is indirect. By reducing ambient temperatures on a building, so that cooling and heating costs are mitigated, there is a significant reduction in the use of fossil fuels for cooling and heating—the combustion of which generates large amounts of carbon dioxide.

• *Economic benefits.* Economic benefits are a little harder to ascertain because so many factors are involved. Although the initial cost of a green roof is greater than that of a conventional roof, over time the green roof prolongs the life of the roof by protecting it from direct exposure to ultraviolet and other harmful radiations. In many cases, the green roof eventually pays for itself. The protection offered by a green roof increases the life of the roof membrane, a major economic advantage to a building owner. As a result, in some instances the manufacturers of roofing systems will increase the warranty on a new roof if it is to be covered by a green roof system. As noted above, energy savings due to the reduced use of air conditioning and heating are another major economic benefit. To the degree that the green roof can be considered either a passive or active recreational amenity for the residents or users of the building, or adjacent buildings, there is also an economic benefit. Green roofs planned for food production have direct economic benefits. The produce harvested for production—and at times enjoyed as a visual amenity by visitors to the roof—is a direct savings in food costs.

On the planning and governmental level, financial incentives and tax reductions (which are institutionalized in many Euro-pean settings) are starting to occur in North America. The use of recycled materials on a green roof may lead to associated lower costs for transportation and manufacturing and sometimes to adjustments in taxes. Some jurisdictions require that a certain portion of new buildings be designated for a green roof, and provide financial incentives to encourage the greening of the city. If a reduction in storm water runoff or a reduction in emissions can be documented, sometimes the regulating governmental authority will reduce the appropriate fee. However, there is a long way to go before incentives and requirements, long established in Europe, are basic code requirements in North America.

• *Increase in the efficiency of photovoltaics.* Some advantages of green roofs come in combination with other new technologies. Photovoltaic panels are often installed on roofs where the solar radiation is the most intense, thereby assuring a high degree of efficiency in converting solar energy to electricity (Fig. 1-15). These panels work best, however, within a certain range of temperatures, without large fluctuations; green roofs help modulate the temperatures within the range that best suits the photovoltaic installations. Green roofs tend to stay much cooler during the day than a standard roof—an advantage for photovoltaic installations.

• *Habitat restoration.* Just as zoological gardens are becoming laboratories for the study, protection, and breeding of endangered species of animals, some green roofs replicate threatened plant habitats, providing an opportunity to study certain plant communities and establish additional ones (Fig. 1-16). The living roof and brown roof projects described later in this book are examples of attempts to create protective habitats for particular species of birds atop roofs. Yet by their very nature as protected environments for the scientific study of endangered communities, some controversy is inevitable because these environments are not made available to people. Open space, whether on the ground or on a roof, is a prized asset. It is not surprising that as green roofs become more common design practice, competition and disagreement will arise over what is the best use for such spaces. Are they for people, for plants and animals, or for all?

• *Environmental monitoring.* As a product of modern technology, some green roofs benefit from the installation of equipment to monitor and test many variables, such as the air temperature and green roof temperature at different times of day, the amount of water absorbed, the storm water runoff, the increase in biomass of the plant materials, the extent of leakage, the exact acoustical and solar insulation, and so on. In time, this accumulation of data will encourage even better results in future installations. When contrasted to similar data for conventional roofing, those data will reinforce the many advantages of green roof installations. Based on the knowledge gained from studying the effects of individual green roof planting installations, scientists are using sophisticated computer models to evaluate and predict the impact of the implementation of green roofs in urban settings on a regional scale.

• *Public education.* Well-designed green roofs provide an opportunity to educate the public on many aspects of the environment. They are often located where educational displays may reach a large audience (Figs. 1-17 and 1-18).

Sustainable Design

Green roofs can be thought of as one component in the large tapestry of processes, design approaches, materials, and construction technologies that comprise *sustainable design*. For this book a working definition of sustainability is important because it has a direct correlation to green roof design. Sustainable design is design that nurtures itself, that uses and recycles all materials and systems so there is no net loss to the environment as a result of implementing the design, and that, once completed, functions without a net drag on the resources and systems on which it depends. Decades before sustainability became a familiar concept, Mahatma Gandhi noted, "Sustainability requires an understanding of how our actions affect our environment, economy and community. We must become the change we wish to see in the world."[28] Green roofs are perhaps one small step in this process.

Yet sustainable design must go well beyond the mere easing or amelioration of environmental problems. It must serve as an integrative process in which connections between people and the built environment are linked in an overarching concept of nature. Perhaps the most far-reaching definition of sustainable design was provided by the noted social ecologist Stephen R. Kellert, who has developed the concept of a restorative environmental design that enriches the human spirit by creating connections between nature and the built environment. He explains:

> Restorative environmental designs avoid and minimize harmful impacts on the natural environment and human health, while also providing positive opportunities for beneficial contact with nature in places of cultural and ecological significance. The major difference from conventional approaches to sustainable design is the tendency only to focus on the first part of the definition (minimizing harmful environmental impacts) while ignoring the inherent human need to affiliate with natural systems, referred to as biophilia by myself and colleagues.[29]

Many of the projects presented in the last three chapters of this book could be categorized as restorative environmental designs, and the important sustainable design features are briefly described.

A correlation to sustainable design is the concept of whole building design, which aims to create a successful high-performance building or project in which all components contribute to the whole. Jan Christiaan Smuts, a South African statesman, philosopher, and author of *Holism and Evolution* (1926), introduced the term "holism," defining it as "the tendency in nature to form wholes that are greater than the sum of the parts through creative evolution."[30] He believed that there are no individual parts in nature, only patterns and arrangements that contribute to the whole. While working on the space program in 1969, the visionary Buckminster Fuller said, "Synergy is the only word in our language that means behavior of whole systems, unpredicted by the separately observed behaviors of the system's parts or any subassembly of the parts . . . The whole is greater than the sum of its parts."[31] Decades later that approach is still essential.

Leadership in Energy and Environmental Design

Leadership in Energy and Environmental Design—known as LEED—is an environmental rating system originally developed by the U.S. Green Building Council to help identify and rate sustainable designs. The Canadian Green Building Council has developed a similar LEED rating system modeled after the original American system. One important aspect of the LEED process is that the design and construction team must document, from the beginning to the end of the building process, compliance with different criteria for sustainability. Even if a building is constructed with many sustainable features, if they are not documented in a step-by-step way, it might not be possible to receive a LEED certification.[32] In either the American or Canadian approach, points (or credits) are awarded for beneficial or positively rated environmental accomplishments in six parts or areas: sustainable site development, water efficiency, energy efficiency, materials and resources selection, indoor environmental quality, and innovation in design. The designers or project managers determine the specific credit within these six parts or areas in order to achieve the full number of points allotted for it. Green roofs could typically earn points for the design in five of these categories—all but indoor environmental quality. A particular green roof design, for example, could reduce storm water runoff, eliminate or reduce site irrigation and water usage, reduce energy usage, use highly rated building materials, and provide innovation in design. Each goal must be carefully documented and verified according to an elaborate process.

In Part 1 of LEED, Sustainable Sites, there are two subcategories of application for green roofs: (1) reduced site disturbance, protect or restore open space; and (2) landscape design that reduces urban heat islands. A project could be awarded points by demonstrating that existing site areas are protected, and damaged areas of the site are restored to provide habitat and promote biodiversity. A green roof that features a restored habitat could demonstrate this requirement in a direct manner. Because green roofs reduce the heat island effect, a substantial green roof that covers at least 50 percent of the roof surface might earn credits under LEED.[33] In Part 2, Water Efficiency, credits are awarded for storm water management, water efficient landscaping, water use reduction, and innovative wastewater techniques. Credits can be earned both for a reduction in the rate and quantity of storm water discharge and for the provision of storm water treatment. Buildings with green roofs in which a collection system to store storm water is implemented may earn credits. If potable water is eliminated as a source for irrigation of the green roof (and other landscape features), then two LEED credits may be earned. Further credits can be earned through methods of reducing potable water use. For example, sometimes storm water can be captured for use in flushing toilets. Still another way to earn credits is to implement wastewater treatment features, such as the incorporation of compost tea or composting toilets. The green roof itself may be designed in a way that helps treat and filter gray water, which is domestic wastewater from dishwashing, handwashing, and bathing (as opposed to sewage contaminated with feces or toxic substances).

In Part 3, Energy Efficiency (sometimes referred to as Energy and Atmosphere), are three important categories: optimize (1) energy performance, (2) renewable energy, and (3) the reduction of ozone-depleting substances. Green roofs that provide thermal insulation and reduce energy consumption demonstrate energy efficiency. LEED emphasizes renewable energy sources instead of traditional ones. The use of photovoltaic cells on a green roof, either to generate electricity for building functions or to power the irrigation system, and the evaporative cooling effect of green roofs may both contribute to LEED credits. Chlorofluorocarbons, when released into the atmosphere, can be a source of chlorine that destroys ozone in the stratosphere. Because ozone absorbs harmful ultraviolet radiation, the reduction of ozone is environmentally damaging. To the degree that it can be demonstrated that the green roof cools the building and reduces the use of refrigerants such as chlorofluorocarbons, LEED credits may be awarded.

In Part 4, Materials and Resources, green roofs may be useful in only one category: the storage and collection of recyclables. For exam-

ple, a green roof could function as a depository for compost, which diverts waste from the local landfill and enriches the growing medium of the green roof. To the degree that materials are recycled or gathered from local sources, thereby reducing transportation costs and the need for manufacturing new materials, the green roof may earn LEED credits.

Part 5, Indoor Environmental Quality, rarely includes categories that relate to a green roof, but, in the future, some indirect applications might apply. For example, carbon monoxide levels are sometimes monitored by the automatic mechanical and ventilation systems of buildings. It is conceivable that future design methods will draw in fresher air from a green roof into the indoor spaces of the building, thereby improving indoor air quality and also reducing energy consumption.

Part 6, Innovation in Design, provides the design team with opportunities to document innovation beyond the predetermined credits from the previous five categories and thereby earn additional LEED credits.

There are four LEED ratings:

Certified	26–32 points
Silver	33–38 points
Gold	39–51 points
Platinum	52 or more

Consultants certified as LEED trained are expert at guiding a project through the LEED process, submitting the test results to the appropriate American or Canadian authority, and helping to gain as many points as possible for each step of the design and building process.

At its best, the LEED system documents for the client, the building owner, and the public that the building, as constructed, has met certain environmental goals. As the world increasingly embraces green design, a LEED certification confers prestige and brings good publicity, perhaps in the same way that the achievement of the tallest building once did. Because the LEED process encompasses design as well as construction, to some degree it can serve as a set of guidelines for the entire project team.

The American and Canadian LEED systems differ in that the latter indirectly provides financial incentives for achieving certain credits. To achieve a LEED certification in the area of energy, the Canadian Commercial Building Incentive Program (CBIP) provides stringent requirements for reducing energy consumption by at least 25 percent and for increasing energy efficiency. If, through the meticulous LEED documentation, calculation, and verification process, a building satisfies these requirements, financial incentives of $60,000–$100,000 are available from CBIP. No such financial incentives are included in the U.S. system. Nevertheless, it is becoming common practice, particularly for federal and state agencies (but also some private developers) to require a minimum level of LEED certification in their new buildings.

The foregoing discussion has introduced you to the LEED process and its vocabulary. The Winnipeg Mountain Co-op Building, in Winnipeg, Canada, in which a LEED certification was achieved, is presented in Chapter Five. There I describe some of the specific credits applied for and the extent to which they were achieved. Several other projects noted in this book have either received a LEED certification or are in the process at the time of writing. The Web sites of both the U.S. Green Building Council and the Canadian Green Building Council include descriptions, some in considerable detail, of many projects that have achieved LEED certifications. Please see www.USGBG.org and www.cagbc.org.

Opposite:
1-19. An installation of photovoltaic panels on a green roof in Basel, Switzerland. (Courtesy of Stephan Brenneisen)

1-20. Another view of the photovoltaic installation at the Exhibit Hall #1 in Basel, emphasizing the expansive scale and vast size of the extensive sedum roof.

CHAPTER TWO

The Green Roof Design Process

Preceding pages:
2-0. A series of green roofs and a recirculating water channel are functional yet decorative elements in a modern housing development in Denmark. (Courtesy of Ulrik Reeh, Veg Tech.)

In many ways the green roof design process is no different from the design process for other multifaceted installations involving many design disciplines. An excellent model of the design process is presented by landscape architect Lawrence Halprin in his book *RSVP Cycles*.[1] The title is his paradigm for the design process: *R* = resources such as information; *S* = scores, making notations of conditions, processes, and designs; *V* = valuation, a combination of evaluation and taking actions; and *P* = performance, the final execution of the design. The following discussion uses an eleven-stage model to describe the specific requirements of a design process for green roofs. Although the stages are presented in chronological order, the process is often a cycle, whereby additional information may have a beneficial impact not only on the stages to follow, but also those started earlier but not yet complete. Whereas Halprin's design process is abstract, the model presented here consists of practical tasks, each of which could be subsumed into one of his categories.

The necessity for a coordinated team effort cannot be underestimated. As noted in Chapter One, a synergistic approach is appropriate. Don

Fowler and Stephanie Viera describe it:

> This is a deviation from the typical planning and design process of relying on the expertise of specialists who work in their respective specialties somewhat isolated from each other. Whole building design in practice requires an integrated team process in which the design team and all affected stakeholders work together throughout the project phases and to evaluate the design for cost, quality-of-life, future flexibility, efficiency, overall environmental impact, productivity, creativity, and how the occupants will be enlivened.[2]

In what follows, various methods and products are described. The purpose is to introduce the materials and vocabularies, not to recommend one product or method over another. For any particular green roof project, the final selection should be based on the accumulated expertise and experience of the design team members. In the case studies of projects in Europe and North America in Chapters Four and Five of this book, specific products and methods of installation are cited. A number of examples in this chapter relate to issues in New York City, but similar issues may well be anticipated in other locations or jurisdictions.

Assemble a Design Team

Green roofs, even small ones, are complex designs that require the seamless integration of many different components, each with its own disparate requirements. Because one of the most common problems in green roof applications is lack of coordination, the first step in designing a green roof is to assemble the design team. This team should include a project manager or coordinator, who may come from one of many different disciplines. He or she should be capable of understanding the vocabulary and potential contribution of each major consultant, should emphasize sharing and communication of all information, and should endeavor to keep the project on schedule. Depending on the complexity and size of the project, various designers and contractors should be part of the design team. For a small project, particularly one in which a green roof is to be situated on the roof of an existing building, the architect, landscape architect, or other consultants might not all be

2-1. An integrated team process and design approach are recommended by the Whole Building Design Group in order to achieve successful projects. (Courtesy of wbdg.org)

necessary. For a large and complex project, the members might include an architect, a landscape architect, an ecologist, a structural engineer, a civil engineer, an irrigation specialist or designer, a LEED consultant (if LEED certification is desired), and a representative of the co-op or condominium association, if the project planned is a residence of this type. The roofing contractor and landscape contractor should also be considered part of the design team and included in all major meetings and coordination activities.

The various manufacturers that provide components of the green roof—the membrane manufacturer, the nursery providing plant materials, the substrate or growing media manufacturer, the irrigation manufacturer, and any special systems provider—should be mined for information about how to best use their products. They may also need to participate in occasional coordination meetings to verify that the way their products are being specified is correct and that they see no problems with the proposed method of installation or how their product abuts or dovetails with another.

As noted in Chapter One, some green roof manufacturers provide an integrated system in which each component is part of a "sandwich" of stacked layers; other systems may have components designed by different manufacturers. Using one supplier's entire system means that only one representative, rather than several, will be on the design team. This method also focuses responsibility for the green roof system entirely on that one company, which will usually have clear testing requirements to verify a correct installation. Furthermore, if a problem occurs, it is hard to blame it on someone else.

Identify Program Goals

The second task in designing a green roof is to develop and refine the program. Le Corbusier once wrote, "To design requires talent, to program requires genius."[3] The more questions that can be generated, and the more thoughtful the answers, the closer the design team will come to a clear program for the project. Answers to questions such as who is going to use the green roof, what is its purpose, how will the public or the private owner benefit, what size will it be, why should it be provided, and so on, will dictate or suggest buildable design solutions.

The most basic question to be answered is, what is the intended use of the roof: Is it for people to use, for aesthetics only, for habitat creation? Will people use it on a regular basis? Will it be accessible or inaccessible? Will there be separate and distinct components, each of which might have different requirements, or will there be a uniform treatment throughout? Will the green roof be extensive only, semi-intensive, only intensive? Is the green roof being built to address a specific problem, such as to reduce storm water runoff, to provide a public amenity, or as a demonstration project?

Conduct Research, Inventory, and Site Analysis

The next task is to gather information. If an existing building is being fitted with a green roof, this information includes an inventory of its conditions and a site analysis. Sometimes city agencies have a building plan dating from the time in which an application for a construction permit was filed. Considerable research may be required to determine if the roof and structural members were built as indicated on the plan. Architects and engineers for a building typically are proud of their creations, and are quite willing to verify which elements in the roof plan were implemented, and which might not have been built as designed. Even if there are significant differences between the plan and existing conditions, the plan is usually invaluable in identifying major components of the roof structure.

When there are discrepancies between what is shown on the plans and site conditions, it is advisable to do test borings or other analysis to determine exact conditions. This might involve peeling away some of the roof membrane to reveal if drains shown on the plan are present at the site. The structural design is the most important element to verify, because relatively small variations in the spacing of structural members may determine whether the roof can support an anticipated design and its required load. If the design is complex and likely to push the load requirements, then it is more likely that such tests will be required.

During this site inventory process, a team should photograph the existing roof, verify the dimensions of the parapet, locate drains and assess how well they are functioning, and determine what other utilities or systems are present.

For example, is there an electrical outlet? Water tanks, mechanical equipment, and other standard objects should be inventoried. The green roof design must respond to all of these site conditions, so the more accurate the information gathered in this stage of the process, the easier it is to avoid problems later.

The feasibility of a green roof must be evaluated by gathering information about loading considerations, the existing or proposed roof membrane for waterproofing, regulatory requirements (which may vary substantially from city to city and to a larger degree on a regional scale), building codes and occupancy requirements, and the life cycle status of key components. Some aspects of building codes may be similar from place to place, such as the height of parapets, usually 36–42 inches (91.4–106.7 cm), and setback distances from the edge of the parapet to the green roof vegetation. However, many cities have unique requirements. Some cities, for example, have strict limits on the use of combustible materials, such as wood, because of concerns about potential fire hazards in a dense urban environment.

Even at this early stage, it is time to anticipate access to the roof for construction. The site analysis should determine the capacity of the freight elevator and the route through the building to bring construction materials and plants to the roof. If no elevator is present, existing stairs may suffice for small installations, but for larger projects materials must be hoisted by crane or pumped to the roof, and the design team must consider this requirement.

Densely built urban sites rarely allow a secure holding area immediately adjacent to the building. Often a portion of the roof itself must be used, at least temporarily, to hold materials, and additional protection of this area of the roof must be anticipated and the logistics included in the plan. Materials must be brought to the site in an orderly way and dovetail with construction operations. The design team must carefully consider these factors as it determines which suppliers and contractors to hire.

2-2, 2-3. Metal planters set atop the parapet at Earth Pledge's green roof comply with building code requirements for height to insure safety while providing space to grow vegetables. (*Bottom photo*: courtesy of Earth Pledge)

Even if a new building is planned, the design team should provide input to the architect early on concerning issues of structural design, drainage, and logistics. Failure to anticipate the green roof as a major design element can be a major failing of new buildings; the contractor installing the roof may find that there is no adequate freight elevator or the access route is difficult. A common problem is a parapet height that matches the minimum of the local building code but does not anticipate the added height of the green roof components, so that once the green roof is installed, the parapet height would be in violation of the code. In such instances, there are two possible solutions: add height to the parapet, at an excessive cost and often with unsightly results, or pull back the green roof installation several feet or more, resulting in an awkward design. It is far better for the architect meeting with the design team to know from the beginning that a green roof of a certain thickness needs to be incorporated into the design.

Balance Costs with Benefits

The fourth stage is to determine the potential benefits to be provided by the green roof as offset by the proposed cost of materials, labor, and regulatory requirements. See Table 2-1 for some infrastructure costs usually associated with traditional roof gardens which may also be applicable to modern green roof designs. As noted in Chapter One, some benefits are obvious. Other benefits are harder to assess but must also be considered. Might the green roof increase property values, thereby justifying some of its costs? Will there be favorable publicity in the media? Will the green roof provide a community function, such as a place for vegetable gardening, that might also justify expenditures in creating the best possible environment for food production?

Material and labor costs may vary substantially depending on the materials and methods chosen or required. For example, is the waterproofing a poured-in-place membrane or a torched-down application? Is it asphaltic or of some other material? What warranty will the roofing supplier give for this application? In some localities regulations limit or forbid certain methods of application.

The structural reinforcement of the roof is a crucial factor. For existing buildings, it is necessary to examine construction documents, particularly civil and structural engineering drawings, and to research building code filings to verify what was built. For buildings being planned, it is important to remember that although the cost of increasing the loading capacity of the roof is expensive, it is much less expensive to build for a certain capacity from the beginning than to retrofit an already completed structure months or years later. If there is any likelihood that a green roof will be added to a new building in the future, it is cost efficient to build into the new structure the capacity to carry the required loads.

Another major cost factor is the substrate used and, to some degree, the other materials of the growing medium. These materials usually include shale, calcined clay, pumice, and nonnative soils.[4] Often local materials are favored because the transportation costs are reduced. However, it is unusual that local soils will provide a viable growing medium on green roofs, unless soils are at least 18 inches (45.7 cm) or deeper. (Some successful green roofs have used local soils, particularly in Europe.) Still, it is cost-efficient to use materials supplied as close as possible to the source.

Local substrate is sometimes a choice for green roofs that will feature local plant communities, because these plants may more readily acclimate on substrate compositions that are similar to their native environment. However, it is a very challenging problem to recreate native flora communities on green roofs, because there are so many conditions that must be studied and replicated, from the type and depth of soil to the range of plant materials. One approach, currently in use in Basel, Switzerland, is to develop indigenous, biologically diverse plant communities.[5] Of course, some tough native plants can be mixed into almost any green roof design.

Usually additive components to the substrate, such as organic matter, aerating materials, or occasional nutrients, are present. Although it is still preferable to use local sources, it is not quite as important because the proportion of these materials in the total composition of the growing medium is not nearly as substantial as the substrate itself. One additional cost consideration is whether the mixing occurs at the site—either on the roof or (more likely) at the base of the building in the construction zone—or whether the materials are

Table 2-1. TRADITIONAL ROOF GARDENS: TYPICAL COSTS: INFRASTRUCTURE
(Assuming 1,000 square foot (92.9 m²) area retrofit on existing roof)

ITEM	QUANTITY	UNIT	UNIT COST	ITEM TOTAL	METRIC
A. Quarry tile removal[1]	1,000	f^2	$12.00	$12,000.00	$129.17/m²
B. Pavers on pedestals—granite or slate[2]	1,000	f^2	$75.00	$75,000.00	$807.32/m²
C. Parapet wall—Repair cap/flashing[3]	150	Lin Ft	$750.00	$112,500.00	$2460/Lin. M.
D. New roof with a 20 year guarantee[4]	1,000	f^2	$25.00	$25,000.00	$269/m²
E. Conduit/utilities underneath pavers[5]	250	LF	$12.00	$3,000.00	$39.36/m
F. Steel guardrail[6]	150	LF	$75.00	$11,250.00	$246/m
G. Irrigation—lump sum[7]	1	LS		$8,000.00	
H. Custom designed planters at parapet[8]	150	LF	$300.00	$45,000.00	$984/m
TOTAL				$291,750.00	

NOTES
1. This many not be necessary, but many old roofs must have pavers replaced, or at least re-set.
2. Precast concrete pavers could be as little as $25.00/$f^2$ ($269/m²); custom selected stone as much as $100.00/$f^2$ ($1,076/m²) or more.
3. This assumes that some amount of repair or treatment is necessary; sometimes none is necessary.
4. A standard manufacturer's roof with guaranteed waterproofing.
5. Installation of copper water lines, conduits for gas or electric, cables for internet, etc.
6. Assume height of 42 inches (1.07 m) to comply with standard building codes; customized designs cost more.
7. Installation of backflow preventer, water meter, zone controller, and drip system.
8. Planters are the most variable in cost: with lattice panels and liners to protect wood, the cost could be much higher; if prefabricated planters are used, without a custom design, the cost would be much lower.
Total costs can easily reach $300.00/$f^2$ ($3,229.25 m²) or more.

Savings for intensive and extensive green roofs can be anticipated: an inaccessible, extensive green roof would not include Items B, F or H, and an extensive roof on a new building would not include items A and C, so that costs could be as low as $36/$f^2$ or $387.50/m². Even an intensive green roof would not include all items from the list.

(Table based on author's professional experience)

premixed and brought to the site. In either case, careful testing must verify that the substrate mixture complies with all requirements (the various percentages of each component and the total weight). A uniform substrate mixture is sometimes easier to verify in premixing that occurs under carefully controlled conditions compared to mixing on site under less controlled conditions (subject to adverse weather, for example, or lack of storage space).

Transportation and shipping costs can add up quickly. Local sources are preferable not only for the substrate and the components of the growing medium and plant materials, but also for structural elements and all green roof components. Nurseries may piggyback the plant materials for a small installation onto the same truck that is carrying plants for a large installation. The nurseries thereby provide a competitive price, but the double booking may require careful timing of the planting schedule. The plantings for both the large and small installation would likely need to be carried out at the same time.

Type and ease of access to the roof affect costs substantially. In some buildings, roof access is available only along circuitous basement corridors to freight elevators, which have limited capacity as to height, width, and weight. In these circumstances it may be necessary to hoist some materials to the roof or use hoses to propel fine substrate mixture and seeds to the roof. Hoisting of large volumes of substrate (for the growing medium) as well as components for planters, arbors, and other structures is typical for intensive roof gardens, but also quite expensive. Depending on the location, the government may require that hoisting occur within certain hours when traffic is minimal (not necessarily the most convenient time for such operations). Sometimes policemen are required to be present to direct traffic and avoid accidents. Charges for hoists and personnel can be accrued per hour or per day.

The choice of plant materials and the method of installing them are basic cost considerations. The limit on the size of plant materials for intensive green roofs may be determined by the size of the planters, the weight of the plants, and how all of them would be brought to the roof. In general, for perennials and shrubs, smaller materials often adapt better to harsh growing conditions than larger, more mature ones, but spaces for specimen trees are still possible in certain expansive designs. Methods of installation for typical

2-4. Hoisting of substrate to the roof of the Botanical Gardens of Augustenborg in Malmö. See Chapter Four for a discussion of this project. (Courtesy of Marten Setterblad and Annika Kruuse)

2-5. Plant materials suitable for green roofs being grown at Emory Knoll Farms, Street, Maryland. See Chapter Three for a discussion of this project.

extensive green roofs may include hydroseeding (in which the seed is part of an emulsion sprayed by a machine over a large area), manual seeding, manual broadcasting of sprigs or cuttings, or planting of individual rooted plants. Often cuttings or sprigs can be broadcast over the prepared substrate bed without additional labor for planting piece by piece. Because so many extensive green roof plants are sedums or other typical plants from common species, the cost per plant, per sprig, or per cutting may not vary that much. Individual rooted plants are more expensive, but if well maintained, may produce faster results. It is likely that labor costs for extensive roofs will vary substantially, depending on the method selected, and have a more significant impact on total project costs than the price of the plant materials themselves.

The schedule for placement of the growing medium mixture and the installation of the plant materials may have cost considerations. A delay between the placement of the growing medium and the installation of the plantings creates a strong possibility that the medium will become contaminated with windblown seeds. Typically, the ideal time for planting in temperate climates is early spring, after the last frost, when the weather is still cool enough to allow plants to adapt to increasingly hotter temperatures. An alternate time is early fall, before regular frosts, when the weather is still warm enough for plants to establish roots, even if growth does not become well established until the following spring. Planting in the intense heat of the summer may result in significant plant losses, particularly if no irrigation is included. Depending on the severity of the loss, replanting or reseeding might be required.

Since green roofs are an evolving industry in North America, contractors may not always be willing to guarantee their work, particularly the planting, since so many factors may affect it. Of course, the cost will be higher for guaranteed work; however, this must be balanced against the cost and inconvenience of replanting significant portions of the green roof should the initial, less expensive installation fail. As the landscape contracting industry gains experience in green roof installation, the inclusion of a guarantee of the plant materials may become standardized.

Maintenance is a major cost consideration. Some green roofs, particularly extensive ones, require less maintenance than others, but *some* level of maintenance is essential. The utopian dream of a maintenance-free design is about as realistic as a putting green of living turf that never needs mowing: there is no maintenance-free green roof. At a minimum, periodic inspections must be conducted to remove seedlings of weeds or undesirable plants, as well as those that could penetrate the root barriers. Often irrigation is not required once the green roof is established, but it may be a necessity during the initial months after installation. Even the hardiest of plants typically used for intensive green roofs require watering during long periods of drought. Many maintenance costs—such as the extent and amount to which fertilizers, herbicides, and pesticides are used—depend on the type of green roof, the palette of plant materials selected, as well as the goals of the design team. It may be part of the maintenance process to exclude fertilization, irrigation, and application of all chemicals. In some designs the "invasion" of the green roof by volunteers that arrive by windborne or animal-carried seeds is greeted with alarm, and every last "weed" must be removed. Other designs welcome them and refer to them as "colonizers" because the goal of the green roof is to let nature take its own course. The former approach implies a higher level of maintenance. Regardless of the design and program, the design team must anticipate a maintenance plan for the green roof and incorporate a budget for maintenance into the total cost of the project.

The previous discussion about costs has focused on comparing and analyzing different items of work and evaluating them on a case by case basis, depending on the design and objectives. An important procedure to follow for green roof design is a life cycle cost analysis (LCCA), which considers "all costs of acquiring, owning and disposing of a building or building system."[6] Although a complete description of LCCA cannot be provided in this book, a summary of the process is warranted. As explained by Sieglinde Fuller of the National Institute of Standards and Technology, LCCA is particularly helpful in comparing alternatives that fulfill the same performance requirements. LCCA is also applicable to "any capital investment decision in which relatively higher initial costs are traded for reduced future cost obligations. It is particularly suitable for the evaluation of building design alternatives that satisfy a required level of building performance but may have different investment costs, different operating and maintenance and repair costs, and possibly different lives." LCCA for a green roof design should be done early in the design process, when the results can guide the design team in seeking the best combination of methods and materials. The numerous costs associated with acquiring, operating, maintaining, and disposing of a building system are carefully evaluated and analyzed. Costs to be considered include: the initial costs of purchasing, acquisition, and construction; fuel costs; operation, maintenance and repair costs; replacement costs; residual values such as resale, salvage, or disposal costs; and finance charges such as loan interest payments and non-monetary benefits. After identifying all costs year by year, they are used to arrive at total life cycle costs for each alternative. Although there are uncertainties in the projections, given that some costs can only be estimated, the results may nevertheless be a useful guide for the design team. LCCA has become so sophisticated that different methods may be used to reveal break-even costs, particular sensitivities to energy and water conservation projects, and other specific applications. LCCA methods may also be used to anticipate inflation and the inclusion of non-monetary benefits or costs which are hard to quantify. The use of computer programs can make the process more efficient and easier to document; some software packages have been developed for LCCA.

Consider Design and Building Codes

The next stage of the design process involves balancing design goals and requirements against the building code restraints. As with the programming process, the most important initial design consideration is the matter of who is going to use the green roof. If more than a small number of people are going to use it on a regular basis, then the application would have to be an intensive green roof—which requires more structural support, deeper depths for planting, guardrail protection at the parapet, and considerably greater costs than an extensive green roof (Fig. 2-6). For example, if a green roof is planned atop an apartment building, and part of the anticipated usage of that roof is for the residents of the building to use all or part of the roof as a recreational amenity, then an intensive green roof design would be necessary. All components of the roof that people would use must comply with often stringent building code requirements for parapet height, design loads, access, safety, and so on.

Access to the roof is a critical design consideration. Even when a green roof is planned for a new building, designers may overlook how people will reach the roof, particularly for extensive green roof designs. Although some extensive green roof designs are accessible for many visitors, it is also typical that only a small number of people, usually maintenance workers, require access. Extensive green roofs can be considered as visual amenities, providing restful views for

2-6. In this modern roof garden, the guardrail includes glass panels, which, when kept clean, give the illusion that there is no barrier at all.

Above left:
2-7. A spiral staircase provides easy access to a green roof at Gemperle Warehouse and Garden Center. See Chapter Four for a discussion of this project.

Above right and right:
2-8, 2-9. A step ladder through the major mechanical space for a hospital might pose difficulties for safety and security, although access to this green roof is limited mainly to scientists, such as Nathalie Baumann, standing at right. Her research is described in Chapter Four. This passageway and roof are at the Rossetti Building, University Hospital, Basel.

people in the building or adjacent buildings, in contrast to typical barren, equipment-encrusted urban rooftops. Yet if there is no clear, accessible access route, the likely result will be poor maintenance, and no matter what the original intent of the design, the aesthetic benefits will deteriorate over time. It is best to have access to the green roof via an elevator reach or a well-designed set of stairs. These approaches become obvious requirements for an intensive application. An elevator or staircase allows for direct access not only by people, but for tools, equipment, and sometimes replacement plants and other significant elements. By contrast, climbing a portable ladder to the top or following a circuitous route up narrow stairs through the building's rooftop mechanical systems will soon create major problems (Figs. 2-7, 2-8, and 2-9). As building code requirements become more standardized, such indirect and limited access will likely constitute a code violation.

Research of all applicable building codes is a major design consideration as well. Some cities, such as Chicago and Portland, Oregon, where major green roof initiatives have been implemented, have clearer codes. New York City is close to implementing one. However, designs should be discussed and reviewed with building code representatives, construction departments, and all applicable agencies that have jurisdiction in the conceptual stages of the design so that agreement about compliance can be reached at the earliest possible time. To the extent that city government provides funding or incentives for green roof designs, it may require certain performance or design standards, such as a percentage of coverage or minimum depth of growing medium.[7]

Portland (Oregon), Chicago, and Toronto —all cities at the forefront of green roof design—have implemented planning guidelines, including incentives for developers. Portland has an Office of Sustainable Development whose mission includes coordination and technical assistance for the implementation of ecoroofs, and there is a Bureau of Environmental Services ecoroof Web site.[8] Homeowners and building owners are eligible for a maximum 35 percent discount on their municipal storm water fee for qualifying ecoroofs. Projects that install eco-roofs in the Central City Plan District are eligible for a floor area ratio bonus, which increases the building's allowable area. The larger the proportional size of the ecoroof built within the Central City, the larger the bonus of additional floor area awarded: one square foot (0.0929 m^2) of additional floor area for each square foot of ecoroofs when they are at least 10 percent of the building's footprint; two square feet (0.19 m^2) for eco-roofs covering at least 30 percent; and three square feet (0.28 m^2) where the total area of ecoroof is at least 60 percent of the footprint. Portland is also planning a storm water discount program, whereby water and sewer bills will be lowered based on the implementation of ecoroofs within the properties. Portland also requires ecoroofs in some districts if the city is providing some portion of the funds for development projects. New city-owned construction projects and major retrofits must meet LEED gold certification, and there are specific certification requirements in such areas as storm water management and water and energy savings that encourage implementation of ecoroofs. Design and construction of all new city-owned facilities must include an ecoroof with at least 70 percent coverage and high reflectivity. Even for city-owned and occupied buildings, a silver LEED certification is required. Portland has more LEED-registered buildings than any other city in the United States. That most are privately owned, rather than city owned, indicates the degree to which its citizens embrace green building design.

Although Chicago has substantial green roofs, there is only one regulatory tool—a density bonus in the city's zoning ordinance—which defines green roofs as a public amenity that improves "the quality of life of city residents, employees and visitors and [is] a benefit to the public."[9] To qualify for the bonus, the green roof must occur within a certain zoning district and cover more than 50 percent of the net roof area (that is, the total area of the roof minus any area covered by mechanical equipment) or 2,000 square feet (185.8 m^2) of contiguous roof area, whichever is greater. The city requires documentation to demonstrate that the building can support the green roof, and the additional loads, and that there is adequate space left for other functions, such as mechanical equipment. The developer must also comply with the Chicago Department of Environment guidelines about plant varieties and growing media and depth;

additionally, the green roof is subject to periodic inspection. The bonuses do not apply for green roofs intended for individual dwelling units. The floor area bonus for qualifying green roofs that meet all the above conditions is calculated as follows: Bonus FAR = (area of roof landscaping in excess of 50% of net roof area ÷ lot area) x 0.30 x Base FAR. The Chicago Department of the Environment, as well as other departments, already requires certain green building initiatives, including green roofs, on buildings that receive public funding, and has incentives for quicker approval processes for projects that meet certain qualifications, such as green roofs.

In Canada, major cities are implementing green roof standards as well. A study by Ryerson University in November 2005, commissioned by the city of Toronto, made recommendations based on a computer model that assumed at least 75 percent coverage on flat roofs more than 3,767.4 square feet (350 m²). Spearheaded by Councillor Joe Pantalone, the Toronto City Council in early February 2006 adopted policies to encourage green roof implementation.[10] Incentives are provided through the Green Roof Incentive Pilot Program with a $200,000 budget for the first year providing a $10/SF ($107.64/ m²) financial incentive up to a maximum of $20,000 per project. There is also a requirement that green roofs be installed on new city owned buildings and on retrofit projects where feasible. Consideration is given to a policy of incorporating a storm water utility charge, a common practice in Europe. This policy might be paired with one to lower water rates for properties with green roofs. Other major Canadian cities are also implementing green policies. Vancouver has LEED gold certification requirements for all public projects and Alberta has LEED silver requirements.

Even when there may not, as yet, be specific planning or construction code requirements for green roofs (or while they are in the process of being implemented), many cities have LEED certification requirements, the compliance with which will often result in the construction of green roofs. Scottsdale, Arizona has a LEED gold certification requirement for all public projects; and the cities of Seattle, Washington; Atlanta, Georgia; Arlington, Massachusetts; Boulder, Colorado; Kansas City, Missouri; Dallas and Houston, Texas; San Francisco and San Diego, and many other cities in California have a LEED silver certification requirement.[11]

Conflicts between different codes may arise. For example, in New York City, if a building is within a landmarked district, regardless of whether the building itself is historic, new, or just old, regulations developed by the Landmarks Preservation Commission require that nothing be visible on the roof from any adjacent view corridor, that is, the full width of any adjacent street from which the building is visible. There is a similar organization in Chicago; other cities have different design-oriented bureaucracies, such as an arts commission, various zoning boards, and community boards that all must be contacted, and to which presentations must be made and approvals granted. For example, in New York City, the Landmarks Preservation Commission often demonstrates some flexibility in considering designs with slightly visible elements if the design provides other elements that are consistent with the design intent of the district and enhance the building or neighborhood. However, it is hard to predict how the commission's staff will react. For example, in the Tribeca district, designated historic for its vintage cast-iron warehouses and industrial buildings, but now an area with many residential buildings, the commission has opposed street tree plantings because they are not typical of the historic vocabulary of the district. The goals of such organizations are often admirable—protecting historic buildings and preventing a clutter of ugly construction that would mar a beautiful neighborhood—yet the rulings and results are not always compatible with solid urban design and modern aesthetic criteria nor with efforts to develop healthy and sustainable design in such neighborhoods.

The New York City Building Department also has stringent requirements that limit the percentage of combustible materials that may be used on a roof. Emergency access must be maintained so that, in the event of a fire, for example, emergency workers have ready access to the roof. Care must be taken if adding pergolas (or other overhead elements with any sort of continuous solid roof) that they are not overly dense, providing so much privacy that the roof is viewed as an additional floor to the building—which is illegal. If public funds are involved in the construction, then approval must be granted by the

New York City Arts Commission, which can require changes to reflect its own criteria for what constitutes appropriate design.

In the United States, a recent development has been the emergence of the International Building Code (IBC) in 1994, which came about as a result of efforts to overcome the highly varied codes then in use, and often in conflict with one another, which were written by three regional associations.[12] The Building Officials and Code Administrators, International, Inc. (BOCA), the International Conference of Building Officials (ICBC) and the Southern Building Code Congress International, Inc. (SBC) merged to form the International Code Council (ICC), which developed the IBC, now in use by all but three states. Many major American cities, including Houston, Philadelphia, Phoenix, San Antonio, Dallas, Seattle, and Denver, use the IBC as the basis for their building codes. California is on the verge of modifying and adopting the IBC. In 2007 New York City revised its building code (the first major revision since 1968) to comply with the IBC, but it must still be approved by the City Council. New York has added a section on sustainability, with incentives such as fee waivers or rebates for the implementation of green roofs, to the IBC.

A final review process may involve the building itself. Co-op boards or condominium associations must approve the design if the building is either. Because sometimes a roof garden design might primarily benefit only the owner of the apartment with direct access to the roof, a co-op board is not always as interested in the most visually exciting or innovative design as it is in one that will have the least negative impact on other residents. Elements such as water features, structures, even drains—all of which might result in leaks or additional penetrations through the roof—are likely to be highly contested by the co-op board or the owners or renters of the apartments most at risk. Sometimes the design is approved only if the client pays for additional protections on the roof that may not be even be necessary. Finally, co-op boards, as well as the building department, will take keen interest in the added weight of what is proposed. It is essential to calculate loads and demonstrate that the completed design will not exceed the maximum calculated load of the roof being used as a base for a roof garden.

2-10. The edge of the green roof atop Chicago's City Hall is pulled back from the parapet in order to comply with the minimum height restrictions.

Because all of these different agencies, public and private, have jurisdiction over the approval of a design for a roof garden, New York City has become home to a whole class of consultants, called expeditors, whose sole role is to present complex designs of different types to the various agencies, streamline the process, and help gain approval for construction. Different and conflicting approvals, recommendations, and requirements by these various agencies must also be resolved. The expeditors' fees are passed on to the client seeking a permit for building a specific roof garden design. There are similar bureaucracies in other cities across North America, so that similar problems and requirements are to be expected.

It is important to be aware of which codes apply and how to take advantage of them. For example, green roofs in Portland, Oregon, have been mandated as part of the long process of reducing peak flow storm water runoff into the Willamette River to protect salmon, green roof designs that retain substantial percentages of the anticipated runoff and retard its discharge, thereby saving costs on the installation of larger storm water systems, will be favored in design review. Similarly, a New York City roof garden that has semi-extensive components will likely receive a favorable review, because the benefits provided by the extensive elements can be considered tradeoffs for the more expensive elements of the intensive design. In Chicago, the

visible from the street. The downside of this solution is that because even the perimeter walk has some thickness to it, the parapet is just below its required height, and visitors to the roof must be carefully supervised. The Chicago government welcomes visitors, but groups can be difficult to handle.

Another example is in Toronto, where Green Roofs for Healthy Cities funded, designed, and built a 6,000-square-foot (557.4-m^2) demonstration garden at City Hall with eight different plots to demonstrate different types of green roof materials, sedum treatment, food production, and approaches to developing habitats for native plants and invertebrates. To preserve historic views of the building from its main public square, the local planning agency did not permit any trees to be used on the green roof.

Green roofs must be safe and secure—a basic design requirement that also is one of the major purposes of most building and zoning codes. However, what is required may vary considerably from place to place. For intensive applications, parapets of 36–42 inches (91.4–106.7 cm) in height or guardrails with clear criteria for each component (the minimum size of each member, and maximum vertical and horizontal spacing) eliminate any chance of a person slipping or falling off the roof. By compliance with these criteria, the guardrails also meet standards for the strength of the railings. Protection at the perimeter edge may be minimal for extensive applications, particularly in Europe, where few people use the roof (Figs. 2-12, 2-13, and 2-14). In North America this minimal protection is sometimes the case as well. If so, it is important to know the liability protections of the building owner's insurance. Often, it is desirable to increase the coverage, if practical. Careful and regular maintenance practices also protect the building owner.

Fire and police departments often have requirements about building access in the event of an emergency. If gates or other security features are present, there must be a way for policemen or firemen to break in easily, whether via some form of automatic control that opens the gates or doors in an emergency or copies of keys that are kept with the fire department. To prevent impediment to emergency workers gaining access to the roof at any point, there may be requirements for an unplanted perime-

2-11. Toronto City Hall's green roof. (Courtesy of Green Roofs for Healthy Cities)

implementation of the green roof on the city hall came up against landmark requirements similar to those in New York City. The historic guardrail on the parapet could not be tampered with; had the green roof been brought to the edge of the parapet, the height of the guardrail would have been substandard. A negotiated solution was to create a walk at the perimeter, immediately adjacent to the parapet, which minimized any reduction in the effective height of the guardrail. The green roof treatment, now inside this perimeter frame, could be built up to suit the different green roof applications being implemented. Because it was set back from the perimeter edge, no aspect of the green roof was

ter edge set in gravel or pavement for a width of 12–36 inches (30.5–91.4 cm). A corollary to this requirement is that, in some applications, all green roof construction must be set back a minimum distance from any exterior wall. For example, if an extension of a building wall continues above the roof, planters may not be set directly against it, and a clear access route may be required between the face of the wall and the rear of the planters.

As the design process moves forward, ecological and microclimatic considerations may gain prominence. Some green roofs are designed to replicate a naturally occurring but endangered ecology in the region. The attempt to build this type of green roof may also be a way to mitigate destruction of similar habitat that is occurring elsewhere. The green roof movement in England started as an attempt to provide alternate habitat for the black redstart, an indigenous bird, a process described in Chapter Four. Scientists can greatly advance their knowledge of green roof methods and applications and of that specific ecology by attempting to recreate it and study it on a roof. Several projects presented in Chapter Five, including the Green Institute and the public library in Minneapolis, the Cedar Hammock Conservation Center near Winnipeg, the Mountain Co-op, also in Winnipeg, and the Neuhoff facility in Nashville, Tennessee, created specific habitats on green roofs. If the green roof is accessible in this type of situation, its use by the building tenants or residents must be balanced against the research needs of the scientists, while also complying with access, safety and all other requirements of the local building codes. Access for most people is not permitted on most ecological green roofs, although the design team may still have to comply with all relevant code requirements, such as having guardrails. Typically, only minimal access is provided for maintenance and research personnel, but the roof provides a pleasing view for those whose offices or apartments face it. On the other hand, some people find such views unappealing or messy.

Many opportunities to take advantage of microclimatic variations, or to attempt to create them through variety, exist within the total area of a green roof. It is rare that building code issues would prevent such experimentation. The plant materials and animals that would likely become established in areas of a green roof that are more sheltered from sun or wind will vary from those in other areas of the roof. If the design team experiments with changing the composition, depth, and degree of slope of the growing medium as well as the range of species planted, then it is likely that the plants and animals that thrive or colonize the green roof will vary considerably. Even if access is forbidden to the public, as long as people are able to view such green roofs, these evolving habitats may be appreciated at a distance for their complexity as well as their visual interest.

2-12. Most green roofs, no matter what the size, require a setback from the edge of the parapet. Requirements for guardrails vary. The gravel walk allows for access for maintenance of the photovoltaic installation atop the Basel Convention Center.

2-13. University Hospital Basel has no guardrail since this roof is viewed by patients and used only for scientific purposes. See Chapter Four for a discussion of this project.

Fig. 2-14. In Rotkreuz, Switerland, a young Northern lapwing (*Vanellus vanellus*) with its mother on a gravel roof about 40 to 50 years old with sparse sedum and moss. The roof was greened in February, 2007, in order to provide more habitat for the birds, who responded by building four additional nests. See Chapter Four for a discussion of this project. (Courtesy of Nathalie Baumann)

Prepare Conceptual Drawings and Construction Documents

Landscape architects are used to preparing drawings from the preliminary to the final stages of the design process. For any design beyond the simplest, a set of drawings to identify the boundaries of the project and materials and methods of construction is necessary. Details in the drawings note areas where dovetailing of different materials and construction trades is required. Because the drawings are typically executed in different phases, from conceptual to design development to final construction documents with specifications, each phase of the drawings, as prepared by one or several consultants or design team members, gives the whole team a chance to carefully review the project. Agreement on a conceptual design should precede more detailed phases of design, and then construction drawings. The early stages of drawings are the most appropriate time to challenge the design and to identify potential problems, so that subsequent drawings will describe a clear, complete, and cohesive design.

A coordinated effort among all the members of the design team is needed to achieve the best possible integration of the green roof design with other aspects of the building. Such issues and details as views of the roof, the use of the green roof, water management, drainage systems, site integration, lighting, energy efficiency, photovoltaic panels, air-conditioning installations, mechanical equipment, access points and the costs of each of these, are all important to understand. Indeed, many of these elements depend on, or are affected by, the location and decisions about other elements. Therefore, the more these interdependent elements are documented on drawings that all design team members review, the better the results are likely to be. Although this process might be tedious in some ways, it promises a design that is integrated with other building functions and is responsive to budget.

Design and construction drawings tend to follow the same process from conceptual and schematic to design development and construction phases. If the concept is fairly simple, schematic design can be omitted. However, toward the end of each design phase, ample time should be allowed for the entire design team to sign off on the concept and details of the design. Once construction has begun, it is very hard to change the design without causing considerable cost overruns and long delays.

Specifications—specific requirements for all of the materials being used with additional directions as to how the materials must be installed to create a specific result—should accompany the drawings. Some specifications allow the contractor to choose the method of installation as long as the results meet the criteria listed. Other specifications require a particular method and do not permit other options. Some specifications allow a range of materials, as long as certain results are achieved, whereas other specifications do not permit substitutions. Five new ASTM standards have been developed for green roofs. In some locations, such as New York City, specifications and requirements are being developed as well. Both shift toward performance specifications, which allow for more flexibility in the use of materials. (Specifications and the ASTM standards are discussed more thoroughly in Chapter Three.)

If the green roof project is going to be bid, then additional documents such as bid forms should be included in the construction documents. Performance bonds, labor and materials bonds, and liquidated damages clauses may be necessary. Bonds are money spent by the contractor at the beginning of the project and returned as long as certain conditions are met.[13] A performance bond, which guarantees that the contractor will execute the work, also usually includes some protection of the owner against defective work by the contractor. A Labor and Materials Payment Bond guarantees that the contractor will pay all bills for labor and materials. In either case, should the contractor not finish the work or default, the surety company that issued the bond pays the amount of the bond to the owner. There can also be bonds that are purely Payment Bonds, without coverage for labor, and Bid Bonds, which guarantee that the contractor will agree to a contract if the bid proposal is accepted. Liquidated damages award the contractor for completing the project according to a specified calendar and penalize the contractor should the work lag behind.

The specifications of the construction documents package should also include warranties and guarantees of products and methods. Sometimes, particularly in a new industry, it is difficult to find contractors willing to guarantee certain types of work, yet it is well worth pursuing, because it tends to weed out those contractors whose level of skill and experience are not compatible with the work being bid.

The overarching purposes of the construction documents—that is, final drawings and specifications—are to assure that all bidders base their costs on the same set of drawings and instructions, to have a record of what is being supplied and installed, and to have some basis for confirming (or verifying) the completion of the work. Without such a set of documents, too much is left to chance. In markets where green roof construction is still emerging, bids tend to come in higher than expected. A clear set of construction documents facilitates the process of negotiating with the selected contractor what revisions, phasing, or adjustments in the design might be considered in order to keep the project within the required budget.

Begin Construction

In some respects, the design and installation of a green roof is no different from the design and installation of a complex landscape architecture project involving many disciplines. The following discussion emphasizes the aspects unique to green roofs.

To the degree possible, construction and installation of the green roof should follow a planned timeline, with planting scheduled at the optimum time of year—either early to mid-spring or early fall in temperate climates—so that plants become established prior to the onset of more difficult weather. Because there is a tremendous amount of climatic variation in North America, the ideal planting time will vary substantially from place to place. Careful coordination is needed between the project manager and the general contractor, who sets the schedule once a contract is awarded.

Once construction begins, the layers of the roof are built from the bottom up. The general contractor must test each layer as it is built, and, once it is finished, protect it. This protection is perhaps most important for the roof membrane system. It may be installed perfectly, but if left unprotected, so that people walk over it or materials are stored on it, it may develop leaks.

Once the waterproofing membrane has been installed, it must be tested by flooding it with water, allowing the water to sit for a set amount of time, and verifying that none has passed through the membrane. Other testing methods and systems were discussed in Chapter One.

The various representatives of green roof component manufacturers should be involved in reviewing the installation and making suggestions to ensure that no warranties are violated. Some manufacturers' "reps" have more expertise than anyone else about the best way to install their product. Their knowledge should not be overlooked or their suggestions ignored. Disagreements should be discussed fully and resolved to the satisfaction of all parties.

The seamless installation of the green roof system itself again depends on the coordination by the project manager and the general contractor with all the trades involved. Although green roof systems that are either prefabricated or whose components are supplied by the same company may be somewhat easier to install, those systems that draw upon different sources of components need not cause problems, because the various elements can be tested for compliance with performance specifications.

Since there is limited storage capacity on a roof, both in terms of weight and area, a staging area for the work should be established as close as practicable to the building, with the major access routes clearly staked out. It is also essential to understand how and where the materials will be stored on the roof, and to verify that concentrations of materials will not exceed the load limits of those areas of the roof. As noted in Chapter One, if hoisting will be required, the exact route for bringing materials to the staging area and hoist should be planned from the beginning of construction. This aspect of the process must be carefully planned, and skilled contractors, experienced with this type of operation, must be used.

Because construction debris can become a major hazard on a roof, even causing injuries, the amount of debris and how it will be collected and disposed of must be specified. Just as the growing medium might be brought to the roof in bags, debris and trash might have to be removed by the same method.

It cannot be overemphasized that safety and security precautions must be strictly enforced, simply because there is so much potential danger of someone falling or slipping off the roof, or of an unauthorized individual causing a terrible incident. There are well-established safety regulations in the United States and Canada, but landscape and other green roof contractors may not be fully aware of them. Before beginning construction operations, it is useful to review and summarize all such requirements for the contractors. Although many construction workers are agile and strong, they still need to abide by strict controls and procedures regulating how work is implemented anywhere close to the parapet or other exposed or dangerous locations. Even though construction hats, harnesses, and safety wires are cumbersome and unwelcome, some combination of these may need to be used at appropriate times. Worker fatigue must be carefully monitored as well. It is one thing to work a few extra hours planting groups of shrubs on an estate and finding that the geometry is slightly off and must be redone. It is quite another to try to finish installing a last pallet of plants and fall off the roof. One way to reduce danger is to complete all parapets and guardrails before any of the layers of the roof are built. However, this method is rarely possible. For example, if hoisting is used, often the hoist must be placed right at the edge of the parapet, obviating the final installation of the guardrail or parapet at that location.

Control Costs

Whereas experienced designers in any field are usually able to give a fairly tight range of unit costs for typical projects—an estate on 6 acres (2.4 hectares), a neighborhood park on 10 acres (4 hectares), a parkway, a storm drainage or storm sewer system, an irrigation system—it is challenging to estimate costs for green roof and roof garden projects. Although 2.5 million square feet (232,250 m²) of green roofs were implemented in 2005 and an estimated 7 million square feet (650,300 m²) were installed in 2006, these projects are scattered in many locations with many different designs and methods of construction. Reliable unit prices are starting to become available, but this will take time. Standards in North America are just being established. The costs may also vary substantially from city to city, depending on whether or not a labor force with the skills necessary for green roof projects has developed in that location. Different factors in different locations may have major impacts on costs.

A design team can control costs in three ways. One is to anticipate a phased implementation in the design, so that if bid costs are considerably higher than expected, some portion of the project can be deferred for months or a few years. For a phased approach, it would be important to consider the phasing carefully through each stage of the design process. If a certain phase of work is deferred, the design team must be confident that subsequent phases of construction will not require the removal and reconstruction of a major portion of what has already been built.

Another way to control costs is to pre-qualify bidders and have a competitive bid process. Anyone choosing to bid the work must demonstrate through a submission of a list of built projects an adequate knowledge of materials, methods, and construction costs. In that way the design team can be confident of the capabilities of the bidders. Such a process is sometimes not allowed in public works on a city, state, or federal level, but it is worth pursuing for privately funded projects.

A final way to reduce costs is through artful use of specifications. Typically, specifications are proprietary for green roof projects; that is, a specific manufacturer's product is required, or that of an approved equal. As designers, manufacturers, suppliers, and contractors gain experience, it would be appropriate to focus more on a performance specification of criteria that must be met—for example, a growing medium that meets requirements as to weight, porosity, percentage of organic matter, pH, additives, and inorganic material; or a green roof system that insulates sound by a certain number of decibels or has the capacity to store a specified annual volume of storm water runoff. By this means of specifications, experienced builders who know shortcuts, hybridized methods, or other innovative products, methods, suppliers, and manufacturers, could significantly control costs.

Green roof costs also tend to be high, and somewhat unpredictable, because so many contractors—roofing, waterproofing, electricians, plumbers, welders, landscape contractors, green roof contractors—must be present in a relatively small space with limited room for storage and

2-15. The ferns planted on the green roof at the Brooklyn Botanic Garden are especially suited to the sloping site and partial shade. See Chapter Six for a discussion of this project.

little tolerance for delays. Selecting a project manager for the design team and a general contractor to supervise all other contractors is important to control cost. These two individuals must have good rapport with one another, as well as an ease in communicating with the other designers and contractors, who must know the schedule in order to execute the work properly.

Install Plants and Irrigation

The intent here is to describe general considerations and planning for planting and irrigation on green roofs; Chapter Three provides more detailed information on principles of planting design, specific plants for roof gardens, and types of irrigation.

The design and program for the green roof will dictate many of the choices for plant materials. If the design is an extensive green roof with highly engineered characteristics, where much of the system is provided by one supplier, the selection and specification of the plant palette may be as simple as incorporating a composition of plant materials recommended by the manufacturer of the green roof system. Often the manufacturer or supplier can recommend the best method of installation and provide a specification. However, many semi-intensive

2-16. Two monitoring stations are visible on the lower green roof at the Minneapolis Library, and are accessible to scientists. See Chapter Five for a discussion of this project. (Courtesy of the Kestrel Group)

green roofs and most intensive ones (and some extensive ones) typically have aesthetic considerations, making the roles of the landscape architect or designer, the ecologist, and the horticulturalist important. Careful consideration must be given to the visual characteristics, growth habits, and compositional qualities of the plant materials. How fast do the plants grow and in what combinations with other materials are they most appropriate? The hardiness of the plant materials must be verified for the particular site, as well as their availability in the specified size. The combination of plant materials finally recommended by these design team members should be carefully reviewed and evaluated by the other team members, particularly the landscape contractor and the representatives of the green roof manufacturer.

Depending on the type of green roof and the carrying capacity of the roof, the number of people and the types of methods used for installation will vary. Where there is adequate capacity, teams of workers, even volunteers, appropriately supervised can spread sprigs or plant individual plants. Where capacity is limited, methods of spreading sprigs or shoots by human or mechanical means may be suitable, or hydroseeding may be applicable.

When plant materials are delivered to a green roof site, they must be stored carefully and protected, but this is not any different from a typical project at grade. The green roof plants tend to be very hardy, durable, and drought tolerant, so that most may be stored, with some protection from sun, and a little watering, for several days to perhaps as long as a week or more prior to planting. Bareroot cuttings and sprigs, with no soil mass to protect the plants, should be planted as soon as possible after delivery to the site.

On extensive green roofs, irrigation is often required during the first one or two growing seasons and then not needed in subsequent years, so the irrigation system can be disconnected or even removed. Intensive green roofs almost always have an irrigation system. In climates with severe weather patterns, it is a wise precaution to include a functional irrigation system for any green roof, or at least hose bibs that could be used intermittently for manual watering during drought periods.

If at all possible, the planting installation should be guaranteed by the landscape contractor for a full year, or at least the duration of the growing season. Although guarantees of planting installation for up to two years are standard for many at-grade landscape architecture projects, roof gardens and green roofs are the exception, due to the many challenging variables including extremes of heat, drought, wind, and exposure. If a guarantee is included, the process is straightforward. The landscape contractor informs the project manager when the work is nearly complete, and the project manager schedules an inspection to verify that all work is complete. During the inspection, the project manager and the landscape architect agree on a checklist of remaining tasks. Then, the guarantee period begins. Usually, the landscape contractor is required to notify the project manager or the owner if any problems, such as inadequate irrigation, occur during the guarantee period, which, if not corrected, would void the guarantee. The landscape contractor is often responsible for maintenance during the guarantee period, for which additional payment is provided. At the end of the guarantee period, a final inspection is held, and it is agreed what plant materials must be replaced at no additional cost to the owner. In the case of green roofs, plantings must be replaced or reinforced with new plantings in areas that do not have adequate coverage. There must be some flexibility in determining what to replant. If almost all of a particular species has died despite normal maintenance, this is a good indication that another species should be planted in its place. The replanted materials must also be evaluated to verify vigorous growth and coverage.

Conduct Postconstruction Evaluation and Quality Control

Because green roof design is a relatively new field in North America, it is important to take stock of the installation as soon as it is complete. To some degree this area overlaps with maintenance, yet is important enough as a task to deserve its own category. The potential users of the site, the building occupants, and representatives of the owner (such as a member of the design team) may all participate in this process as well. They should note which plant materials thrive and which do not, any signs of leaks or construction issues, and, depending on the extent of use and the type of green roof, any signs of overuse or underuse. As the guarantee period nears its end, a thorough evaluation of the design should be conducted, with an attempt to rectify problems and improve upon the design to the extent possible within the budget and available tools.

One long-term method of improving the quality of green roof designs is to install monitoring equipment to measure the result. Because some green roofs are designed for particular purposes, such as to reduce storm water runoff or peak discharges, on projects where research is needed, some specific monitoring equipment might be included in the installation costs (Fig. 2-16). This equipment should be set in place by scientists and monitored by them and their assistants or volunteers. Over time, as data are gathered, it may be possible to adapt or revise some aspects of the design to improve the performance of certain components of the green roof. The more data that can be gathered and shared throughout the green roof industry, the greater the potential for correcting mistakes, finding solutions to unexpected problems, and improving designs for future installations.

Maintain the Green Roof

Who will maintain the green roof, and what the maintenance will consist of, should be determined during the design phase and included in the specifications of the bid. The specifications should require a guarantee of plant materials, at least in terms of coverage. Within a certain period of time (say, one year) there will be a certain percentage of continuous plant material coverage, depending on the both the plant materials and planting methods. A certain percentage of the planting budget (for example, 5–10 percent) should be set aside for plant replacements and maintenance. Although the design team may be dissolved as construction is completed, the design process must include a maintenance plan and a budget for funding it for several years. A five-year maintenance plan is best because it establishes a long-term approach to maintenance; it becomes a standard part of building operations over many years, not something added at the last minute, when funds may or may not be available.

There is an incentive to hire the same company for maintenance that is doing the planting installation. Because the company is required to guarantee its work, it is in its interest to do an excellent job of maintenance to avoid having to replant areas of the roof that have not thrived.

2-17, 2-18. Pavers on pedestal systems allow for creating a dead level pavement system and the placement of utilities underneath the pavement where they can still be readily accessed for maintenance.

terms of maintenance, find another company to take over, and for the two to overlap in their activities for at least a few weeks.

There are some traditional construction techniques that result in easier maintenance, and these should not be overlooked when intensive green roofs are being designed, or some combination of intensive/extensive green roof where visitors may look at the fenced-off extensive installation from an intensive green roof or more traditional roof garden. Maintenance often involves checking utilities, such as electrical, gas, and water lines, to verify that there are no breaks or leaks. Also, planters may need to be moved short distances in order to access utilities, check the flashing at the base of the parapet, or study other problems that may be beneath them. Pavers on pedestals are a long established technique for creating a level outdoor space over a sloping roof. Each pedestal can be adjusted so that the paver resting on a group of three or four pedestals is held dead level in relation to the pitch of the roof. If the roof has a slight or manageable pitch, it is sometimes preferred to have each pedestal set at an identical height and have a paved surface with the same slope as the roof. Either way, the advantages of the pedestal system is that water drains between the open joints between each paver and utilities can be run underneath them where they are kept out of sight while being quite accessible. A maintenance worker merely lifts up one of the pavers to gain access to the utilities. The pavers selected are usually square or rectilinear in order to match a pedestal layout in a grid. The wider the distances that the pavers bridge, the thicker they need to be, up to 1½ to 2 inches (3.8 to 5.1 cm), so that a granite or limestone paver 24 inches by 24 inches (61 cm by 61 cm) by 1.5 inches thick could easily weigh enough, from 60 or 70 pounds (27.2 to 31.8 kg) so that it could not be easily moved, but with a proper tool, a stainless steel hook to pry it off the pedestal and two sets of hands, the lifting can be accomplished.

Similarly, planters may need to be portable. Sometimes, when code requirements demand that planters be set back away from a major wall, portable planters may be acceptable, since access is still possible. They are often set against the parapet, where the capacity to support weight is greater. To access the pavers below them and also to save on weight, some planters

However, some landscape or green roof contractors may specialize in construction and planting installation but do not have the staff to provide maintenance on a long-term basis. It might be useful to require in the specifications that the landscape contractor, prior to the end of any

are built with false bottoms, and the frame is covered with a removable fascia and cap so that once disassembled, the individual planter or group of planters can be easily moved. Sometimes, the frame supports wheels so that the whole planter can be rolled like a shopping cart. A galvanized metal or plastic liner holds the growing medium in place well above the finish grade of the roof garden. Once the parapet or the utilities underneath the pavers have been checked, the planters are slid back in place and reassembled, often with minimal disturbance to the plants themselves. With drip irrigation systems, emitter lines are typically brought up behind the planters and rest on the surface of the growing medium. The emitters can easily be removed and lifted back into place when maintenance is complete.

Some people believe that extensive green roofs, once established, need minimum maintenance. But even those installations where the roof is permitted to grow wild with just about anything, as long as it grows and does not threaten to penetrate the root barrier, still require periodic inspection of drainage, waterproofing, and irrigation systems, monitoring of the guardrails and other important safety elements, and occasional removal of thatch or other debris. As in most aspects of life, a small investment in prevention is worth a great deal compared to the cost of repairs or changes after a serious problem.

From conceptual design to maintenance, from specifications through installation, green roof design demands an integrated approach. The Whole Building Design Guide provides an excellent definition: "A truly successful building is one where goals are identified early on and held in proper balance during the design process; and where their interrelationships and interdependencies with all building systems are understood, evaluated, appropriately applied, and coordinated concurrently from the planning and programming phase. The end result is a high-performance building."[14]

2-19, 2-20. Mark Davies of Higher Ground Horticulture demonstrates how planters on wheels with removable top rails can be moved for maintenance. The false bottoms reduce the volume of the growing medium and save on weight when loads are a concern.

CHAPTER THREE

Plant Materials, Irrigation, and Specifications

Plant materials—appropriately selected, correctly specified, properly planted, and well maintained—have the potential to be the most attractive and visible elements of a green roof. This chapter discusses design criteria for the selection of plants for intensive and extensive green roofs, a description of green roof nurseries, and some typical plant lists. Basic information is also included on green roof irrigation and specifications, two necessities for successful plantings.

Plant Materials for Intensive Green Roofs

A large variety of suitable plant materials is available for projects in which an intensive, rather than extensive, installation is being implemented. Unlike perennials used for extensive green roofs, the plants for an intensive-style modern roof garden may be woody, with significant weight. They may also have large root systems that would penetrate or incapacitate a root barrier in an extensive system but readily fit inside a sturdy wood, metal, or plastic planter. Despite more relaxed selection criteria than those for extensive green roofs, there are still some limitations. Following are fourteen considerations for selecting plant materials for intensive green roof designs and insuring the success of the installation.

Avoid Messy Plants

Eliminate plants that are messy, that is, ones that require a lot of cleanup—for example, some specific species or varieties of trees, such as willows and crabapples, and some herbaceous plants, such as hollyhocks. Even though these plantings can be quite attractive, the dead leaves from trees that shed all season can clog a

Preceding pages:
3-0. A display of sedums thriving atop the green roof at Emory Knoll Farms in Street, Maryland, shows off their varied colors and textures. Visitors can evaluate potential choices of green roof plants in growing conditions typical of what might be encountered in an installation.

3-1, 3-2. Intensive green roof installations are typically in individual planters, often set near the parapet where there is more structural loading, or in continuous plantings, with a consistent or variable depth. These two examples are on the same roof garden in New York City.

drainage system or a water feature. The fruit of crabapples, although particularly decorative and ornamental in the winter, can pose a hazard when it starts dropping. It can stain the pavement, leave a pulpy mess that attracts insects and even rats, cause tripping, and require considerable cleanup time. Some newer varieties of crabapples, such as Sugartyme, have been developed that drop dessicated leavings. By the time the fruit falls, it has deteriorated to a miniature dry bead, easily ignored or removed. Hollyhocks add a lot of color and height to perennial borders at grade. However, they are coarse, can grow quite tall, and might require staking within the windy confines of a roof garden. Furthermore, they are biennials, blooming on the second year's growth. In a spacious at-grade garden, this pattern can add a delightful characteristic: hollyhocks that seed themselves all over and with an array of colors and heights. On a roof garden, however, this seeding might seem chaotic.

Avoid Large Plants

Trees and shrubs that grow very large are often not advisable, although some adapt better than others: this can be called the bonsai challenge. The Japanese art of bonsai, which involves an artful pruning and shaping of both roots and branches and a limited amount of soil, stunts even species such as pines and maples, which would typically grow quite large. Placing a tree in a planter with a limited amount of space in a modern roof garden under severe conditions of exposure will naturally produce stunted growth compared to the results if it were planted in a sheltered, large open space in deep soils. Pines, maples, and even some oaks adapt more naturally to this than sycamores, lindens, and beeches. Still, the risk of planting a shrub or tree that grows too fast or gets too large is that it will likely have to be removed, and that can be an arduous process.

Some design situations call for large plants (Fig. 3-3). The designer must verify that a mature tree of the selected species will not exceed the load limits of that specific location. It makes no sense to plant a tree whose total weight at planting is only slightly below the maximum weight permitted. Nature does not make freeze-dried trees whose weight remains the same from year to year.

Avoid Brittle Plants

Plants that are brittle and could break in high winds, such as Bradford pear, ailanthus, and some willows, should not be planted. If in doubt about the durability of a species in this regard, do not use it. Windy conditions are so typical of roof gardens that even if research reveals only occasional instances of the wood breaking or the tree losing its anchoring in wind, it is still best not to use it. The cost of repairing damage caused by fallen or broken limbs, as well as the cost of replacing the plantings after the damaged species has been removed, can be quite high.

Avoid Trite Selections

Some species are used so often that it is hard to change common practice. For example, Bradford pears, valued because of their symmetrical oval shape, lustrous medium-textured foliage, and early white flowers, are widely planted as street trees and in urban gardens, but these trees also have a habit of developing many lateral branches that diverge from the main trunk at the same place. If some of these are not pruned as the tree grows, a weak area develops. On a roof garden, with intense winds, the possibility of significant damage is high. Bradford pears and other species with weak limbs or weak spots prone to breakage should be assiduously avoided. Other common species, even if suitable, may not have such obvious defects, but might still be avoided, given that there is such a wide choice of suitable plants with unique characteristics available.

Research Hardiness

Using plant materials that are extremely hardy is a basic consideration of any roof garden. One class of generally hardy plant materials is those native to alluvial environments; these plants are used to flooding and have cells along their trunks that bring oxygen to the roots, so they function well as street trees in compacted soils or roof garden plantings, even in drought. For example, in New York City, where the average life of a street tree is a mere seven years, such species as magnolias, hollies, pin oaks, river birches, and sweetgums do quite well as long as they are winter hardy for the region. In Atlanta, these same species thrive, along with water oaks and others adaptable to the milder climate.

The designer must maintain a flexible attitude toward hardiness classifications. As a result of international warming trends, some species are advancing into regions previously too cold for them to survive in, while others are retreating from areas that are now too warm. Oleander, usually found in the warm coastal plain of Georgia, is now typically found as far north as Atlanta, a city at an elevation of over 1,000 feet (304.8 m) above sea level with a climate that used to be too cold for such plant materials. Many species of azaleas and rhododendrons, once a mainstay of the planting palette in Atlanta, must now be limited to cool exposures.

Because plant materials on roof gardens typically experience much more severe conditions than they would encounter in a garden in the same location at grade, a practical rule of thumb is to lower the hardiness zone rating by one for any plant material being considered for a roof planting. A good example is *Lagerstroemia indica,* crape myrtle. It is quite hardy throughout the southeastern United States and as far north as New York City, where many fine specimens grow at the Brooklyn Botanic Garden. Yet only very hardy varieties would withstand the extreme conditions of a roof garden in New York City.

Consider Bamboos and Grasses

Bamboos and grasses are increasingly popular and readily available. Bamboos are among the most tenacious of plant materials. However, even planting them at grade, it is often advisable to build an underground concrete "bathtub," or use polyethylene sheeting with a similar contoured shape, to contain the roots and prevent

3-4. Crape myrtles are splendid small trees with unusual interest—exfoliating bark, striking blooms in mid- to late summer with sometimes a second bloom in early fall, and bright red fall color—but they can also grow quite large, such as these specimens at the Brooklyn Botanic Garden. Hardy ones may be suitable for roof gardens where there is adequate space.

them from spreading to adjacent areas of the garden. In a roof garden in which the plant materials are in planters, the planter itself prevents the bamboo from spreading to another planter. However, the bamboo typically sends up new rhizomes and shoots that fill the planter entirely rather quickly (within a few years). Also, it may be difficult to combine bamboos with other plants that may not be able to compete. One additional drawback of bamboos is that they grow so thick that they may need to be thinned after a certain number of years. This thinning may involve removing the entire root mass by cutting it out of the planter, trimming down the size of the roots and replanting—a labor-intensive technique that can be justified by the elegant effects of mature plantings. A final concern about bamboo, an important one, is that because the roots grow aggressively, they can sometimes penetrate a roofing membrane that is not particularly durable.[1] Consultation with the green roof manufacturer to specify an appropriate containment system resolves this problem.

Bamboos are highly variable in color, height, texture, and hardiness, so those intended for roof gardens must be carefully selected with these characteristics in mind. Both clumping and spreading (or running) varieties can be considered equally, depending on their design characteristics. Clumping species multiply by expanding out from the center, so they tend to be less invasive than the spreading varieties, which typically send rhizomes as far as 12–18 inches (31–46 cm) horizontally from the parent plant to start a new plant. Common species of spreading bamboo are *Phyllostachys, Sasa, Indocalamus,* and *Pleioblastus*; *Fargesia* is the most common species of clumping bamboo. The whole array of plants includes varieties that range from ground covers to specimens that grow several stories tall, or more, under ideal conditions. One important characteristic of many bamboos is that although they tend to be evergreen in many southern climates, in northern ones they are often deciduous and tend to leaf out later in the spring than many deciduous trees. Depending on the design characteristics sought, this pattern can be an advan-

3-5, 3-6. Grasses adorn planters and add rich color and texture to the composition of this roof garden in New York City. (Courtesy of Robert Martin Designs)

tage or a disadvantage. If the bamboo is intended as a privacy screen, there could be a problem. Conversely, if a dappled pattern of light is desired to highlight the surface, than bamboo can be an excellent choice.

Other grasses are even more suitable, such as *Pennisetums*, *Fescues*, and *Miscanthus* species. They also spread readily and completely fill up a planter; however, they can be much more readily removed and transplanted than bamboos. In temperate climates, most grasses are deciduous and die back in the winter. In subtropical and tropical climates, the growing season is much longer, but there still may be periods when plants are dormant, and appropriate maintenance is necessary. The accumulation of foliage, particularly on grasses, may require thinning and pruning since it may continue growing for longer periods than in temperate climates. Many grasses look best in the late summer or fall when their colorful efflorescences accent the landscape. These remain on the plants through the winter—a desirable ornamentation for some people, a nuisance for others. The stalks that remain after the grasses die back in winter are dry and dead. Usually they should be cut back and removed to avoid a fire hazard. However, this practice should be dependent on the overall maintenance plan for the entire garden. In a public space where there are many visitors and people might be smoking, removal of thatch might be desirable, whereas a private client might enjoy the effect. Another potential maintenance issue is that some grasses, as well as other perennials, are readily self-sowing and can spread indiscriminately around a roof.[2] Depending on the type and style of design, this spreading could undermine a tight organization of planting materials and also require considerable extra weeding.

Provide Seasonal Interest

One important design element for roof gardens is seasonal interest, and it should be a factor in the selection of almost all of the plantings, trees, and shrubs, as well as perennials and annuals. Again, because the amount of space is limited, it is important to provide locations for displays of color, bloom, texture, and fragrance that show off the plant materials to their best advantage. As in an at-grade garden, there is no need to display something of interest at all times in every space, but a pleasing sequence should be possible as different plant materials in different locations wax and wane in interest value.

Consider Special Characteristics, Good and Bad

Because space is usually so limited, it is crucial to be aware of specific positive and negative characteristics, such as fragrance and special season of interest as well as thorns and poisonous aspects. Thornless varieties of popular species are available sometimes, such as hawthorns and locust. Just as a children's playground should be free of poisonous plants, particularly flowering plants that might entice a curious youngster, poisonous plants should be avoided in the accessible locations of roof gardens where children might be present. Similarly, it is common to include a grouping of kitchen herbs on a roof garden near a kitchen or some easily accessible area where the attractive textures and spicy fragrances are enticing. Such plantings should exclude anything that is not edible, because a child or even an adult ignorant of culinary horticulture might pick something inedible or poisonous by mistake. Where space is limited, espaliers (pruned trees or shrubs trained flat against a wall) are effective. Some fruit trees, such as apple and pear, and shrubs with pliant branches, such as witch hazel, are good choices (Figs. 3-7, 3-8, 3-9, and 3-10).

Use the Full Range of Plant Materials

The plant world is remarkably diverse. Unless a specialized garden is being designed, it is important to sample from the whole spectrum. Use evergreen as well as deciduous materials. Use a few trees as well as shrubs, ground covers, and bulbs. Many bulbs do extremely well on roof gardens, and many species are hardy. Most bulbs require freezing temperatures to reinforce a period of dormancy; then as the earth warms in the spring, they send out new growth and flowering stalks. On roof gardens the insulated top of a building may retain some heat, even during a very cold winter, so that some bulbs, such as crocus and daffodils, will send shoots through the growing medium several weeks to a month earlier than they would in an at-grade garden. As long as the species is hardy, this is no reason not to use them.

Daffodils are often used in the at-grade

3-7, 3-8, 3-9, 3-10. Espaliers provide rich rewards in an economy of space. In the aerial view at left, witch hazels are trained against the brick wall and the close-up below shows ferns planted at their base. The two middle views show a roof garden with espaliered apple and pear trees. (*Middle left:* courtesy of Wouter Deruytter)

landscapes of parks and estates because they naturalize and spread. Crocus return every year, although they may not multiply. Other species, such as tulips, decline over the years; new bulbs must be planted for effective displays. On roof gardens where the amount of space and the volume of growing medium is limited, daffodils and crocus may last several seasons, if not permanently.

Vines are often overlooked as choices. Most roof gardens have walls as defining boundaries, or there is the possibility of an overhead canopy or arbor at an entrance or some sheltered location. Vines are often excellent choices to soften and enhance such places. Designers must check the growth characteristics of the vines; some will cling to masonry whereas others must have supports around which to twine; some will bloom within a year of planting, and others may take several years. There is debate about whether species such as Boston ivy (*Parthenocissus tricuspidata*) and English ivy (*Hedera helix*), which cling to masonry or other surfaces, damage those surfaces over time. However, if the designer prepares for them by using support structures like arbors or lattice, these are hardy and durable plant materials. Many flowering species of vines, such as clematis, wisteria, and hydrangea, carefully researched and chosen, can be excellent selections for highlights.

Expand the Palette

Despite the wide variety of plant materials that are suitable and available, it is still worthwhile to try to expand on what is typically specified. Occasionally experiment with something untried in a place where it will not be a terrible problem if it dies and must be replaced. However, if it does well, then you can add it to your planting palette. Sumacs (*rhus sp.*), mahonias (*mahonia sp.*), and Korean dogwoods (*Cornus kousa*) are all striking and effective plant materials that are useful on roof gardens, although they are relatively recent introductions. A roof garden might greatly benefit from an underutilized, little known, or even weedy plant that takes on special characteristics in this exposed setting.

Listen to the Client

Although modern roof gardens offer the opportunity to employ a great array of design styles and give the designer a chance to explore a wide palette of pavements and plant materials, it is still important to listen to the client. This is possibly harder to do for a private than a public client. If the client doesn't like your favorite plant, then find another. For public roof gardens, which serve many people and are significantly larger than private roof gardens, it may be more difficult to decide which species of plant materials to implement, yet it is still important to provide what the client has requested, unless there are specific reasons to eliminate a species because it could endanger the public health and safety. If the designer still feels that a plant is appropriate, in spite of the reservations of the client, it might be possible to include a few in a more secluded area of a larger garden as long as the reasons for using that particular plant can be explained clearly.

Develop a Plant List and Specifications

If the installation is large enough for a contractor's bid, then it is necessary to develop a plant list following the most recent edition of the *American Standards for Nursery Stock*. Costs for hauling plants to the site, navigating them through the access routes to the roof, carefully preparing the planters, and installing the plants will be quite high compared to standard, at-grade locations where access and installation are routine. It is all the more important to have an accurate list of what is to be planted, with little room for interpretations by different contractors that might yield widely divergent costs.

A set of specifications, or at least a set of notes and instructions giving the basic requirements and intent of the planting design, should accompany the plant list. The lines of authority should be indicated; that is, who is in charge of each phase of the work with whom the landscape contractor might need to interact, such as the irrigation, lighting, and general contractors. References to the quality of the plant material, the anticipated schedule for planting, and who will inspect the work to verify its completeness should be included.

Incorporate a Guarantee

If possible, require that the plantings be guaranteed. For most private and public installations of parks, residences and standard projects, it is routine for the landscape contractor to guarantee plant materials for at least one growing season past the date of acceptance, the point at which the landscape architect certifies in writing that the planting is complete. In competitive environments, a two-year guarantee is often required of bidders. By contrast many landscape contractors who install roof gardens try to avoid guaranteeing plant materials, because they argue that it is unfair to hold them accountable for plant losses when there are so many variables beyond their control. However, because the cost of replacement may be considerable, particularly if the logistics have changed—for example, it might no longer be possible to carry plant materials through an unfinished apartment, and the only option is to hoist them to the roof—then a guarantee is important to incorporate. Often, it is possible to negotiate with the landscape contractor who installs the garden to do the maintenance for the first year or so. This arrangement gives the contractor more incentive to follow through with all maintenance requirements.

Plan for Maintenance

Typically maintenance requirements are the same as for at-grade gardens but much more stringent, due to the impact of wind and exposure. Plantings must be pruned, fertilized, irrigated, weeded. Particularly if lightweight soil mixes are used to avoid taxing the load limits of the roof, it may be necessary to fertilize regularly because some of these soils do not hold nutrients well. In temperate climates it is advisable to use a slow-acting fertilizer in the spring, at the beginning of the growing season, and a faster-acting fertilizer around the beginning of September. The goal is to achieve balanced growth over the entire season, not spurts of growth or bloom.

Plant List for Intensive Green Roofs

Table 3-1 provides a list of trees, shrubs, and perennials that are adaptable to intensive roof gardens in the eastern United States, a temperate climate.[3] Many would do well in other areas of the United States and Canada, but it is important to verify hardiness requirements in other regions. (Mexico, with its own wide-ranging climate and habitats, has an entirely different palette of plant materials, which should be studied carefully.) An experienced landscape architect, designer, or horticulturalist should be able to consider this list and adapt it for local conditions. The amounts of sun and shade, the frequency and direction of high winds, temperature extremes, water requirements, the rate of growth and the size and depth of planting must all be considered. Even one hardy species may exhibit different characteristics at different ends of its natural range. For example, sweetbay magnolia, *Magnolia virginiana*, tends to be evergreen in the southern United States and deciduous in the northern United States. In either setting it has beautiful foliage

Table 3-1. RECOMMENDED PLANT LIST FOR INTENSIVE GREEN ROOFS[4]

BOTANICAL NAME	COMMON NAME	SIZE	ROOT	NOTES
I. TREES				
Acer palmatum	Japanese maple	3–4 feet (1 m) or larger	B&B or cont.	Many varieties
* Amelanchier canadensis	Shadblow or amelanchier	6–8 feet (2 to 2.5 m) or larger	B&B or cont.	Multitrunk
Betula nigra	River birch	6–8 feet (2 to 2.5 m) or larger	B&B or cont.	Multitrunk
Carpinus betulus 'Fastigiata'	European hornbeam	6–8 feet (2 to 2.5 m) or larger	B&B or cont.	Great for hedge rows
* Cornus florida	American dogwood	5–6 feet (1.5 to 2 m) or larger	B&B	Partial shade
Cornus kousa	Korean dogwood	4–6 feet (1.2 to 2 m) or larger	B&B	Partial shade or sun
Crataegus phaenopyrum	Washington hawthorn	4–5 feet (1.2 to 1.5 m) or larger	B&B	Partial shade or sun
Lagerstroemia indica	Crape myrtle	6–8 feet (2 to 2.5 m) or larger	B&B or cont.	Many colors and varieties; verify hardiness
Magnolia soulangiana	Saucer magnolia	5–6 feet (1.5 to 2 m) or larger	B&B	Partial shade or sun
* Magnolia stellata	Star magnolia	4–5 feet (1.2 to 1.5 m) or larger	B&B	Partial shade or sun
Magnolia virginiana	Sweetbay magnolia	4–5 feet (1.2 to 1.5 m) or larger	B&B	Partial shade or sun
* Malus floribunda	Japanese flowering crabapple	4–5 feet (1.2 to 1.5 m) or larger	B&B or cont.	Partial shade or sun
Malus 'Sugar Tyme'	Sugar tyme crabapple	4–5 feet (1.2 to 1.5 m) or larger	B&B or cont.	Partial shade or sun
Pinus virginiana	Virginia pine	4–5 feet (1.2 to 1.5 m) or larger	B&B	Partial shade or sun
Pinus thunbergii	Japanese black pine	4–5 feet (1.2 to 1.5 m) or larger	B&B	Sun
II. SHRUBS				
Aucuba japonica	Japanese aucuba	24–30 inches (61 to 76 cm)	3 or 5 gallon (10 or 20 L)	Shade solid green, also 'Picturata' and 'Golddust,' tender, EG
Berberis juliana	Wintergreen barberry	24–30 inches (61 to 76 cm) or larger	3 or 5 gallon (10 or 20 L)	EG
Berberis thunbergii	Japanese barberry	24–30 inches (61 to 76 cm) or larger	3 or 5 gallon (10 or 20 L)	Red foliage, other varieties
* Buxus sempervirens	Common boxwood	24–30 inches (61 to 76 cm) or larger	3 or 5 gallon (10 or 20 L)	Partial shade or sun, EG
Cotoneaster dammeri	Bearberry cotoneaster	15–18 inches (38 to 46 cm) or larger	3 gallon (10 L)	Sun, semi-EG
Forsythia suspensa	Weeping forsythia	24–30 inches (61 to 76 cm) or larger	3 or 5 gallon (10 or 20 L)	Partial shade or sun
* Hamamelis mollis	Arnold promise or J'Elena witch hazel	24–30 inches (61 to 76 cm) or larger	3 or 5 gallon (10 or 20L)	Partial shade or sun
Hydrangea quercifolia	Oakleaf hydrangea	24–30 inches (61 to 76 cm) or larger	3 or 5 gallon (10 or 20 L)	Partial shade or sun, coarse
Hydrangea sp.	Lacecap or others	24–30 inches (61 to 76 cm) or larger	3 or 5 gallon (10 or 20 L)	Sun
Ilex glabra	Inkberry	24–30 inches (61 to 76 cm) or larger	3 or 5 gallon (10 or 20 L)	Sun or shade, multistem
Ilex meserve	Blue girl holly	24–30 inches (61 to 76 cm) or larger	3 or 5 gallon (10 or 20 L)	Partial shade or sun, tender, EG
* Ilex verticillata	Winterberry	24–30 inches (61 to 76 cm) or larger	3 or 5 gallon (10 or 20 L)	Sun, multistem
Mahonia bealei	Mahonia	24–30 inches (61 to 76 cm) or larger	3 or 5 gallon (10 or 20 L)	Partial shade, multistem, EG
Myrica pennsylvanica	Bayberry	24–30 inches (61 to 76 cm) or larger	3 or 5 gallon (10 or 20 L)	Prefers sun, EG
Pieris japonica	Japanese andromeda	24–30 inches (61 to 76 cm) or larger	3 or 5 gallon (10 or 20 L)	Partial shade, sun, multistem, EG
Rosa sp.	Roses	24–30 inches (61 to 76 cm) or larger	3 or 5 gallon (10 or 20 L)	Choose carefully
Skimmia japonica	Japanese skimmia	24–30 inches (61 to 76 cm) or larger	3 or 5 gallon (10 or 20 L)	Partial shade or sun, EG
Spiraea vanhouttei	Bridal wreath	24–30 inches (61 to 76 cm) or larger	3 or 5 gallon (10 or 20 L)	Sun or shade
Syringa vulgaris	Common lilac	3–4 feet (1 m) or larger	3 or 5 gallon (10 or 20 L)	Sun
Viburnum opulus compactum	Dwarf cranberry bush	3–4 feet (1 m) or larger	3 or 5 gallon (10 or 20 L)	Partial shade, sun, multistem
Viburnum plicatum tomentosum	Doublefile viburnum	3–4 feet (1 m) or larger	Cont. or B&B	Partial, shade or sun, view from above; may grow too large
Viburnum rhytidophyllum	Leatherleaf viburnum	3–4 feet (1 m) or larger	Cont. or B&B	Shade or sun, EG, droopy; may grow too large
Viburnum 'Winterthur'	Winterthur viburnum	3–4 feet (1 m) or larger	Cont. or B&B	Prefers sun
Taxus baccata 'Repandens'	Spreading English yew	12–15 inches (30.5 to 38 cm) or larger	Cont.	EG, partial shade
Taxus hicksii	Hick's yew	3–4 feet (1 m) or larger	B&B	EG, sun

BOTANICAL NAME	COMMON NAME	SIZE	ROOT	NOTES
III. PERENNIALS, GROUND COVERS, BAMBOOS, GRASSES, BULBS				
Achillea sp.	Yarrow	Quart or gallon (1 or 4 L)	Cont.	Many varieties, colors, heights
* Aster novae-angliae	New England aster	Quart or gallon (1 or 4 L)	Cont.	Very hardy, other species
Echinacea sp.	Coneflower	Quart or gallon (1 or 4 L)	Cont.	Pink or purple available
Festuca ovina glauca	Blue fescues	Quart or gallon (1 or 4 L)	Cont.	Many others available
Fothergilla gardenia	Fothergilla	Quart or gallon (1 or 4 L)	Cont.	Partial shade, other varieties
Helleborus niger	Christmas rose	Quart or gallon (1 or 4 L)	Cont.	Shade, white, EG
Helleborus orientalis	Lentenrose	Quart or gallon (1 or 4 L)	Cont.	Shade, EG, variable color
Hemerocallis sp.	Daylilies	Quart or gallon (1 or 4 L)	Cont. or Bareroot	Many varieties
Heuchera 'Palace Purple'	Palace purple heuchera	Quart or gallon (1 or 4 L)	Cont.	Other varieties
Hosta sp.	Plantain lily	Pint, quart, or gallon (½, 1, or 4 L)	Cont.	Many varieties
Hypericum calycinum	Aaron's beard, St. John's wort	Quart or gallon (1 or 4 L)	Cont.	Many varieties
Liriope muscari	Big blue liriope	Quart or gallon (1 or 4 L)/flats	Cont./BR	Many varieties, one variegated
Miscanthus sp.	Grass genus	Quart or gallon (1 or 4 L)	Cont.	Many types
Ophiopogon japonicus	Dwarf lilyturf	Pint or gallon (½ or 4 L)/ flats	Cont. BR	Fine textured, part shade, sun
* Opuntia fragilis	Prickly pear cactus	Gallon (4 l)	Cont.	Full sun
Pachysandra terminalis	Japanese spurge	Pint or gallon (½ or 4 L)/ flats	Cont./BR	EG
Phlox subulata	Garden phlox	Quart or gallon (1 or 4 L)	Cont.	Many varieties
Phyllostachys aureosulcata	Yellow groove bamboo	4–5 feet (1.2 to 1.5 m) or larger	Cont. or B&B	EG
* Phyllostachys nigra	Black bamboo	4–5 feet (1.2 to 1.5 m) or larger	Cont. or B&B	EG
Pennisetum alopecuroides	Japanese fountain grass	Gallon (4 L)	Cont.	Many varieties; showy efflorescences
Rudbeckia hirta	Black-eyed Susan	Quart or gallon (1 or 4 L)	Cont.	Long bloomer
Sedum spectabile	Sedum	Quart or gallon (1 or 4 L)	Cont.	Many varieties
Vinca minor	Periwinkle	Pint, quart, or gallon (½, 1, or 4 L) or flats	Cont.	EG, other varieties
* Tulips, bluebells, daffodils, iris, crocus, lily-of-the valley, lily	Hardy bulbs	Bulbs	Bulbs	May sprout earlier due to heat from the roof
Herbs: thyme, sage, rosemary, basil, etc.		Pint, quart, or gallon (½, 1, or 4 L)	Cont.	May be rotated periodically
Ferns: Dennstaedtia punctlobula, Polystichum acrostichoides, Thelypteris noveboracensis	Hay-scented fern, Christmas fern, New York fern	Pint, quart, or gallon (½, 1, or 4 L)	Cont.	Many others; some may be too tender for exposures of roof gardens
IV. VINES				
Akebia quinata	Five leaf akebia	12–15 inches (30.5 to 38 cm) runners	Cont.	Hardy, dense
Campsis radicans	Trumpet creeper	12–15 inches (30.5 to 38 cm) runners	Cont.	Coarse, may damage wood
Clematis paniculata	Sweet-autumn clematis	12–15 inches (30.5 to 38 cm) runners	Cont.	Fragrant
Clematis texensis	Scarlet clematis	12–15 inches (30.5 to 38 cm) runners	Cont.	Many other varieties
Hedera helix	English ivy	Variable	Cont. or B&B	EG, tough
Hydrangea petiolaris or anomala	Climbing hydrangea	12–15 inches (30.5 to 38 cm) runners	Cont.	Slow to get started
Lonicera sp.	Honeysuckle	12–15 inches (30.5 to 38 cm) runners	Cont.	Many varieties, colors
Parthenocissus quinquefolia	Virginia creeper	12–15 inches (30.5 to 38 cm) runners	Cont.	Striking fall color
Parthenocissus tricuspidata	Boston ivy	12–15 inches (30.5 to 38 cm) runners	Cont.	Very hardy
Wisteria sinensis	Japanese wisteria	12–15 inches (30.5 to 38 cm) runners	Cont.	Fragrant

NOTE: B&B = Balled and burlapped, BR = bare-root, EG = evergreen, Cont. = container, L = Liter, * Image provided.

3-12. A star magnolia (*Magnolia stellata*) blooms in early spring at Sniffen Court. See Chapter Six for a discussion of this project.

that is silvery underneath, so that a shimmering effect is created by a breeze, and it has large and fragrant (but not prolific) flowers. However, a suitable use in the South might not be appropriate in the North, and vice versa. On an even more local scale, the microclimatic conditions of a particular roof garden might produce thriving plants in one area but struggling or dying plants in other areas.

For each species included in Table 3-1, a typical size is given. Depending on budget and design requirements, the sizes could be larger or smaller. If hoisting to the roof is not a possibility, then the landscape architect and contractor must be aware of the narrowest space in which all plants must fit along the route through the building. If there are no major limitations with the access route, the size of the planters will determine the maximum size of the plant materials. Finally, the designer must also keep

in mind the load limits so that no problems arise if a specified plant doubles or triples in size over time. To have to remove a spectacular specimen just as it matures because it weighs too much is costly and a sign of poor design. Plan ahead.

Plant Materials for Extensive Green Roofs

In contrast to the great diversity of plant materials that adapt and thrive on an intensive green roof or roof garden, there is a far more restricted palette of plant materials for extensive green roofs. The growing medium is very shallow, ranging from only 2 to 6 inches (5.1–15.2 cm). Whereas complex intensive green roofs are typically irrigated with appropriate zones for plant materials that have different watering requirements, extensive green roofs often have no irrigation at all. They may be irrigated during the first growing season to help establish the plant materials, but the irrigation system is often disconnected after the first year. Occasionally, supplemental irrigation is provided during extreme drought, but this is not always the case. Therefore, the plant materials used on extensive green roofs must survive extremes of temperature, exposure, wind, and drought. In addition, a habit of growth that is more horizontal than vertical is preferred, because the goal of an extensive green roof is to have complete coverage of the growing medium and to add minimal weight to the structure. The best plants for extensive green roofs also should be relatively low in nutritional requirements, because the less fertilization that occurs, the less potential for adding nutrients to storm water runoff. Plants should have lateral roots rather than taproots to avoid penetration of the root barrier, and seeds should not be disseminated by the wind (to avoid spreading to adjacent properties). The most adaptable groups of plants that have been found to grow well in such conditions are sedums, succulents, and related species. However, as the green roof industry evolves in North America, it seems likely that many additional herbaceous species, including some grasses, will be found suitable for extensive green roof installations. Several projects that replicate native plant communities, such as prairies, are discussed in Chapter Five (Figs. 3-19, 3-20, and 3-21). As the full range of species for a range of plant communities becomes available through seeding or cuttings, and it is verified that these species are stable and suitable for green roofs, the palette will greatly expand beyond sedums and succulents.

One of the main suppliers of extensive green roof plant materials in the United States is Emory Knoll Farms, in Street, Maryland (about a two-hour drive north of Washington, D.C.).[5] The two owners are Ed Snodgrass, a fifth-generation farmer living with his wife, a writer, in a beautiful farmhouse on the site that dates from 1881, and John Shepley, the business manager, who has a background in electrical engineering and accounting. They have embraced the concept of sustainable design throughout the farm: the business office features a composting toilet by Sun Tech; the walls of the business office are homosote (a product composed of paper pressed together with binder to form wall board, which is typically used as insulation); carpets are made from recycled materials. Solar electric panels generate almost 50 percent of their electricity in the spring and almost all during the summer. Their solar hot water heater also runs on biodiesel fuel; supplementary fuel is generated from vegetable oil, which they collect free from local restaurants. They use recycled cardboard to package some of the nursery products and anticipate relying on soy-based ink in the future.

The most obvious feature of the business office is its green roof. A visitor can easily climb up and look at neat rows of sedums and other succulents, with varying colors and textures, thriving on its gentle slope. Many select what they will specify on their own green roofs based on observations of what is growing there—and, of course, thorough discussion with their own design team on a particular project.

In many ways Emory Knoll is like a standard nursery that grows and ships plant materials on demand. The trays are similar to those used in other nurseries, except that at Emory Knoll Farms, most of these materials are recycled. The trays are not biodegradable but are recyclable. After repeated uses they can also be melted down and recast for reuse. (Experiments are being done with corn plastic from corn sugar, which may become a future option for the plug trays. They could then be composted as they wear out.) The bottom trays, in which the plug trays fit, are polystyrene and can be reused; many are secondhand, because Emory Knoll Farms often finds used ones available from other nurseries.

The explosion in the demand for extensive green roof plants is clearly indicated by the quantity sold by Emory Knoll Farms. In 2000 they sold plants to cover 3,000 square feet (278.7 m²); in 2001, 10,500 square feet (975.5 m²); in 2002, 180,000 square feet (1,672.2 m²); in 2003, 136,000 square feet (12,634.8 m²); in 2004, 206,000 square feet (19,138 m²); and in 2005, 500,000 square feet (46,450 m²).

Emory Knoll Farms grows up to five hundred varieties of suitable plants, but they grow only about forty to fifty species in substantial

Below:
3-13. A thicket of bamboo makes an ideal planting for a roof garden in New York City. (Courtesy of Higher Ground Horticulture).

Bottom:
3-14. Boxwoods give a strong architectural accent to this narrow roof garden in New York City. Courtesy of Wouter Deruytter)

		Table 3-2. PLANT LIST FOR EXTENSIVE GREEN ROOFS	
BOTANICAL	COMMON NAMES	CHARACTERISTICS	NOTES
Allium schoenoprasum	Chives	6–12 inch (15–30 cm) height, clumping, nice flowers. Hardiness zone 4–8	Globular, clover-like clusters of pale purple flowers
* Delosperma nubigenum 'Basutoland'	Yellow ice plant	3 inch (8 cm) height 10 inch (25 cm) spread, Hardiness zone 6.	Very high drought tolerance, low moisture tolerance, very high shade tolerance. The hardiest of this genus, this plant has great ability to absorb rainwater after a dry period. It has thick, fleshy leaves and brilliant yellow flowers in early summer.
Sedum acre 'Aureum'	Gold-moss stonecrop	3 inch (8 cm) height 10 inch (25 cm) spread. Hardiness zone 4.	Very high drought tolerance, high moisture tolerance, very high shade tolerance. Responds well to cooler weather. The foliage tends to stay bright green throughout the winter, but most growth occurs in the early spring and late autumn during cooler weather. Not suitable for use south of the Mason–Dixon line due to its intolerance for high summer heat.
Sedum album	White stonecrop	4 inch (10 cm) height 12 inch (30.5 cm) spread. Hardiness Zone 4.	Very high drought tolerance, no shade or moisture tolerance. Very persistent ground cover, turns red to russet in the winter.
Sedum album 'Murale'	White murale stonecrop	4 inch (10 cm) height 12 inch (30.5 cm) spread. Hardiness zone 4.	Very high drought tolerance, no shade or moisture tolerance. A selection of Sedum album, it has red foliage during periods of drought stress and cold.
Sedum floriferum 'Weihenstephaner Gold'	Bailey's gold stonecrop	4 inch (10 cm) height 10 inch (25 cm) spread. Hardiness zone 3.	Very high drought tolerance, no moisture or shade tolerance. Excellent ground cover for roofs and at grade; notable for its yellow flowers.
Sedum kamtschaticum	Russian, kamschatca, or orange stonecrop	6 inch (15 cm) height 10 inch (25 cm) spread. Hardiness zone 4.	Very high drought tolerance, good moisture and shade tolerance. Remarkably tough and drought-tolerant plant for its size. Tends to be taller than most other sedums listed here.
Sedum reflexum	Blue stonecrop	4 inch (10 cm) height 8 inch (20 cm) spread.	Very high drought tolerance, no moisture or shade tolerance. Has the appearance of a miniature blue spruce tree, so adds a nice texture of blue/gray to the plantings.
Sedum sexangulare	Watch-chain or tasteless stonecrop	4 inch (10 cm) height 8 inch (20 cm) spread. Hardiness zone 4.	Very high drought tolerance, no moisture tolerance, good shade tolerance. Similar in appearance to Sedum acre, but a much tougher plant.
Sedum spurium 'Fuldaglut'	Fuldaglut two-row stonecrop	6 inch (15 cm) height 8 inch (20 cm) spread. Hardiness zone 4.	Very high drought tolerance, moisture and shade tolerance. One of the most reliable of the red foliage spuriums. (Another is 'Voodoo.')
Sedum spurium 'John Creech'	John Creech two-row stonecrop	4 inch (10 cm) height 10 inch (25 cm) spread. Hardiness zone 5.	Very high drought tolerance, moisture and shade tolerance. A nice low-growing habit.
Sedum spurium 'Roseum'	Red or pink two-row stonecrop	6 inch (15 cm) height 8 inch (20 cm) spread. Hardiness zone 4.	Drought tolerance very high, moisture and shade tolerance. Pink flowers.
Sedum spurium 'White Form'	White blooming two-row stonecrop	6 inch (15 cm) height 8 inch (20 cm) spread. Hardiness zone 4.	Very high drought tolerance, moisture and shade tolerance. White flowering form.
* Talinum calycinum	Fame flower or round-leaf rock flower	12 inch (20.5 cm) height 7 inch (18 cm) spread. Hardiness zone 6.	Very high drought tolerance, no moisture or shade tolerance. An American native widely distributed throughout the Midwest, this plant self-sows freely, but doesn't displace other ground covers as much as grows between them. Once it starts blooming, it flowers every afternoon from approximately May to September.

(Courtesy of Ed Snodgrass)   NOTE: Metric equivalents are approximate. * Image provided.

quantities. Ninety percent of the plants grown and shipped are sedums, in many varieties. In spite of the diverse array of plants grown at Emory Knoll Farms, only about fourteen species represent most of their business. See Table 3-2. This plant list represents sedums and related species recommended for extensive green roofs in the eastern United States. Although all of the plants on this list are grown at Emory Knoll Farms, designers will need to consider general climate and site specific conditions before making a final plant list for a particular installation.

On several areas of the farm, near the residence, the owners are growing various sedums on design elements such as a curving dry laid stone wall. The sedums grow out of the crushed gravel or other stone that is used in the construction; it is an experiment to see how they will grow and adapt to extreme conditions. Similarly, in an extensive rock garden at the residence, Ed Snodgrass observes new species and may test ones that seem to grow well as green roof plant. A German company, Jellitto, has a catalog of over three thousand varieties, and Emory Knoll Farms is methodically experimenting with testing several hundred to see if they will grow well and survive in the United States in 3–4 inches (7.6–10.2 cm) of growing medium.

Emory Knoll grows most of the plants for green roof installations as landscape plugs with a 3.25-inch (8.2 cm)-deep root ball, with 72 cells per flat. Some flats are larger, with 36 or 50 cells per flat in custom sizes. The standard growing medium is Fafard Super Fine (Fafard is a major U.S. supplier of planting soils and related products). The plants are not grown in any standard green roof media because of the additional shipping weight that it would contribute; for example, crushed shale, slate, or other similar media would be quite heavy by comparison. Several large greenhouse sheds also house many other green roof plants, grown in standard flats.

One final method of green roof planting used at Emory Knoll Farms involves the use of mats. Mats of specified species are grown and harvested like sod, then rolled into large cylinders that are hoisted onto trucks. However, once the mats are delivered to the site for installation, they cannot stay rolled up for more than a day without starting to die back. The advantage of mats is that they give instant coverage of the roof,

thereby creating a complete appearance from the beginning, as well as minimizing loss of the growing medium to wind erosion. Because there is complete coverage, the likelihood of weeds taking root is significantly reduced. Due to the limitations of storage on most sites, the logistics must be planned so that the mats are shipped at the same rate that they are planted on the roof.

Just as a large sod industry for turf has developed in the United States, other growers of green roof plants will develop this method once the reliability of and demand for certain species or combination of species are verified. It is already common practice for some nurseries to offer mats of single species such as blueberry,

Top:
3-15. *Delosperma nubigenum* 'Basutoland' or yellow ice plant, has brilliant yellow flowers and the ability to absorb a lot of water during sudden rains.

Above:
3-16. *Talinum calycinum*, fame flower or round leaf rock flower, has beautiful flowers. These are non-sedum species suitable for extensive green roofs. (Courtesy of Ed Snodgrass)

3-17. Plants in various containers being laid out at the Minneapolis Library in preparation for planting on the extensive green roof. (Courtesy of the Kestrel Group Inc.) See Chapter Five for a discussion of this project.

3-18. Prickly pear cactus at the Minneapolis Library will adapt to either extensive or intensive planting. (Courtesy of the Kestrel Group Inc.)

and summer annuals, but mats of perennials are not widely available because perennials tend to be grown individually, at a higher and more profitable cost.

Emory Knoll Farms ships in boxes, each holding about 100 square feet (9.3 m^2) or 200 plants. The maximum capacity of one box is 108 square feet (10 m^2) or 216 plants—the total number of plants in three flats of the standard 72-cell-size tray—which weighs only 118 pounds (53.52 kg). A pallet holds 32 of these boxes, or from 6,700 to 6,912 plants. A 53-foot-long (16 m) tractor trailer, which is hired to deliver their larger orders, holds 24 pallets or almost 161,000 plants. Emory Knoll Farms ships all over the United States. Some of the farm's plants are native, but the great majority are not. "One of the ironies of growing natives," explains Snodgrass, "is that they require more inputs than succulents, much more water, fertilizer and heated greenhouses." Often the natives need deeper soils to get established, which requires extra strength in the structural system on the roof—not often available in projects with limited budgets. Natives may also require additional water and fertilizer, whereas many of the succulents manage well without these elements. Many green roofs designers, he reports, are "anti-irrigation, anti-fertilizer," because they wish to minimize the impact of releasing excess water and dissolved fertilizer into storm water pipes and riparian systems.

Snodgrass often travels across the United States to supervise installations or discuss possible designs. Substitutions between what is ordered and what is shipped are made freely, with the permission of the designer, based on reasonable boundaries. He tries to keep records of what was successful and what was not. He feels that a feedback mechanism is well established in landscape architecture but not green roofs. "In landscape architecture, we have standard ways of evaluating whether plants are successful or not, but not in green roofs. We are speaking about the difference between emerging and mature markets." For green roofs, professionals are still evaluating what makes a successful plant: Is it one that thrives on its own with minimal help but tends to take over less hardy species? Is it one that migrates—that is, seeds itself randomly over the entire installation while dying out where originally planted? Is it one that grows well for one or two seasons but then appears only sporadically? Is it one that encourages other plants and/or animals to become established with it? All of these possibilities are common, yet each presents both problems and opportunities. In time, clear criteria for evaluating green roof plants will emerge.

Of the two owners, Ed Snodgrass in particular has participated in the design process on many green roof installations. Most of the installations grow well in a growing medium of 80 percent expanded shales and slates and 20 percent compost. He tends to advise a laissez-faire attitude toward the maintenance of established green roofs. "It's more helpful to look where the problem is," he says, "rather than where it isn't in order to fix things." If plants are thriving in certain areas of a green roof, but the exact ratio of species is quite different, he doesn't perceive a problem. Some landscape architects who conceive of a fixed palette or stable installation might not appreciate this perspective. He even suggests that adding occasional drifts of herbaceous annual plants can be a nice touch. "If they die after a few seasons, so what? They've added some interesting color and texture to a green roof." Public perception may be slow to adapt to evolving aesthetics of green roof applications, however. For example, he happens to like the changing colors and textures of native plant aesthetics, such as a prairie or meadow treatment, but many people are so inured to the traditional irrigated lawn that they have problems with plantings that have dormant or less active periods of growth. "One of the inhibitors in expanding natives and grasses on roofs is the general population's definition of beauty. I like the meadow look and don't mind a period of dormancy, but the marketplace isn't there yet."

Irrigation

In many ways, irrigation for green roofs, if it is provided, is no different from that incorporated into standard at-grade installations. Particularly for simple extensive green roofs, in which no irrigation is anticipated after the first year of installation, watering might consist of a temporary hose system with manual sprinklers, which are moved from place to place until the entire area is thoroughly watered. When the green roof is well established the hoses can be removed or stored and only reused during a period of drought or other difficulty. The hose-bibs for the water should be durable, vandal-proof, and frost free, to provide maximum protection from the elements.

Code Compliance

Compliance with local codes is important. Usually, this compliance requires (even for simple systems) a "backflow preventer" that prevents water in the irrigation system from backing up into, and possibly contaminating, the potable water supply. Backflow preventers come in a variety of sizes and types, based on the amount of water flow and the complexity of the irrigation system. A water meter may be another requirement so that, if there is a charge for water usage, the exact amount can be determined automatically. As an irrigation system becomes more complicated, there are a series of controllers, or timers, that can be installed to provide a set amount of water to each zone of the irrigation system. A *zone* is an area in which irrigation is received at a certain time for a set duration. Ideally, an irrigation zone should receive consistent solar exposure and have similar plantings, which therefore have the same irrigation needs, so that a uniform irrigation application will achieve good results. It is important that the backflow preventer, controller, and water meter be located in an area that is both protected from vandalism and accessible for maintenance and inspection. Code requirements sometimes dictate the maximum distance of the backflow preventer and water meter from the water supply line. This is usually a more rigid requirement in at-grade gardens, where a city inspector might be expected to make routine inspections on a regular basis and expects to find these elements in predictable, easily reached locations. There may be more latitude on a roof garden or green roof, but still the locations should be approved by the appropriate city or local agency.

Other important components include filters to prevent particles of sediment or other elements from clogging the irrigation lines. Because green roof growing media usually include long-lasting—even permanent—inorganic materials such as shale, slate, or brick, which often fracture into minute particles, filters are particularly important. Although most buildings have water supply systems within reasonable pressure ranges, occasionally pumps are

required to bring water to the roof or increase pressure. In some cases special valves are necessary to decrease pressure, depending on the type of irrigation system used. All of these components should be carefully discussed and selected by an expert, either the landscape architect or an irrigation consultant who should be included on the design team.

Spray, Drip, and Flood Systems

Generally, there are four types of irrigation systems: spray, surface drip, basal drip, and flood. All have some applications for green roofs.[6] Spray systems include pop-up-type sprinklers, set in overlapping patterns, which distribute a mist of water, generated by fairly high water pressure, over different areas of plantings. Spray systems are perhaps the most commonly used irrigation systems for estates and parks, because nozzles and sprinkler heads of various sizes can be used to provide coverage over large areas. However, there is significant loss to evaporation or wind as the mist is thrown up to varying heights by the sprinklers. The same problem should be expected if a spray system is used on a green roof, except the losses would be even greater because the exposure to intense sunlight and wind is typically greater. As water conservation measures have become necessary and in some locations are even required by law, a movement toward more efficient systems, particularly drip, has emerged.

Drip systems are now widely used in agricultural and large residential landscapes. Compared to spray systems, drip systems are effective at maintaining optimum soil moisture, are relatively easy to transport and install, and are adaptable to the application of liquid fertilizers. Drip systems feature a network of *emitters*, which are small, flexible pipes of rubber, plastic, PVC, or other such material with a pattern of tiny holes in them. Other types of emitters are very small sprinkler heads, which tend to be considerably less expensive than the larger, more complex ones used for spray systems.

From the top:
3-19, 3-20, 3-21. Pasque flower, prairie smoke, and blue campanula adorn green roof plantings at the Green Institute to recreate a prairie landscape. See Chapter Five for a discussion of this project. (Courtesy of the Kestrel Group)

3-22. Sedum plantings on the green roof at Emory Knoll Farms.

The emitter lines can be laid in parallel rows, a grid pattern, or even concentric patterns of loops or ovals at the surface of the plantings, and send a low-pressure trickle of water to the plants. Theoretically, drip systems, especially basal drip, are much more efficient and less expensive than spray systems, because little water is lost to direct evaporation, and there are no sprinkler heads, which are expensive and require regular maintenance.

If there is a drip irrigation system, or even if there is only manual watering, it is helpful to group plants with similar light, watering, and fertilization requirements together, so that the plants have the best chances for survival with the application of routine maintenance. A garden with a drip irrigation system in which each zone includes plants with widely varied water needs will surely suffer, because most plantings will receive either too much or too little water.

Surface drip or spray irrigation may be required on intensive green roofs where plant root depths vary widely. If a green roof has a large, complex planting, even on an extensive

3-23. Ed Snodgrass, Emory Knoll Farms. The green roof over the office is directly behind him.

roof, then a more complex drip system, which included various valves, pressure gauges, filters, and a pump, will be needed.

For extensive projects, basal drip is the practical choice because widely spaced emitters can irrigate broad roof areas. The basal drip method relies on fabrics with high capillary potential to distribute moisture evenly across the base of the green roof. The emitters, which are buried within the growing medium, are protected by filter fabric or insertion in slotted casings. The surface drip method can be problematic with extensive green roofs because the spacing density of the emitters may become too tight to be practical. Drip systems of all types must be designed and installed by experts, such as irrigation consultants, to minimize the potential for clogging by particles or dirt and to ensure that all plants receive optimal water.

Flood systems, which are much more common in Europe, maintain a shallow depth of water at the bottom of the green roof, that is, the drainage layer with retention cells. However, there are some notable examples in the United States, including the Oaklyn Branch of the Evansville Library, described in Chapter Five. These systems are only viable for green roofs with a total profile thickness of 8 inches (20 cm) or greater. Water is replenished at the bottom of the system as it is drawn up by the plants. This approach could be termed "on-demand" irrigation, because water is furnished at the rate that plants withdraw it. These systems are inexpensive and can be installed on roofs with pitches up to 2 percent (.25:12). Like basal drip systems, they minimize direct evaporation and reduce the tendency for weed germination. They are ideal for turf and for intensive green roofs incorporating shrubs and small trees. Excess water can be stored within the drainage layer or drained to cisterns, from which it is pumped back to the roof when needed. Water is absorbed via capillary action into the growing medium and the roots of the plants; as the roots become established, they eagerly suck up the water. Little water is lost to direct evaporation.

Although maintenance is greater to prevent clogging, the subsurface systems, whether basal drip or flood, have two major advantages over spray or surface drip. They eliminate tripping hazards, which could be a concern on any accessible green roof where the occasional pedestrian might catch a shoe or heel in a surface line. For all types of roof settings, which typically experience high winds, there is no evaporation loss from drifting or atomization of spray.

Regardless of which irrigation system is used, it is typically drained at the end of the fall and reactivated in the spring to prevent any damage from freezing during the colder months. Typically, water demands of plant materials are greatly reduced in the winter because plants are dormant. However, some green roofs, exposed to intense sunlight for long periods of time, may grow actively during the winter. In such situations, it can be helpful to have an alternate manual watering system, such as a hose, at least for the first year or so of the installation, to provide water when the irrigation system is not functioning.

To Irrigate or Not

Proponents of different types of green roofs make many different claims about the desirability, feasibility, or necessity of irrigation. Some feel that irrigation is essential. Others argue that if the green roof's purpose is to simulate a natural habitat, then there should be no artificial means of providing water, so that nature is allowed to practice natural selection on the plantings. In fact, some municipalities forbid the use of irrigation. Although this approach is essentially sustainable, practical considerations may apply. What if the installation of the planting occurs at the beginning of, or in the midst of, a long drought? Without irrigation of some kind, almost everything could die. Eventually, seeds might germinate on their own, but it could take months to generate coverage over the entire roof, and winds might wreak havoc with the whole installation. Green roof designers should learn from landscape architecture practice: Even if a palette of native plant materials is specified on an at-grade landscape, irrigation of some kind—whether manual, spray, drip, or subsurface—is provided for the first few years at least to allow the plants to become established. Once they have "taken," then the irrigation system can be dismantled or, more likely, used only on occasions where weather patterns demand it. In short, it can well be argued that a little irrigation goes a long way.

Specifications

Four major types of technical specifications play a role in green roof applications.[7] A *descriptive* specification gives step-by-step requirements for materials, methods, and workmanship for the installation of the item. This type of specification gives the designer the most control. A *performance* specification is used to match an existing condition, such as a particular pavement, finish, or even planting; traditionally, this specification allows the contractor considerable latitude in the way the specified item is constructed, as long as the standards for verification are met. A *proprietary* specification requires a specific product by a particular manufacturer. These are the types of specifications that typically include the clause "or equal," because some government contracts forbid the use of only one product, to avoid potential corruption or price gouging and ensure fairness and competition. (Some might refer to this type of specification as a performance specification in that the "or equal" clause can only be verified if there are accepted testing methods and standards to prove that the material being suggested is, in fact, equal to the one originally specified.) Finally, the *reference* specification refers to an established standard for identifying a material, mode of installation, or testing method. The most common reference standard in the United States, as mentioned, is ASTM, the American Society for Testing and Materials. CSA, the Canadian Standards Association, is the Canadian equivalent. In 2002 ASTM changed its name to ASTM International, and as it sets international standards, much discussion may be expected with other international organizations such as DIN (Deutsches Institut für Normung), the most cited European standards organization. Other such organizations go by the acronyms ANSI (American National Standards Institute) and TMECC (Test Methods for the Examination of Composting and Compost). At present FLL (*Forschungsgesellschaft Landshaftsentwicklung Landschaftsbau E.V.*) has the most extensive compilation of test methods and standards that is relevant to the green roof industry.[8]

In 1998 the ASTM established a subcommittee, E06.71, on sustainability. Subsequently, a task group was established, called the Green Roof Task Force, chaired by Michael F. Gibbons, FCSI, of Architectural Systems, Inc., Dallas, Texas, to develop standards for green roofs.

ASTM follows a consensus process that emphasizes cooperative and group efforts.[9] These new standards should go a long way toward standardizing green roof construction in the United States.

The methods described in the new ASTM International standards establish a common basis for measuring critical material properties of green roofs, such as maximum weight and moisture retention potential, under conditions similar to those encountered in the field. The five standards, which include important thresholds for safety and quality, allow a designer, landscape architect, architect, or engineer to specify green roof systems in such a way as to differentiate among similar products, and require testing to verify compliance with the new specifications. Staff from a Penn State University laboratory are members of the ASTM subcommittee. At the time of writing, the Penn State laboratory is one of the few in the United States that is implementing both FLL and ASTM testing methods for green roof media.

The five new standards appear in the *Annual Book of ASTM Standards*, Volume 04.12. The following summary is taken from the ASTM Web site, www.astm.org, and information shared by Roofscapes, Inc. The standards can be purchased directly online from the ASTM Web site.[10]

1. E2396 Standard Testing Method for Saturated Water Permeability of Granular Drainage Media [Falling-Head Method] for Green Roof Systems

2. E2397 Standard Practice for Determination of Dead Loads and Live Loads Associated with Green Roof Systems

3. E2398 Standard Test Method for Water Capture and Media Retention of Geocomposite Drain Layers for Green Roof Systems

4. E2399 Standard Test Method for Maximum Media Density for Dead Load Analysis [which includes tests to measure moisture retention potential and saturated water permeability of media]

5. E2400 Standard Guide for Selection, Installation, and Maintenance of Plants for Green Roof Systems

These five new standards represent three testing methods, one practice, and one guide. According to ASTM's criteria, an active standard supersedes previous versions of a standard. However, these standards are the first of their kind, so they will probably be revised and superseded in the future. Testing methods provide procedures for measuring properties of a building material, such as growth media. Practices provide a systematized method of evaluating a condition; in the case of Standard Practice E2397, measurements of media density and porosity are used to formally establish the dead and live loads associated with a green roof system. Guides provide recommendations for construction procedures.

The typical scope of work, called Section 1.1, is provided for the following ASTM International Standards. Section 2 (Materials) and Section 3 (Execution) complete each standard.[11]

E2396 1. Scope

1.1 This test method covers a procedure for determining the water permeability of coarse granular materials used in the drainage layers of green roof systems.

E2397 1. Scope

1.1 This practice covers a standardized procedure for predicting the system weight of a green roof system.

1.2 The procedure addresses the loads associated with green roof systems. Components that are typically encountered in green roof systems include: membranes, non-absorptive plastic sheet components, metallic layers, fabrics, geocomposite drain layers, synthetic reinforcing layers, cover/recover boards, insulation materials, growth media, granular drainage media, and plant materials.

1.3 This procedure also addresses the weight of the green roof system under two conditions: (1) weight under drained conditions after new water additions by rainfall or irrigation have ceased (this includes the weight of retained water and captured water), and (2) weight when rainfall or irrigation is actively occurring and the drainage layer is completely filled with water. The first condition is considered the dead load of the green roof system. The difference in weight between the first and second conditions, approximated by the weight of transient water in the drainage layer, is considered a live load.

E2398 1. Scope

1.1 This test method covers the determina-

tion of the water and media retention of synthetic drain layers used in green roof systems.

1.2 This standard is applicable to geocomposite drain layers that retain water and media in cup-like receptacles on their upper surface. Examples include shaped plastic membranes and closed-cell plastic foam boards.

E2399 1. Scope

1.1 This test method covers a procedure for determining the maximum media density for purposes of estimating the maximum dead load for green roof assemblies. The method also provides a measure of the moisture content and the water permeability measured at the maximum media density.

1.2 This procedure is suitable for green roof media that contain no more than 30% organic material, as measured using the loss on ignition procedure Test Methods F1647, Method A.

E2400 1. Scope

1.1 This guide covers the considerations for the selection, installation, and maintenance of plants for green roof systems.

1.2 This guide is applicable to both extensive and intensive green roof systems.

Another new ASTM International standard, ASTM E2114 (the Standard Terminology for Sustainability Relative to the Performance of Buildings) merits inclusion because it was developed by the same subcommittee. As green roof design advances in North America, it is important to have a contextual framework within which green roof design and other aspects of sustainable design can be defined and tested.

E2114 1. Scope

1.1 This terminology consists of terms and definitions pertaining to sustainable development and, in particular, to sustainability relative to the performance of buildings.

1.2 The purpose of this terminology is to provide meanings and explanations of terms applicable to sustainable development. In the interest of common understanding and standardization, consistent word usage is encouraged to help eliminate the major barrier to effective technical communication.

1.3 It is recommended that terms used only within an individual standard, and having a meaning unique to that standard, be defined or explained in the terminology section of that individual standard.

1.4 Certain standard definitions herein are adopted from other sources. Each is an exact copy. The source is identified at the right margin following the definition, and is listed in Section 2.

1.5 Terms are listed in alphabetical sequence. Compound terms appear in the natural spoken order.

"Sustainability," as defined in ASTM E2114, is "the maintenance of ecosystem components and functions for future generations." And "sustainable development" is, "development that meets the needs of the present without compromising the ability of future generations to meet their own needs."[12]

Despite all of these advances, it is still important to recognize what the ASTM International standards are *not*. The work done by ASTM is focused almost exclusively on providing definitions and standard methods to measure material properties. It remains for the designer to specify the properties required. Except for the plant guideline, ASTM says nothing about what constitutes appropriate properties. As of 2007, only the FLL provides any useful time-tested guidelines for green roof construction. As Charlie Miller, a member of the committee and an expert on green roofs, notes:

> No standardized method or guideline, for example, provides this information. Rather, estimates of the performance of a green roof system in controlling storm water are provided by the providers of these systems. There is no broadly accepted method or computer program to compute performance either. Roofscapes uses a German computer program to predict storm water performance. Some American green roof manufacturers have developed methods of their own. None of these has broad industry acceptance. When it comes to performance of green roofs as stormwater or energy conservation measures, the industry is sorely in need of standard methods.[13]

Because green roof applications are relatively new in North America, there are some limitations to the use of descriptive and performance specifications. An expert in green roof design might be able to use a descriptive specification, but unless those specific materials and methods have been successfully used within a short distance of that location, potential risks remain. What if the green roof installation method required does not work in a slightly different climate? Serious consequences could arise for the designer. Conversely, a performance specification might give too much latitude to the contractor, who may lack experience with green roofs. If both general and bid conditions establish a prequalification process, whereby a contractor must verify green roof installations previously completed as a precondition for entering the bid process, then performance specifications may be a safer option.

Proprietary and reference specifications are probably the safest approach until green roof installations are routine in North America. A specification requiring a green roof system by a particular, experienced manufacturer often includes a time-tested specification by that manufacturer. If the "or equal" clause is included, then having a detailed manufacturer's specification may give the designer considerable control over the evaluation of a comparable product before construction begins. Reference specifications refer to the testing institution, which has presumably researched materials and methods, consulted with experts, and consolidated results. A reference specification often includes some built-in safeguards for verifying that certain results have been achieved. In a green roof system designed to retain a certain level of storm water runoff, a designer can verify results by using a reference specification. As the green roof industry matures in North America, the use of reference specifications will become essential in concert with the development of industry-wide specifications for different types of green roof applications. Similarly, performance specifications will be used more frequently as enough green roof projects are completed that contractors can readily match certain built conditions achieved elsewhere.

CHAPTER FOUR

Green Roofs in Europe

4-0. The 92,493 sq ft (8,500 m²) green roof at Schipol Plaza at Amsterdam's airport. The moss-sedum system Type XF300c (Xero Flor R) weighs a maximum of 7.2 lbs/sq ft (35 kg/m²) and reaches a maximum height of about 1.2 inches (30 mm). (Courtesy of Mostert De Winter BV, the Netherlands)

4-1. Thatch roof, Donegal, Ireland; perhaps a precursor of some green roofs. (Courtesy of Joseph M. Dunn)

For any study of green roofs in North America, it is necessary to acknowledge our predecessors. Vegetated roofs have been a tradition in Europe for hundreds of years. Sod and thatch roofs, for example, are common vernacular materials in Norway and Ireland, respectively, and in other countries. Green roofs have evolved in Europe over centuries, from thatched huts to sophisticated modern gardens. The aim for earlier designs was to insulate a residence from cold weather during fierce winters. Grass sod or thatch was not regarded so much as a vegetative material as it was a good insulator. Another type of green roof—the *Holzzementdächer*, made of wood and cement—evolved in Germany.[1] In typical constructions in some German cities in the late nineteenth century, soil was placed on flat roofs to protect the roof membrane from exposure to potentially catastrophic fires—a major concern as the country became more urbanized.

In the twentieth century, Le Corbusier introduced the concept of the rooftop as a building's "fifth façade." On the flat roof of the Villa Savoye (1927–31), which is lifted off the ground on his trademark pilotis, Le Corbusier placed a roof garden mimicking the land beneath the building.[2] The Austrian artist/eco-architect Friedensreich Hundertwasser (1928– 2000) helped to establish a tradition of green roofs in European housing.[3] Like Le Corbusier, who started his career as an artist, Hundertwasser evolved from inventive, fanciful, and idiosyncratic art installations to naturalistic architecture. Among his wonderful architectural designs, which eschew any formal square geometry, is the Hundertwasserhaus Vienna. Completed in 1985, this low-income apartment complex features a rolling grass meadow punctuated by large trees that protrude at 45-degree angles from inside the rooms, with limbs extending from the windows. A strong ecological movement swept through Europe in the 1980s, which resulted in the incorporation of ecological goals into the construction industry. Research gradually proved that green roofs were not a problem for the roof membrane, because the membrane could be waterproofed and made impermeable to vegetative roots. As a result of increasing competition in the industry, green roofs began to compete with simple "graveled" roofs, and green roof design took off.

In modern Europe, a region of dense population with little space left over for new buildings, planners and designers have often rehabilitated old structures or adapted them to accommodate environmental requirements, such as storm water management. In many European cities, green roofs are required on all new construction, and recognized as a necessary environmental requirement, with no financial, zoning, or other incentives to reduce the cost. In Stuttgart, as much as one-fourth of all buildings with flat roofs have green roofs. In Linz, Austria, green roofs have been part of the required design vocabulary of buildings since 1985.[4] In both Basel and London, the development of wildlife habitat has become a driving factor in requiring the implementation of green roof projects, on both existing and new construction.

Many different ways of designing green roofs in Europe have evolved over decades. The most common are typical extensive roof systems, with a uniform cross-section applied over a large area. One alternative approach, pioneered by Stephan Brenneisen of Basel and others, varies the depth of substrates and uses native substrates, resulting in a more diverse range of vegetation and insects. At the same time, many advocate for purely sedum roofs, although they may be challenged by those who recommend a more diverse selection of plant materials, or even an approach in which native seeds are spread over substrate and nature is allowed to

4-2. Hundertwasserhaus, Vienna, Austria, completed in 1985 by Friedensreich Hundertwassser, is a precursor of modern green roofs in Europe. (Courtesy of Mark Zanzig)

be the gardener. Indeed, many installations recreate a particular plant community. Because the roofs are so diverse, so are the suppliers. Many manufacturers provide standard materials for roofing, waterproofing, root barriers, and so on, and follow the specifications of the FLL. Construction techniques are often standardized, whether for flat or sloping roofs, so that it can be as common to install a green roof on multiple sloping roofs in a new apartment complex in Basel, for example, as it is to install gutters in U.S. housing structures. Nurseries specializing in sedums are willing to ship plants all over Europe. By contrast, some nurseries grow plants and provide seeds that are adapted to a narrower spectrum of local conditions and are not suitable throughout the region.

Green roofs are added for a variety of reasons, and each design responds to that specific set of circumstances and requirements. Led by Dusty Gedge, an entire green roof movement has sprung up in London as a way to provide nesting habitat for the black redstart, an endangered bird. Industrial sites are characterized by brown roofs such as the one recently installed on top of a building at the botanical gardens in Malmö, Sweden. Collaborative efforts between some of these different approaches will no doubt yield even more exciting results. At the same time, Europeans often focus urban design efforts on elaborate intensive roof gardens that are major draws for tenants. In London, developer Charles Green designed a green roof as an amenity for the tenants in his newly renovated building. The garden on top of the LIFFE Building, near St. Paul's Cathedral in London, provides a lovely outdoor space for tenants and is also rented out for parties, weddings, and special events. Schools use roofs as sites for gardens and educational projects, and many major airports include green roofs on vast warehouses and terminal buildings. Resorts and recreational facilities sometimes emphasize the aesthetic effects of green roofs, even if they also have environmental functions. In short, complex projects involving many design disciplines provide green roofs of many different sizes, scales, and types as aspects of major efforts in urban design. The following section provides an overview of the diversity and expertise demonstrated by Europeans in their practice; their creations should be considered models by practitioners in North America.[5] More information about products and manufacturers that are occasionally referenced in the text can be found in the Notes and Appendix B.

4-3: A view of the Moos Utility Building. The green roof extends behind it. (Courtesy of Stephan Brenneisen)

4-4: Among the hundreds of species established are these orchids. (Courtesy of Stephan Brenneisen)

Continental Europe

Moos Lake Water Filtration Plant, Wollishofen (Zurich)

The modern European green roof movement can perhaps be traced to Zurich, Switzerland, where in 1914, one of the first ferroconcrete buildings was constructed to house a water filtration plant.[6] Water from a nearby lake was pumped and slowly filtered through a layer of sand, then stored inside the building. From the beginning the planners anticipated cooling the building with an earth cover, because they knew that *E. coli* bacteria could contaminate the water if it was not kept cool. The existing roof consists of concrete slab beams 3.2 inches (8

cm) thick with a 0.8-inch (2-cm) layer of asphaltic waterproofing and a natural crowned cross-section, very much like a wide roadway with a highpoint in the center. A drainage layer of about 2 inches (5 cm) of gravel covers the waterproofing. About 6–8 inches (15–20 cm) of native topsoil from the construction site was lifted onto the top of this roof and allowed to grow. The only maintenance involves mowing the roof once a year; a lawn mower is lifted by an adjacent pulley/crane system attached to one side of the building.

Over ninety years of growth has produced a roof meadow rich in plant species and flowers; 175 species have been documented on this almost 10-acre (4-hectare) roof garden, including nine species of orchids. Many of these species are rare or endangered in the eastern Swiss plateau of which Zurich is a part. There are over ten thousand individuals of *Orchis morio*, an orchid species otherwise extinct in the surrounding area. Other rare species that bloom in spring and summer include *Campanula patula, Centaurium umbellatum, Epipaeris palustris, Fillipaendula hexopetala, Gymnadenia conopea, Koeleria pyramidata, Listera ovata, Orchis incarnaia, Orchis latifolia, Orchis maculata, Ochis militaris, Platanthera hifolia, Primula veris, Roelaria pyramidata, Sanguisorba officinalis*, and *Sieglingia decumbens*.[7] Many of the rare and endangered plants on the roof meadow may be traced to the original topsoil hoisted there years ago, which was full of native seeds. An inventory of species in the nearby Wollishofen highway junction area showed that of the forty-five species initially inventoried, twenty-four are established on the green roofs of the water filtration structures.

Scientists inventorying both the plants and the insects that inhabit the area have found that the two layers of substrate (the drainage layer and the topsoil) have merged, without any negative impact on the site. In many ways, it exhibits the characteristics of a site with a perched water table in which, under natural conditions, water is held close to the surface by a hardpan, or impermeable layer. In this case, of course, the roof is the hardpan. Because water drains toward the edges of the roof, the site is drier in the center and moister at the perimeter edges, all of which encourage the rich diversity of plants and insects. The only repair needed over the years involved rewaterproofing one edge along the length of the building. This required digging up the full depth of the substrata to the existing asphaltic layer, and might be necessary on the opposite side. This effort allowed scientists to study the full depth cross-section of the substrate.

As the city has expanded, additional water treatment facilities have been built nearby, using the same method of establishing a meadow. Some topsoil and seeds from the existing meadow were used to help establish the new ones. The site has become a powerful visual, aesthetic, and environmental image for Zurich. The Swiss geobotanist Elias Landol even suggested giving these green roofs regional nature conservation status.[8]

Zurich Train Station

The Zurich train station sits within one of the denser urban areas of this city, and four additional platforms had to be added to accommodate more passengers.[9] Already a complex urban design task, the challenge grew when the entire area was mapped as a sensitive region for a range of insects and animals, including a rare species of lizard. Their natural environment consisted of almost desert-like spaces, but they had adapted to using the gravel-laden spaces between the railroad tracks. Because Swiss law prohibits the destruction of endangered natural habitat without replacement, the designers developed the innovative solution of recreating the habitat on rooftops over the new platforms. These roofs were developed as green roofs. In hot summers, the roofs have, of course, given the added benefit of shade to thousands of railroad passengers.

Special problems arose with the challenges of providing ready access to the roof for the less mobile insects and animals and encouraging the mobile ones to use the roof. One device was a gabion system—a series of steel mesh cages encasing stacked rocks—through which small lizards and insects could climb to reach the roof. Planted fences were also implemented as

4-5. A view of the hardscrabble green roof over the Zurich train station. (Courtesy of Reid Coffman)

4-6. Rock-filled gabions give lizards a route to climb to the roof. (Courtesy of Reid Coffman)

a way of providing a linear route for moving along the site.

The growing medium, typically at a depth of 3.2 inches (8 cm) with small hills up to 1 foot (30.5 cm), was a sandy loam and gravel mixed with some organic materials. The small hills were proposed as places of refuge during severe weather, either intense heat or cold. The roof membrane was by Sarnafil, one of the major European green roof manufacturers. It was difficult to place the material on the roof; after trying different methods, the contractor used a crane to hoist about half the material. Coarse gravel presented a problem because it could not be handled easily. To resolve the issue, it was mixed with wood chips, which made it possible to blow it up to the roof with a concrete pump over a distance of 656.2 feet (200 m). The roof continues to be monitored for insects and lizards. To date, insects are flourishing, although only a limited population of lizards has been noted. It may take longer for the lizards to adapt to the new environment, and they may have had difficulty reaching the roof. Moreover, until recently there were no shaded areas, so that the lizards—if they reached the roof during the hot summer months—could not stay there for long. This led the designers to place materials that produce shade—such as old wood branches and flat stone plates—over the stable parts of the roof, to see if these make a difference.

The designers attempted to establish *Sphingonotus caerulans*—a species of lizard that is rare north of the Swiss Alps—on the roof. It is typically a southern alpine species that thrives on sandy river shores and sandy, sunny slopes with less than 20 percent vegetative cover. The population in the main railroad station is one of the biggest in the northern part of the Alps. It has been hypothesized that the vibrations from arriving trains might disturb them on the green roof; however, as Dr. Regula Boesch explains, "I am sure that the lizards are not disturbed by train vibrations. Along all the tracks we can find a lot of lizards less than 1 meter from the railroad bed and also in the coarse gravel of the track itself. They are not running away if a train

is passing the site."[10] Further study must be done to determine how to adapt the green roof design to attract more of these lizards. Nevertheless, this habitat, though in the middle of a major urban district, has become well established.

University Hospital, Basel

The University Hospital complex in Basel has the character of a campus, with groupings of buildings organized around a large intensive garden built over an underground parking garage, as well as a series of buildings with green roofs, constructed at different times. On any day with favorable weather, one can walk through the main hospital entrance and into the interior park, where beautiful gardens with clear pedestrian routes provide quiet places for private visits between families and patients. The part also features cafes, water features, major sculptures, and seating areas. It is common to see patients walking by themselves; clearly, being amid the garden contributes to healing. As one patient (whom the author met while visiting the grounds) commented, "In Basel people come to this hospital to get well. In most places, people go to the hospital to be sick."[11]

In 1990, Clinic 1 (Klinikum 1), originally built in 1937, had green roofs added on most of its buildings to provide convalescing patients with views of green open space instead of flat gray rooftops. In 1978 Clinic 2 (Klinikum 2) was built, and green roofs were installed on all of the flat roofs. In 1998, by the time a new green roof application was considered, research work by Stephan Brenneisen at the University of Basel had advanced beyond a consistent style of green roof design. He sought to develop bioroofs to create the best possible conditions for diverse plant species and animal populations. Instead of providing a uniform cross-section over the entire roof with a uniform drainage configuration, a substrate of uniform depth, and uniform plantings primarily of sedums, a much wider range of flora and fauna was made possible by varying the depth of the substrates and adjusting the cross-section. This green roof was therefore designed to attract invertebrates as well as birds. Native substrates of a sandy loam and gravel mixture were used, in a range of depths. Treatment at the surfaces also included areas of bare gravel, exposed directly to full sun, and occa-

Opposite:
4-7. View of the interior courtyards at University Hospital in Basel, where a series of intensive green roof gardens link buildings at the campus.

sional dead logs. Rather than planting this roof, it was allowed to "plant itself" from the germination of the seeds distributed within the substrates. Some overseeding was done with a seed mixture specifically designed for the low and high water retention soils in Basel. There is no irrigation.

This roof is substantial in size, about 32,280 square feet (3,000 m²), and is situated below a tower building that houses many patients. When the green roof was renovated in 2003, the old substrate was temporarily removed to allow for new waterproofing and related elements such as lightning protection, and then reinstalled on the new green roof. It is an L-shape that wraps around an interior courtyard with its own garden that serves as a light well for the building. The depth of substrates varies between 3.2, 6, and 10 inches (8, 15, and 25 cm, respectively). As the vegetation evolves, it is expected that a mix of habitat, from dry meadow to more open, sparse areas, will evolve, each attracting its own predominant vegetation and animals. Despite a dry summer with no irrigation, the 2003 installation, considered in 2005, read as a rich grassland, with some areas as high as 1 yard (approximately a meter), and many insects and birds.

At the same hospital campus is the Rossetti Building, designed by Swiss architects Jacques Herzog and Pierre De Meuron. Sheathed in green glass, the building provides a visual link to the older hospital buildings across the street, one of which is clad in a similar, but less reflective material. Because the location is about 328 feet (100 m) from the Rhine River, the designers of the green roof sought to recreate the habitat of a river bank, and the project became a habitat restoration. The local substrate used on the roof consists of 60 percent stones, gravel, and sand, with some finer soils and organic matter added, mainly humus. The depth of the substrate varies from 3 to 15 inches (7.6–38.1 cm).

4-8. An aerial view of Clinic #2 of University Hospital, just after the green roof was planted. The goal of achieving variable results is evidenced by the variation in forms. (Courtesy of Stephan Brenneisen)

4-9. View of the green roof at University Hospital in Basel in September, 2005. Since access is limited, there is no parapet protection.

Small hills of the substrate were built to a height of 10–15 inches (25.4–38.1 cm), contrasting with other areas only 2.8 inches (7 cm) thick. As a result, the areas of deeper substrate are covered in vegetation similar to species in a rich dry meadow, whereas the thinner sections are more sparsely vegetated, primarily with sedum species and thyme (*Thymus pulegioides*).

Different plant and animal species thrive in these different conditions. Part of the approach is to provide a basic structure on which nature can finish the garden that people have started. At both this green roof and the Clinic 2 roof, plant and animal species from the surrounding area have seeded and colonized the areas that suit their habitat requirements. At the Rossetti Building, for example, a rare species, the jumping spider (*Pseudeuophrys lanigera*), has established a thriving population.[12] These spiders prefer an open land with low vegetation because their hunting strategy is to hide and pounce on their prey, which includes beetles and other insects. The gravel areas with their sparse vegetation suit them. The wasp spider (*Argiope bruennichi*) is also found on the roof, although it prefers stronger structures than the jumping

spider, which it uses to weave its webs. The wasp spider nests in the taller grasses and preys on grasshoppers. The most prominent spider found on the roof is *Pseudomaro ainigmaticus*, a very small spider that typically lives in macro pores under stones along gravel beds in natural river banks. Two individuals of this species have been found on the Rossetti Building, findings that represent only the third or fourth time that this species has been recorded anywhere in Switzerland. Such records could establish the potential of green roof designs, with adapted materials from the natural surroundings, to provide habitat.[13] The focus on the installation of micro habitats may lead to a real habitat restoration on a rooftop. Lastly, over fifty-two species of beetles have also been found on the roof of the Rossetti Building. The green roof is primarily used for scientific purposes.

Stephan Brenneisen became initiated into green roof design in 1995. "I knew that we had a flat roof at the institute near the Rhine River (at the University of Basel), so I talked with the owner of building and organized money, got permission from government. . . . As a scientist, it was clear to me that one should not make it all the same."[14] Brenneisen was advised to use three types of substrate, sand, and gravel, and volcanic and garden soil at depths of 2, 3.5, and 4.7 inches (5, 8, and 12 cm) over an area of 1,076 square feet (100 m²). Everything was seeded the same, so that measurements could be taken over nine different fields. The development was quite different on each test field. The results showed that it was the type and depth of substrate that determined what would grow; in other words, diverse substrate conditions generate species diversity. This result belied the approach of seeding with a diverse mixture, because many of the seeds might not germinate, depending on the type and depth of substrate.

Dr. Brenneisen gradually progressed to studying animals on the roof, as a way of exploring nature conservation issues, because the animals tend to arrive at the roof naturally. After some work with a colleague who was an expert on beetles and spiders, he began to evaluate populations on green roofs. His research showed that the sand–gravel mixture typically used on green roofs in Basel was too dry, and that its water retention was poor. He started experimenting with local substrate, rather than the volcanic material from northern Germany, and added both finer soil and organic material. Finally, at the Rossetti Building, he made small hills.

Dr. Brenneisen's research led to changes in the guidelines and laws on green roofs in the canton district, including the city of Basel. Now, all flat roofs on new buildings must be green roofs. The substrate must be natural soil from local sources. Different depths of substrate must be used within a single green roof design. No watering is permitted, and no fertilizer or herbicide may be applied. (Fertilizer and herbicides are permitted only on ground-level spaces.) Brenneisen reports that the best time to seed is usually early autumn until October, and by early spring there is already considerable growth. Seeding in the spring, after May, may not be successful because seedlings can desiccate during short dry periods. Seeding half in the autumn and another half early in the spring may reduce the risks for both periods. Some seeds and seedlings planted in autumn may die off because of hard winter conditions, whereas some of the seeds from early spring will sprout late, grow less, and fail to produce ripe seeds before the summer drought occurs.

Research on Endangered Bird Species

In Switzerland, much open habitat has been lost to building development, and significant river and wetland habitat has been lost to channelization or water management projects. Green roofs are one major way to restore habitat for invertebrates such as spiders and beetles; undisturbed, generally dry land that is not regularly maintained and mowed is quite suitable for them. In turn, these sites attract birds that prey on the invertebrates and take advantage of the same habitat for nesting.

Brenneisen developed a study in which birds were watched on sixteen different green roofs by birders, every two weeks for one hour. The birders recorded what kinds of birds would come and what they did on these various roofs. Bird species that relied on the roof's plant or animal species came frequently, but those whose food supply was not present, even if those birds were quite common in the city, did not alight on the green roofs. (The findings of this research were the basis of later cooperation with Dusty Gedge in London, profiled later in this chapter.)

Nathalie Baumann, a scientist at the Zurich University of Applied Sciences in Wädenswil, Switzerland, is studying a range of five flat-roofed green roof projects in different regions of Switzerland to identify suitable habitats for endangered bird species. Three ground-nesting bird species of Switzerland—the skylark (*Alauda arvensis*), the little ringed plover (*Charadrius dubius*), and the Northern Lapwing (*Vanellus vanellus*)—have been threatened by development pressures but have been observed on green roofs in Switzerland. Each species has slightly different habitat requirements in terms of food sources, nesting, and breeding (the little ringed plover and the northern lapwing typically nest in wetland sites, whereas the skylark prefers meadows). Both of these habitats could be recreated on a green roof.[15]

Baumann's research may help establish the criteria for determining how best to create alternate habitats for these birds on flat green roofs. Scientists need to know which bird species, in addition to the previously mentioned ones, will nest on such green roofs, what types of substrate (natural soil, sand, gravel or stone) will attract them (color, texture), what types of vegetation will attract enough of the insects on which the

4-11, 4-12. Two sites where Northern Lapwings (*Vanellus vanellus*) are nesting. The first is in Rotkreuz, where the birds have nested for about ten years on an existing roof which was later re-greened. The second is Steinhausen, where roof soil, cut dried meadow grass, and seeding are tested in different combinations and studied to determine biomass growth. (Courtesy of Nathalie Baumann)

young birds feed, and what ecological conditions are optimum for maintaining viable populations of different bird species. According to Baumann, "These birds can find a new habitat in the urban landscape. They can find a way to overcome the pressure from other habitats." She adds that "the standard green roofs with sedum mats will not be good enough, particularly for young birds to get enough food to grow; there will be a need for more biomass and different structures in order for them to survive."[16]

One corollary to this approach is to create maintenance-free natural habitats on green roofs: there would be no mowing, not even once or twice a year, and no irrigation. The concept is to simulate a natural environment and see whether certain species can survive. If they do, fine. If not, then further experimentation is necessary to see what changes should be made to allow those species to survive. For example, the substrate may be a clay material that holds water—during periods of drought, some species may be able to access the moisture in this material. These green roofs are works in progress, and over time flora and fauna may adapt to them in different ways.

4-13. A Northern Lapwing chick hiding among sedums. (Courtesy of Nathalie Baumann)

4-14. A male adult bird standing guard near the edge of a green roof; his chicks are hidden. (Courtesy of Nathalie Baumann)

4-16. The chickens wander at ground level, but some also reach the green roof. (Courtesy of Reid Coffman)

Asphof Rothenfluh, Basel Canton

Situated in the countryside outside the city of Basel, the organic farm Asphof Rothenfluh features a unique chicken coop with a green roof modeled after Norwegian-style sod buildings.[17] On two different buildings, a farm shed and a henhouse, the farmer has installed green roofs. The existing load-bearing capacity of the roofs for both buildings was limited to 20.5 pounds per square foot (100 kg/m²). Therefore, the substrate used, rather than an inorganic material of considerable weight or a manufactured drainage mat, was a native reed applied in a layer 6 inches (15 cm) thick, which could retain water filtered through the 2-inch (5-cm) layer of local farm topsoil that was placed on top. The whole roof is raised above the walls of the structures to allow for ventilation; brambles were planted at the outer perimeter as a way to achieve a thicket of growth that would discourage chickens, or other farm animals, from alighting on the roof. The first plant seeded was *Phacelia*, which grows fast and is known to improve the soil. Mown grass was slated to be used to create a dry meadow on the top of the roof; instead of this approach, however, the interior areas of the green roof were planted with hemp plants, grown for medicinal purposes. The roof has had a dramatic effect on the temperature and ventilation of the henhouse; the temperatures are moderated in the summer by as much as 45° Fahrenheit (7° C) compared with

4-17. A view of the top of the sloping green roof with wooden boards providing a landing for visitors.

4-18. Warehouse and garden center, Basel suburb. A view of the sloping roof of the warehouse from the side.

the outside temperature due to cooling from evapotranspiration from the roof and its insulating effects. The air circulation has improved, and ventilation during the winter has improved. The hens are allowed to roam throughout a large fenced area surrounding the building, but also seem quite comfortable inside. The numbers of eggs laid has increased. The green roof over the storage shed is handled in a similar manner and is functioning well. After one year, the volume of the reed mat had compressed from a thickness of 6 inches (15 cm) to 4 inches (10 cm). Some chickens do manage to reach the roof, and perhaps they enjoy the view.

Warehouse and Garden Center, Basel Suburb

In rural areas green roofs are not necessarily a requirement of building codes, but they can still provide environmental advantages; the warehouse and garden center in Sins, a suburb of Basel, provides an array of green roofs over Alex Gemperle's warehouse and garden center and demonstrates to customers different green roof materials and applications.[18] Four separate but linked accessible roofs have different purposes. Nearest the entrance is a flat roof bearing a gazebo containing a kitchen and ample space for entertaining. Adjacent to it is a full-size bocce court for parties. From this roof one can look to the adjacent large warehouse building, with its three styles of roof, each treated differently. The center of the building is covered by a large, two-sided, steeply sloping roof, planted as an extensive green roof. This roof forms a backdrop for the flat roof on the near side, which holds displays of green roof materials in linear beds, so that customers interested in purchasing them can see the height, color, and texture of the plant materials; they can also observe these plant materials in well-established plantings on the sloping green roof directly above them.

Raised beds adjacent to the warehouse building entrance are planted with additional hardy plantings.

Visitors can walk through the warehouse (underneath the sloping roofs) to a terraced area on the far side of the building and climb a brightly painted spiral staircase to the large green roof on the other side. Here Gemperle has laid out an array of extensive green roof plantings subdivided according to types of substrate and depth. At one end are ponding areas to retain water and develop yet another type of planting—substrates with their feet wet, which will be planted with

water-loving plants. A walk of steppingstones laid out in a curving loop allows access to all the varied plantings and connects to the base of the steep V-shaped roof, should visitors wish to climb it as well.

Top:
4-19. A wooden platform connects the sloping extensive roof to the new, flat extensive roof on the lower level, shown under construction in September 2005.

Above left:
4-20. The wet extensive roof under construction in September 2005.

Above right:
4-21. After installation is complete. German technology is sufficiently advanced that achieving a water garden on a roof is almost routine. (Courtesy of Alex Gemperle)

Cave Houses, Dietikon, Switzerland

An area of focus for architect Peter Vetsch in Dietikon is the development of earth houses, or cave architecture, which he has been involved in for over thirty years.[19] He has developed and refined construction techniques—which took a while to gain acceptance by building inspectors and zoning reviewers—that guide his continuing practice. Over the years he has defined nine artistic principles, or postulates, that guide his current practice: to integrate a building into its environment as much as possible and to return to nature a substantial part of what construction disturbance takes away; to provide for the roof a living surface (living roof, that is) arising from vegetation growing on adjacent parts of the site; to achieve integration into the landscape—as many outer walls as possible, in addition to the roof, should be covered with earth and with a living surface; to integrate a building into nature—an earth-covered greened box does not suffice—organic forms are needed; to regulate and rehabilitate the landscape by mitigating deconstruction and urban sprawl; to promote integration, protection, and safety; to promote community and privacy; to provide suitable public buildings; and to make it possible to reach setback and property line edges by earth covering and rooftop greening.

Vetsch did not want to restrict the types of vegetation that could grow on the roof, so he developed a structural reinforced concrete system that allowed for considerable weight and soil depth. In turn, this structural capacity allowed him to continue the pattern of landscape already established at the site by transplanting and reestablishing it on the roof of new buildings. The roofs are covered with anywhere from 16 to 32 inches (41–81 cm) of growing medium, often native topsoil from the site. In some cases, depending on site conditions, he designs houses in which an entire side of the building is buried into the rear or side of the site, even as an orientation is chosen for the houses that lets in ample natural light. The earth covering keeps the interiors cool during the summer and insulated during the winter. At the same time, houses are grouped around common spaces, such as courtyards or ponds, to encourage interaction among the residents. At a housing estate in Lattenstrasse, for example, nine earth houses are placed around a pond and wetland habitat. The living areas of the houses face southward and have high-arching interior walls and large openings that receive abundant light, whereas the bedrooms are oriented to the north. The bathrooms are in the intermediate zone between the living and sleeping areas, and receive additional light from skylights. Terraces face out toward the pond, encouraging residents to socialize and embrace the natural habitat. A seamless landscape seems to flow over the houses and into the pond.

In other buildings, depending on the program for the site, Vetsch may change which areas receive the most light. For example, the Guldimann House in Lostorf is situated within a forest. Canton regulations require a setback of at least 49 feet (15 m) from the edge of a forest. The architect designed a structure of two main floors and a basement on a south-facing slope; the client asked that the ground level include living areas, the upper floor the bedrooms, and the basement the garage, cellar, and storage area. By careful coordination with the building inspectors, Vetsch was permitted to build closer to the forest edge by carrying a living surface of new forest over the roof of the underground portion of the residence. In this way the client got more space within the building envelope while the habitat was protected and extended.

Vetsch's earth or cave houses are less obtrusive and intrusive than standard construction. Also, the living surfaces and the organic forms of the rooms, with curving vaults and arches and many rounded edges, not only provide direct protection from the wind and inclement weather, but also contribute to a sense of psychological safety, well-being, and privacy.

The general methods of construction that Vetsch has perfected often include domes, inherently strong structures that are connected to glass-covered atria to let in natural light. The main structures are usually created by spraying concrete, in much the same way that gunite (sprayed concrete) swimming pools are constructed in the United States and Canada. The domes and other walls are insulated with polyurethane foam, 5.9 inches (15 cm) thick and covered with geotextile fabric. Over the years Vetsch has determined that using poor or native soil (as opposed to nutrient-enriched soils with a lot of added humus) is better for natural plantings where nature becomes the gardener. Yet

4-22. Guldimann Residence, cave architecture. (Courtesy of Peter Vetsch)

4-23. In spite of extensive side and roof coverage, the interiors are still light and airy. (Courtesy of Peter Vetsch)

the system is flexible enough to allow for more elaborate gardens or even swimming pools to be built above it. Another advantage is that the construction of armature-sprayed concrete is an excellent shelter against earthquakes and hurricanes.

The inherent advantages of standard green roofs—roof protection, habitats for plants and small animals, protection from solar radiation and infrared light, reduced heating and cooling requirements, reduced storm water runoff—all apply to Vetsch's unique structures. It can be quite difficult to tell where the architecture ends and the green roof begins.

4-24. A building under construction. (Courtesy of Peter Vetsch)

4-25. In Lattenstrasse, grouping of cave houses around a pond gives an impression of community and security.

MAG-Galerien, Geislingen, Germany[20]

Dating back over a thousand years, the town of Geislingen, near Stuttgart, is situated in a valley, with most development occurring along the gentle slopes near the bottom. The steeper slopes are left alone due to the construction challenges that they present. Any major new construction must be compatible with the historic architecture of the town center but also provide for future needs. Over time, additional recreational, shopping, and parking facilities were needed but almost no land was available that could be used without severe environmental impact.

In the center of the town was MAG (Maschinenfabrik Geislingen), an old factory that was to be replaced by a new shopping development. As a result of a long planning process and a design competition, the architectural firm Haring und Zoller, of Stuttgart, developed a design for a new building that would tie into the historic town architecture and provide for construction of a multiple-story shopping complex containing a large grocery store, a health club, a parking garage, and a roof with green space and recreational areas for different age groups. A total elevation change of 77 feet (23.5 m) is gracefully handled with a series of stairways, escalators, bridges, and ramps that connect the various levels of the MAG Galleries to the roof.

The new structure follows the edge of the valley, with entrances at the higher levels into a parking garage, so that people can arrive by car and gradually descend into the building to use the various facilities. Essentially, the green roof (ZinCo) is a public park on top of a privately owned shopping center. On the roof is an intensive green roof of 54,000 square feet (5,017 m²), subdivided into planting beds with trees, shrubs, and perennials of 36,000 square feet (3,344 m²), gravel walkways of 10,000 square feet (929 m²), a street ball facility of 6,500 square feet (604 m²), an area of 1,000 square feet (93 m²) for children's play with a sandbox, seesaws, and benches, and some transitional areas with walkways and trellises. The substrate is as deep as 3 feet (0.91 m). Beautiful views extend from these gardens down into the heart of the town. Because the different areas are clearly defined and appeal to diverse groups, the roof has become a community center, with different groups peacefully coexisting. Teenagers favor the street ball areas, whereas mothers and toddlers congregate at the children's play area. Others stroll through the gardens.

4-26. Aerial view of the new building with its green roof in Geislingen, Germany. The large scale is apparent even though the structure fits the contours of the valley. (Courtesy of ZinCo)

The semi-intensive and intensive designs are integrated into one area; the intensive treatment supports larger plant materials, such as trees and shrubs, and the semi-intensive is planted with perennials. From the upper-level entry, as visitors approach these gardens, they appear to be at grade. It is not until one reaches the edge, several stories above the town streetscape below, that it is clear this is a roof garden.

Separated from the intensive green roof areas by a fence is an extensive green roof (approximately 26,000 sq ft, 2,415 m^2) inaccessible to the public, that is planted in sedums. Two additional semi-intensive green roofs follow the slope of the ramps down from the parking garage into the shopping areas. Originally, the main extensive roof did not receive any irrigation and had to be hydroseeded on two occasions to help establish a permanent vegetative cover. Maintenance of the sedum roof is carried out only once a year, whereas the intensive green roof is thoroughly maintained by the town of Geislingen as a showplace. The intensive roof has a regular irrigation system, a well-established lawn with perennial beds, and trees organized in clear patterns.

The small amount of runoff that is not absorbed by the plantings and substrates goes into the sewage system. Although there was discussion with town officials about tying into the storm water system, it was determined that the cost would be prohibitive.

A high level of cooperation and coordination flowed between the town planners, the architectural firm, the client, Kaufland Stiftung Co., KG, and the landscape contractor, the Gartner Froning Company. Construction of the estimated 58,125 square feet (5,400 m^2) of intensive green roof and 27,986 square feet (2,600 m^2) of extensive green roof was achieved in several months.[21]

From the top:
4-27, 4-28. Geislingen: Two different phases of construction, the first showing the spreading of the substrate, and the second after construction is complete and planting is about to start. (Courtesy of ZinCo)

4-29. The completed installation at Geislingen. Without viewing the edge, it is difficult to see that one is on a roof garden. (Courtesy of ZinCo)

Adler Thermae Spa, Tuscany, Italy[22]

Located in the very heart of the Val d'Orcia Natural Park in Tuscany, about 118 miles (190 km) from Rome, the Adler Thermae Spa and Wellness Resort is an elegant facility in the ancient village of Bagno Vignoni, where a thermal spring was used for centuries by the Etruscans and Romans. The modern resort offers indoor and outdoor thermal baths, saunas, steam rooms, mud baths, waterfalls, and pools for all age groups as well as fine dining, antistress programs, and massages—in short, almost any service desired by someone seeking relaxation. All of the resort facilities feature a natural bioclimatization system that regulates humidity.

The architects and brothers Hugo Demetz and Hans Peter Demetz designed and developed the resort. On one side it is cut into a hillside, blending seamlessly with the natural environment and disguising the size of the resort, while also contributing to a sense of enclosure. The main building of the hotel is a villa built in a typical Tuscan style. The rooms, facing either the central park or the Tuscan hills, are integrated with the surroundings and are partially covered with grass on the sides. Considerable underground parking is available, and some of the pool facilities and gardens are intensive green roofs built directly on top of it. (The pools have hot thermal water with a temperature of 97 degrees Fahrenheit [36 degrees C], which

4-30. The architect's sketch of the green roof cross section, including a horse. (Courtesy of Hugo Demetz and Hans Peter Demetz, architects)

4-31. A bird's-eye view of the resort. Green roofs cover the matching side wings of the main building. A glimpse of the underground parking, which extends beneath the swimming pools and recreational areas, can be seen as well. (Courtesy of Adler Thermae)

4-32. The thermal pool. (Courtesy of Adler Thermae)

compares to 122 degrees Fahrenheit [50 degrees C] at the source, the spring of Bagno Vignoni.) The pools are surrounded by a serene park of 32,292 square feet (3,000 m²), part of it an intensive green roof. Befitting the sublime setting, the seams where the built up gardens meet the existing topography are invisible.

Brown Field Roof, Malmö, Sweden

In Europe brown field sites, old industrial areas of warehouses, docks, gravel-laden railroad yards, quarries, and abandoned buildings are among the last to be redeveloped as a result of intense pressure for urban development. Prior to this new development, these abandoned areas had evolved their own rich landscapes,

4-33. A plan of the brown roof at Malmö. (Courtesy of Marten Setterblad and Annika Kruuse)

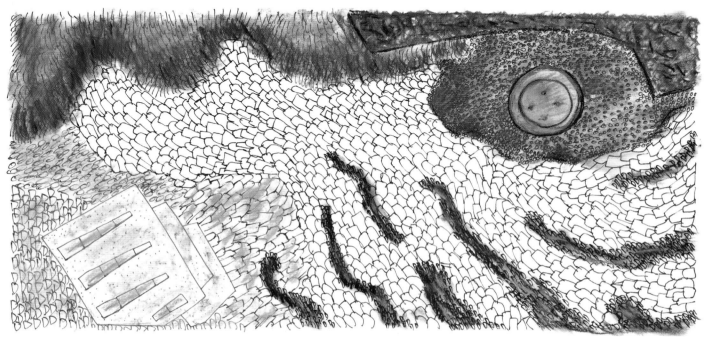

replete with plants and animal species, and well worth conserving as complete habitats.[23]

An innovative approach to brown field roofs was designed by Marten Setterblad, a landscape architect at the Swedish University of Agricultural Sciences, and Annika Kruuse af Verchou, a biologist at the city of Malmö's Department of Parks and Streets, an ideal team blending design and science. Their site is the roof of the Botanical Roof Gardens of Augustenborg, in Malmö.[23] The climatic conditions on the roof are ideal for a brown field concept—a harsh climate with rapid changes in temperature and the high winds also typical of the natural conditions of a brown field site at grade. Their goals were to provide conditions that would encourage a diverse range of species on the roof as well as an aesthetically pleasing design, and to let the garden evolve in much the way that a brown field would, with some plants flourishing and others dying, some colonizers establishing themselves, and dynamic change overall.

This brown garden is on top of a two-story public building and covers 2,152.8 square feet (200 m²). Public access was planned from the beginning, so that both scientists and the general public can observe and enjoy the garden. The design concept is to embody the contrast between force and contra-force, which is how brown fields form; repeated rough management of the land by humans results in continuous responses by nature, creating a unique brown field landscape. The land is constantly excavated, filled, built, and abandoned, leaving concrete foundations, brick fragments, and local materials. Nature responds with plant materials that colonize the disturbed sites and adapt to difficult conditions. A balance between these counteracting forces—culture vs. nature—results in a rich diversity of both plant and animal species. Natural succession occurs, but only to a point, as new disturbances by machines and people recur. The designers sought to replicate this process on the roof.

They chose chalk from local sources as the principal substrate, because the Malmö region has been the center of many quarries, and the mineral is abundant. Placed to a depth of 5.9 inches (15 cm), the chalk base is of variable texture; pieces range from nearly 15.7 inches (40 cm) in diameter down to a range of typically gritty material, all unprocessed and raw. There-

4-34, 4-35, 4-36. Two views of the brown roof at Malmö, and (*left*) a closeup of the iron pond or "button." (Courtesy of Marten Setterblad and Annika Kruuse)

foot-deep (30.5 cm) layer of organic material was added to provide an appropriate base for a rich range of perennials. The surface of the land is modeled to create miniature hills and valleys, thereby increasing the potential for varied conditions, each of which will attract certain species. Water basins were also a goal, and these were achieved by creating an iron pond designed as an oversized button. The designers sought to play on the concept of scale within the ruderal landscape, characterized by plants growing on rubbish or wastelands. Just as the button is very large, the designers remind visitors that the essence of the ruderal landscape includes organisms ranging from the microscopic to supermacro. A roof garden without any water is not ideal from an ecological point of view; the button's main use is to collect rain water. The rain water eventually evaporates and the pond dries up. Birds need it for cleaning and drinking, and it is also useful for insects. This is a very small water collector, but it is functional; it may be compared with fissures or small cavities in a rock, which would occur in a natural landscape. There is a nursery as well, set up as an experiment to grow and breed threatened species of brown field plants. Finally, various mixtures of gravel, brick, iron, sand, and inorganic and organic materials are organized to provide as diverse a setting on a roof as could be imagined.

Particularly in the chalk area, some perennials, trees, and shrubs were actually planted, with small root balls containing organic materials, but it was decided not to replenish the organic materials for these plants, so that only the toughest would survive. However, for the bulk of the garden the designers created a natural seed bank by using raw chalk, supplemented by mature plants gathered from nurseries and other sources.

As the first brown field roof garden built in Sweden, it has the educational goal of showing the public that such gardens can be both practical and beautiful. At the same time, it is providing a base for research into the ecological processes that govern brown fields and for assessing the variety of plant and animal species that has become established so far. The garden is expected to be a major contributor to the urban landscape, and a special feature of the botanic garden.

4-37. The garden captures the view of a shelter on an adjacent site in Malmö. (Courtesy of Marten Setterblad and Annika Kruuse)

4-38. The plantings at Malmö, like the patterns of substrate, are varied. (Courtesy of Marten Setterblad and Annika Kruuse)

fore, the base includes seeds of many tenacious plant materials that would typically be able to survive. To provide for a variety of environments within this garden, in some areas the chalk base is complemented with other materials. A dry meadow was created with prefabricated material over about one-fifth of the surface, where a 1-

Sedum Roofs and Green Roof Planning in Sweden

Like other regions of Europe, southern and middle Sweden has a long tradition, dating from the seventeenth and eighteenth centuries, of using sod roofs on buildings. However, modern green roof systems began only in the 1980s with direct imports from Germany, and have been used primarily for mitigating storm water runoff.[24] As the systems have become more sophisticated, a standardization of the process, through the use of thin, extensive sedum green roofs, has occurred. (Semi-intensive or grass roofs are rarely used due to national policies limiting the use of any material that might spread fire.) A wider interest in using green roofs as a planning tool throughout a district or region has also emerged. As the amount of undeveloped land has decreased, green roofs have become one method for maintaining green space within urban developments and contributing to a sense of connection between buildings.

School buildings and recycling centers, which often have a favorable environmental image as a result of their educational functions and programs, are the most common building types to have green roofs in Sweden. Schools may offer environmental education programs, and a green roof itself can serve as a teaching tool. Because two of the common problems of urbanization are increased storm water runoff and a decline in biodiversity, green roofs are examples of effective solutions. The monitoring of runoff retention on the green roof or a census of plant and animal species can become subjects of school science experiments. In Sweden, the school itself may become an example of sustainable design.

Recycling center buildings in southern Sweden are located on every block for residents to dispose of plastics, metals, paper, packaging, and glass. These buildings are usually operated by housing firms or cooperatives that seek to

4-39. The green roof on the head office of the bank SEB in Stockholm, Bankhus 90, was built in 1991. (Courtesy of Tobias Emilsson)

4-40. A school building in Lund, Sweden with a sedum roof. (Courtesy of Ulrik Reeh, Veg Tech.)

4-41, 4-42. Two views of a school building in Lund with a sedum roof. (Courtesy of Tobias Emilsson)

promote sustainability. It is important that the buildings look residential and fit into the character of the neighborhood. Often, they form one side of a courtyard or are part of the view from adjacent apartment windows. Because these structures are small, a green roof can be applied at a modest cost.

Although there are few planning requirements or economic incentives for increasing green roofs in Sweden, the city of Malmö has implemented a "green space factor" system, modeled after a system previously used in Berlin. In 2001, Malmö held a planning fair, called Building Expo Bool, one of the goals of which was to begin to transform the city toward sustainability. The planners sought methods that would create a more attractive urban environment, encourage biodiversity, and improve storm water management. The green space fac-

tor is calculated by multiplying every area within a lot by a value between 0 and 1, depending on its value for green space. A higher numerical value is associated with a higher value for green space. Therefore, a small surface with a high environmental quality may have the same value as a much larger surface of low environmental quality. A developer is free to allocate which types of green spaces or structures are to be included in the lot, as long as the required green space factor for the entire lot is achieved. For the expo site in Malmö, the green space factor was set at 0.5, meaning that 50 percent of the lot should be covered by high-quality green with a value of 1.0, with an average of 0.5 over the entire lot. This system has considerably increased the use of vegetated roofs throughout Malmö.

In Stockholm the municipal water company, Stockholmvatten, introduced a system of variable storm water fees based on the annual amount of storm water discharge. Green roofs may reduce or eliminate stormwater discharge; therefore, these fees are incentives to install green roofs. (Such systems are also widely used in Germany, sometimes even with greater financial incentives.) If all storm water is treated on the lot and there is no discharge to the storm sewer system, a significant reduction in annual fees results. The fees are also tied into the size of the building through a floor space index, so that the larger the building, the larger the potential savings. If the discharge is delayed through detention, there is a 50 percent reduction in the annual fee.

London

Origins of Green Roofs

The major impetus to construct green roofs in England started in London with a small bird, the black redstart (*Phoenicurus ochruros*).[25] The bird breeds in vacant lots that are typically littered with the debris of warehousing and construction, such as gravel pits, railroad side yards, docks, and abandoned industries, in what is referred to as brown fields. Despite their abandoned nature, these are rich landscapes—complete habitats replete with many plant and animal species—well worth conserving. A "protected" species, according to the criteria of the English Wildlife and Countryside Act, the redstart rose in population immediately after World War II, as bomb sites in the city of London became habitats. However, as available London real estate became more scarce, developers began revitalization projects in these sites, thereby eliminating much of the bird's habitat. Legislation protects the "birds, its eggs and nestlings from killing and injury, and damage or destruction to its nest," but only while it is breeding.[26] Ironically, once the breeding season is over, there is no longer any formal protection. Given the bird's abandoned, industrialized habitat, it was hard to set aside conservation lands to protect the species. Finally, in 1997 the London Biodiversity Partnership (LBP), a group of environmentalists, challenged a proposed development, Deptford Creek in southeastern London, by suggesting that habitat for the birds could be

4-43. Canary Wharf is a large, modern urban development in London, adjacent to the Thames.

provided by installing green roofs in the new development. After a protracted period of legal wrangling and tense negotiations, the LBP helped reinforce local planning regulations that require developers to include consideration of protected species in the planning of future developments.

As the Deptford project moved forward, ecologists found that two pairs of black redstarts were breeding in locations that were part of the proposed development site, an old power station and an abandoned aggregate recycling complex. Because there was no planning or architectural reason to save these buildings, it was decided to move the habitat that attracted these birds to the roof of the proposed new buildings by moving some of the rubble that was habitat for the birds to the roofs, and spreading it in variable depths. Over time, as more development examples followed, the LBP initiated the use of the term "brown roof" to describe a green roof of the particular style being implemented. "Brown roofs are essentially extensive green roofing systems that seek to replicate the original ecological footprint prior to development. Essentially the roofs should be constructed of aggregate material associated with well drained brownfield land low in nutrients," and the material should be derived, if at all possible, from the original site prior to development, so that local characteristics are recreated on the new roof.[27] Another critical requirement of the process is not to sterilize the material in any way. Better still is to store it at the site for an indefinite period, so that it accumulates seeds and populations of invertebrates that will form the base for new plant and animal communities on the roof.

Dusty Gedge, one of the members of the LBP and an expert birder, became a leading proponent for green and brown roof installations, which he called living roofs, in other proposed developments throughout London. He has become a fierce, if entertaining and witty, advocate for brown roof systems, as opposed to the sedum systems that are most common in London. Over the last several years, he has initiated joint research efforts with Stephan Brenneisen of Basel, Switzerland, to determine if modified extensive green roof designs, featuring varying depths of rubble or other local substrate, would provide appropriate bases for new habitats for birds, invertebrates, and plants. This

research has confirmed the speculation that varying the depth and character of the substrates results in a greater diversity of species. Gedge's research also assessed whether some traditional sedum green roof projects in London were providing diverse habitats compared to some existing brown fields. The research focused on spiders because if they are present in a site, one may assume that there are adequate food sources upon which they prey. Found on the roofs were a little more than a fourth of the spider species known to exist in London, a figure that represented almost 10 percent of the total number of spider species nationwide. One new species of spider was discovered and also a rare beetle. These results suggest that the much greater diversity of plants and animals found in brown fields could gain a foothold if similar conditions were created on the roofs.

Prior to the collaborative efforts led by Dusty Gedge and Stephan Brenneisen, the green roof industries in London and Basel were quite divergent. In Basel, as in all of Switzerland, green roofs are mandated, and there are legal frameworks for reviewing installations and verifying that they comply with requirements. Within the canton are extensive brown field sites that are experiencing intense development pressures. In response, Brenneisen undertook studies, completed in 2000, to investigate whether green roofs with particular design parameters could be designed to provide habitat for invertebrates, birds, and other specific species. His results were positive, and the canton adopted construction requirements for green roofs to provide for invertebrate habitat. Design parameters were included; for example, vary the depth of the substrate, use local substrates, and provide a certain amount of bare or open space. By contrast, although the black redstart movement has jump-started the green roof industry in London, there is still a tendency to rely on extensive green roofs with uniform substrate depths and sedum installations. There is still not agreement as to whether sedum green roofs of uniform depth, or brown roofs (living roofs) of variable depth are better solutions. The joint British–Swiss research effort should continue to yield a wealth of information about how best to build green roofs for biodiversity.[28]

Since the initial development at Deptford Creek, LBP now has a legally mandated advisory and constraining role in many other proposed developments. By 2002 over 161,400 square feet (15,000 m²) of green roofs were constructed for black redstarts in these proposed developments. Many of the roofs are not accessible or visible to the residents or office workers within the buildings. Nevertheless, the vocabulary of green roof design is establishing a strong foothold in London.[29] It is a measure of how explosively this movement has caught on that, by the fall of 2005, approximately 3,766,000 to 4,304,000 square feet, or 86 to 99 acres (350,000–400,000 m²), are proposed in diverse developments, from the Olympics to Silver Keys to Thames Gateway to the Greenwich peninsula.

A final factor in promoting green roof development in London is Great Britain's Environmental Agency, the British equivalent of the U.S. Environmental Protection Agency. In London, this agency regulates all developments along the tideway, essentially the Thames River. The agency has become quite powerful and is a strong proponent for these developments. Since 1997 a black redstart survey is required for virtually any development in central London; if birds are present, a green roof is required, even if the criteria for such roofs are not yet well established or budgeted.

Canary Wharf

The development at Canary Wharf is one of the largest roof garden complexes in Europe. Encompassing 97 acres (39 hectares), it covers part of the Isle of Dogs. (The complex is named not after the bird species, but for the Canary Islands, the source of the imports into the docks that once flourished there.) Planning began in 1981 when the vast area, in tremendous physical decline, was declared an enterprise zone to encourage development. There are now approximately 14,000,000 square feet (1,300,600 m²) of space in over thirty office buildings with four retail malls, a department store, and sports and health clubs. The tallest building is the fifty-story One Canada Square which, at 800 feet (244 m) high, is the tallest in Great Britain. Ninety thousand people are employed in the hundreds of businesses, shops, and restaurants.[30]

There are sedum green roofs atop some very tall buildings, but Canary Wharf is most notable for a series of major linked intensive public gardens, five in all, covering 20 acres (8 hectares). Each garden has a different theme and connects through pedestrian walks and plazas to the various buildings. With a project so large, a range of different designers and landscape architects is

4-44. Dusty Gedge, founder of Livingroofs.org, stands in the middle of the experimental green roof atop the tallest building in Canary Wharf.

reflected in the outcomes. For example, Canada Park is a formal layout, planted entirely with North American species, primarily trees and ground covers with some massing of shrubs. Jubilee Park, by contrast, is undulating and more informal. It consists primarily of large *Metasequoia glyptostroboides*, dawn redwoods; well over two hundred are planted. There are no flowering shrubs, a few flowering cherries, but basically, the theme is to be *green*. When these parks first opened, they were animated with seasonal displays of annuals, but the budget for these flowers was cut to save money.[31]

Alec Butcher, the landscape manager of Canary Wharf Management Ltd (CWML), is "responsible for parks, gardens, and street trees throughout the estate. The whole estate is one whole roof top garden. It's difficult to imagine but all underneath all of the structure you've got retail shopping areas, truck tunnels, and car parks below the landscaped areas."[32] The major trees are planted in huge concrete boxes that are 5.25 feet (1.6 m) deep by 32 square feet (3 m²). The lawn areas are much thinner, with a depth of topsoil of about 12 inches (30 cm). The shrub beds range in depth from approximately 3.2 feet (1 m) deep to 12–20 inches (40–51 cm). An extensive irrigation system is installed throughout the entire development. The sites are irrigated from mid-March to mid-October. There are separate spray head sprinklers for grass and local shrub areas, and a drip system for

4-45, 4-46, 4-47. Three images at various scales of Jubilee Park at Canary Wharf.

major trees. Separate zones are designated for windy areas as well as for very shaded versus sunny areas—a typical condition given that the tall buildings generate large shadows.

The sedum roofs are fertilized once a year and weeded periodically, but there is no irrigation. The plants have generally reacted quite well, although growth has been sparse in some areas exposed to very high winds. Some areas have struggled a bit, particularly in the last few years, as a result of drier weather. The overall results for these green roofs are good. Visitors looking down on the green roofs at lower levels have noted how they change colors with the season, with flowering in a range of yellow hues through late spring and early summer. For the range of species used in this project see page 118.[33]

Two species—*Saxifrage granulata* (meadow saxifrage) and *Saxifrage tridactylites* (rue-leaved stonecrop)—have self-sown and because their growth properties are similar, have not been weeded out. As the season dries out toward the end of summer, the color of the sedums changes toward red. None of the sedum roofs are accessible for safety and security, but some of them are visible from various locations within the building complex.[34]

The intensive plantings, which represent a much greater percentage of space, are more challenging to maintain. The plant materials, although adaptable, do not always respond as well as Butcher would like to the extremes of both sun and shade. Strong winds, particularly in the winter season, can be quite destructive. The winds, as well as strong sunlight at other times, burn tender areas of the plant materials

4-48. A view of sedum roofs at lower levels of the office buildings at Canary Wharf.

CANARY WHARF PLANT LIST	
Sedum acre	Biting stonecrop
Sedum album	White stonecrop
Sedum hispanicum	Spanish stonecrop
Sedum pulchellum	Stonecrop
Sedum reflexum	Reflexed stonecrop
Sedum selskianum	Stonecrop
Sedum spurium, "Album Superbum"	Stonecrop
Sedum spurium, "Summer Glory"	Summer Glory stonecrop

and stunt growth. The west end of the development is calmer, and better suited to less hardy plants. Because tall buildings keep many of the planting beds in shade, many plants are shade tolerant.

To develop more information on how green roofs can be planned for biodiversity, CWML has funded a field station on top of one of its buildings, where its researchers study substrate types and depths, orientations, and planting methodologies. Because a rare beetle has been identified at Canary Wharf and the development is already mandated to provide habitat for the black redstart, there is impetus for research. The concept of developing rubble roofs into habitat for diverse species is still controversial; some researchers, still favoring extensive sedum green roofs, doubt seriously that diverse species can become established on a rubble roof. Other researchers, such as Dusty Gedge and Stephan Brenneisen, feel that their preliminary research suggests that a diverse green roof will result in a diversity of species.

Visible from the roof of the Barclays Bank building—one of the tallest buildings in Canary Wharf—are other existing and proposed projects, often vast in scale, that are slated to have green roofs for the black redstart: the Isle of Dogs; the King's Cross Channel Tunnel; the Olympics; Silver Keys; the Thames Gateway; the Greenwich peninsula; and even a large power station. The green roof at Barclays Bank is the first in the Canary Wharf area to illustrate the cross-fertilization of Stephan Brenneisen's and Dusty Gedge's ideas. The Londoner explains, "There were compromises on this roof based on what this building purportedly could take."[35] Because it is a retrofitted green roof, the weight that could be supported was limited. At the same time, it was necessary to include some

sedums even in what would be a natural-type installation. This green roof is about 4,304 square feet (400 m²) and is 525 feet (160 m) high. The substrate is the ubiquitous roofing shingle, fractured into pieces, as per the concept of using native materials near the site. Also included are recycled brick and concrete, with some pine bark as biomass to comply with FLL. Overall, in the growing medium there is approximately a 50–50 mix of pine bark with the inorganic shingles, brick, and concrete. Because the site is so high and exposed, and subject to strong winds, the entire bed was covered with an erosion control mat, and the area was seeded with a calcareous grassland mix. To counter concern about how the substrate would bind with the erosion control mat, Gedge artfully added some corn flowers (*Rudbeckia sp.*) along its edges to help hold it in place. Down the center, like a formal axis, stretches a 6.5-foot (2-m)-wide planting of sedums—the only ones in the Canary Wharf development that are on substrate, instead of being set on almost bare drainage mats and subbase (Fig. 4-4). As a result of the substrate, this sedum is quite green. Finally, neatly inscribed circles of exposed materials, which are kept bare, are expected to attract invertebrates. There is no irrigation, as Gedge explains: "It will turn into whatever it wants to be. By the time winter hits, it should be quite green." The only maintenance is to remove tree seedlings, but essentially "the system will weed them out naturally."[36] Research of several years' duration will evaluate how successful this new, natural green roof is in attracting nesting black redstarts, as well as spiders, beetles, and other fauna and flora.

From one corner of this green roof site, one can see large red circular buildings with diverse roof gardens and green roofs in the distance. One sedum mat design on crushed brick, installed two years ago, was taken away. Standing at the site of the new Barclays Bank green roof and looking out across the vast urban fabric of the city of London, Mr. Gedge commented, "You can see with the naked eye that all sedums are taken away. Birds, winds, God knows? But again, my argument is, 'Do the sedum systems really work?'"[37]

To date in London, few developers are willing to pay for environmental expertise, and what passes for a green roof, per the planning guide-

lines, may not suffice to support either plants or animals. Mr. Gedge emphasizes that, depending on the type of system, biodiverse roofs are at least 25 percent and sometimes as much as 50 percent less expensive to install than generic sedum green roofs. One reason is that the bioroofs are typically seeded, which is much less expensive than shipping and planting sedum plugs. Gedge suggests that "in general, use a substrate appropriate to that circumstance in terms of biodiversity."[38] Most of the crushed brick used in London comes from a source 100 miles (161 km) away, and then it is sent 100 miles (161 km) farther for processing, and then finally shipped back 200 miles (322 km) to London. A biodiverse roof that is planned and installed using substrate from a local source or the site itself is immediately more economical.

Komodo Dragon House, Zoological Society

Although the sedum green roofs at Canary Wharf are visible to the public, the living roof experiment atop the Barclay's Bank building is accessible only to scientists and maintenance staff. It is not visible to the public because there are no taller, adjacent structures from which to view it. By contrast, at the Zoological Society of London (ZSL), the Komodo Dragon House was designed by the architects WharmbyKozdon and

4-49. The Komodo Dragon House under construction. (Courtesy of ZinCo)

4-50. The finished Komodo Dragon House.

4-51. The bioswale engineered and planted by the side of the Komodo Dragon House.

includes a specially designed living roof.[39] Stephan Brenneisen and Dusty Gedge provided the design concept for the roof. The roof is an integral part of the Green Roofs–Urban Biodiversity and Science Technology Transfer Project between Switzerland and the United Kingdom. It demonstrates how living roofs in an urban context, especially London and Birmingham, can provide habitats for black redstarts (*Phoenicurus ochruros*) and invertebrate species associated with brown field land. The growing medium of the living roof lies on a moisture retention mat and consists of various blends of crushed brick and concrete. All the material is from a secondary aggregate source. The depth of aggregate varies throughout the roof, and some of it is covered with topsoil from the original site excavation. The use of crushed brick and concrete as the basis for the growing medium is characteristic of soil types on brown field land. The green roof on the Komodo Dragon House replicates the ecological circumstances of brown field sites in urban areas of the United Kingdom. The green roof has been seeded with an appropriate seed mix, and was maintained by ZSL staff over the first two years to establish a varied plant community.

The building and its living roof stand as a good example of the ZSL's efforts to demonstrate environmentally sensitive design. The entire roof, with its diverse components, is fully visible to zoo visitors entering the Komodo Dragon House, or walking by it to see other exhibits. On one side of the building, the land has been gently sculpted into a wide bioswale planted with a rich community of plant materials that evoke the tropical environment of the Komodo dragon (*Varanus komodoensis*). A bioswale is a drainage ditch engineered at a fairly gentle gradient of no more than about five percent, to allow it to filter silt and pollutants from stormwater runoff. Particles in the stormwater settle in the ditch, or are filtered by plant materials or biological processes. Any overflow is released into the storm drainage system. In an urban environment such as London's, a bioswale, like a green roof, can have a significant impact on water quality, as well as the quantity of runoff.

Other components of the green roof not only enrich the environment visually, but provide a more varied habitat for invertebrates.

Two additional features are partially buried logs, log piles, and branches, in the existing growing medium, as well as sand dunes, an important invertebrate habitat. In the original design "ribs" of sand were part of the growing medium. The "sand dunes" are located on the "bridge," and the border at the top provides a barrier for any movement due to wind. The materials come from locations within the zoo site. Another proposed sand element is a 3-inch (70 mm) high "sand cliff" made of a combination of sharp sand, sand, and concrete as a bonding agent.[40] The cliff could be achieved by using a temporary curb, against which the damp mix could be applied. The curb would be left for a week to dry out and then removed.

LIFFE Building

The LIFFE Building, situated in the midst of a dense historic district of London, not far from St. Paul's Cathedral, is a new office structure with an intensive green roof that is rented out for special events such as weddings, parties, and films. The roof is also used by the tenants of the building.[41] The roof garden is anchored between two historic tower structures; thus, the roof garden itself has become a landmark.

The garden features elegant lawns and clipped hedges of boxwood and yew, which help to define spacious outdoor "rooms." Blooming perennials such as lavender are unifying elements. A water feature graces the entrance, and to one side along the length of the garden (but often out of sight) are several small, tent-like structures for accommodating groups of people for catering, dining, entertainment, or other activities. There are few trees, because the shrub specimens and hedges define spaces well and there is no need for trees that require deeper planting depths. The roof includes pavers on pedestals as well as mortared sections and curbs, which provide a clear pedestrian route around the entire perimeter of the site. Because this garden has heavy pedestrian usage, a full parapet and handrail have been installed. A sturdy spiral staircase, which rises two stories to one end of the garden, provides roof access. A full-time maintenance crew prunes, waters, fertilizes, and weeds the entire roof garden, as would be the case with any garden of a similar design at grade.

4-52. The site of the LIFFE building roof garden, visible from a great distance, is anchored between two towers on the Thames River.

(All images on this page are by author, courtesy of Cannon Bridge Properties LTD)

Left:
4-53. The LIFFE roof garden is planted elaborately with areas of lawn, pavement, and beds for shrubs and perennials.

Below:
4-54, 4-55. A close-up of some rich plantings at LIFFE. St. Paul's Cathedral is visible in the background.

Green Roofs in Europe

King's Cross Building

Although the roof of a building being rehabilitated does not seem to represent a rural environment, the living roof that was developed on a structure in King's Cross, London, became a focal point for many "country" activities of children and the building's tenants. Charles Green, a developer with The Office Group, and Global Generation, an educational charity that seeks to provide educational opportunities (including direct experience with nature) in rural environments for urban children and young people from London, formed a partnership to redevelop a building in a way that would encourage people to come together as a community and make positive changes in London's urban environment.[42]

Green acquired a building in King's Cross, a part of London heavily affected by the Channel Tunnel Rail Link. Many people have been displaced, yet there are considerable opportunities for renewal. Green's company acquires vacant freehold buildings in central London, carries out comprehensive refurbishments, and then rents the space to a variety of small and medium-sized businesses. A forward-looking planner, Green decided to engage in a partnership with Global Generation to build a living roof instead of a mobile phone mast atop his building. Dusty Gedge, the London Biodiversity Partnership, six biology students from the Sainte Union Secondary School, and local children from Calthorpe Community Garden (across the road from the building) all participated in developing a design.

The building was acquired by The Office Group in October of 2004. An initial inspection established the roof as easily accessible, a possible site for recreational functions, and an outdoor space that would be an attractive amenity for the tenants and the community. The Office Group saw this living roof as having the potential to set their development apart from their competition—a clear marketing advantage.

The program for the site was thorough. The final design needed to comply with Department

4-56. The layout's organic forms naturally make the sequence of spaces feel larger.

4-57. The brightly painted mural welcomes visitors and contrasts with the perennials blooming below.

Left and below left:
4-58, 4-59. Sawed-off pieces of wood are used to create one of the pavements.

Below:
4-60. Display bins reveal the materials used to construct the surfaces of the roof garden, crushed brick and concrete and used filter sand at right, and carbonated sewage and clean filter sand at left.

of Health and Safety regulations, create a separate area for outdoor tenant meetings in an attractive environment, promote biodiversity, provide a process to include the local community, and be completed on a limited budget.

Adjustments to the existing handrail on the roof to comply with building code requirements were carried out at a low cost. The roof was made watertight. Evaluations by engineers determined that up to thirty-five to forty people could be on the roof at one time without problems. Global Generation provided supervisors for the children, and older children took the lead in helping to implement the plan developed by Dusty Gedge. Because much of the work was carried out during business hours, there was some concern about potential disruption to the tenants. However, knowing that a garden was being created, tenants were generally tolerant of occasional disruptions. Some minor maintenance issues have arisen, primarily problems with runoff, but careful monitoring should minimize future issues.

The roof features organic forms paved with recycled materials such as glass, rubber, and other media, placed to a limited depth. Sawed-off logs set on end create a circular seating area. On display in plastic bins are some of the materials used as substrates on the roof, including recycled glass, crushed brick, and stone. The seed mix used contained local plants; because the weather was exceptionally dry, an additional seeding was planned for the following fall or spring. Within less than six months of installation, a nicely blooming group of perennials and additional plants had already colonized the roof. A small ancillary building houses maintenance equipment, and a brightly colored mural decorates the side facing the entrance to the roof garden.

After completion of the living roof, several additional tenants decided to move into the building. Many of the tenants enjoy the cachet of feeling that they are contributing to the environmental improvement of their neighborhood by renting in a building with a living roof. Green is so confident about the results that he intends to implement a similar process on The Office Group's next rehabilitation project, which is a significantly larger building. He believes that "if green roofs are to be increased in number, the design has to be almost a balance between the intensive and extensive, where the roof can be a bio-diverse environment and at the same time be designed well and most importantly, be useable, livable space for the occupiers of the building."[43] His team is also considering using geothermal heating and cooling as opposed to air conditioning. The Office Group is "motivated by environmental concerns. We recycle paper, use low-energy lamps, and the living roof was an opportunity for our firm to go further in the environmental area. But an equal, probably greater motivation is that adding a commercial element to the building gives us an advantage over everyone else." People like that they are able to contribute to the environment by renting space. As he explains, he is excited by the prospects: "I'm using dead space for a break-out social space for use by tenants. I'm creating value. It's effectively adding to the space used by the tenant."

North Harringay Primary School

The North Harringay Primary School, in Harringay, one of thirty-two outlying boroughs of London, is an old school building with a new green roof.[44] Melissa Ronaldson, an avid gardener, herbalist, and parent, collaborated with parents and grandparents at the school, including Anne Gilman and Deborah Peacock, to develop a roof garden for students. Ms. Gilman has seen several of her grandchildren progress through the school. Many of the children and families have limited space and resources for a garden in a dense urban environment such as London. Ms. Ronaldson sought to develop educational programs around gardening that would have special appeal for these students. Like many public schools, this one is surrounded by high, even menacing, fencing for security purposes, with the only entrances at a few controlled points. Gardening softens this stark appearance.

Ms. Ronaldson was asked to run a gardening club. Seeking opportunities for outdoor classroom settings, she "went up to the roof one day to pick up some pots that someone said were lying around scattered up there" and immediately saw an opportunity. "There is something magical about a garden on a roof," she said. Fortunately, there was easy access up the stairs. An engineer determined that structural loads on the roof were adequate to build up to 2 feet (61 cm) with planters and soil, so this is an intensive green roof. The garden has been built a step at a time and is constantly evolving. It has become so successful that the parents and teachers are planning to build a small enclosed meeting area in one corner, against the parapet walls where there is the most structural support. Eventually, they hope to "create an outdoor classroom that could be transformed into a performance space for the community."

The garden brims with examples of inventive people applying ingenuity to develop usable and beautiful results with an economy of means. The three women went to the Chelsea Flower Show in search of garden sculptures or topiary but found that even small examples were prohibitively expensive. Instead, one of them constructed a graceful giraffe made of chain link mesh and steel. They may plant a fine-textured vine on it to cloak it in greenery and give it more character. Vigorous clumps of herbs grow in

4-61, 4-62. Two views of the garden as a wonderland.

planters made from rubber tires painted in bold colors with graceful, abstract forms. Brick pavers and planter walls have been hand-painted by students so that each has made a contribution to the garden. Salvaged rubber tires are painted to make planters for perennials and annuals. There are also some "stand-alone" wooden planters with fruit trees, which can be reached from all directions by children walking through the garden.

Every season a new theme serves as a focus for students and classes. For example, a recent project focused on vegetables from all over the world; the students grew tomatoes, sweet peppers, pumpkins, corn, and potatoes. "Parents shared in one big harvest from the garden, and we had a big feast," Ms. Ronaldson said. The focus on gardening stimulated parents to buy organic vegetables (however, the garden can sustain only occasional harvests for parents and children).

Students decorated fences with glass mosaics and designed and fabricated other ornaments. A small water feature accenting the center of the garden is set off by colorful tile mosaics. All the plants are either edible vegetables or medicinal plants. Tropical and indigenous, some of the plants have historical, others contemporary medical use. The students teach one another about their origins and how they are (or might be) used in contemporary London.

4-63. A giraffe made of chain link mesh and steel will be trained with a fine textured groundcover to create a fanciful effect, or left as is in contrast to the luxuriant plantings.

Right and opposite:
4-64, 4-65. Details include the use of many everyday objects, such as rubber tires, painted and re-used as planters, and elaborate mosaics.

Inn the Park, St. James Park Restaurant[45]

The St. James Park was established by King Henry VIII in 1532 and is now a Grade 1 listed Historic Park and Garden. Encompassing over 85 acres (34.3 ha), it is one of eight Royal Parks in London, which together include over 5000 acres (2,023.4 ha) of wide green spaces, lakes, ponds, monuments, and gardens.[46] The park is maintained and conserved by The Royal Parks, a government agency set up in 1993. One of the agency's programs has been to create a network of eating establishments that reflect the heritage of their historic locations. Inn the Park, located on the site of the former Cakehouse, faces the tree-shaded areas of the lake in St. James Park, not far from the royal parade grounds, where the Changing of the Guards takes place. The face of the building curves to match the edge of the lake. An outdoor terrace concentric to the building provides a delightful setting when the weather cooperates. Inside are spacious dining rooms. All the food served is British, with the ingredients—such as fresh fruits, vegetables, juices, meats, and dairy products—supplied by local farms.

The sides of the building face either the lake or the historic Nash landscape, dating from 1827, with verdant lawns marked by groups of flowering bulbs, shrubs, and large shade trees. The rear of the building blends into this landscape, which flows directly over the building as a green roof. Several skylights allow adequate light and air into the dining areas, and are the only element of construction visible in the swath of lawn that sweeps over the roof. London plane trees nearby further disguise the artifice; when approaching from the rear, the walk appears to lead through a meadow to a lookout platform with a view of the lake. A continuous wood bench and railing form the edge, and the outdoor eating area concentric to the restaurant is immediately below. The green roof is planted with a rich mixture of grasses, perennials, and wildflowers that tie into the surrounding park landscape. One can easily imagine that some of the food served in the restaurant could have been harvested nearby.

4-66. The landscape of the park sweeps by the Inn, which is nestled into the expanses of lawn and trees.

4-67, 4-68. Skylights allow light to penetrate into the dining areas below, and an elegant wood deck, accessible by stairs from the rear of the building, provides views outward.

Because they occupy large amounts of space with huge expanses of pavement for parking, runways, and storage, and because they have many flat-roofed buildings, airports are a natural choice for green roofs. Airports are heat islands, with temperatures often many degrees higher than the surrounding open spaces and less concentrated developments. Airports also generate significant noise, air, and water pollution. Even with carefully designed storm water infrastructure systems to provide fast and efficient removal of storm water from all paved surfaces, and containment systems for capturing de-icing solutions, major storm events such as heavy rains can overwhelm the capacity. Therefore, many major European airports have a tapestry of green roofs over terminals, concourses, maintenance buildings, and other structures. These green roofs provide benefits and respond to all of these environmental problems without jeopardizing airport security and passenger safety. Despite the network of green space that comes with these installations, there has been no increase in problematic bird populations or other animals that might interfere with aircraft operations or personnel. This achievement is due to careful initial selection of the plant materials, monitoring of the results, and adequate maintenance.[48]

Airports feature unique site design challenges that affect animal populations. Typically, airport surroundings include large areas of undeveloped lands, which are desirable as they mitigate noise and air pollution and provide a margin of safety for landing planes. These areas, if not carefully managed, can become semi-natural and attract large birds, which can be sucked into jet engines with potentially disastrous results.[49] Land use policies over many years have been developed to discourage animal populations from settling in these buffer areas. For example, plants are selected that do not produce flowers, berries, fruits, or seeds that attract animals. Grass height is carefully regulated, as tall grass attracts rodents, which, in turn, attract birds of prey. Grass cut too low attracts birds such as geese. Furthermore, animal populations are dynamic, not static, and in the last several decades species such as sea gulls and pigeons have increased dramatically, so that measures must be taken to discourage them. The design of green roofs at airports must respond to all of these concerns.

Three major airports in Europe—Schiphol International Airport, Amsterdam, The Netherlands; Kloten International Airport, Zurich, Switzerland; and Frankfurt International Airport, Frankfurt, Germany—have a network of green roofs that has responded to these environmental challenges in different ways, while also providing many environmental benefits.

Schiphol International Airport

At Schiphol International a system of canals and dense hedges encloses the areas around new runways to provide security and blend into the natural surroundings. Species of grasses that grow tall deter most non-predatory bird species; as a further line of defense against bird strikes, specially trained teams of dogs are used to chase away the birds. The number and type of species of bird strikes are carefully monitored.

The airport has three buildings with extensive green roofs totaling 143,483 square feet (13,330 m^2) and two buildings with intensive green roofs totaling 4,306 square feet (400 m^2). Within the Schipholrijk neighborhood, of which the airport is a part, six other buildings have intensive green roofs totaling 645,835 square feet (60,000 m^2). That the airport's green roofs are more than 20 percent of the total for the entire neighborhood emphasizes how pervasive green roof planning is in this area.

Dating from 1994, the Schiphol Plaza green roof was built over the main terminal building, which includes a parking garage and a train station. The total green roof area is 91,493 square feet (8,500 m^2). The substrate is a formula (Xero Terr) with a depth of only 1.6 inches (40 mm) and a saturated weight of 7.2 pounds/square foot (35 kg/m^2). A patented, airport-specific moss–sedum system (Xero Flor, one of the major European green roof manufacturers) was used.[50] Two other extensive roofs at the airport also have green roofs with sedum mats (XeroFlor). The sedums do not attract large birds, and maintenance requirements are limited. Although the sedum mats grow into a continuous blanket of plant materials, shrinkage can occur between the mats, and additional substrate must be used to fill in the gaps.

Two small intensive green roofs, totaling 4,306 square feet (400 m^2), are located inside the departure and arrival buildings at the airthe

port. Although intended for people using the terminals, these roof gardens (by ZinCo, using a Floradrain system) are not easy to visit due to strict security restrictions.

4-69, 4-70. Two views of sedum green roofs at Schiphol Airport, Amsterdam, the Netherlands. (Courtesy of Mostert De Winter BV, the Netherlands)

Kloten International Airport

The largest airport in Switzerland is Kloten International Airport in Zurich. Situated in a nature conservation area of 180.4 acres (73 hectares), the airport has two large green roof projects, Dock E and Car Park B. Dock E is a new dispatch building, located between the takeoff and landing runways. The green roof measures almost an acre in size, 43,056 square feet (4,000 m²). It is a (ZinCo) system with a substrate 3.2 inches deep (8 cm), the construction and coordination for which took considerable planning. Prior to installation of the green roof, there was already a 46-foot-wide (14 m) photovoltaic system on one side of the roof. To avoid damaging this system, a pneumatic pump was used to bring the substrate and gravel material to the roof, where it was then spread manually. The planting consisted of sedum shoots placed at the rate of two to three pieces per square foot (twenty to thirty pieces per square meter). Drought and frost-resistant species were chosen. Completed in 2002, the roof has been successful. Maintenance includes weeding twice a year and occasional fertilization.

The multistory Car Park B also has an extensive green roof. As with Dock E, a pneumatic pump was required to bring the gravel and substrate to the roof, which is 164 feet tall (50 m). This green roof totals 86,111 square feet, almost 2 acres (8,000 m²). The planting was a combination of sedum shoots and hydroseeded sedum seeds. A jute control net was installed after seeding to prevent wind erosion.

4-71, 4-72. Extensive green roofs at the Kloten International Airport in Zurich, Switzerland. (Courtesy of ZinCo)

Frankfurt International Airport

Europe's largest airport is Frankfurt International in Germany. Set in a densely populated area, the airport covers 4,942 acres (2,000 hectares). The open space between runways equals approximately 1,234 acres (500 hectares), or a quarter of the entire airport, and it is important conservation land because plants and animals endangered elsewhere in Germany live there. In contrast to other international airports, Frankfurt International focuses on land management rather than scare tactics to deter birds. There are over three hundred plant species on the airport grounds, designed in such a way as not to attract birds. Much of the vegetation is maintained as a heath, with no watering and no fertilization. The ericaceous materials attract some rare and endangered bird species, but they are not ones that threaten air traffic.

The airport has green roofs atop Terminals 1 and 2, the cargo building, and Terminal B. Together, these green roofs total at least

4-73, 4-74, 4-75. Extensive and intensive green roofs at Frankfurt International Airport, Germany. (Courtesy of Fraport AG and Optigrün)

Right, below, and opposite:
4-76, 4-77, 4-78. These photos show the progression in the installation of a sedum green roof at Cophenhagen Airport, Denmark. (Courtesy of Ulrik Reeh, Veg Tech.)

322,917 square feet (30,000 m²).[51] Of this, a small amount, 25,838 square feet (2,400 m²), is intensive, whereas the balance is extensive. Most of these green roofs use an Optigrun system. The intensive roofs have a substrate depth of 16–24 inches (41–61 cm), and the extensive green roofs have a substrate depth of 3–4 inches (7.5–10 cm). Excess rainwater is captured from these roofs and used for other purposes on site.

Opinion in Europe regarding the implementation of green roofs at airports is not unanimous. Some experts are cautious, worrying, for example, about the impact of large populations of sea gulls, as has occurred in urban areas of London. Some are concerned that plant species over a certain height are too welcoming to birds. Nevertheless, the green roofs described here have been successful, and it is likely that more will be planned and implemented. A green-roofed building recently opened at the Copenhagen airport. Roofs spread with gravel seem to be more attractive to birds, particularly large species such as gulls, than green roofs with low- to medium-height vegetation. In the United States, more than 75 percent of recorded bird strikes causing damage to civil aircraft are waterfowl (32 percent), gulls (28 percent) and raptors (28 percent). One area of current research in London is focused on determining the minimum gravel size that can be used as a substrate, but is too heavy for gulls to pick up.[52] Carefully designed green roofs at airports present opportunities for mitigating many environmental problems without increasing the risk of bird collisions.

Europe has embraced the concept of green roofs, whether brown, living, or actually green, so that they are as commonplace as well-designed terraces are in North America. Green roofs are part of the design vocabulary and are required by many city or regional governments across Europe. As scientists have become involved in green roof research—and particularly, habitat studies—bioroofs, in which diverse habitat is created on a roof, have become a major part of contemporary green roof practice. Scientists have the potential to mitigate a whole range of standard environmental issues while providing much needed habitat for endangered species. What perhaps is still needed in Europe are more developments in which extensive-style green roofs are combined with intensive green roofs in an integrated design that provides increased recreational opportunities for people as well.

In a book that presents a selection of green roofs throughout North America, it is difficult to determine which ones to include. The following examples are representative of the remarkable developments that are underway. Each one has a particular history, context, focus, or application that gives it significance.

The projects are grouped chronologically (by the date completed) into two sections: multiple projects by one designer and individual projects by different designers. Some designers are specialists in green roof design, and it is instructive to explore a range of projects with different purposes and approaches. For example, Charlie Miller is a civil engineer in Philadelphia who brings his expertise to a diverse array of green roof projects. Three are explored: an office building, a chiropractor's facility, and a school library. Green roof design is a recent development in Mexico, and the research efforts at the Autonomous University of Chapingo, on the outskirts of Mexico City, and green roof projects within the public schools there, demonstrate hopeful beginnings. Diana Balmori of New York City focuses her attention on green roof projects within the urban fabric of that city; each of her projects—the Solaire Building, Silvercup Studios, and Gratz Industries—responds to the site and program of the particular client. The Kestrel Group in Minneapolis emphasizes a strong collaborative approach, with an ecological bent to its projects; the Green Institute and the Minneapolis Library are examples. Finally, the work of Cornelia Oberlander from Vancouver is considered. She has been in landscape architecture practice for many decades. The Robson Square and Vancouver Public Library projects were completed near the middle and the zenith, respectively, of her long career.

In the second section of this chapter, the individual projects discussed are no less diverse. The Oak Hammock Conservation Centre near Winnipeg, Manitoba, resulted from a collaboration between Ducks Unlimited, Canada, and the Provincial Government to develop office space and a learning center, to interpret for the public the importance of habitat conservation and the value of wetland ecosystems. The headquarters of the Gap in San Bruno, California, has a roof whose undulating shape recalls the topography of the mountains in the background. The demonstration green roof on the Peggy Notebaert Nature Museum in Chicago was a retrofit onto a relatively new building; it came about as a result of a program decision by the museum staff to take a green approach throughout the entire facility, and led to additional green roofs there. The Ford River Rouge Plant in Dearborn, Michigan, has a large, flat green roof atop its truck manufacturing facility. In Nashville, Tennessee, an endangered plant community was recreated on top of a former slaughterhouse building within a mixed-use development near the Tennessee River. In Beaverton, Oregon, the water quality center provides high standards for water quality and design for a regional facility serving a large metropolitan region. In San Francisco, the North Beach Place project, a mixed-use residential development, created a whole series of diverse spaces atop a large green roof within a complex of new buildings, on the site of former public housing which had deteriorated badly. Millennium Park in Chicago, a collaborative effort of many designers, planners, contractors, and philanthropists, provides an array of exciting facilities on a large, almost 25-acre (10.1 ha) green roof adjacent to historic Grant Park. Richard Kula, a scientist in Winnipeg, spearheaded a long process for a new green-roofed building, on the site of several smaller structures, for a cooperative selling camping equipment and other gear; the entire process was documented for a LEED certification. At Sarah Lawrence College in Bronxville, New York, the client who endowed the new arts building insisted on a green roof. Finally, at the California Academy of Sciences in San Francisco, the green roof resulted after the entire institution was rebuilt in a different location within Golden Gate Park, due to severe earthquake damage to the village of buildings that had previously housed the museum. Architect Renzo Piano evolved a green roof as a pivotal design feature: a magic carpet hovering above the surrounding forest.

The material is organized as follows:

Design team: Key participants are listed. Additional information is provided in Appendix B.

Context and concept: The history and background of each project are described, and how the green roof became part of the program is explained.

Layout: The basic organization in space of the green roof design is provided; for larger sites, the design of major elements is also described so that the location of the green roof is understood in relation to other major features.

Green roof: Information is provided on the manufacturer and composition of the green roof layers, including the growing medium.[1]

Other features: As many of these projects are complex, integrated designs, a description is provided of important additional elements, many of which are examples of sustainable design.

Planting and irrigation: The methods and time of irrigation and planting are described. A plant list of botanical and common names is provided. Many of these projects include sedum species, only some of which have widely used common names. Therefore, the term "stonecrop species" is often used when there is not a common name in wide use.[2]

Post-planting and maintenance: There is a description of any additional work on the green roof that has occurred since the original installation. A summary of maintenance is provided.

Throughout the text, measurements are provided in imperial units with metric equivalents in parentheses. Figures are rounded. A conversion chart is provided in Appendix F.

Heinz 57 Center; Life Expression Chiropractic Center; Oaklyn Branch Library

DESIGN TEAM
Architect: Burt Hill Kozar Rittlemann Associates, Pittsburgh
Green roof provider: Roofscapes, Inc., Philadelphia
Waterproofing supplier: Carlisle Syntec, Carlisle, Pennsylvania
Waterproofing installer: Burns & Scale Co. Bridgeville, Pennsylvania
Owner: The Huntley Group, Pittsburgh
Tenant: Heinz Company, Pittsburgh

Charlie Miller and his company Roofscapes, Inc., is one of the leaders in green roof design in the United States. His portfolio of projects ranges from the public to the private sector, from large to small installations, both intensive and extensive. The three projects presented

5-1, 5-2. Two views of the Heinz building. Even at a considerable distance, the diversity of plant materials is apparent. (Courtesy of Roofscapes, Inc.)

here underscore the diversity of green roof applications. The Heinz 57 Center in Pittsburgh is a renovation of a building that was vacated in 1988 but came back to vibrant life in October 2001. For the Life Expression Chiropractic Center, constructed in 2001, the green roof was conceived as a crown to the clean architectural appearance of the building. Finally, the Oaklyn Branch Library, constructed in 2002, is a two-story building in which the green roof evolved as an educational, yet fully functional, feature of the building program.[3]

Context and concept

In the heart of Pittsburgh's most densely populated business district, this fourteen-story building is the former Gimbel's Department Store. It features a wealth of classical detailing and is a major visual anchor to the district. As has been typical in urban areas across the United States, the department store closed and the building was completely vacated in 1984.

Fourteen years later, Burt Hill Kozar Rittlemann Associates was hired to develop renovation plans for the structure. A 50-foot (15.2 m) diameter octagonal atrium, cut through the building from the top floor down to the seventh floor, was the most ambitious element of their design. The dramatic increase in interior light was one of the enticements for the Heinz Company to locate their North American operations headquarters on the top seven floors.

A key aspect of the architect's concept was to complement the atrium with a green roof on the 30-foot-wide (9.1 m) terrace wrapping around the executive offices on the fourteenth floor, to provide dramatic and enjoyable views of the plantings as well as a setting for outdoor meetings and informal gatherings. The carpet of ground cover would also provide an acoustical damper in the brick-and-glass environment on the rooftop.

Layout

The final design of the outdoor space included high-density recycled plastic lumber decking, constructed in four locations that are integrated with paved terraces so that visitors use the terraces and seating areas without walking on the adjacent plantings. The construction is organized to encourage water striking the pavement to flow towards one of the five concealed roof drains within the vegetated areas. The granular media selected for this garden facilitate internal drainage.

5-3. One of the Heinz green roofs soon after planting; terraces and steppingstones are integrated into the design. (Courtesy of Roofscapes, Inc.)

5-4. A view of one of the Heinz green roofs after the plant materials have become established. (Courtesy of Roofscapes, Inc.)

Miller explains, "In two-media media assemblies, such as the one installed at Heinz, the coarse granular layer (in this case 2 inches or 5.1 cm thick) provides the drainage function. When drainage paths to a roof drain are long, we will install perforated conduit (like French drains) in the coarse granular layer to promote rapid dewatering during large storms. Our criteria for the coarse granular drainage layer are specific: a) it must have a saturated water permeability of at least 25 in/min or 63.5 cm/min (ASTM E-2396); b) satisfy grain-size distribution requirements, which include 99 percent of particle larger than 1 mm (#18 sieve); c) hard and frost resistant; and d) non-carbonate. These requirements ensure that the material will not clog fabrics or silt up, will have a high drainage potential, and will continue to perform indefinitely."

Green roof

Covering 12,000 square feet (1,114.8 m²) or slightly more than a quarter of an acre, this extensive green roof, installed over a concrete deck, uses a two-layer assembly (Roofmeadow Type III: Savannah). Three inches (7.6 cm) of growth media over 2 inches (5.1 cm) of engineered drainage media give the roof good drought resistance. Waterproofing (Carlisle Syntech 045 EPDM), supplemented by a polyethylene root barrier, provides adequate protection. (Based on European experience with similar systems, it is expected that the green roof will double or triple the life of the underlying waterproofing.) The high walls surrounding the entire roof garden result in some highly variable and intense microclimatic conditions. It is often hot and dry as well as windy. The range of plants selected tolerate this xeric, or very dry, regimen quite well.

Other features

The decking and paving areas provide complete access to the roof's amenities. Even though the green roof materials do not tolerate pedestrian traffic, the landscape can be appreciated from the variety of seating spaces and terraces.

Planting and irrigation

A range of plant material was selected within the context of the Roofmeadow Type III, a predetermined mixture based on the site condi-

HEINZ 57 CENTER PLANT LIST	
Allium schoenoprasum	Chives
Anthemis tinctoria	Golden marguerite or golden chamomile
Campanula rotundifolia	Bellflower
Carex alba	White sedge
Carex annectens	Yellow fruit sedge
Carex buchananii	Fox red curly sedge
Carex rosea	Rosy sedge
Chrysanthemum leucanthemum	Oxeye daisy
Delosperma nubigenum	Ice plant
Dianthus carthusianorum	Clusterhead pinks
Dianthus deltoides	Maiden pink
Festuca glauca	Blue fescue
Hieracium pilosella	Mouseear hawkweed
Pennisetum alopecuroides	Rose fountain grass
Petrorhagia saxifraga	Saxifrage pink
Phlox subulata	Creeping phlox
Potentilla verna (neumanniana)	Cinquefoil
Sedum acre	Golden-carpet, gold moss stonecrop
Sedum aizoon	Aizoon stonecrop
Sedum album	White stonecrop
Sedum ewersii	Pink stonecrop
Sedum floriferum	Gold stonecrop
Sedum reflexum	Blue stonecrop
Sedum reflexum pinifolium	Blue spruce stonecrop
Sedum spurium	Two-row stonecrop
Sedum telephium	Vera Jameson stonecrop
Sedum ternatum	Woodland stonecrop
Stachys byzantina	Lamb's-ears
Stachys monieri	Betony
Teucrium chamaedrys	Germander
Tradescantia bracteata	Prairie or longbract spiderwort
Veronica officinalis	Speedwell

tions and the type of green roof. A summary of Roofmeadow media types is contained in Appendix D. This selection included 32 xeric species from nineteen plant genera, including six North American natives; approximately one-third of the plants are sedums, and the balance is a range of herbs, meadow grasses, and meadow perennials that provide differences in plant height, texture, and bloom color. The plants were established from plugs and seed and were protected from the strong winds at the fourteenth-floor roof level by a photo-degradable wind blanket that biodegraded (or decomposed) into the growing medium. No irrigation was installed. Above is a complete plant list.

Work was completed in the fall of 2001. The

plants had already achieved approximately 50 percent coverage by July of 2002. The rate of coverage was slowed by the drought conditions of the summer, yet coverage was 90 percent by May 2003. In thin, unirrigated projects such as this one, it is important to allow the plants to establish gradually, from the stage of plugs or cuttings. This helps them acclimate to the growing conditions on the roof and develop into a robust, drought-tolerant landscape.

Post-planting and maintenance

Some maintenance of the plant materials is necessary, but no irrigation is required. After a 24-month period of establishment a light weeding is done twice a year, in the spring and fall, and there is one annual light fertilization.

Life Expression Chiropractic Center, Sugar Loaf, PA

DESIGN TEAM

Architect: Van Der Ryn Architects, Sausalito, California

Green roof provider: David Bros. Landscape, Worcester, Pennsylvania

Waterproofing supplier: Sarnafil, Inc., Canton, Massachusetts

Waterproofing installer: Houck Services, Harrisburg, Pennsylvania

Context and concept

For a new chiropractic center, Van Der Ryn Architects sought a design that would harmonize with the clean lines of the building's architecture, accommodate considerable pitch, and

5-5. The entire roof of the Life Expression building is a green roof. (Courtesy of Roofscapes, Inc.)

appear as a living structure within the landscape. They saw the green roof as a way of blending the building seamlessly into the surrounding landscape. The owner went a step further and asked that the vegetation extend to the edge of the roof and cascade over the eaves.

Layout

The entire 6,000-square-foot (557.4 m^2) roof is covered. The dead load of the cover had to weigh no more than 28 pounds/square foot (136.7 kg/m^2) when fully saturated. The layout, using reinforced waterproofing (Sarnafil G-476 PVC), accommodated pitches on the deck ranging from 3 to 12 (25 percent or 14 degrees) to 7 to 12 (58 percent or 30 degrees).

Green roof

The total depth of the vegetated cover for this extensive green roof is 5 inches (12.7 cm) in a single layer. The lightweight medium was engineered to absorb and retain rainfall while remaining fully drained. The green roof system (Roofmeadow Type 1) is adapted to a sloping roof. The roof itself is a plywood deck over glulam rafters, that is, layers of lumber glued together. The waterproofing was a loose-laid PVC membrane (Sarnafil G476), 0.08 inches or 2.0 mm (80 mil) thick, which was adaptable to the varying slopes.

Several engineering challenges had to be overcome, such as: reducing load as much as possible by using lightweight media; maintaining uniform moisture conditions on the pitched deck; and protecting media from wind scour. However, the overriding challenge here was slope stability. Several techniques were required to achieve slope and dimensional stability for the vegetated cover. Depending on the local slope conditions, these included the use of roof battens (thin strips of wood), slope restraint panels, and reinforcing mesh.

This green roof is compatible with electric leak survey methods, that is, electric field vector mapping (EFVM). An evaluation of the water-tightness of the waterproofing membrane may be carried out without disturbing the established green roof vegetation. In order to render this deck compatible with EFVM, a conductive layer of metal mesh was installed under the membrane and connected to a building ground point (e.g., plumbing).

Other features

To create the effect of a waterfall going over a weir during rainstorms, it was agreed that the runoff would be permitted to sheet-flow off the roof along the length of the eave. Creating a gap of a half inch (1.3 cm) in the fascia produced a weir of that dimension. Some unconventional waterproofing details were required to create a watertight solution in this location. As the vegetation matured, it grew past the edge of the eave and overhangs the fascia. The cover reduces the rate and quantity of runoff

5-6. Thriving sedums grow over the eave of the Life Expression building; water flows over this eave as a sheet during heavy rains, but the flow is restrained due to the absorption by the vegetation of most of the rainfall. (Courtesy of Roofscapes, Inc.)

5-7. The green roof of the Life Expression building, with a profusion of vegetation, much of which shows seasonal colors at different times of the year. (Courtesy of Roofscapes, Inc.)

LIFE EXPRESSION CHIROPRACTIC CENTER PLANT LIST

Allium schoenoprasum	Chives
Dianthus deltoides	Maiden pink
Sedum acre	Golden carpet or gold moss stonecrop
Sedum album 'Coral Carpet'	Coral carpet stonecrop
Sedum floriferum 'Weihenstephaner gold'	Weihenstephaner gold stonecrop
Sedum oreganum	Green stonecrop
Sedum reflexum	Blue or Jenny's stonecrop
Sedum sarmentosum	Stringy stonecrop or bunge
Sedum sexangulare	Tasteless stonecrop
Sedum spurium v. 'Fuldaglut'	Fuldagut stonecrop
Sedum spurium v. "Tricolor'	Tricolor stonecrop
Thymus serpyllum	Creeping thyme

because it absorbs a considerable amount of water, but the duration of the runoff is prolonged, to acheive the curtain effect desired by the owner.

Planting and irrigation

The planting emphasizes a drought-tolerant plant collection that creates a dense and uniform low ground cover. Ninety-five percent of the plants are flowering sedum varieties. They were planted as plugs installed on 12-inch (30.5 cm) centers, and coverage was complete within one year. There was no irrigation, emphasizing the xeric conditions on the roof, but weed germination has been limited.

To protect the roof from wind erosion until the plants were established, the surface of the growing medium was covered with a photo-degradable wind blanket mesh, fastened securely to the base of the green roof construction; it has long since disappeared into the mat of vegetative cover.

The species *Thymus serpyllum* is absent from the mature plant community, but its initial growth helped provide an appropriate base for other plants to become established.

Post-planting and maintenance

After the 18-month establishment period, the only maintenance consists of light weeding. The roof is estimated to retain up to 55 percent of annual rainfall.

DESIGN TEAM
Architect: Veasey Parrot Durkin & Shoulders, Evansville, Indiana
Landscape architect: Storrow Kinsellaa Associates, Indianapolis
Green roof provider: Enviroscapes, Madison, Indiana
Waterproofing supplier: Sarnafill, Inc., Canton, Massachusetts
Waterproofing installer: Midland Engineering Company, Evansville, Indiana

Context and concept

For a new two-story library building, the architects took advantage of a sloping site that enabled them to blend the roof into the landscape on the uphill side. The landscape design for the project was a mesic (indicating moderate moisture) meadow prairie—a native plant community that would cloak the entire site. The prairie is integrated into the entire site: the challenge was to blend in the roof design as well.

Layout

The prairie is edged with a graceful swath of turf that sweeps down to the lower level of the site. Informal groupings of red oak and flowering viburnums grace the side slopes of the building and create a transition to the lower level. The parapet walls for the green roof are the same masonry as the building, and a paved perimeter path of compatible materials helps to harmonize with the palette of natural plant materials.

Green roof

Roofscapes selected a two-layer green roof system (Roofmeadow) that combines a base layer of granular drainage material with an upper layer of growing media. The total depth of this intensive system is 12 inches (30.5 cm).

The roof of the building is a steel deck. The waterproofing, a loose-laid PVC (polyvinyl chloride) membrane (Sarnafill G4765) 0.08 inches or 2.0 mm thick (80 mil), consists of two watertight membranes. An upper PVC protective membrane is separated from the primary waterproofing membrane by a felt layer. Roofscapes took advantage of this waterproofing method to create a riffled surface required as part of the irrigation trickle system (Optigrüen International AG).

The roof deck pitches uniformly at a rate of 3 percent toward one edge of the building. To minimize long-term maintenance requirements, there are no drains; runoff discharges from the low edge of the roof into a meandering grass swale. The green roof itself incorporates an internal drainage network of perforated rectangular conduits that intercept water during heavy rainfall and discharge it to the storm sewer.

Other features

The site was a sloping one with some access problems. This project was the first in the U.S. to utilize pneumatic methods to pump and disperse the green roof media onto the roof. Both the drainage layer and the growth medium layer were installed using blower trucks.

Planting and irrigation

The plants were established on the roof from a combination of plugs and seeds. The growing medium was protected during the establishment period by a hydro-mulch cap. The plant materials were selected to reach maturity in approximately two years.

Irrigation is provided by a base level trickle system (Optigrüen International AG). Water is furnished at the bottom of the green roof, rather than at the surface level, and only at a rate demanded by the plants themselves. As a result, water loss due to evaporation is negligible, and it

OAKLYN BRANCH LIBRARY PLANT LIST	
Andropogon scoparius	Little bluestem
Bouteloua curtipendula	Sideoats grama or mosquito grass
Campanula rotundifolia	Bluebell bellflower or Scottish bluebell
Carex annectans	Yellow fruit sedge
Carex bicknellii	Bicknell's prairie sedge
Centaurea cyanus	Garden cornfloweror or bachelor's button
Coreopsis tinctoria	Golden tickseed
Elymus canadensis	Canada wild rye or Canadian dime grass
Liatris spicata	Blazing star or spike gay-feather
Phlox drummondii	Drummond's anual phlox
Phlox pilosa	Downy phlox
Sphaeralcea coccinea	Scarlet globemallow or red false mallow or prairie mallow
Sporobolus heterolepis	Prairie dropseed

is not necessary to monitor the moisture level of the growing medium. This method is particularly efficient because minimal water is wasted. This irrigation system actually approximates the natural conditions associated with shallow soil over a shale bedrock—the natural environment that the green roof is intended to mimic. This green roof is the first within the U.S. to have this type of irrigation system.

Post-planting and maintenance

Since the 24-month establishment period ended in 2004, maintenance for this project has consisted of twice-a-year inspections of the irrigation system, twice-a-year mowing, and light fertilization annually, or as needed.

5-8. An illustrative rendering of the proposed Oaklyn Library building and landscape. The vegetation of the green roof connects seamlessly to the adjacent plantings. (Courtesy of Roofscapes, Inc.)

5-9. The green roof of the Oaklyn Library under construction. (Courtesy of Roofscapes, Inc.)

5-10. The finished green roof of the Oaklyn Library with well-established vegetation. (Courtesy of Roofscapes, Inc.)

DESIGN TEAM

Horticulturist: Ulrike Grau (researcher, Chapingo)

Director of research: Dr. Gilberto Navas Gomez (supervisor, Xochimilco)

Biologist: Michael Siemsen (researcher, Chapingo)

Coordinator: Tanya Muller Garcia (Xochimilco)

Two Europeans collaborated with a Mexican biologist in implementing the first green roofs in Mexico in 1994. Ulrike Grau, from Humboldt University in Berlin, has worked at the Autonomous University of Chapingo, in surburban Mexico City, for considerable periods. Dr. Gilberto Navas Gomez has joint degrees from the same two universities. Michael Siemsen has studied biology at the Christian-Albrecht University of Kiel and at Humboldt University. Starting in 2004 Tanya Muller Garcia, drawing on the knowledge and experience gained in these earlier efforts and assisted by Dr. Gomez, began to coordinate and design green roofs for public schools in Xochimilco, the first of Mexico City's sixteen school districts to include green roofs as part of its program to improve air quality and educate people about sustainable design.[4]

Context and concept

Mexico City, one of the world's largest urban areas with a population of 25 million people, is also one of the most polluted: it is surrounded on three sides by mountains that tend to trap particulates, and has experienced several decades of rapid, uncontrolled industrialization, multi-laned highways, and population growth. Annual precipitation, almost all rainfall, of 20–32 inches per year (50.8–81.3 cm) is the same as that of central Europe and parts of Germany. However, the distribution is drastically different in Mexico City. Instead of a relatively even pattern throughout the year, the city experiences extremes: only 5 percent of the rainfall occurs during the winter, and as much as 8 inches (20.3 cm) per month fall during the rainy season from June to mid-October, with torrential downpours of almost 2 inches (5.1 cm) commonly occurring within a few hours. Xochimilco is situated within the basin of Mexico City, but in a less densely populated area.

In the early 1990s, Gilberto Navas Gómez collaborated with a group at Humboldt University to implement the first green roofs in Mexico City at the Autonomous University of Chapingo. They intended to develop an extensive green roof system requiring low maintenance and min-

5-11. Experimental green roof plantings on the roof of a classroom building in Mexico City are divided into squares. (Courtesy of Gilberto Navas Gómez)

imal irrigation beyond the initial installation. Because Mexico has a high diversity of succulent plants, including many sedums, they also wanted to study a range of green roof plants and monitor how they responded to typical conditions.

Layout

The design team selected four adjacent sections of a flat roof on a building on the university campus. The roof area planted was approximately 5,380 square feet (500 m²) out of a total roof area of 6,778.8 square feet (630 m²). The roof is approximately 16.4 feet (5 m) high, with a uniform 3 percent slope across the surface from north to south, and two drains on each of the four sections of the roof. No additional roof reinforcement was required.

Green roof

A system was installed incorporating different components by different German manufacturers. A gravel perimeter buffer from the parapet, about 20 inches (50 cm) wide, facilitated drainage and fire control and permitted access for maintenance. Starting at the bottom, the roof had a PVC waterproofing membrance sandwiched between two layers of filter fabric, a drainage layer manufactured of variable depths, covered by another filter fabric for fine soils, then the growing medium and the plant materials. The drainage layer was an expanded-clay product imported from Germany, and it was installed at four different depths—0.6, 0.8, 1.2, and 1.6 inches (1.5, 2.0, 3.0, and 4.0 cm)—on each of the four roofs. The growing medium comprised three native materials: tezontle (a very porous volcanic material), coconut fibers, and sugarcane residues. These were mixed with Lavalit, a volcanic mineral imported from Germany. Eight different mixtures of these components were used, and the depth of the growing medium on each roof was increased gradually from 1 to 2.75 inches (2.5–7.0 cm).

Planting and irrigation

The planting palette was quite limited. Rooted cuttings of *Sedum moranense* (red stonecrop) were first gathered from nearby hills and prop-

5-12, 5-13. *Sedum moranense* followed by a thicket of sedum plantings. (Top, courtesy of Ulrike Grau. Bottom, courtesy of Gilberto Navas Gómez)

agated for rooted cuttings. Specimens of the cactus family were also used, as well as some *Kalanchoe daigremontiana* (Good luck plant or Mother-of-thousands).

Post-planting and maintenance

After several years, it became apparent that a green roof was a practical choice in Mexico City, even with its extreme climatic conditions. However, a careful evaluation of the results led to some major renovations from 1998 to 2001, carried out by participants from Humboldt University and the Autonomous University of Chapingo in an interdisciplinary course on sustainable urban development through green roofs. Ulrike Gran and Michael Siemsen, under the direction of Dr. Gómez, were responsible for implementing the renovations and scientific studies.

The green roof was renovated in stages. At first the plant materials were salvaged and transferred to a greenhouse, where they could be protected, and propagated for further planting. Then the filter fabrics and growing medium were removed to expose the leakage in the waterproofing, which was most severe around air-conditioning units and the parapets. It was determined that the intense solar radiation, typical of Mexico City's climate, had caused distortion in the waterproofing and the root-repellent membrane. A zinc sheet was installed underneath the new membrane to prevent future leakage. Instead of the German expanded clay previously used for the drainage layer, the local volcanic product, tezontle, was employed.

It was decided to use only native products in the substrate even though no commercial supplier of a substrate mix existed in Mexico City. All the principal inorganic components were volcanic materials of different mineral composition and color: tezonite (red-brown), tepojal (gray-white), and pumice (light gray). A high percentage of light-colored components was used to reduce the absorption of solar radiation and limit the amount of evaporation. Organic components were also incorporated: coco fiber, wood chips, and worm compost, along with imported peat moss. Using these seven ingredients, the design team composed fifteen different growing medium mixtures and distributed them on the roofs in a checkerboard pattern, about 5 feet (1.5 meters square). The substrates

AUTONOMOUS UNIVERSITY PLANT LIST

Cylindropuntia imbricata	Chain-link cactus
Mammillaria gracilis	Thimble cactus
Opuntia sp.	Pricklypear cactus
Sedum griseum	Stonecrop
Sedum moranense	Red stonecrop
Sedum praealtum	Greater Mexican or green stonecrop
Sedum x luteoviridae	Stonecrop
Sedum x rubrotinctum	Christmas cheer stonecrop

were separated by plastic foil strips, and most were installed to a depth of 4 inches (10.2 cm), with a few areas at depths of about 2.5 inches and 5.5 inches (6.4 and 14 cm, respectively).

The selected plant materials were more diverse this time, including not only two hybrid and three standard species of sedums, but several other hardy native plants.

Supplemental irrigation was supplied during the first two months, until the rainy season began. Maintenance was limited and primarily consisted of weeding, which was substantial, in part because the worm compost had not been sterilized, so it was full of seeds that readily germinated. Nevertheless, within ten months a vigorous mat of plants almost completely covered the roofs.

Some of the plant species responded better than others to the long dry periods typical of Mexico City's climate. During a one week period in November, 2002, substantial frost caused more damage to some of the plantings than the periods of drought.

One of the four roofs was equipped with a range of standard instruments so that scientists could measure factors such as rainfall, storm water runoff, temperatures underneath the roof membrane with and without a green roof, evaporation, and condensation. These data provide additional guidance for the implementation of future green roofs and a baseline for demonstrating the benefits of green roofs. In 2003 the local government of Mexico City approved, for the first time, the use of financial incentives for developers who improve environmental conditions and create green areas. As the green roof industry matures in Mexico City, more sophisticated strategies are likely to be implemented.

5-14. A sedum roof at a public
school building in Chapingo.
(Courtesy of Tanya Muller Garcia)

Xochimilco Public Schools

Context and concept

The ongoing experiments in green roof design carried out at the Autonomous University of Chapingo generated wide interest and led to programs elsewhere in Mexico City. Starting in 2004, the central city government allocated funds for installing green roofs on certain schools within the most urban areas of the district. One prominent example is the Xochimilco district. Two goals guide this project: to improve the local environmental conditions and to educate and train students in technologies of sustainable design.

Because most of the schools selected for green roofs were old buildings, for which green roofs were never planned and in which the infrastructure was often in need of repair, only extensive green roofs have been implemented. Over a fifteen-month period starting in May 2004, green roofs totaling 20,559 square feet (1,910 m²) were installed on eight public schools.

Planting and irrigation

Consisting primarily of sedums native to the valley of Mexico City, 133,700 plants were used. The plantings were a mixture of *Lampranthus spectabilis* (trailing ice plant), *Sedum amecamecanum* (native stonecrop, high altitudes), *Sedum moranense* (red stonecrop), and *Sedum praeltum* (native stonecrop). Planting occurred just as the rainy season was beginning in mid-May. The sedums were planted at a density of approximately six per square foot (65/m²). All the sedums were nursery grown, at a location in Xochimilco, for about two months prior to planting, then harvested for planting when they were about 2 inches (5.1 cm) tall (except *S. prealtum*, which is planted at a height of 4 inches [10.2 cm]). Until mid-October, when the rainy season ends, the plantings receive regular rainfall, and a slow-release fertilizer (15-15-15) (ratios of nitrogen, phosphorus and potassium, key nutrients) is used. Once the rainy season ends, no additional maintenance is provided in order to conserve resources and test which species survive the best. A dry period ensues for up to eight months. Tanya Muller Garcia and her design team determined that the first two sedum species survived the drought period quite well but that *Sedum amecamecanum* and *Lampranthus spectabilis* did not. On future green roofs, she expects to try two other sedum species, *Sedum rubrotinctum* and *Sedum griseum*.

Post-planting and maintenance

Public education programs and methods include photographs showing the step-by-step installation and transformation of a school, as well as the Web site of the school greening organization, which provides a clear and concise explanation of green roofs and their benefits, particularly those most relevant to people in Mexico City, such as the positive effects on the heat island. Invitations are regularly sent to local government officials and any interested people from other parts of the city to observe or participate in the process. Recently, two additional districts within the school system began installations. After planning efforts are complete, it takes approximately five weeks to implement a green roof on a school, during which time there are numerous opportunities to include teachers, parents, and students in the construction process and educate them about the plants native to their region of Mexico. Because the urban fabric is so densely built and lacking in green space, the green roof becomes a measurable and identifiable sign of the improvement in the environment.

The Solaire Building, Silvercup Studios, and Gratz Industries

DESIGN TEAM

Client: Albanese Development Corporation for Hugh L. Carey, Battery Park City Authority

Design team: Balmori Associates, Inc., Diana Balmori, principal

Architects: Cesar Pelli & Associates

Associate architects: Schuman, Licktenstein, Claman, Efron

Landscape contractor: Steven Dubner

Balmori Associates is a New York-based landscape and urban design firm with a reputation for innovative designs that integrate modern technologies with strongly conceived compositions in both traditional and urban settings. The firm has designed green roofs for new constructions and retrofitted ones for existing buildings. Diana Balmori has coined the term "fifth façade" to suggest the potential impact of green roofs on the urban landscape.[5]

Balmori Associates is committed to drawing attention to the fifth façade through education and demonstration projects and by encouraging local funding, tax credits, and incentives for green roofs. In 2002 the firm developed a plan, called "Long Island (Green) City," to create a network of green roofs for a mixed residential and industrial neighborhood in Queens. As the first part of this plan, two demonstration projects, totaling over 46,000 square feet (4,273.5 m^2) of green roofs, have recently been completed. These are the first scientifically monitored green roofs in New York City.

The Solaire Building, NY

Context and concept

For the Solaire Building, Balmori Associates collaborated with architect Rafael Pelli, at Cesar Pelli & Associates, on two green roofs for this new residential tower in Battery Park City in Lower Manhattan, New York City. There are two types of green roofs on top of the Solaire: an intensive, accessible green roof garden of about 5,000 square feet (464.5 m^2) on the nineteenth floor and an extensive, inaccessible green roof of about 4,800 square feet (445.9 m^2) on the top, twenty-eighth floor. The Solaire represents the first step toward a new kind of urban "smart" development that unites architecture, landscape, and the urban setting into a sustainable system. The green roofs were integrated into the building's hydrological systems: excess water not absorbed by the vegetation or growing medium collects and drains into a cistern in the basement. There the water is filtered and reused, in combination with treated gray water collected throughout the building, in Teardrop Park (directly behind the building) and to irrigate the intensive garden, as needed.

Layout

The intensive green roof on the nineteenth floor provides functional, aesthetic outdoor space where building residents can enjoy views of Battery Park and the Hudson River. It is organized on a grid with a central axis that generates clear pedestrian routes, and from which views are created. The design centers on four large stands of bamboo that can be seen from the street level. The plantings were chosen for their visual interest throughout the seasons, but also for their

SOLAIRE BUILDING PLANT LIST

SHRUBS AND SMALL TREES

Euonymus kiantschovicus	Spreading euonymus
Juniperus procumbens 'Nana'	Dwarf spreading juniper
Phyllostachys bissetti dwarf	Bissetti dwarf bamboo
Pinus mugo 'Mops'	Mops mugo pine
Rosa sp. 'Carpet White'	Carpet white rose
Spirea japonica 'Little Princess'	Little princess spirea

GROUND COVERS, PERENNIALS, VINES, AND GRASSES

Alchemilla mollis	Foam flower
Antennaria dioica	Pussy-toes
Clematis Montana 'Rubens'	Rubens anemone clematis
Cotoneaster dammeri 'Royal Beauty'	Royal Beauty cotoneaster
Delosperma cooperi	Hardy ice plant
Euonymus fortunei	Wintercreeper euonymus
Geranium sanguineum 'Johnson's Blue'	Johnson's blue geranium
Hedera sp.	Climbing ivy
Hypericum x 'Hidcote'	Hidcote St. Johnswort
Lonicera sp.	Honeysuckle
Lotus coriculatus	Bird's-foot trefoil
Miscanthus sinensis 'Gracillimus'	Gracillimus Japanese silver grass
Pennisetum alopecuroides 'Hameln'	Hameln fountain grass
Perovskia atriplicifolia	Perovskia or Russian sage
Sagina subulata	Irish or Scotch moss or awl-leaf pearlwort
Sedum requienii	Miniature stonecrop
Sedum spurium 'Autumn Joy'	Autumn Joy stonecrop
Thymus serphyllum	Thyme

ability to resist strong, drying winds and intense solar radiation. The grasses, perennials, shrubs, and trees are grouped into masses of different colors and textures. A grove of bamboo is situated in the center of the garden, where the elevation is slightly higher.

Stone pavers, used for walkways and seating areas, were laid directly on top of the growing medium, which supports a lush carpet of ground covers and sedums. Vertical aluminum screens, planted with honeysuckle and ivy, surround mechanical and other utility structures, helping to integrate the mechanical equipment with the growing space. Through evapotranspiration, the plantings create a microclimate that is several degrees cooler than the surrounding rooftops. The bamboo also acts as a windscreen for the seating areas and provides some shade. Because this entire space is accessible, it is bounded by a continuous parapet with handrail.

By contrast, the extensive green roof on the top floor is an inaccessible installation planted with a variety of sedums. It is visible from adjacent buildings, providing views of a plane of flowering green space. However, its main functions are environmental: to absorb storm water runoff, to insulate the building and reduce the amount of air conditioning required during the summer and heating required in the winter, to clean the air of pollutants, and to produce oxygen. Together with the intensive green roof on the nineteenth floor, the plant materials and growing medium absorb at least 75 percent of the rainwater.

Green roof

Both the intensive and extensive green roofs at The Solaire Building were built with the layered Garden Roof Assembly™ (American Hydrotech). The installation components, from the bottom up, consisted of the following: a hot, applied, rubberized asphalt waterproofing membrane, a root barrier and protection course, 4 inches (10.2 cm) of Dow Styrofoam insulation, a recycled polyethylene drainage and water retention layer (different profiles were used for the two roofs), and a filter fabric.

Lightweight engineered soil (growing medium) of various depths was then poured into place over the surface of the roof, over the layered green roof system. The growing medium was composed of 70 percent expanded shale (Solite) and 30 percent organic materials. On the deeper planting beds on the nineteenth floor, a bark mulch was spread over the growing medium. In the intensive green roof, the growing medium began at a depth of 6 inches (15.2 cm) to support the ground covers, sedums, and smaller perennial plants. Held in place by low planter walls made from recycled composite plastic, the growing medium reaches a depth of 12 inches (30.5 cm) for a variety of shrubs, grasses, vines, and perennials. The bamboo (Phyllostachys bissetti) was planted in root control bags (a nonwoven polypropylene fabric bag that limits a plant's root structure) and set in raised beds with 18 inches (45.7 cm) of growing medium. The saturated weight of these different levels of engineered soil ranged from 25 pounds/square foot to 100 pounds/square foot (122.0 to 488 kg/m^2). The extensive green roof has 4 inches (10.2 cm) of growing medium, deep enough for the sedum mix planted there. A gravel trench surrounds the perimeter of both green roofs and acts as an extra drainage layer near the edge of the waterproof membrane and as an anchor to the layered installation.

Planting and irrigation

A drip irrigation system that saves water by minimizing evaporation was installed on both rooftops. The sedums used in the extensive green roof did not need additional irrigation after the first few growing seasons; however, the irrigation system was left in place in case of long periods of drought.

Post-planting and maintenance

When the intensive garden was finished, the owner, the Albanese Development Corporation, removed some of the amenities, some of the pavers, and the bamboo, thus limiting the original design scope of the green roof. The bamboo was replaced with groups of *Amelanchier Canadensis* and *Betula nigra*, shadblow or serviceberry and river birch respectively, which leaf out earlier and therefore provide screening and shade in the spring.

The nineteenth-floor intensive green roof is maintained much like an at-grade garden would be: some weeding and pruning are necessary through the growing season, and the soils are checked for composition and moisture. As necessary after inspections, nontoxic pesticides, herbicides, and fertilizers are used. The extensive green roof was designed to require very little maintenance and irrigation after the sedums became established.

The Solaire Building won a gold LEED rating and received New York State's green building tax credit. In addition, in 2002 the building was one of five projects selected by the U.S. Department of Energy to represent the nation at the International Green Building Challenge in Oslo, Norway, a conference to share information on sustainable design for buildings.

5-15, 5-16. The main green roof of The Solaire under construction (*top*) and the finished edge, with guardrail and seating with a path of stepping-stones. (Courtesy of Balmori Associates)

5-17, 5-18. The bamboo being planted at The Solaire at a slightly higher elevation than its surroundings, and another view after it became well-established. (Courtesy of Balmori Associates)

Long Island (Green) City, Queens, NY

Context and concept

In Long Island City, Balmori Associates has pioneered "Long Island (Green) City," a large-scale planning project to build a 30,000,000-square-foot (2,787,091 m²) network of green roofs. Much of this mixed-use neighborhood, which incorporates industrial, warehousing, business, and residential buildings, is composed of low structures with large flat roofs ("pancake buildings"), ideal candidates for extensive green roofs. Stuart Match Suna, president of Silver-

cup Studios, and Roberta Brandes Gratz, the owner of Gratz Industries, offered their buildings for pilot projects.

Planning green roofs for Silvercup Studios and Gratz Industries was a collaborative effort involving many public and private entities, including business owners, consultants, engineers, and nonprofit organizations. Working with the Long Island City Business Development Corporation (LICBDC), Balmori Associates received funding from Clean Air Communities, a program initiated by Northeast States Center for a Clean Air Future and Northeast States for Coordinated Air Use Management (NESCCAF/NESCAUM), committed to implementing air pollution reduction and energy efficiency strategies in low-income New York City communities.

For the Gratz Industries green roof, Balmori Associates collaborated with the Pratt Institute Center for Community and Environmental Development (PICCED) on their proposal, "Manufacturing Green." For this project the team received funding from the New York State Energy Research and Development Authority (NYSERDA) and the Rockefeller Brothers Fund, a philanthropic organization working to promote social change and a more sustainable world. It also benefited from a low-interest loan from the New York Energy Smart Loan Fund program, based on the proposed improvements from the green roof.

Silvercup Studios, Queens, NY

DESIGN TEAM
Client: Silvercup Studios, Inc.
Designer: Balmori Associates, Inc., Diana Balmori, principal
Architects: Shalat Architects P.C.
Landscape contractor: Greener by Design

Layout

Silvercup Studios is a television and production facility. The campus—a historic building and former bakery—is a complex of rambling, interconnected buildings with rooftops at various heights. Balmori Associates developed a design plan incorporating several different roofs, covering a total of 35,000 square feet (3251.6 m²), making it the largest green roof built to date in New York City. This project is visible to thousands of commuters from the Queensboro Bridge and adjacent on- and off-ramps. For its first demonstration project of Long Island (Green) City, Balmori Associates wanted to cre-

SILVERCUP STUDIOS AND GRATZ INDUSTRIES PLANT LIST	
Delosperma nubigenum 'Basutoland'	Basutoland yellow ice plant
Orostachys aggregatum	Fish mouth stonecrop
Orostachys boehmeri	Fish mouth stonecrop
Sedum acre aureum	Gold moss stonecrop
Sedum aizoon	Aizoon stonecrop
Sedum album 'France'	France white stonecrop
Sedum 'Bertram Anderson'	Bertram Anderson stonecrop
Sedum cauticola 'Lidakense'	Likadense dwarf stonecrop
Sedum floriferum	Gold stonecrop
Sedum hybridum 'Immergrunchen'	Immergrunchen stonecrop
Sedum lanceolatum	Lanceleaf stonecrop
Sedum pluricaule 'Rose Carpet'	Rose Carpet stonecrop
Sedum reflexum 'Blue Spruce'	Blue Spruce stonecrop
Sedum rupestre 'Angelina'	Angelina stonecrop
Sedum sexangulare	Tasteless stonecrop
Sedum sieboldii	Siebold's stonecrop
Sedum spurium 'John Creech'	John Creech two-row stonecrop
Sedum spurium 'Roseum'	Pink two-row stonecrop
Sedum spurium 'Voodoo'	Voodoo two-row stonecrop
Sedum spurium 'White Form'	White Form two-row stonecrop

5-19. A rendering of the proposed green roof patterns at Silvercup. The bands of red and orange fabric act as unifying elements. (Courtesy of Balmori Associates)

Case Studies   155

ate a low-maintenance, inexpensive green roof , to show that even a simple, extensive one that is only visually accessible can still make a strong aesthetic statement. The firm developed a design based on "textiles," that is, grouping sedums with similar leaf colors into linear strips that break into larger geometric forms, suggesting fabric patterns.

Green roof

Balmori Associates chose to use interlocking green roof modules (Green Tech) to form a continuous planted surface. For added protection for the existing waterproof membrane and roof surface, a layer of Amergreen 50, a two-part prefabricated sheet drain to protect the waterproofing and facilitate water flow, was laid down before the modules were set into place. The modules, approximately 4 square feet (0.37 m^2) and 8.5 inches (21.6 cm) deep, were filled at an off-site location and trucked to the building, where they were set in place and planted with twenty varieties of sedums and similar plants. Each module was filled with precut Styrofoam insulation pieces, a layer of filter fabric and 3 inches (7.6 cm) of growing medium, topped with a biodegradable, coarse jute mat

that acted as a wind blanket as the plants got established on the roof. The growing medium was composed of 80 percent expanded mineral (Solite) and 20 percent organic material.

Other features

To help unite the diverse building elements, orange, red, and yellow panels of outdoor mesh fabric serve as strong visual accents. A gravel path edges the green roof installations, and aluminum siding on the outside edges gives the roof a more finished look.

Post-planting and maintenance

The green roof projects for both Silvercup Studios and Gratz Industries are monitored by a group of scientists known as GRIS (Green Roof Infrastructure Study) working with Earthpledge. Data from unvegetated control areas of the rooftops will be compared to readings taken from the green roofs to study the absorption and flow rate of storm water, and temperature differences on the green roof and in the buildings below. The data will be collected for a period of one year, analyzed by the GRIS scientists, and then made public as part of an educational outreach program.

DESIGN TEAM
Client: Gratz Industries
Designer: Balmori Associates, Inc., Diana Balmori, principal
Architects: Pratt Institute Center for Community and Environmental Development (PICCED) and Pratt Planning and Architectural Collaborative (PPAC)
Landscape contractor: Greener by Design

Layout

One block away from Silvercup Studios is the demonstration project atop Gratz Industries, a light-metal manufacturer and fabricator specializing in the production of Pilates exercise equipment. For this building, Balmori Associates conceived of the roof design as a painting in motion where severe Mondrianesque rectilinear grids of color will eventually blur into nonlinear patches of color. Ellsworth Kelly was also an influence on the aesthetic. Diana Balmori describes the design as "the abstract patterns fitting the stark reality of the roof of an industrial building and morphing into a looser planted organization."[6] This pixillated pattern covers three quadrants of the 11,000-square-foot (1,022 m²) roof surface. The fourth quadrant is not vegetated and acts as a control for the monitoring study.

Green roof

The structural engineers determined that additional weight of only 10–25 pounds per square foot (48.8 to 122 kg/m²) could be added to the Gratz Industries rooftop. The design team chose a built-in-place layered green roof system (Soprema). On top of tapered insulation and protection boards, a new asphalt waterproof membrane was installed. Then a drainage/aeration layer and a water retention mat were laid

5-21. The structural plan at Gratz: different rectilinear areas were designed to support loads of 10, 15 and 25 pounds per square foot (48.8, 73.2 and 122.1 kg/m², respectively) with a control area with no green roof modules. (Courtesy of Balmori Associates)

5-22. In this graphic enlargement of the planting plan at Gratz, the use of bands of fabric is clear. (Courtesy of Balmori Associates)

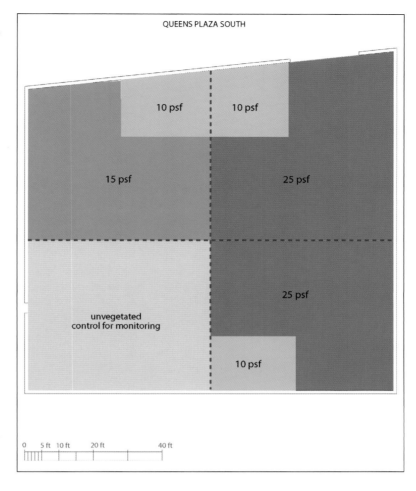

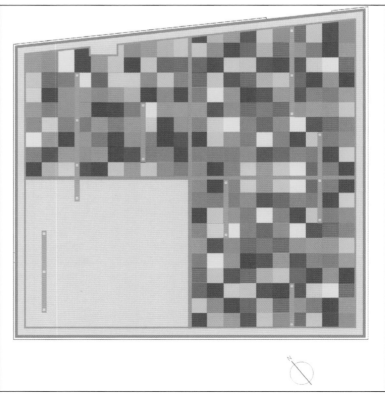

into place before the growing medium was spread out in depths ranging from 2 to 4 inches (5.1–10.2 cm). A .5-foot square (.15 m per side) aluminum grid was spread over the vegetated surface to protect it.

Planting and irrigation

The plant palette, which is the same as that used for Silvercup Studios, was chosen to achieve a maximum variety of foliage, color, and bloom times. The drip irrigation system was used only as needed during the first growing season.

Balmori Associates is implementing green roof designs of different types and settings within the New York City region. Over time, they will be able to compare the results of modular versus nonmodular systems, as well as the vocabulary of plantings, to develop a sense of what works best. From a design perspective, Diana Balmori and her colleagues are interested not only in developing green roofs as sustainable design elements within the landscape, but also as major aesthetic components emerging out of longstanding traditions in fine arts and landscape architecture.

The Green Institute and Minneapolis Central Library

The Green Institute and the Minneapolis Central Library are two major institutions in Minneapolis with green roofs that have contrasting programs and methods of implementation. The Green Institute is a project in sustainability with many different innovative features, whereas the library features green roofs of different kinds. The design model for both projects was dolomite prairie (or bedrock prairie) and bluff prairies, analogs from scientific and natural areas within the Twin Cities metropolitan area. Bluff prairies are typically at the top of bluffs or hills or along slopes by major streams. Dolomite bedrock prairies typically occur where rocky glacial materials have been exposed as a result of erosion or if dolomite bedrock is near the surface. Since dolomite is similar to limestone, these prairies are often very alkaline. Ten thousand years of natural selection have created plants and plant communities specially adapted to cliffs, bedrock, and scree beds. The harsh growing conditions in these places are similar in

5-23. The plan of the Green Institute shows the strong axial relationships that respond to the site and the design concept. (Courtesy of the Kestrel Group)

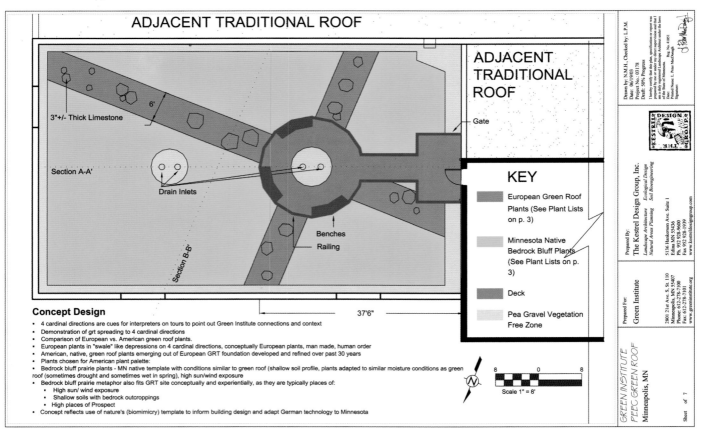

ADJACENT TRADITIONAL ROOF

ADJACENT TRADITIONAL ROOF

3"+/- Thick Limestone

6'

Section A-A'

Drain Inlets

Section B-B'

Benches
Railing

Gate

KEY

European Green Roof Plants (See Plant Lists on p. 3)

Minnesota Native Bedrock Bluff Plants (See Plant Lists on p. 3)

Deck

Pea Gravel Vegetation Free Zone

Concept Design

- 4 cardinal directions are cues for interpreters on tours to point out Green Institute connections and context
- Demonstration of grt spreading to 4 cardinal directions
- Comparison of European vs. American green roof plants.
- European plants in "swale" like depressions on 4 cardinal directions, conceptually European plants, man made, human order
- American, native, green roof plants emerging out of European GRT foundation developed and refined over past 30 years
- Plants chosen for American plant palette:
- Bedrock bluff prairie plants - MN native template with conditions similar to green roof (shallow soil profile, plants adapted to similar moisture conditions as green roof (sometimes drought and sometimes wet in spring), high sun/wind exposure
- Bedrock bluff prairie metaphor also fits GRT site conceptually and experientially, as they are typically places of:
  - High sun/ wind exposure
  - Shallow soils with bedrock outcroppings
  - High places of Prospect
- Concept reflects use of nature's (biomimicry) template to inform building design and adapt German technology to Minnesota

37'6"

N

8   0   8
Scale 1" = 8'

Drawn by: N.M.H. Checked by: L.P.M.
Date: 06/19/03
Project No.: 03178
Draft: 50% Progress

I hereby certify that this plan, specification or report was prepared by me or under my direct supervision and that I am a duly registered Landscape Architect under the laws of the State of Minnesota.
Date:
Printed Name: L. Peter MacDonagh   Reg. No. 41851
Signature:

KESTREL DESIGN GROUP

Prepared By:
The Kestrel Design Group, Inc.
Landscape Architecture   Ecological Design
Natural Areas Planning   Soil Bioengineering
5136 Hankerson Ave. Suite 1
Edina MN 55436
Ph. 952 928-9600
Fax 952 928-1939
www.kestreldesigngroup.com

Prepared For:
Green Institute
2801 21st Ave. S. St. 110
Minneapolis, MN 55407
Phone: 612-278-7100
Fax: 612-278-7101
www.greeninstitute.org

GREEN INSTITUTE
PEEC GREEN ROOF
Minneapolis, MN

Sheet   of   7

many ways to those found on rooftops: hot, dry, windy environments with shallow, free-draining soil profiles. Nevertheless, these native plants thrive. Green roofs designed using a "native analog approach" (that is, utilizing naturally occurring plant communities to inform planting) provide a habitat for many insect and bird species. This design method can also enhance a sense of regional identity by recreating a local aesthetic. Native plant materials that grew within a 200-mile (322 km) radius of the city, with additional European or non-native species added as required, were chosen. The proportions of plant materials on each green roof were based on studies of intact plant communities in that region.[7]

Green Institute, Minneapolis, MN

DESIGN TEAM
Client: The Green Institute
Landscape Architect and Green Roof Specialist: The Kestrel Design Group, Inc., Minneapolis, MN: L. Peter MacDonagh and Nathalie M. Hallyn
Architect: LHB Engineers and Architects, Minneapolis, MN
Roofing System: American Hydrotech

Context and concept
The Green Institute lives up to its name. In addition to the green roof, it has a biofiltration system that processes water in the parking lots and the largest solar array in the upper Midwest. The roof features considerable plant diversity. Storm water runoff was monitored by the Kestrel Design Group for two years. The design metaphor for the building is an installation that surfs on solar energy; that is, it harvests energy from sunlight and rainwater.

5-24. The bluff prairie of Minnesota is the analog for the green roof designs at the Green Institute and the Minneapolis Central Library. (Courtesy of the Kestrel Group).

5-25. The recycled plastic deck and interpretive signs at the Green Institute interpret the "Meadow in the Sky." The elevated light rail system, which affords passengers an excellent view of the green roof, can be seen in the background. (Courtesy of the Kestrel Group)

5-26, 5-27. The completed installation at the Green Institute in the spring and fall. (Courtesy of the Kestrel Group)

Layout

A light rail system, which transports about 38,000 riders per day, runs within roughly 50 feet (15.2 m) of the building, so the green roof is extremely visible and appreciated; both tenants of the building and people from the neighborhood visit. The green roof is 35 feet (10.7 m) above the ground yet is accessible to anyone entering the building. A major structural beam runs down the center of the roof, and the designers "put a deck on top of that beam and a little circle to walk around, and it can take live loads of 200 lbs/f^2 (976.5 kg/m^2)."[8]

Green roof

The extensive green roof (ZinCo/American Hydrotech) covers 4,000 square feet (464.5 m^2). About half of the roof has a substrate depth of 6 inches (15.2 cm); the other half is only 2 inches (5.1 cm) deep. The substrate was a lightweight mix of expanded shale, compost, and sand, all available within 40 miles (64 km) of the site. Eighty-five percent of the growing medium is the substrate, with the remaining 15 percent a mixture of organic additives and superabsorbent polymers.

Plantings and irrigation

Of the total twenty-nine plant species, about eighteen species are grouped on an open field or prairie in the deeper growing medium. In contrast to the undulating areas of prairie are bands of European plants, primarily sedums, set in the shallower areas. The designers wanted to "push the limit on that"—that is, to test what minimum depth of substrate would be needed to sustain a vigorous growth of sedums. The prairie plants became established more quickly, possibly because the deeper level of substrate used for them is able to store more moisture and nutrients.

There is no irrigation, but the plantings (all plugs) were hand-watered during the first growing season. The planting occurred in May 2004, and was coordinated by the Institute and volunteers. Plant monitoring was done by the Kestrel Design Group. Planting was conducted in the early spring, the ideal time because the plant materials had a chance to acclimate for several months before the intense summer heat set in. A limited amount of replanting was done in the second year.

GREEN INSTITUTE PLANT LIST

FORBS (NON-WOODY PLANTS, SUCH AS HERBACEOUS PERENNIALS)

Allium stellatum	Prairie wild onion
Anemone patens	Pasque flower
Asclepias verticillata	Whorled milkweed
Aster sericeus	Silky aster
Campanula rotundifolia	Harebell
Geum triflorum	Prairie smoke
Liatris aspera	Rough blazing star
Opuntia fragilis	Brittle opuntia
Penstemon grandiflorus	Large flowered beard tongue
Ruellia humilis	Wild petunia
Sisyrinchium campestre	Blue eyed grass
Solidago nemoralis	Gray goldenrod
Tradescantia occidentalis	Western spiderwort

GRAMINOIDS (GRASS AND GRASS-LIKE PLANTS)

Bouteloua curtipendula	Side oats gramma
Bouteloua gracilis	Blue gramma
Koeleria macrantha	June grass
Schizachyrium scoparium	Little bluestem
Sporobolus heterolepis	Prairie dropseed

PEEC GREEN ROOF TRADITIONAL PLANT SPECIES

Allium schoenoprasum	Chives
Dianthus deltoides	Pinks
Papaver alpinum	Poppy
Sedum album	White stonecrop
Sedum floriferum	Gold stonecrop
Sedum hybridum	Stonecrop
Sedum reflexum	Blue stonecrop
Sedum sexangulare	Tasteless stonecrop
Sedum spurium	Two-row stonecrop
Sedum ternatum	Woodland stonecrop
Sempervivum spp.	Hens-and-chickens

Other features

The green roof here is typically an ideal setting for photovoltaic installations because it regulates temperatures, keeping them more uniform. This uniformity improves the efficiency and prolongs the operating range of the photovoltaics, which function best when temperatures are between 85 and 95 degrees Fahrenheit (29 and 35 degrees Celsius, respectively). When the surrounding air temperature is around 90 degrees (32°C), the green roof tends to hover around 92 degrees (33°C) but not warmer. Therefore, the optimal operating temperatures for the photovoltaics are extended through a longer period each day. Electricity from the photovoltaics is stored in batteries in the building for later use. Excess electricity is hooked up to the electric grid and sold back to the local utility company. During peak demand periods in the summer, which occur after 4 P.M., the photovoltaics have typically provided a surplus energy for the building so that the balance can be sold. In the Minneapolis region there is a range of thirteen to thirty days when temperatures reach 90 degrees (32°C) or higher, so there can be substantial applications from photovoltaics.

Post-planting and maintenance

The Kestrel Group directs a grant-funded monitoring program, to evaluate four factors on the green roof: storm water volume, storm water rate, percentage of plant cover, and the degree of species richness and diversity. Two ecologists of the Kestrel Group are using Hobo data loggers, which are remote sensing equipment. A rain gauge, in combination with more sophisticated instruments, helps them determine, for example, how much rain fell, how much was discharged from the green roof, at what rate it was discharged, and its total volume.

Minneapolis Central Library, Minneapolis, MN

DESIGN TEAM

Landscape Architect: The Kestrel Design Group, Inc., Minneapolis, MN; L. Peter MacDonagh and Nathalie M. Hallyn
Architect: Cesar Pelli & Associates
Architect of Record: Architectural Alliance, Minneapolis
Roofing Sytem: Henry Company

Context and concept

As befitting a major facility in the heart of downtown, the Minneapolis Central Library by architect Cesar Pelli has much larger green roofs than the Green Insitute. The green roof spans approximately 18,400 square feet (1,709 m²) on several different levels. The goal was similar to the Green Institute's: to create green roofs that serve as analogs to native plant communities in surrounding areas. At the Central Library, extensive research determined that Minnesota's "Bedrock Bluff Prairie" would be the most suitable analog for green roof planting. The Central Library roof planting mix was

5-28. The plan for the green roofs at the Minneapolis Library responds to the complex geometry of the architecture. (Courtesy of the Kestrel Group)

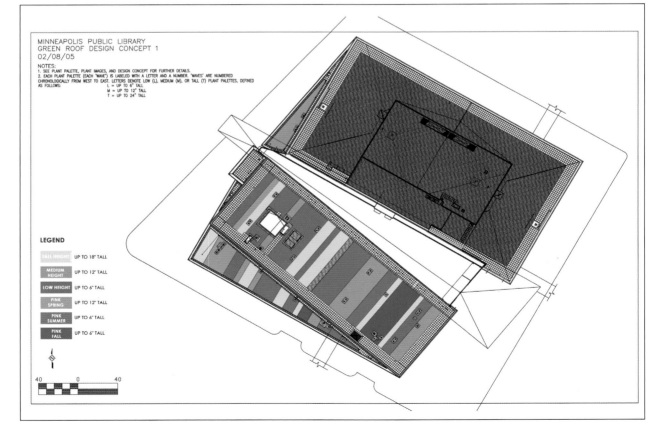

informed by actual plant species composition, abundance, frequency in Bedrock Bluff prairies, by this ecosystem's general visual and aesthetic character, and by individual plant adaptations to this harsh environment. Forty-two species of selected native plants were then complemented by twenty-one species of proven green roof plants, to ensure success. The Kestrel Group completed construction documents and provided construction observation. Architectural Alliance was the Architect of Record for the entire building.

The site will be accessible to people on the Minneapolis Skyway system, a series of elevated pedestrian bridges that connect various buildings downtown. The bridges are particularly useful during winter, allowing people to move from building to building without venturing outdoors into arctic conditions. Vehicular traffic passes underneath the Skyway.

The building is six stories on a site that is one city block square. At the street entry level is a major urban plaza, an abstract geometric pavement featuring paths that are black and silver,

with plantings of white birches below. Much of the pavement is asphalt squares on a pedestal system over an underground garage and utility systems. Black washed Mexican stone is also used. During the summer, the site heats up a great deal, due to the extensive use of black.

The building itself is less stark. The architect wished to be guided by the Minneapolis grid system, which is deeply influenced by the meanders of the Mississippi River and the falls of St. Anthony, where the city was founded. The Minneapolis Central Library straddles two street grids: the Nicollet Avenue grid and the older Hennepin Avenue grid. The two terminal blocks of these two grids morph into one odd-shaped block.

A large atrium roof joins the north and south halves of the building block. The three green roofs are currently installed on the three roofs of the south portion of the block. The north portion of the building awaits a planetarium addition and sky garden. The conceptual design for the green roof recognizes the Mississippi River bend that rotates Minneapolis' street

5-29. The conceptual graphic shows the intent to create waves of prairie on the green roof of the Minneapolis Library. (Courtesy of the Kestrel Group)

MINNEAPOLIS CENTRAL LIBRARY PLANT LIST

TRADITIONAL PLANT LIST

Allium schoenoprasum (L)	Wild chives
Papaver alpinum (L)	Alpine poppies
Sedum 'Green Spruce' (M)	Green Spruce stonecrop
Sedum album (L, Fa, M, Sp, Su, T, Ps)	White stonecrop
Sedum album 'Chloroticum' (L, T, Ps)	Baby's tears white stonecrop
Sedum album 'Murale' (L, Fa, M)	Murale stonecrop
Sedum divergens (L, M)	Spreading stonecrop
Sedum ewersii (L, Fa, M, Sp, Su, T, Ps)	Pink stonecrop
Sedum floriferum 'Weihenstaphauer Gold' (L, Fa, M, Sp, Su, T, S)	Bailey's gold stonecrop
'Weihenstaphaner Gold' (L, Fa, M, Sp, Su, T, Ps)	Bailey's gold stonecrop
Sedum hybridum 'Immergrauch' (S, Su, Ta, Ps)	Immergrach stonecrop
Sedum kamtschaticum (M, Sp, Ps)	Kamschatka stonecrop
Sedum pluricaule Rose Carpet (Sp)	Sakhalin stonecrop
Sedum reflexum (L, Fa, M, Sp, Su, T, Ps)	Blue stonecrop
Sedum sexangulare (L, Fa, M, Sp, Su, T, Ps)	Tasteless stonecrop
Sedum sichotense (L, M)	Stonecrop
Sedum spurium 'Fuldaglut' (F, Ps)	Fuldaglut two-row stonecrop
Sedum stenopetalum (T)	Wormleaf stonecrop
Sempervivum mix (L, Su, T)	Hens-and-chickens

NATIVE PLANT LIST

Allium canadense (M)	Meadow garlic
Allium stellatum (Su, Ps)	Autumn onion
Andropogon gerardii (T)	Big bluestem grass
Anemone cylindrica (M, Sp, Ps)	Candle anemone
Anemone patens (L, Fa, M, Ps)	Pasque flower, praire crocus
Antennaria neglecta (L, Fa)	Field pussytoes
Aquilegia canadensis (Ps)	Wild red columbine
Arenaria stricta (Sp)	Rock sandwort
Asclepias verticillata (M, Sp)	Whorled milkweed
Aster ericoides (T)	Heat aster
Aster oolentangiensis (T)	Sky-blue aster
Aster sericeus (T)	Silky aster
Astragalus canadensis (Ps)	Canadian milk-vetch
Astragalus crassicarpus (T)	Ground plum milk-vetch
Bouteloua curtipendula (T)	Side-oats grama
Bouteloua gracilis (L, Fa)	Blue grama
Campanula rotundifolia (Su, Ps)	Scottish harebell
Carex pensylvanica (Ps)	Pennsylvania yellow sedge
Cassia fasciculata (T)	Partridge pea
Coreopsis palmata (M, Sp)	Prairie coreopsis or tickseed
Dalea purpurea (M, Sp, Su)	Purple prairie clover
Delphinium virescens (T)	Prairie larkspur
Fragaria virginiana or vesca (Ps)	Virginia or wild strawberry
Geum triflorum (L, Fa, M, Sp, Su, Ps)	Prairie-smoke
Hedyotis longifolia (L, Fa, Su)	Long-leaved bluets
Heuchera richardsonii (L, Fa, M, Ps)	Prairie alumroot
Koeleria macrantha (T)	June grass
Liatris aspera (T)	Tall blazing star
Liatris cylindracea (T)	Cylindrical blazing star
Liatris punctata (T)	Dotted blazing star
Lobelia spicata (Sp, Su)	Pale-spike lobelia
Opuntia fragilis (L, Fa)	Brittle prickly pear
Penstemon grandiflorus (Sp, Ps)	Large beardtongue
Ruellia humilis (M, Sp, Su)	Fringeleaf wild petunia
Schizachyrium scoparium (T)	Little bluestem
Solidago nemoralis (T)	Gray goldenrod
Sporobolus heterolepis (M, Sp, Su)	Prairie dropseed
Talinum parviflorum (L)	Small-flowered Prairie fameflower
Talinum rugospermum (F)	Prairie fameflower
Tradescantia occidentalis (T)	Prairie spiderwort
Viola pedata (L, Fa)	Birdfoot violet

grid, as well as the influence of that grid shift on the library building design. The planting design therefore operates in four dimensions: two for the street grid and resultant library footprint, and two (verticality and time) for the river.

The Kestrel Group's original concept for the green roof described it as a metaphor for an ancient Mississippi River, a glacial formation in the bottom of a canyon. In earlier geological periods, great floods filled up the canyon two out of every three years, and these floods spread over what is currently the city of Minneapolis. The landscape architect explained his vision: "We wanted to use this wave pattern of that memory of the great river and the lake that spread over there. We came up with a curved wave design pattern which connected the three roofs and reflected Pelli's set of ratios, which governed the frit patterns and geometry of the library windows. The client and the design committee approved it. Pelli, however, didn't approve it, because he felt that the green roofs should be more geometric and less representational."[9]

The design was revised in an innovative way to accommodate Pelli's request. Bands of native species are used in geometric patterns, but the varying heights, textures, and colors of the materials, as emphasized by shadow patterns, still suggest waves within the rectilinearity of the grid. Twenty to thirty species are grouped and organized to create wave effects in each band. The wave patterns change seasonally because certain species are more apparent at different times of year when they are in bloom. For example, a wave of color moves across one roof starting in April from one end and reaches the far end by October, like the flow of the river. "Seasonal wave movement is also superimposed on three-dimensional wave patterns by a purple and pink burst of color that moves from west to east from spring to fall in accordance with the flow of the Mississippi River. All three green roofs have this wave effect."[10] The way that the green roof design mimics the city and the river symbolizes the positive impact the green roof has on the Mississippi River, as it mitigates the effects of urban stormwater runoff.

Green roof

The south-facing roof also has four floors of reflected glass above it, making it extremely hot

5-30. The architecture of the Minneapolis Library resolves the conflicting grids of the city, as it responds to the Mississippi River. (Courtesy of the Kestrel Group)

from all the energy reflected off the glass as well as direct solar gain. The client uses it for evapotranspirative cooling. An irrigation system was installed there and it uses water harvested from the other green roofs and other parts of the library that now have green roofs. Cisterns in the parking garage below the building collect the water.

All of the green roofs have a substrate depth of 4 inches (10 cm). The soil is a lightweight mix of expanded shale, compost, and sand. The percentage of organic constituents in the growing medium is a little lower, about 5–10 percent by comparison. There are mycorhizae (beneficial fungi which are in the root-systems of plant species, and serve as a secondary root-system; while living off the host plant's sugars, they extract mineral elements and water for the benefit of the host plant) in both projects.

The largest green roof is on the sixth floor, about 16,000 square feet (1,486 m²), and there are two smaller ones, 2,000 square feet (185.8 m²) and about 1400 square feet (37 m²) on the second floor. The larger one on the second floor is visible from the Skyway.

The layers of waterproofing and other materials were simplified, based on the experience at the Green Institute where some layers were found to be unnecessary. The central library installation conforms to a performance-based specification in terms of the amount and type of cover, ability to hold and release water, and vegetation diversity. This difference gave more flexibility to the results.

Planting and irrigation

The planting design included a base of European succulents, because no data was available on the long-term performance of native bedrock bluff plants on green roofs. Then a mix of sedums and native species was used in geometric bands. These bands vary in vegetation height, texture, and time of flowering, creating a perception of waves.

Planting was originally scheduled for April and May but did not occur until July and August, the hottest months of the year. A combination of cuttings and plugs was used. A minimal amount of planting was done in the second year.

In the list on page 164, L represents low, M is medium, T is tall, Sp is spring flowering, Su is summer flowering and Fa is fall, and Ps is partial sun. The plants are grouped by these categories on various areas of the green roofs, but the organization of the plant lists is by traditional and native species. All the plants in these lists were minimum 1.5-inch (3.8 cm) plugs, and a minimum of 4 inches (10.2 cm) tall. By type of plant, the following areas were planted: L: 6,842 square feet (635.6 m^2); M: 2,319 square feet (215.4 m^2); T: 4,055 square feet (376.7 m^2); Sp: 1,136 square feet (105.5 m^2); Su: 1,136 square feet (105.5 m^2); Fa: 1,786 square feet (165.9 m^2) and Ps: 938 square feet (87.1 m^2) with a total of 18,212 square feet (1,692.0 m^2).

Four species of sedum (*Sedum album*, *Sedum floriferum*, *Sedum reflexum* and *Sedum sexangulare*) were planted in equal proportions as cuttings and applied at a rate of 25 pounds per 1,000 square feet (122.1 kg/m^2).

The south-facing roof gets the most reflected heat. It is irrigated with pop-up sprinklers. Moisture and temperature sensors control irrigation. The other two roofs are irrigated with a drip irrigation system, which is controlled by moisture sensors.

Other features

Because these roofs are on a library with a major educational function, a range of materials is in place to help the public see and appreciate the installations. The designers are expecting insects, spiders, beetle, butterflies, and even a few species of nesting birds to colonize the roof.

Post-planting and maintenance

Different roof surfaces were tested on a 90-degree (32°C) day . A green roof was 92 degrees Fahrenheit (33°C); a roof with white reflective tile with high albedo was 125 degrees Fahrenheit (52°C); when a darker color ballast was used, the temperature rose to 145 degrees F (63°C); a portion of the roof left in asphalt was as hot as 170 degrees F (77°C).

The Kestrel Group has assisted the client in writing grant applications for monitoring storm water because the City of Minneapolis has implemented a storm water utility fee. Federal rules from the National Pollution Discharge Elimination System require controls not only for the rate of storm water runoff but also the volume and quality. Because the library has a green roof, the facility is assessed a lower fee than non-green buildings.

Robson Square and Library Square, Vancouver, Canada

These two major projects, built almost thirty years apart, share the artistry, dedication, and expertise of landscape architect Cornelia Hahn Oberlander, who collaborated in the design of both projects, with different design teams.[11]

DESIGN TEAM
Architect: Arthur Erickson
Landscape architect: Cornelia Hahn Oberlander

Context and concept

The landscape for the provincial government complex was intended to bring nature into the city. Completed in 1979, the three-block-long Robson Square, bookended by the courts of the provincial government and an art gallery in a former courthouse built in 1910, is an eye-catching urban oasis. Constructed over offices and parking structures, its intensive roof garden is a major destination for visitors to the city. As the dynamic area has attracted new development, new buildings have cast shadows on some spaces that were previously sunlit, yet the overall effects are still spectacular.

Due to its scope and scale, an important requirement of this project was a close collaboration among architect, landscape architect, engineer, and client. The provincial government sought a showplace for its complex of buildings and courts. The design team was challenged to develop a unified design vocabulary that would lead people through a series of spaces, suggest and replicate natural settings, including waterfalls, while responding to the immense technical challenges of a roof garden. Arthur Erickson first conceived the design as a tower laid on its side, with all the interesting configurations that would result as one sought to climb or traverse it.

Conceptual planning began in 1974, and many studies were conducted to determine the carrying capacity of the roofs of the many offices and parking structures. Various means of waterproofing and protection against root penetration were investigated. Oberlander wanted a plant vocabulary that suggested nature but also contained a repetition of masses for a unified effect. In the spring, she used

accents of blooming flora, such as magnolias and rhododendrons, against masses of dark or lustrous green foliage, such as Zabel laurel. Careful study was given to the methods and means of irrigation, fertilization, and the type and depth of the growing medium.

Layout

The streets bordering the site are lined with allées of Red Sunset maples, planted at a dense spacing of 15 feet (4.5 m) on center, thus giving a clear green definition to the edge. Linear and geometric spaces were created with 3-foot (0.9 m)-deep planter boxes and beautiful patterns of diverse, reinforced concrete pavements. A series of giant waterfalls suggests mountain retreats or natural settings, and the sound of rushing water masks street noise (Figs. 5-33, 5-34, and 5-35). A short distance away are additional pedestrian spaces, plantings, and cafes. As the roof garden crosses over the streets below it, dramatic flying planters create an effect of hanging gardens that step up out of sight. Yet there is still restraint in the use of both construction materials and plantings. Through the repetition of materials and the uniformity in treatment, a remarkable and tranquil urban space emerges.

Green roof

At the time Robson Square was built, a limited number of products for waterproofing and water retention were available in Canada and the United States. The waterproofing used was EPDM (ethylene propylene diene monomer), a type of rubber applied in overlapping sheets, but it was considered reliable for only about

5-33, 5-34, 5-35. Despite being in the heart of a major city, the enclosure provided by the architecture and a limited palette of planting at Robson Square gives a feeling of serenity. By contrast, there are spectacular water features, like the massive waterfall, whose roaring turbulence masks street noise.

ten to fifteen years. A gravel layer was laid down to allow for subdrainage through the planters. Large changes in elevation were built up with Styrofoam, a material still commonly used for that purpose today. Even then, it was clear that a normal loamy soil would be much too heavy, so a lighter-weight product called Terra Mix (W.R. Grace & Co.) was used.

Over the years, as the waterproofing had to be replaced, the landscape architect worked to find modern substitutes. A growing medium of ingredients available from local sources has been used, consisting of one-third sand, one-third pumice, and one-third Humus Builder, a composted product of food waste from local restaurants. Rigid, waffled drainage systems glued onto nonwoven filter mats are the modern replacement for the gravel and drainage systems. Before the old waterproofing is removed, the plant materials are carefully salvaged and stored, then replanted in the same configuration to maintain design continuity.

Other features

Among the many unique features of this spectacular urban design are pavement patterns—rectilinear slabs of granite set in linear patterns—to direct pedestrians from one space to the next. Near the waterfalls crashing into pools are "stramps," stairs combined with ramps, which accommodate steep changes in grade in a safe but adventurous way. Although they would probably not comply with today's more rigorous standards for handicap access, they still present a fanciful solution for directing people up a steep, paved slope gracefully and artfully.

From a horticultural standpoint, this project

demonstrated that roof gardens with deep planters have the potential to be as rich in full, dense plantings as anything planted at grade, just as long as great care is taken in planning and execution. In addition to specimen trees, masses of shrubs, and ground cover are walls of vines that cloak some concrete walls of buildings.

ROBSON SQUARE PLANT LIST	
Acer rubrum 'Red Sunset'	Red Sunset maple
Acer japonicum	Japanese maple
Clematis montana rubra	Clematis
Hedera helix	English ivy
Magnolia soulangiana	Saucer magnolia
Pinus contorta 'Contorta'	Contorta shore pine
Prunus laurocerassus 'Zabeliana'	Zabel laurel
Rosa wichuraiana	Memorial rose
Rhododendron sp.	Rhododendron in varieties
Taxus media 'Hicksii'	Hicks yew

5-36. An allée of shade trees at Robson Square defines the edges, and quiet pools of water foreshadow major water features inside the square.

Considerable areas of fine lawn, raised in mounds to a higher elevation, have become landmarks that people walk around or sit upon rather than walk across. Scuptures are carefully situated in prominent settings, reinforced by either plantings, or the architectonic vocabulary.

Given the tendency for so many innovative projects to accrue large cost overruns because much that is being implemented is new and unexplored, one surprising aspect of this project is its cost. When conceptual planning began, the budget was $1.8 million (Canadian), but when work was completed in 1979, the total cost came to only $1.2 million.

Planting and irrigation

For such a large series of gardens, the planting palette is restrained, and features masses of dark evergreen foliage with flowering or contrasting accents.

The original irrigation system was installed with spray heads activated by a computer. This system has been converted to drip irrigation, activated by a sophisticated computer system with different settings for different zones.

Post-planting and maintenance

The plantings have succeeded in a spectacular way. The allées of trees form a continuous canopy around the edges of the square, and the shrubs, trees, and vines within the planters have formed solid masses that provide enclosure and fill all the spaces. Perhaps because of the constraint in the use of exotic plant materials, occasional efforts have surfaced to add striking annuals for color displays—these, unfortunately, mar the serenity of the setting. Citizens and city officials need to plan changes to preserve and maintain successful green roofs for future generations in consultation with either the landscape architect or the architect. Disregard for the original plans is typical when projects have been so successful in providing prosperity to a region that the projects start to be tampered with without recognition of what has been provided or what may be undermined by unconsidered changes.

Library Square, Vancouver, Canada

DESIGN TEAM
Architect: Moshe Safdie + Downs/Archambault & Partners
Landscape architect: Cornelia Hahn Oberlander with Elisabeth Whitelaw

The architect Moshe Safdie, renowned for his housing development Habitat 67 in Montreal at Expo 67, was commissioned to design the new main branch of the Vancouver Public Library and collaborated with Cornelia Hahn Oberlander.

Context and concept

The new branch and its square offer strong yet graceful urban design at the street level and a remarkable green roof, an echo of the region's Fraser River, which flows through the Greater Vancouver Regional District. The design team began work on the building in 1992; it opened in 1995. The location was not previously a major public district, but thoughtful design and consideration of pedestrian access routes has already humanized the previously bleak environment. By incorporating a curved and stepped amphitheater opening to the street, the entrance plaza is artfully graded and sculpted to neutralize a 20-foot (6 m) grade change across one side of the site, almost a 5 percent slope. The generous stepped platforms encourage visitors and passersby to slow down and enjoy the space. By contrast, a curving arcade sculpts the plaza at the other entrance and leads visitors into the building.

Below:
5-37. At Robson Square considerable elevation changes are handled gracefully by combinations of steps and ramps called *stramps*.

Opposite:
5-38. The view from any intersecting street at Robson Square is suggestive of hanging gardens. The towers in the background were built in later years.

5-39. The entrance plaza at the Vancouver Library. The green roof is not visible from the street.

ment within a static environment. According to the designer, "The planting reflects the changing patterns of light and shadow."[12] Two varieties of fescue represent the Fraser River and the adjacent land, while the bearberry represents the higher elevations of the land.

Green roof

The continuous waterproofing membrane, warranteed for fifteen years (American Hydrotech), was applied hot, as a rubberized asphalt (a special formulation from refined asphalts, synthetic rubber, and inert clay filler). A prefabricated drainage mat (Nilex) was used, with a waffled drainage core bonded to a layer of nonwoven filter fabric. The drainage capacity of the core, together with the water absorption capacity of the 14-inch (35.56 cm) depth of growing medium, creates a total volume on the roof of 33,000 cubic feet (934 m^3)—a substantial amount in terms of storm water absorption.

The growing medium is the same used for the renovations at Robson Square, a weed-free mixture of one-third sand, one-third pumice, and one-third Humus Builder. Its weight does not exceed 76 pounds per cubic foot (1,217 kg/m^3). Although the depth of the growing medium suggests that this is a nonextensive roof, it is referred to as an extensive roof because it is meant to be viewed from above and is not open to the public.

With a limited palette of plant materials, two grasses and one perennial, the plantings are massed in clear, concentric forms. Morgan Japanese maple trees at the eighth floor are planted continuously on one edge of the green roof and provide additional enclosure. The same species is situated in individual planters on the same level as the green roof, and adds character.

Other features

A composting station was added to process waste materials from the green roof. This facility has not been fully utilized because the work is dependent on maintenance staff, but this might change if the roof is redesigned to be accessible—a possibility that is under consideration at the time of writing.

Large tulip trees (*Liriodendron tulipifera*) are planted along each of the streets in a continuous trench, bridged by pavers for pedestrian access. This method promotes faster growth

Layout

An extensive-style green roof crowns the top of this nine-story building. Accessible only to maintenance workers and occasional authorized visitors by a ladder from the floor below, the curving, concentric forms seem to sweep over the roof like a flood of water; no parapets extend above the grade of the roof. The total area is 30,000 square feet (2,787 m^2), of which 2,000 square feet (185.8 m^2) consists of pavement. Occasional visitors must be wary of swooping sea gulls, who seem to have included the roof in their territory.

When viewed from adjacent buildings, an abstract river design appears with adjacent washes of grasses and ground cover, suggesting move-

because the roots are not confined by individual tree pits.

Planting and irrigation

The premixed growing medium was lifted in buckets by a crane to the rooftop during periods of low vehicular traffic, 3 P.M. to 11 P.M. The growing medium was applied to a depth of 14 inches (35.6 cm).

Plugs, the smallest available rooted material, were used. Approximately 16,000 plugs of the two varieties of grasses and 26,000 plugs of bearberry were used over the 28,000-square-foot (2,601.2 m²) roof. The average spacing was about 1.5 plugs per square foot (16 plugs/m²).

An irrigation system was used during the first year. In subsequent years it has been used weekly, only in periods of drought.

The total cost of installation for the growing medium and plants in place was about $270,000 (Canadian) in 1995.

Post-planting and maintenance

Because the growing medium contained no weed seed, there has not been a significant problem with weeding. The amount of weeding

LIBRARY SQUARE PLANT LIST	
Acer 'Morgan'	Morgan Japanese maple
Arctostaphylos uva ursi	Bearberry or kinnikinnick
Festuca ovina glauca v. 'Elijah Blue'	Elijah blue fescue
Festuca ovina glauca v. 'Solling'	Solling green fescue

5-40. The fluid forms of the green roof at the Vancouver Library contrast with the rigid geometry of the architecture.

5-41. Japanese maples anchor one edge of the green roof at the Library; similar trees planted in individual planters have grown more slowly.

5-42. The design is simple and bold. Since the plant palette is limited, weeds are easily identified.

is expected to diminish as the ground covers and grasses form a continuous cover on the roof. One advantage of a design in which the palette of plant material is both so limited and so clear in definition—blue and green grasses and a finely textured ground cover—is that weeds are easily identified. There is no risk of culling the wrong plants by mistake. An unexpected impediment to weeding has been

swooping birds, usually sea gulls. Maintenance also includes removal of thatch.

The Japanese maples planted in one long row in a continuous planter are already twice as large as the same trees planted in individual planters. This outcome further validates the technique of street tree planting in a continuous trench rather than in individual tree pits around Library Square along Georgia Street.

The annual cost of maintenance is about $15,000 (Canadian). The contract for maintenance has been rebid by the city each year, a fairly standard practice in the case of a green roof for which there is little history. Once a firm has maintained a roof for a year it is likely to want a higher fee. With rebidding, therefore, there may be a new maintenance firm each year and each new firm has to plow through a learning curve.

Public Works and Government Services (PWGS) Canada is conducting research projects to monitor storm water runoff. In 2003 Kerr Wood Leidal Associates Ltd. of Burnaby, British Columbia, was hired as a consultant to quantify storm water runoff benefits from the green roof on the public library and another green roof compared to a traditional flat roof. The storm water runoff from the library green roof showed a 28 percent reduction in volume. At first this does not seem to be a large reduction; however, when compared to the maximum possible reduction for natural, predevelopment conditions, the reduction from the green roof is 48 percent; about 20 percent of the roof is still impervious. If the entire roof were a green roof, the actual reduction in storm water volume would be as much as 70 percent. Measurements show that the green roof was also able to attenuate summer peak flows by greater than 80 percent and smaller winter peak flows by approximately 30 percent. The green roof was unable to limit peak flow from large storm events, which were defined as greater than a two-year storm (one whose volume and intensity occurs an average of every two years, but over a short period of time may occur more frequently or not at all). Nevertheless, the green roof appears to mimic natural hydrologic conditions effectively and significantly reduce the impact of storm water runoff.[13]

The Oak Hammock Marsh Conservation Centre, Manitoba, Canada

DESIGN TEAM

Architect: Number TEN Architectural Group, Winnipeg, Robert Eastwood, principal

Scientist: Ducks Unlimited specialists and the Manitoba Department of Natural Resources

Landscape architect: Gary Hilderman, Hilderman, Thomas, Frank E. Cram (Winnipeg Water treatment design for the lagoons was by the UMA Engineering Group.)

Reclamation and planting: Brent Wark of Native Plant Solutions (affiliated with Ducks Unlimited Canada).

Well water cooling design: MCW Engineers, in Winnipeg.

Context and concept

Situated in a rural area just north of Winnipeg, in the vast interlake region of central Manitoba, the Oak Hammock Marsh Conservation Centre straddles both prairie and marsh.[14] In 1973 the rehabilitated marsh and surrounding uplands were designated as a Wildlife Management Area (WMA) by the province of Manitoba; in 1987 the area, which consists of about 5.5 square miles (14 km²) of restored wetland and about 8.5 square miles (22 km²) of managed uplands, was designated a Ramsar Site, a wetland of international importance for wildlife and people. Ramsar refers to the IUCN (The World Conservation Union) Convention on Wetlands, based on a conference held in Ramsar, Iran, in 1971. This area is one of Canada's thirty-six designated Ramsar sites, which represent almost 20 percent of the wetland areas designated worldwide under the Convention to date. Oak Hammock has also been designated one of Manitoba's eight Heritage Marshes and has been recognized as a globally significant Important Bird Area (IBA) by Bird Studies Canada and the Western Hemisphere Shorebird Reserve Network.

The building in this conservation zone serves as the headquarters for Ducks Unlimited Canada (DUC), a private, non-profit conservation organization established in 1938 and a

5-43. Model of Oak Hammock showing the integration of the building with the landscape. (Courtesy of Number TEN Architectural Group)

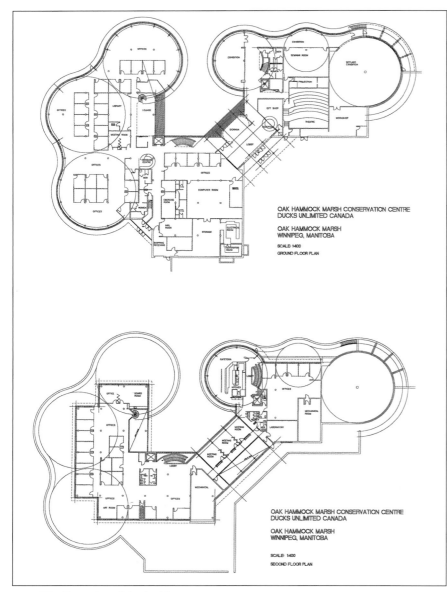

OAK HAMMOCK MARSH CONSERVATION CENTRE
DUCKS UNLIMITED CANADA

OAK HAMMOCK MARSH
WINNIPEG, MANITOBA

SCALE: 1:400
GROUND FLOOR PLAN

OAK HAMMOCK MARSH CONSERVATION CENTRE
DUCKS UNLIMITED CANADA

OAK HAMMOCK MARSH
WINNIPEG, MANITOBA

SCALE: 1:400
SECOND FLOOR PLAN

5-44. The floor plan of the building at Oak Hammock, with the flanking wings of the Ducks Unlimited office facility and the public conservation exhibits. (Courtesy of Number TEN Architectural Group)

world class interpretive center operated jointly by DUC and the Province of Manitoba, which attracts over 200,000 visitors from around the world annually. The center has received numerous awards for the quality of its programs and public service, including the Best Outdoor Site in Canada Award from Attractions Canada and the British Airways Tourism for Tomorrow Award as global winner in the environmental experience category.

Historically, this region was dominated by an extensive 181.4-square-mile (470 km^2) wetland and mixed prairie area known as St. Andrews Bog, which extended from Winnipeg north to Teulon between Lake Winnipeg and Lake Manitoba. In the 1930s, the land became

almost dry as a result of prolonged drought and large-scale drainage for agricultural uses. During World War II the remnants of St. Andrews Bog were used by the airforce as a bomb target area, and when marsh restoration work was undertaken in the 1980s the military had to first sweep the area for undetonated ordnance.

In the late 1980s, DUC needed a new national headquarters and partnered with the Manitoba Department of Natural Resources (MDNR, now called Manitoba Conservation), which had plans to develop a major wetland education facility. The DUC headquarters had been located in urban Winnipeg since 1938, but a joint proposal called for a new facility, along with an interpretive center, at Oak Hammock Marsh, in the midst of the restored wetland and prairie habitat. A design competition was held in 1989 and won by Number TEN Architectural Group in Winnipeg. Two of the competition entries had green roofs.

The building housing both the DUC headquarters and the interpretive center was designed in 1990 and completed in 1992. Extensive public hearings were held, and several citizens groups were strongly opposed to the project, because they believed that the building would encroach on the natural habitat and that increased visitation to the area would disturb wildlife. However, after a process of public hearings and environmental impact assessments, the project was approved. One of the important determining factors was that the footprint of the building, when completed with its green roof, would be less visible; furthermore, the green roof would provide nesting habitat for ground-nesting birds. It was also intended to function as an observation platform from which to view and study birds in a natural setting. The building would actually re-create habitat and be inconspicuous from the air.

Despite the severe Canadian winter climate, there was no shut-down of the site as a result of weather conditions. However, as a condition of the license, construction had to halt for two different three-week periods that coincided with critical periods in the life cycle of the birds. Between May and June, the birds nest and nurture young, and from September to October, the major fall staging and migration occurs. Therefore, foundations were formed and poured in the summer, after the first critical period. There were stringent requirements to prevent any significant effects on the marsh. No fuels could be stored on site, other than propane tanks and burners used for heating during winter construction; equipment had to re-fuel off site. Burning of construction materials was prohibited on site, and trash had to be removed as soon as possible. The impact on wildlife was minimal. Even during construction, birds could be seen perched along the parapets of the bermed roof areas. To this day, wildlife exists in close proximity to the structure and the people who visit it.

Layout

Three sites were considered within the marsh area. The site finally selected allowed the building to be constructed outside the marsh dikes, which limited the impact on the marsh itself. The building is sited beside the smallest of the six marsh cells that are part of the restorations by DUC. The architectural mass features long, flowing curves that recall the sinuous configuration of the marsh shoreline. Some earthwork was done so that, at the last stage of construction, a small piece of the marsh could extend up to and into the courtyard of the building. In the event of a fire, contaminants from the building and fire-fighting activities could be restricted to this more contained area to reduce the impact on the marsh. To reduce bird strikes on the building, faceted glass is set in the building curves, and deep roof overhangs break up the reflected images of the sky and plantings.

The building is clad in Manitoba limestone, which is called Tyndalstone, after the location of the quarry in a town in Manitoba, about 50 miles (81 km) away. Originating from depositions in glacial Lake Agassiz, the stone is sedimentary, with many visible large fossils. The fractured layer from the bottom of the quarry had a texture and golden color range that matched the color and texture of the *Phragmites* (common reed), as well as other grasses

5-45. An aerial view of Oak Hammock shows the artful camouflage of the building, which allows it to blend into the network of wetlands and prairie landscape. (Courtesy of Number TEN Architectural Group)

5-46. The curving forms of the building at Oak Hammock embrace the wetlands around it, and birds soar in and out of the spaces.

5-47. From the parking lot at Oak Hammock, the building (except its main entrance) is hidden from view by graceful berms planted in prairie with scattered trees.

and cattails in the marsh and the surrounding tall grass prairie in the late summer and early fall. The building is virtually invisible at this time of year, completely camouflaged by the layers of stone and the prairie growth on the two green roofs.

From the parking lot and arrival drop off points, visitors see only the upper roof line where large berms intervene, planted with prairie grasses and small native trees and shrubs. The soil for the berms was excavated from specific areas of the site where "prairie potholes" were being created as nesting locations for waterfowl. For the entire site, there was a balance of cut and fill. Visitors enter the building through a gap in these berms, which disguise the height and also define the edge of the building. Immediately inside are the flanking wings of the Ducks Unlimited office facility and the public conservation exhibits. Swallows and other birds soar through the mini-marsh-ponds between the wings of the building, and muskrat and aquatic birds swim and feed in the water. There is no obvious emergency access point from the roofs; the berms extend to the edge and provide a means of escape from the building in the event of a fire or other emergency. They also provide paths for the waterfowl that nest on the roofs; the parents lead their hatchlings along the berms to the marsh

below to feed and bathe. There have been no reports of predators using these paths.

Green roof

The total building area is 50,000 square feet (4,645.0 m²) on two levels, with a footprint of 28,400 square feet (2,638.4 m²), all of which is planted. Both the upper and lower roofs are planted with prairie grasses, with the exception of spaces immediately adjacent to office areas on both levels, which have small paved areas or are planted with standard grasses. The only roof area of the building not planted is the 400-square-foot (37.2 m²) elevator tower. All runoff from the roofs flows towards the prairie side of the building.

The green roofs originally consisted of a ballasted, loose-laid, ethylene propylene (EPDM) sheet with welded joints, lapped over the structure and insulated. The roofs were flood-tested to a depth of over a foot (0.30 m). A heavy-duty filter fabric was placed over the insulation and waterproofing membrane. Drains at the surface and the bottom were installed; both types were needed because the whole system can freeze solid in the winter, leaving only the subgrade drains to function. The lower-level drains are connected to interior pipes that drain to the treatment lagoons bordering the parking lots. When the system is frozen, the soil has less insulation value, but snow cover functions as a thermal buffer. Scuppers (spouts projecting past the face of the building) are also installed to allow water to flow off the roof edges in a few locations in the event of very heavy rainfalls. The scuppers also accent the linear geometry of the architecture. The total cost of the building including the green roofs was about $100/square foot ($1,076/m²) in 1990 Canadian dollars.

The growing medium was essentially a sandy clay loam. Brent Wark of Native Plant Solutions (NPS) explains, "In this part of the world, where it's not uncommon to be 40 below Celcius (-40° F) in the wintertime, I had great concern that we'd get all this stuff growing, only to have it winter kill. We brought the individual components, blended it and moved it up there. You need some clay for moisture efficiency; some sand to move water through to scuppers and drains and get it out of the system. Also, we didn't want it to turn into a small lake when we have a prairie thunderstorm. The soil was somewhat different than the areas we planted at grade, such as the berms, which had Manitoba gumbo Red River soil, which has a lot of clay. On the roof we had to add some sand for tithe and permeability. They built the roof to hold my dirt."[15]

The depth of the growing medium on the green roofs is almost 6 inches (15.2 cm) for the standard grasses at the staff areas, and 16 to 24 inches (40.6–61.0 cm) for the prairie grasses. The native soils were mixed and screened before they were brought to the site.

Other features

A network of two lagoons and a tertiary cattail lagoon form a water treatment system near the parking lots. The cattail lagoon naturally processes waste material and salt from the building, and even removes minerals from the water. Clean water drains back from the tertiary lagoon to the marsh. Because the lagoons border the parking lots, the cattails are well located to absorb any heavy metals or other toxins from automobile emissions, thereby protecting

water birds and other aquatic life. In winter, the cattails are harvested above the plane of the ice and processed into cattle feed. There is a separate settlement lagoon for solids in addition to the three previously described.

5-48, 5-49. Berms wrap around the building at Oak Hammock to reduce its visibility. Areas for staff are on the second level, and the prairie landscape thrives on the third level.

In the summer the green roofs, architectural overhangs, and operable windows keep the building mass cool, so less air conditioning is needed, although a system is provided. The large concrete frame stores heat and dampens temperature fluctuations. In the evening, it emits heat so that there is less need for continuous heating. A well-water loop in the air handling equipment for cooling eliminated the need for a cooling tower or exterior condensers. Well water at 40 degrees Fahrenheit (4° C) is pumped from one well into the building and returns to another well at approximately 45 degrees Fahrenheit (7° C). Well water is also used for water supply. All the domestic water is recycled in the closed loop cooling system. Except for electricity and some supplemental heating, the whole utility system is self-contained.

Because noise would interfere with the proper functioning and visitor appreciation of the marsh site, all mechanical systems are located internally within heavy concrete walls for buffering insulation, and acoustic lining is used on all intake and exhaust air ducts. All mechanical equipment is inside the building frame, and none is on the roof. Unfortunately—at least visually—several satellite dishes have been added on the roof to connect the facility with other education centers around the world.

Another goal was to minimize interference with the observation of the night sky, because star gazing is an important public program. A low level of exterior lighting ensures safe movement along the sidewalks and parking lots and cutoffs within the fixtures prevent the light beams from spreading over a large area. All lighting is reflected to the ground from poles or bollards.

Around the building is a series of ponds, marshes, and prairies managed by biologists from DUC and Manitoba Conservation. An intricate network of small dikes and ponds regulates the elevation of water to maximize the quality of the habitat for wildlife. Fresh water supplies are directed into the marsh through ditches that also tap into an artesian groundwater system. On a carefully developed cycling schedule, different areas are flooded and de-watered periodically. Habitat is both inundated and regenerated in a natural way that makes maximum use of the water available and prevents any one area from being overtaken by dense cattail growth. Historically, the area was beset by botulism that killed many thousands of aquatic birds, but enhanced water management has now all but eliminated this threat, even in the driest of years. A series of small, artificial islands were positioned throughout the marsh to provide safe nesting sites for birds. The marsh and adjacent uplands are regulated as no-hunting area.

Most electrical power in Manitoba is water-generated. Within the building, electric baseboard heaters are installed around the perimeter, with supplemental electric radiant ceiling panels at critical, exposed areas such as doorways. For the entire project, no fossil fuel is burned to provide energy either on the site or on generating locations. Similarly, no building function is dependent on fossil fuels.

Planting and irrigation

The establishment of the plants on the roof was less challenging than the development of the growing medium. Brent Wark explains, "We went with seed mixes. We just employed the same methodology that we've employed in 150,000 acres (60,703 ha) of upland that we have planted over the years for waterfowl nesting cover out in the prairies. We went with diligent pre-planting weed control, used standard seed drills on the berms, but we also had to come up with some modified equipment for the roof. Once the planting was done, there was another round of diligent weed control."[16] Proper weed control insures the establishment of the preferred seeded plant materials; once established, the plants can compete naturally with weeds and other species.

A high prairie seed mix was developed on the green roof, because this seemed most suitable based on the soil's relatively low moisture levels. The mix contained the first six species in the list opposite. These main components are primarily low-growth form native species. As Brent Wark explains, "If you go out to the top of a high dry hill in prairie Manitoba, that's what you find growing on top. That was put out as a seed mixture." Later on, after a final year of weed control, forbs—the last four species in the list—were added for aesthetic purposes. Forbs are non-woody flowerings plants that are not grasses. Most perennials are forbs. Trees and shrubs are not.

Prairie restoration

To complete the careful re-vegetation of the disturbed areas of the site, and to complement the high prairie seeded on the green roof, low and middle prairies were established in the drier areas of the prairie and on the berms that tie into or screen the building and the lower areas adjacent to the wetlands. The tall grass prairie was planted on the lower slopes of the berms where there is more moisture, although DUC has found that once prairies are established, they require no irrigation. NPS has found that planting tall grass and cattail edges where the prairie plantings meet the wetlands reduces the presence of Canada geese, because they do not feed on the tall grasses and feel more vulnerable to humans, dogs, and other potential predators. Brent Wark described the process of establishing the different plant zones: "The roof would be categorized as a high prairie situation in terms of its moisture efficiency and plants that can grow there. The side slopes would be a mid-prairie ecozone with a little bit better moisture situation. Those plants are a little bit more robust and are a little bit taller, and at the base of the complex you'd be in a low prairie situation, and grading right into the wetlands. Each of those zones has different vegetation groups that thrive there. So we went out, and we had a look at the site, determined what we would call high, mid and low prairie and then put together the mixes that would provide the site appropriate vegetation."[17] (Note: High, middle and low prairies refer to the relative elevation of the prairie above a base datum, not the relative height of the plant materials themselves. Tall-grass or tall prairie and short-grass are the terms used to indicate height.) An important goal of the prairie restoration plantings was to create smooth transitions from one prairie area to another. Mr. Wark said, "It's very important so that you don't get these detectable lines in the planting, you have to kinda smear these things together. So this is why you will carry some of the species from the top of the knoll and the green roof, down into the upper part of the mid prairie zone. The best analogy is to take a pencil, and draw a mound, and with colored pencils draw

OAK HAMMOCK MARSH CONSERVATION CENTRE PLANT LIST

HIGH PRAIRIE

Andropogon scoparus; Schizachyrium scoparium	Little bluestem
Bouteloua curtipendula	Side oats grama
Bouteloua gracilis	Blue grama
Elymus canadensis	Canada wild rye
Koeleria cristata	June grass
Nasella viridula	Green needle grass
Achillea sp.	Yarrow
Crocus sp.	Crocus
Echinacea purpurea or pallida	Coneflower
Geum triflorum	Prairie smoke

MID-PRAIRIE

Andropogan gerardi	Big blue stem
Panicum virgatum	Switch grass
Surghastrum nutans	Indian grass
Andropogon scoparus	Little blue stem
Bouteloua curtipendula	Side oats grama
Bouteloua gracilis	Blue grama
Calamovilfa longifolia	Prairie sand reed
Elymus lanceolatus	Northern wheat grass
Koeleria cristata	June grass
Nasella viridula	Green needle grass
Pascopyrum smithii	Western wheat grass
Elymus Canadensis	Canada wild rye
Elymus trachycalulus sub trachycaulus;	
Agropyron trachycaulum	Slender wheat grass
Elymus trachycalulus sub. subsecundus;	
Agropyron trachycaulum v. unilaterate	Awned wheat grass
Rosa woodsii	Wood's rose
Symphoricarpos occidentalis	Western snowberry
Achillea sp.	Yarrow
Bergamot sp.	Bergamot
Echinacea sp.	Coneflower
Helianthus maximillianii	Maximillian sun flower
Petalostenum candidum; Dalea candida	White prairie clover
Petalostenum purpurum; Dalea purpurum	Purple prairie clover
Solidago sp.	Goldenrod

LOW PRAIRIE*

Bechmania syzighacne	Slough grass
Calamagrostis inexpansa	Northern seed grass
Scholochloa festucacca	Whitetop
Spartina pectinanta	Prairie Cordgrass
Andropogon scoparus	Little blue stem
Panicum virgatum	Switchgrass

*The low prairie mix, adapted to the wettest and thickest soils, included the first four species in this list typical for wet areas, and two species from the mid-prairie zone.

high, middle, low prairies zone, and take your thumb along the interface and smear it. You don't get a straight line. There are no straight lines in nature. That's what you have to try and overcome when you're designing and managing these things."[18]

In the mid-prairie zone, which has better moisture efficiency and thicker soil, and is the mainstay of vast prairies in Manitoba, three species predominate: *Andropogon gerardi*, or big blue stem, *Panicum virgatum*, or switch grass, and *Sorghastrum nutans*, or Indian grass. The secondary group featured in the accompanying list are five of the species that were components of the high prairie and were also included in the mid prairie seed mix, although in smaller proportions, along with several other related grasses. Three early seral stage grasses (a transitory plant community gradually replaced by other species) along with two significant shrubs, are included in the list's penultimate grouping. Finally, as with the prairie established on the green roof, the last group is a list of perennials added for aesthetic purposes.

Post-planting and maintenance
Over time, the EPDM sheet moved slightly because of differences in temperature at the deck level and parapets. This caused movement and openings at the joints along the parapet, and water leaked under the membrane. Since the parapets were above the green roof soil, they grew warmer than the sheltered deck structure. The freeze/thaw cycle of the soil may also have caused movement. The membrane under the green roof was therefore completely replaced with a new system, consisting of a two-ply (Suprema) membrane. There is a drainage layer over the membrane. The load limit for the Suprema system is 150 lbs/square foot (732.4 kg/m^2). The replacement was done sequentially, one area at a time, so as to minimize disturbance to the waterfowl. The planting was fully re-established within one year and birds resumed nesting on the roof. A maintenance fund has been established for future repairs or replacements.

Prairies in nature are maintained in part by fire, usually from lightning strikes that occur during summer months when the prairie grasses are dry. The fires effectively remove excess thatch, encourage the germination of seeds and tillering from existing plants in the fall or the following spring, while also killing off many species that are not adapted to fire. Fire is used for the same purpose on the green roofs. The fire department expressed some concern about the areas immediately adjacent to windows of the building, so no tall prairie grasses were planted there. The fires were set in calm weather, with ready access to water. Not much smoke was generated. It was what observers called a "cool" fire, without intense heat or destructive power. The prairie responded positively, as anticipated. The process will be repeated every five to seven years, with different areas of the green roofs scheduled for a burn at different times.

The $11-million wetland Interpretive Centre at Oak Hammock Marsh opened in May, 1993; that year 100,000 visitors toured the site. The next year 180,000 people visited. The project became, in one sense, a victim of its own success. There were so many visitors that a few green roof areas were removed and replaced with pavers, to accommodate more visitor observation areas on the upper roof.

On October 1, 2005, the *Winnipeg Free Press* reported that the Center was "welcoming about 500,000 birds daily in their seasonal migration south. Visitors eager to check out swooping geese and splashing pelicans can visit Oak Hammock Marsh Interpretive Centre to check out the wildlife." The center's Web site is www.ohmic.ca. The sounds alone of the many birds create a remarkable din, echoing over the vast landscape. This remarkable facility, which has created waterfowl habitat accessible to the public, will continue to draw those wanting to explore the natural world.

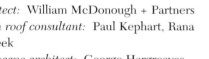

5-50. Aerial view of GAP Inc. shows the entrance to the building and the sweeping curves of the green roofs. (Courtesy of Mark Lutringer)

5-51. Large trees were planted in the foreground of one side of the GAP Inc. building and give a nice contrast to the curving geometry of the green roofs. (Courtesy of Mark Lutringer)

5-52. From an interior lounge, visitors and staff have a refreshing view of the constantly changing patterns of the green roof. (Courtesy of Mark Lutringer)

Gap Headquarters, San Bruno, CA

DESIGN TEAM

Architect: William McDonough + Partners

Green roof consultant: Paul Kephart, Rana Creek

Landscape architect: George Hargreaves

Structural/mechanical engineer: Ove Arup

Context and concept

In 1994 Gap Inc., the developer of Banana Republic, Old Navy, and Gap clothing stores, realized that its various leased headquarters buildings were filled to near capacity. The company decided to develop and build a 12-acre (4.9 ha) site adjacent to other company offices. Because this was the first time that the company had developed its own real estate, despite its thousands of stores and support facilities on leased land, a major design statement reflecting the values and ideals of its employees was developed. Gap Inc. has always emphasized its commitment to maintaining a high-quality environment for its employees.[19]

The site selected in San Bruno is only a few miles from the San Francisco International Airport, yet it includes a landscape of rolling hills with scattered clumps of oaks and fields of scrub sage and grass, all disappearing under the tide of development. Also present were eucalyptus trees and other non-native vegetation, as

5-53. A view of the green roof at Gap Inc. The landscape has evolved gracefully. (Courtesy of Rana Creek)

5-54. In this view of the green roof at Gap Inc., the individual prairie plants, with all their varying texture and color, can be appreciated. (Courtesy of Rana Creek)

well as a grove of mature live oaks, one of the few remaining in the area, which was preserved. The company held a design competition and selected William McDonough + Partners, of Charlottesville, Virginia, as design team leader. The green roof consultant, Paul Kephart, brought an expertise in California Mediterranean plants and ecosystems. Large

areas of California and the West Coast have a climate similar to what one might encounter in coastal areas of Italy, Greece, Spain, or Africa.

The design team sought ways to blend the building with its site while also providing comfortable working space for employees. William McDonough said, "We believe that people want to feel like they've spent the day outdoors in a beautiful place, so we designed a building full of daylight and fresh air to invigorate the mind, body, and spirit."[20] The design of this complex project took place from 1994 to 1996; construction was completed in 1997. The two-story glass, steel, and reinforced concrete building accommodates a grade change, helping to absorb underground parking for more than five hundred cars.[21] The architects designed a fitness center with a swimming pool in addition to a range of other amenities for employees—a café, a commons area developed around the grove of oak trees, and a private, outdoor plaza.

Layout

The architect's concept for the building was to have a completed site in which, "from a bird's perspective, nothing's changed"—as if the entire native landscape had been miraculously lifted up and the building placed underneath it.[22] The savanna ecosystem was to be transported to the roof. The completed building is almost 200,000 square feet (18,580 m²) and consists of three connected bays of offices and work stations built around a two-story landscape atrium. The green roof sweeps over the building's outline in a series of smooth, undulating forms.

Green roof

Originally, the green roof was conceived of as a rolling surface of native sedum, including gardens and paths accessible to employees. As the design evolved, it became an extensive green roof of native grasses, reflecting the foothills. beyond the Gap site. Aesthetically, it has the quality of a Japanese *shakkei*, or borrowed scenery garden, in which distant landscapes, such as the foothills, are brought closer to the site by being recalled in the new design.

The fire department needed assurance that the roof would not become a fire hazard (fireworks are legal in San Bruno, and there was concern that a stray rocket might ignite dry plantings in mid summer, for example, at a Fourth of July celebration).[23] It was agreed that a series of openings on the roof for access, with small compartments for storing fire hoses, would be provided. An irrigation system was also included to facilitate the planting and to maintain moisture during extremely dry periods.

The green roof system (Hydrotech) includes a monolithic membrane which was fluid-applied and flexible. It fully adheres to the deck and has no seams, thereby minimizing leaks, and is also resistant to most fertilizers and acids.

Natural soil was used, gathered from the surrounding site and sterilized. The installation is an extensive green roof with a depth of approximately 6 inches (15.2 cm).

Other features

The building includes many features that make it a comfortable work environment. The windows actually open, and a simple exhaust system draws out oxygen-depleted air and other pollutants and supplies a continuous flow of fresh air that is pulled across the concrete base of the building which heats up during the day and prevents the air from becoming too cool. Another benefit of this system is that the floor plenum is in direct contact with the concrete floor deck, which is cooled with night air. The deck then provides a cooling effect on the air circulating throughout the building during the day, thereby reducing air conditioning loads. The atrium bays admit a generous amount of daylight, and the layout of offices and work stations is designed so no one sits more than 30 feet (9.1 m) from a perimeter window or atrium.[24]

Energy-saving features abound. Sensors adjust the intensity of interior lighting to compensate for the dimming outdoor light and automatically turn off lights when rooms are not occupied. Windows are coated with a heat-blocking agent and are double paned to keep the building cooler in summer and warmer in winter.

Planting and irrigation

Twelve species, selected by Paul Kephart and the design team for their variety of texture, color, and adaptability, were planted. They later added a few native grasses found growing in the nearby San Bruno foothills.[25]

Irrigation occurred periodically, but not excessively. Mowing was also carried out, because of concerns about fire.

Post-planting and maintenance

In 2004, almost all the plantings on the green roof died due to moisture insufficiencies associated with a malfunction in the irrigation system. Even though many of the species were adaptable to long periods of drought, many died in

---

GAP HEADQUARTERS PLANT LIST

Agrostis densiflora	California bent grass
Carex texensis	Texas sedge
Castilleja exserta v. exerta	Purple owl clover
Castilleja mutis	Indian paintbrush
Deschampsia holciformus	Pacific hair grass
Eriophyllum lanatum	Wooly sunflower or Oregon Sunshine
Eschschlotzia californica	Golden poppy
Festuca rubra	Red fescue
Festuca idahoensis	Idaho fescue
Layia platyglosa	Tidytips
Lupinus nanus	Dwarf lupin or sky lupine
Nassella cernua	Nodding needlegrass
Nassella pulchra	Purple needlegrass
Sidalcea malveflora	Checkerbloom
Sisyrinchium bellum	Blue-eyed grass

these extreme conditions. Paul Kephart direct-ed the replanting.[26] He reported to the design team that, from a biological diversity and regenerative standpoint, the roof had thirty-two more species than in the original planting mix. About two summers ago there had been a heat wave, and these additional materials were adapting to those conditions, which were made more extreme by the irrigation malfunction. Just as the California climate changed to a more drastically arid one, the plants that grew on the green roof began to reflect this. However, since the original grassy meadow had been so successful, Gap Inc. wanted the original plant material re-planted. It turned out that the amount of damage was overstated, because once there was a watering, a great deal of the plant material regenerated. There was some overseeding, but a complete restoration occurred within one growing season.

Today, the planting reflects the change in the seasons—that is, it is not always green—and continues to evolve. What is remarkable about this green roof, compared to traditional plant-ings, is that it continues to function environ-mentally—that is, it reduces the volume of storm water run-off, and provides insulation against noise and heat—while its precise make-up and the proportions of various species change from season to season or year to year. The employees have the pleasure of seeing a prairie evolving on their very roof.

As the first building of its kind in the United States, Gap Inc. has found over the years that it is not only important to construct a green build-ing, but it is just as important to operate it in a manner that minimizes its environmental impact. It is essential to have an educated oper-ations staff that understands and maintains the design intent of the building and its control sys-tems. The building staff and occupants also play a role, as they are encouraged by management to reduce waste and conserve energy whenever possible. Through the creation of a design with a well-trained operations staff and dedicated employees, Gap Inc. has achieved its goal of pro-viding a building that inspires growth and cre-ativity.

Peggy Notebaert Nature Museum, Chicago, IL

DESIGN TEAM
Conservation Design Forum (CDF), Elmhurst, Illinois, David Yocca, principal; Bruce Dvorak, project manager
Architect: Perkins and Will, Ralph Johnson
Structural Engineer: C.E. Anderson
Green Roof Planting: Valleycrest Contractors
Green Roof Materials and Construction: Roofscapes, Inc.
Peggy Notebaert Nature Museum: Stephen Bell, Director, Laurene van Klan, new presi-dent and CEO

Context and concept
The Peggy Notebaert Nature Museum, which opened in 1999, is the public face of the Chica-go Academy of Sciences.[27] The Academy, the city's first museum, was founded in 1857, and opened to the public in 1865, as the home for the collections of papers and specimens from prairie, wetlands, woodlands, and other ecosys-tems that were disappearing as a result of agri-cultural activities and settlement. Today, these collections contain about 250,000 specimens and include extinct species (such as the passenger pigeon, the Carolina parakeet, and the ivory billed woodpecker). After the Great Fire of 1871 destroyed the museum, specimens from all over the world were sent to be housed in a new muse-um located in Lincoln Park, near the city's zoo. In the 1980s the academy began training pro-grams for Chicago public school teachers and students. As public interest grew, the board wanted a facility that would help it embrace nature, and it chose a new building on another site by the North Pond in Lincoln Park. In 1999, the Peggy Notebaert Nature Museum, designed by architect Ralph Johnson of Perkins and Will, opened as the new public face for the academy at the corner of Fullerton Parkway and Cannon Drive. The modernist, interconnected structures of the museum (inspired by the wings of a but-terfly) are marked with striking roof lines and face toward different areas of the site.

Features of the museum tie into the theme of a living building, in which all the exhibits relate to the ecology of the Midwest and the specific challenges of creating and protecting the environment within a large urban area. The

major exhibits include a butterfly garden (where as many as 250 species can be observed), river works, a wetlands exhibit, and a science teaching lab where groups of students may conduct experiments. A restored prairie landscape and other native landscape features can be found on the museum grounds. There are also interpretive displays and walks around the perimeter of the pond, as well as occasional sculptures.

The academy's mission is "to inspire people to learn about and care for nature and the environment," with a focus on the Midwest, particularly its prairies and other unique landscapes. The directors of the museum sought ways to embrace Mayor Daley's greening initiatives for the city and hired Conservation Design Forum (CDF), an interdisciplinary firm specializing in the creative integration of environmentally and culturally sustainable land planning, design, and development initiatives based in Elmhurst, Illinois, as a consultant. Together with the board of the museum, CDF helped to design and implement an ambitious program called "Greening of the Nature Museum."[28]

The initial phases identified in the master plan for immediate implementation included four different elements: green roofs, a south wall garden, a sculptural tree trellis, and vines on walls. Green roof systems were proposed to cover four existing roof sections over different parts of the museum complex—virtually all of the building's roof space except for an area

devoted to a solar array. The initial portion of green roof was proposed to be a demonstration garden that would be easily accessible to the public and viewable from other areas of the museum. Even though the Nature Museum was a relatively new building, the demonstration green roof, which opened in 2002, was a retrofit, added in response to the green mission. Although the design team had to work with the limitations of the structure, the demonstration green roof is an imaginative series of gardens of great diversity. Subsequent green roofs were installed on much larger roof areas on the wings of the building and two small areas over entrances. The blank south wall facing Fullerton Avenue was proposed to be resurfaced with a "living wall," evocative of cliff habitats native to the region, in which dolomitic limestone is exposed, weathered, and gradually vegetated. The area at the base of this wall was envisioned as a small gathering space immersed in a wetland garden. A tree trellis and vines were intended to cloak the museum with vegetation when viewed from almost any direction.

The museum boasts no less than 17,000 square feet (1,579.3 m²) of rooftop gardens, extensive water conservation systems, solar rooftop panels, exhibits, and amenities constructed of recycled and renewable materials, and more. These facilities include elevated walks for the observation of birds and trees and access to the green roof.

The initial demonstration green roof, cover-

entrance, but only maintenance workers and scientists on special projects may enter.

Green roof

Each room of the demonstration green roof has a different depth of growing medium, a different level of moisture retention, and a different planting palette. Starting at the south end, the first space has 2–5 inches (5.1–12.7 cm) of growing medium over 4 inches (10.2 cm) of gravel; the second 5–6 inches (12.7–15.2 cm) of growing medium over 2 inches (5.1 cm) of gravel; the third has 6–8 inches (15.2–20.3 cm) of growing medium over 2 inches (5.1 cm) of gravel; and the final one at the north end has 8 inches (20.3 cm) of growing medium over 2–10 inches (5.1–25.4 cm) of gravel. From the south end to the north, therefore, there are four types of green roof systems: a wetland, an extensive green roof, a semi-intensive green roof, and an intensive green roof. Within the first extensive garden is a small pool with a water depth of 4 inches (10.2 cm), so that only the top 2.5 inches (6.4 cm) is unsaturated. Aquatic plants and water-loving prairie plants are planted here. The varying depth of cover of growing medium and gravel reflects the change in the maximum additional dead load permitted on the existing roof. At the southern end of the roof, the additional dead load was found to be 40 pounds per square foot (195.3 kg/m^2), and at the northern end, where the overlay is deeper, the additional dead load is 90 pounds per square foot (439.4 kg/m^2).

The growing medium for the demonstration green roof is primarily perlite, with some organic material added. The waterproofing of the original building was peeled off. The green roof system is an Optima system (Roofscapes) on top of a 60-mil (0.06 inches or 1.5 mm)-thick waterproofing system (Sarnafill) with root barrier, moisture management fabric, gravel drainage with edging against the parapet, and a biodegradable blanket to protect against wind-blown erosion.

In 2004, the much larger and more simply-designed southeast and northwest green roofs were installed and placed over the existing waterproofing of the building. The lower one, on the northwest wing of the building, is 8,700 square feet (808.2 m^2), visible from the second story catwalk, and accessible from the demonstration garden via a ladder. The upper green

5-56. At the Peggy Notebaert Nature Museum's demonstration green roof, diagonal walks separate different types of green roof plantings and also make the garden seem larger.

ing 2,400 square feet (223 m^2) in a long narrow rectilinear shape 12 feet (3.65 m) wide by 200 feet (61.0 m) long, appears much larger because a zigzagging pattern of parallel diagonal walks cuts across the geometry, which subdivides the space into four rooms or compartments. Fortunately, because it is visible from other areas of the museum, the green roof remains a focal point. Visitors can peer into it from several vantage points including the gate at the south

roof, on the southeast wing, is 5,900 square feet (548.1 m²), less accessible, and not visible to museum visitors (Fig. 5-59). Neither of these green roofs has guardrails, but supervised groups of as many as twenty students and scientists may visit. There are also two smaller green roofs, each about 350 square feet (32.5 m²) over two separate entrances (Fig. 5-60). These four extensive green roofs (Sarnafill) have a growing medium 3 inches (7.6 cm) deep and a slight amount of pitch, at 4 degrees. One of the small green roofs facing south over the ravine is planted in cacti, as there is no irrigation and the solar exposure is intense, while the other three green roofs are planted in sedums. There is manual irrigation only, which was useful during the drought conditions of the summer of 2005.

The demonstration green roof has one solar panel that provides enough electricity to power a small pump. It circulates enough water in the wetland pool to prevent stagnation and algae growth. It also fills the pool during periods when there is water loss due to evaporation.

Other features

Effective interpretive displays that emphasize the advantages of green roofs are placed within the museum and by the entry point to the demonstration green roof at the elevated walk. An overhead camera with connections to the museum allows visitors inside the museum to go on a virtual tour of the green roof.

The living wall or cliff garden was implemented as a cliff with built-in pockets for planting, with a series of ledges that push back into the landscape at the base (Fig. 5-61). The design makes it seem as though the wall emerges seamlessly from the landscape and blurs the edges of the building. The overhead green roof panel overflows onto the wall, and the water not absorbed by the green roof slowly trickles down the stone, mimicking natural seepage and replicating the natural hydrological system that would normally cycle water to cliff plantings. This water provides moisture to some of the planting pockets set within niches of the wall, and is augmented with a drip irrigation system using surplus rainwater harvested from the green roof, stored in a cistern below the roof. There is a small wetland garden at grade at the base of the wall which provides a natural setting for a stone seating area.

The wetland is kept constant with the stored rainwater.

There is an array of photovoltaic panels on the northeast roof (not a green roof), which provides some electricity for the building's operation. These were not incorporated into one of the green roofs because funding was awarded through separate grants.

Planting and irrigation

This discussion focuses on the demonstration roof garden, since it is far more complex than the later extensive green roofs. For a small garden, the wealth of plant materials is remarkable. The plant list on page 190 is subdivided into three categories: extensive, intensive, and wetland. On the semi-intensive roof, plants are

5-57. The demonstration green roof at the Peggy Notebaert Nature Museum is nestled among the angular geometric forms of the steel and glass building.

5-58. An educational display is posted at the entrance to the demonstration green roof, which is only open to the public during guided tours.

PEGGY NOTEBAERT NATURE MUSEUM PLANT LIST

EXTENSIVE[29]

Achillea millefolium 'Heidi'	Heidi yarrow
Achillea 'Schwellenburg'	Schwellenburg yarrow
Allium canadense	Wild onion
Allium cernuum	Nodding wild onion
Amorpha canescens	Leadplant
Andropogon scoparius	Little bluestem
Anemone patens wolfgangiana	Pasque flower
Aquilegia canadensis	American columbine
Asclepias tuberosa	Butterfly weed
Asclepias verticillata	Whorled milkweed
Aster azureus	Sky blue aster
Aster laevis	Smooth blue aster
Aster ptarmicoides	Upland white aster
Aster sericeus	Silky aster
Baptisia leucophaea	Cream wild indigo
Bouteloua curtipendula	Side oats gramma
Buchloe dactyloides	Buffalo grass
Campanula rotundifolia	Harebell
Carex bicknellii	Bicknell's sedge
Coreopsis palmata	Prairie coreopsis
Danthonia spicata	Poverty oat grass
Dianthus allwoodii	Helen carnation
Dianthus gratianopolitanus	Spotty carnation
Dodecatheon meadii	Shooting star
Geum triflorum	Prairie smoke
Helianthus mollis	Downy sunflower
Helianthus occidentalis	Western sunflower
Heuchera richardsonii	Prairie alum root
Koeleria cristata	June grass
Lavandula angustifolia 'Hidcote'	Hidcote lavender
Liatris aspera	Rough blazing star
Petalostemum candidum	White prairie clover
Petalostemum purpureum	Purple prairie clover
Phlox bifida	Sand phlox
Phlox pilosa	Downy phlox
Sedum acre	Goldmoss stonecrop
Sedum album	White stonecrop
Sedum kamtschaticum	Orange stonecrop
Sedum 'Mochren'	Mochren stonecrop
Sedum spurium	Two-row stonecrop
Sedum 'Vera Jameson'	Vera Jameson stonecrop
Sempervivium arachnoideum	Hens and chicks
Solidago speciosa	Showy goldenrod
Sporbollus heterolepis	Prairie dropseed
Stachys byzantina	Large-leafed Helene von Stein Lamb's ear
Thymus serphllus	Creeping thyme

INTENSIVE

Aster sagitarius drumondii	Drummond's aster
Blephilia ciliate	Ohio horse mint or downy wood mint
Carex gravida	Common sedge
Carex pennsylvanica	Pennsylvania sedge
Echinacea purpurea	Purple coneflower
Elymus villosus	Silky wild rye
Geranium sanguineum 'Max Frei'	Max Frei cranesbill
Geranium sanguineum var. striatum	Bloodred cranesbill
Hemerocallis 'Little Wine Cup'	Little Wine Cup daylily
Hystrix patula	Bottlebrush grass
Parthenium integrifolium	Wild quinine (also extensive)
Penstemon pallidus	Pale bear tongue
Quercus imbricaria	Shingle oak
Polemonium reptans	Jacob's ladder
Rhus aromatica 'Gro-low'	Gro-low sumac (shrub)
Smilacina racemosa	False Solomon's seal
Solidago flexicaulis	Broad-leaved goldenrod
Tradescantia ohiensis	Common spiderwort

WETLAND

Acorus calamus	Sweet flag
Alisma subcordatum	Common water plantain
Asclepias incarnata	Swamp milkweed
Caltha palustris	Marsh marigold
Carex cristatella	Crested oval sedge
Carex lacustris	Common lake sedge
Equisetum arvense	Horsetail
Eupatorium maculatum	Joe Pye weed
Helenium autumnale	Autumn sneezeweed
Iris virginica shrevei	Blue flag iris
Juncus dudleyi	Dudley's rush
Juncus effuses	Common rush
Juncus torreyi	Torry's rush
Lobelia cardinalis	Cardinal flower
Lobelia siphilitica	Great blue lobelia
Panicum virgatum	Switch grass
Pontedaria cordata	Pickerel weed
Sagittaria latifolia	Common arrowhead
Scirpus atroveriens	Dark green rush
Scutellaria epilobiifolia	Marsh skullcap
Solidago riddellii	Riddell's goldenrod
Sparganium eurycarpum	Bur reed
Spartina petinata	Prairie cordgrass
Spiraea alba	Meadowsweet
Verbena hastata	Blue verbena
Vemonia fasciculata	Ironweed
Veronicastrum virginicum	Culver's root
Zizia aurea	Golden Alexanders

VINES

Celastrus scandens	American bittersweet (vine)
Clematis virginiana	Virgin's blower (vine)

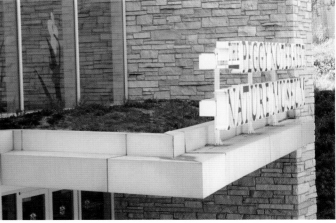

Top and above right:
5-59, 5-60. Two of the three green roofs at the Peggy Notebaert Nature Museum, the large one with the backdrop of the city skyline, and the other a small overhang at an entrance. (Courtesy of Conversation Design Forum)

5-61. At the Peggy Notebaert Nature Museum, water from a scupper draining one of the green roofs seeps down the face of a cliff garden. (Courtesy of Conservation Design Forum)

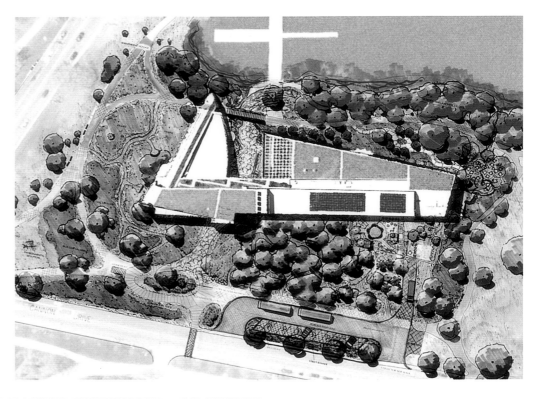

5-62. An illustrative plan of the design for the entire site of the Peggy Notebaert Nature Museum. Piers jut out into the pond, vegetation wraps around the building, and the narrow demonstration green roof is in the center with the large extensive green roofs on either end. (Courtesy of Conservation Design Forum)

5-63. This as-built aerial photograph shows how closely the greening of the museum followed the conceptual plan. (Courtesy of Conservation Design Forum)

used both from the extensive and intensive lists. Except for a few vines, shrubs, and one tree, all plants were 2-inch (5.1 cm) plugs. The single oak tree in the northernmost intensive garden is planted over a structural support beam in the building below. The planting was completed in the summer of 2002. A drip irrigation system is used as needed. It is drained at the end of the fall, and the system is restarted in the spring after last frost.

Post-planting and maintenance

Since its completion in 2002, maintenance on the demonstration green roof has consisted of removal of old plant growth from all of the perennials, and occasional pruning of the shrubs and the oak. It is expected that the oak, 5 to 6 feet (1.5 to 1.8 m) tall when planted, will grow only to a limited height because the depth of the growing medium is limited. The larger sedum green roofs have manual irrigation used for periods of drought, but there is no regular automatic irrigation.

The museum was awarded a grant from the Illinois Environmental Protection Agency to monitor storm water and other factors on the demonstration green roof, namely: storm water runoff; storm water runoff reduction; water quality; precipitation; and particulate matter on different depths of growing media and gravel. The control system for the study will be one of the remaining conventional roofs of the museum.[30] Measurements over several years show that the green roofs delay peak flow by as much as an hour following substantial rainfall.

DESIGN TEAM

Architect: Roger Schickedantz, Roger McDonough + Partners

Ford representatives: Roger Gaudette and Donald Russell

Michigan State University Department of Crop and Soil Sciences: Dr. Brad Rowe, Dr. Clayton Rugh, Mike Monterusso (research on plants and media)

University of Oklahoma: Reid Coffman, Professor of Landscape Architecture, and Graham David, researcher, insect studies

Context and concept[31]

In 1915, the Ford Motor Company acquired the 1,100-acre (445.2 ha) River Rouge site in Dearborn, Michigan, a short distance from the original Model T factory in Highland Park. Henry Ford's goal was to produce everything at one site, thereby minimizing shipping of materials and components from other sources. Decades later a unique brownfield property remained— but what could be done with it? In 1999, Bill Ford, Jr. pledged to convert the property into a model of a sustainable manufacturing center. A design team was assembled with the aim of "reestablishing habitat, greening the site, preserving buildings with historic importance, cleaning impacted soil using phytoremediation and managing storm water discharges."

Because so much of the site was paved, with few outlets for runoff water and few natural areas, the architect suggested topping the new truck assembly plant proposed for the site renovation program with a green roof. The scale and scope of the project were significant—10.4 acres (4.2 ha) of green roof.

The design team first experimented with

5-64. Workmen place sedum mats on the roof of the River Rouge Ford plant in June 2002. (Courtesy of Ford Motor Co.)

5-65. An aerial view of the River Rouge Ford plant's large green roof. (Courtesy of Ford Motor Co.)

and houseleek. Expanded slate was determined to be the preferred choice for growing medium; the superabsorbent polymers were to be used sparingly, because they competed with other materials for moisture instead of making it available to the plants.

The trays had shortcomings: the projected weight of a tray with mature sedum plants in expanded slate would be 19 pounds per square foot (92.8 kg/m²). Since each tray was approximately 9 square feet (0.8 m²), the weight of a full tray would be at least 171 pounds (77.6 kg), difficult to maneuver onto a roof. Furthermore, the polystyrene material of the trays deteriorated after only one year of exposure to ultraviolet radiation. Therefore, the modular tray approach was abandoned.

Next the team evaluated established, commercially available green roof systems. Drainage systems by American Hydrotech, Sarnafil, Siplast, and Xero Flor were installed on twelve platforms and different blends of growth medium were evaluated: heat-expanded slate, sand, compost, and peat moss. The platforms were set at a 2 percent slope, and runoff was collected in aluminum troughs at the low end. Sedum plugs, native plugs, and sedum seeds were all tested. The percentage of rainfall retained by the different systems was found to vary from 39 percent (Xero Flor) to 58 percent (Siplast). The depth of the Xero Flor system was only .78 inches (2 cm), whereas the Siplast system was 3.93 inches (10 cm) deep. Sedum growing in the shallower substrate tended to crowd out weeds or other plants and retained over twice as much rainwater as a conventional roof system would, so the Xero Flor system, with sedums as the plant material, was selected.

Layout

Using a 15-acre (6.1 ha) site a few miles from the River Rouge plant, in May 2002 the design team established a farm for growing a sedum blanket to apply to the roof of the new building. It consisted of a layer of plastic placed over freshly graded and contoured ground, covered by a thin layer of fleece with a material of plastic coils holding the substrate, which was applied by a mechanical spreader. Russell explains, "The water retention fleece is a fabric material produced from a blend of recycled, synthetic fibers with a saturated weight of not

5-66, 5-67. Two views of different areas of the green roof at the River Rouge Ford plant. (Courtesy of Ford Motor Co.)

modular systems because it seemed an advantage to fully establish plant growth at the ground level before moving the system to the roof. Starting in 2000, sixty-four modular trays were filled with varying depths of four types of substrate: rice hull ash, coco-peat, expanded slate, and standard topsoil as a control. A 1-inch-thick (2.54 cm) blanket of superabsorbent polymer was added to absorb water. Twelve species of plants were evaluated, including *Buchloe dactyloides* (buffalo grass), *Linaria purpurea* (purple toadflax), *Mentha spicata* 'crispa' (crisp mint), and *Petalostemum purpureum* (purple prairie clover). Later some sedums were included, from plugs as well as seeds, such as *Sedum spurium* 'coccinuem,' *Sedum kamtschaticum*,

more than 1.5 pounds per square foot. (7.3 kg/m^2). It serves as a water reservoir for the vegetation. The coils, facing downward, are part of a product which serves as a drainage layer. The same material, with the coils facing up, acts as the base for the vegetation blanket. The drainage mat is a lightweight, flexible composite material made up of a drainage core of looped polyamide filaments bonded to a specially perforated nonwoven filter fabric" (Figs. 5-69, 5-70, and 5-71). A mixture of sedum seeds was shipped from Germany (the origin of all the green roof layers); sedum cuttings came from Michigan nurseries. A water-permeable shade cloth covered the entire field for several weeks until the plants started to become established. The field was watered daily and fertilized as needed.

After one major weeding in midsummer, the sedum mats began to fill in rapidly. A target area of 70 percent coverage had been preset as the minimum necessary before harvesting the blanket. By late August the available material was sawed into into 3.3 by 3.3 foot (1 x 1 m)

sedum squares, which were stacked on pallets and transported to the new assembly building.

Green roof

Three layers of materials were installed on the roof before the sedum vegetative mats were applied. Part of the original roof installation was

RIVER ROUGE FORD PLANT LIST	
Sedum acre	Gold moss stonecrop
Sedum album	White stonecrop
Sedum floriferum	Gold stonecrop
Sedum kamtschaticum	Russian or orange stonecrop
Sedum kamtschaticum ellacombianum	Stonecrop
Sedum kamtschaticum sp kamtschaticum	Stonecrop
Sedum middendorffianum diffusum	Diffusum stonecrop
Sedum pulchellum	Lime stonecrop, widowscross
Sedum reflexum	Blue stonecrop
Sedum spurium 'Coccineum'	Coccineum two-row stonecrop
Sedum spurium 'Fulda Glow'	Fulda's glow stonecrop
Sedum spurium 'Superbum'	Superbum stonecrop
Sedum telephium	Purple stonecrop

5-68. A bioswale, part of the other sustainable design features implemented on the River Rouge Ford site. (Courtesy of Ford Motor Co.)

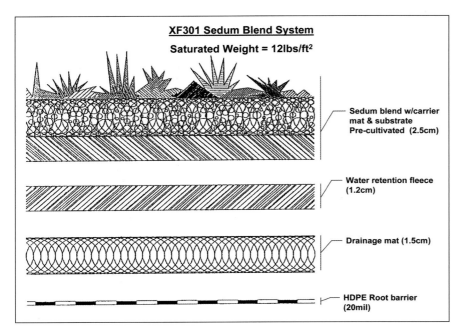

XF301 Sedum Blend System
Saturated Weight = 12lbs/ft²

Sedum blend w/carrier mat & substrate Pre-cultivated (2.5cm)

Water retention fleece (1.2cm)

Drainage mat (1.5cm)

HDPE Root barrier (20mil)

a modified bitumen moisture-resistant membrane (Siplast). A root-impermeable membrane was placed over it; then, a drainage layer (Xero Flor) was applied, followed by a layer of water-absorbing fleece. In September sedum vegetative mats were placed on top of the fleece. The growing medium was a mixture of heat-expanded slate, sand, compost, and dolomite.

Other features

Additional aspects of the greening plant were implemented, such as a greenbelt parkway, natural water-treatment wetlands, vegetated drainage swales (Fig. 5-68) and wildlife habitat. Extensive arrays of photovoltaic panels, on the roof of the new visitor center, provide supplemental electricity. Solar collectors on the ground heat water for the building.

Planting and irrigation

The sedum vegetative mats consist of a mixture of thirteen sedum species (list on page 195).

An irrigation system was installed over the whole roof. A slow-release, palletized fertilizer is applied once a year at the beginning of the growing season.

As this large green roof has become established, it has also become the subject of numerous studies and has drawn the attention of many visitors. Reid Coffman, a professor of landscape architecture at the University of Oklahoma, and Graham David, a researcher with a background in entomology and insect taxonomy, initiated a single-season survey of the insect and avian fauna of the green roof at the River Rouge plant in 2004. They identified and recorded twenty-nine insect species, seven spider species, and two bird species in a 2-acre (0.8 ha) area. The birds, nine *Contopus cooperi* (the olive-sided fly catcher) and one *Charadrius vociferous* (killdeer), in combination with almost nine hundred specimens of insects and spiders, suggest that a community of fauna is becoming established on the roof.[32]

5-69, 5-70, 5-71. A cross section through the River Rouge Ford green roof showing its components; a close-up photo showing the same components as installed; and an overview of colorful sedums. (Courtesy of Xero Flor America)

DESIGN TEAM

Landscape architect: Eric Shriner, Pivot
  Architects

Nashville Cultural Arts Project: Helen Nagge
  and Mel Chin

Owners: Stephen McRedmond and Anita
  Sheridan

Roofing contractor: Houston Herbert, R. D.
  Herbert & Sons

Horticulturalist and landscape contractor:
  Mike Berkeley and Terri Barnes, Gro Wild

Structural engineer: Robert Whitaker, Ross
  Bryan Associates

Context and concept

The Neuhoff meat processing plant is located
in an area of Nashville known as Old German-
town, historically an ethnically diverse neighborhood.[33] Currently it is rapidly revitalizing
after years of use and abandonment as a light
manufacturing and industrial area. Owned by
the McRedmond family, the Neuhoff plant
became the centerpiece for a wide-ranging
effort in community development. Stephen
McRedmond and his sister Anita Sheridan
sought to redevelop it as a mixed-use entity
through a nonprofit organization they encouraged to use space in one of the buildings. The
Nashville Cultural Arts Project (NCAP) began
to hold a series of lectures on innovations in the
fine arts, design, and ecology there. Altogether
there are seven brick masonry buildings
encompassing 700,000 square feet (65,032 m²)
on 14 acres (5.7 ha); there are only three major
buildings, but they include some unusual elements. The building selected for the green roof
is two stories high and triangular in shape. A
giant smokestack towers over the whole complex.[34]

Landscape architect Eric Shriner and Mel
Chin, an installation artist and one of the
founders of NCAP, came up with the idea of creating a demonstration project that would use
architectural redevelopment as a tool for ecolog-

5-72. An existing cedar glade landscape in rural
Tennessee, a site threatened by development
pressures. (Courtesy of Eric Shriner)

5-73. The Neuhoff green roof soon after planting.
(Courtesy of Eric Shriner)

5-74. The Neuhoff green roof after the vegetation has become well-established. Other industrial buildings on the site can be seen in the background. (Courtesy of Eric Shriner)

5-75. Close-up of the Neuhoff green roof with well-established vegetation. (Courtesy of Eric Shriner)

ical conservation.[35] They sought to use plant materials from the cedar glade, an endangered plant community native to the hills of Tennessee, on the roof of buildings being redeveloped for a range of uses (Fig. 5-72). The cedar glade community is found only in an area 6 miles (9.7 km) in diameter in Tennessee, which is being increasingly developed for housing and NASCAR (car-racing). The plants are in nutrient-poor, inadequately drained soils that experience periodic inundation followed by stretches of drought. Because these are two conditions that typically occur on a roof, the goal of establishing a cedar glade community on a green roof seemed practical. Eric Shriner took on the role of project manager or coordinator. McRedmond established the NEU Development Corporation as NCAP's profit-making wing and then collaborated with others in seeking funding for more extensive work on other buildings.

Layout

The green roof, enthusiastically embraced by all these different individuals and budding organizations, was a pilot project costing $25 per square foot ($269.00/m²). Because the budget was limited, no design drawings were prepared; instead, everyone worked from an as-built drawing of the existing roof, prepared by the German manufacturer's representative in Virginia, Mike Perry of Building Logics. The scope of work involved tearing off the old roof and installing a new roof with insulation and planting; Shriner coordinated.

Green roof

With the plan of the existing roof in hand, Eric Shriner proceeded to schedule all of the necessary functions. The existing drainage on the roof, a fairly simple system, was retained and no additional drains were added. The team settled on the simplest planting system they researched (FAMOS) because it had no drainage mat. Gro Wild, a nursery that grew native plants, had direct experience with landscape restoration, and was enthusiastic about the project.

Robert Whitaker, the structural engineer from Ross Bryan Associates, determined that the original concrete deck consisted of reinforced concrete 7 inches (17.8 cm) thick with #4 rebars (steel reinforcing bars 1/2 inch or 1.3 cm in diameter) set 12 inches (30.5 cm) on cen-

ter in both directions. He estimated that the roof could support as much as 80 pounds per square foot (390.6 kg/m²). It was estimated that the proposed green roof system, including the planting medium and plants and all components, would weigh only about 18 pounds per square foot (87.9 k/m²). Although a thicker growing medium than the agreed-on 5-inch (12.7 cm) depth could have been considered, it was felt that the additional material would increase the cost to a financially unfeasible point. Similarly, the specified size and type of plant materials could also have been larger, but the design team went with the green roof industry standard of bare root materials, plugs, and small pots.

The installation occurred in two phases: repair of the parapet walls and existing roof and the installation of the base layers of waterproofing and insulation in June 2002, and the green roof installation, the following October. After initial repairs, a conventional roofing base was installed: a vapor barrier (Famobit P-3), a 2-inch (5.1 cm) thick isocyanurate (R13), a .75-inch (1.9 cm) thick layer of perlite insulation (R3) and a waterproof membrane (Famobil P-4). Although originally all construction was to occur in sequence, the gap between the first and second phases allowed time to verify that the new roof was functioning well, with no leaks. In October it took four days to install the roof membrane (Famogreen Ret-CUP4), which consists of a modified bitumen with a copper foil root barrier sandwiched inside. To absorb water and provide protection against drought, hydrogel crystals adhere to the surface of a polyester fabric that forms the top layer of the membrane.

The growing medium is fairly high in organic materials, which might be expected to cause problems. It consists of 40 percent pine bark, 30 percent peat moss, 15 percent perlite, and 15 percent vermiculite, mixed at the site and applied in a uniform layer 5 inches (12.7 cm) thick.[36]

Other features

As part of a complex of buildings that will include public organizations, the green roof has been adopted by several organizations, including representatives from the World Wildlife Fund and the Consortium for Living Watersheds, a nonprofit organization focusing on watershed issues, because a building's roof is a watershed in microcosm. Additional affiliations were formed with the Cumberland River Compact, the National Environmental Protection Administration, and the Tennessee Valley Authority. The Consortium for Living Watersheds eventually hopes to connect educational exhibits about the green roof to an access way to the nearby Cumberland River, where a museum, called the Center for Watershed Research, will be housed in a barge permanently moored in place. The barge will have its own green roof and incorporate features to recirculate water from the green roof to the building. Depending on the success of the entire Neuhoff development, additional barges or boats may be brought to the riverside docking area.

A curved building that housed the slaughterhouse will be a mixed-use five-story residential building. The water tower will have a restaurant with views of the entire site and the river. John Prine, the popular country music star, already has a recording studio in another building.

Planting and irrigation

The green roof planting was implemented in October 2002, a good season for planting in the Southeast; the weather cooled off, and many plants became dormant but could still actively establish root systems. Twelve hundred plants from fifteen species were planted in an assortment of 4-inch (10.2 cm) pots, plugs, and some bare root liners. Treatment with a mycorrhizal root growth inoculant was administered to encourage plant growth, nutrient intake, and the growth of organisms beneficial to a new plant community on virgin soil. Finally, because the site was quite exposed, a biodegradable erosion-control mesh fabric was placed over the plantings to act temporarily as a mulch to retain moisture.

At the time installation was finished in 2002, the 2,600-square-foot (241.5 m^2) installation was the only green roof in the region using plants from an endangered plant community. The plantings survived an unusually cold and wet winter, and there was vigorous growth the following spring.

Post-planting and maintenance

The owner is currently doing fairly minimal maintenance; the main goal is to weed out invasive species. However, it is expected that other appropriate species may become established, seeded via birds or wind dispersal, so that the composition of the evolving plant community may change over time. Stephen McRedmond has a 10-acre (4.0 ha) farm in downtown Nashville, with extensive plantings of several species of coneflowers, from which the planting on the roof may be replenished. At the time of writing, the roof was clearly a work in progress.

Shriner reports, "There was an issue with establishment of invasive weeds as well as native broomsedge, and their establishment interfering with the establishment of the nonnatives. The endangered plants we planted are still on the roof, perhaps with some blown-in others. Initial and ongoing weeding became a significant issue for establishing the desired plant palette. We believe the primary reason for this is that the growing medium that we ended up using was higher in organic material than the typical soil associated with the cedar glade plant community. In short, the planting medium is too rich for the endangered plants to outcompete the other plants, requiring weeding to maintain the desired plant palette."[37]

Clean Water Services Field Yard, Beaverton, OR

DESIGN TEAM
Architect: WBGS Architecture & Planning, PC, Eugene, Oregon
Landscape architect: Murase Associates, Dan Jenkins, principal
Civil engineer: URS
General contractor: Skanska USA Building Inc.

Context and concept

The Clean Water Services Field Yard in Beaverton is the agency responsible for storm water and sanitary sewers for twelve cities in Washington County, Oregon.[38] The crews of the Field Operations Division of Clean Water Services maintain a range of sanitary and storm drainage pipe facilities within the 122-square mile (316 km[2]) service area. The agency's leadership sought to have their new field operations headquarters facility demonstrate innovative erosion control and water quality treatment. They preferred a central location within Washington County to reduce the travel time per crew in their large district. The agency serves the greater Portland metropolitan region and is under strict federal guidelines for controlling storm water runoff. (Although the city of Portland is part of the metropolitan region, it is not part of the district served by Washington County; it has its own regional sewer and storm water management bureau.) If the agency's most visited facility could be a model for stormwater runoff reduction, erosion control, and improved water quality, it would offer a significant public education benefit, showing individuals the advantages in tangible terms.

Clean Water Services leased from TRIMET, the regional transportation agency for buses and light rail facilities, a 5-acre (2 ha) site adjacent to a 92-acre (37.2 ha) park, Tualatin Hills Regional Nature Park, in Beaverton, a rapidly growing suburb with considerable urban development. TRIMET wanted to replace its aging fueling facilities and parking for its bus fleet on land immediately adjacent. Clean Water Services agreed to provide storm water measures for both properties including future transit-oriented development in return for use of TRIMET's site for their new facility. A master plan, developed by WBGS Architecture & Planning, PC, and

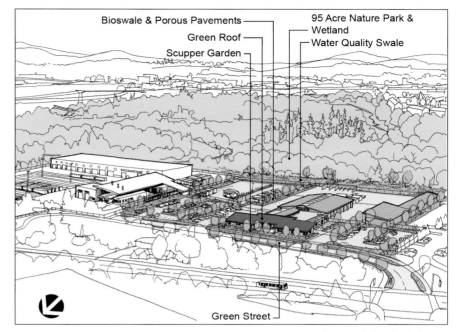

Murase Associates (landscape architects) incorporated new facilities for TRIMET, and new headquarters for Clean Water Services, and resolved water quality issues for the adjacent natural park. All runoff from the Clean Water Services site would eventually drain into the natural park.

As the work focused on the Clean Water Services headquarters, the design team sought to create a showcase—even though the program required large parking areas and storage yards, which would typically generate a lot of storm water runoff. The single-story concrete block and steel building contains administrative offices totaling 18,000 square feet (1,672.2 m[2]), 15,000 square feet (1,393.5 m[2]) of heated, indoor vehicular parking, and 13,000 square feet (1,207.7 m[2]) of unheated outdoor carport parking. Included in the final construction are a green street, landscaped swales, water quality or bioswales, porous pavements, scuppers, native plant materials, and a green roof. Originally, the green roof was intended to cover the entire building, but it was later scaled back to cover 25 percent of the building due to budget restraints. Here the term *ecoroof* is preferred to green roof because the roof is not green all year round and provides many ecological benefits, about which Clear Water Services sought to educate the public.

Layout

A green street forms the entrance road from the

5-76. In this aerial sketch of the complex of buildings at Beaverton, they fit gently into the landscape with the green-roofed administration building visible in the foreground. (Courtesy of PIVOT Architecture)

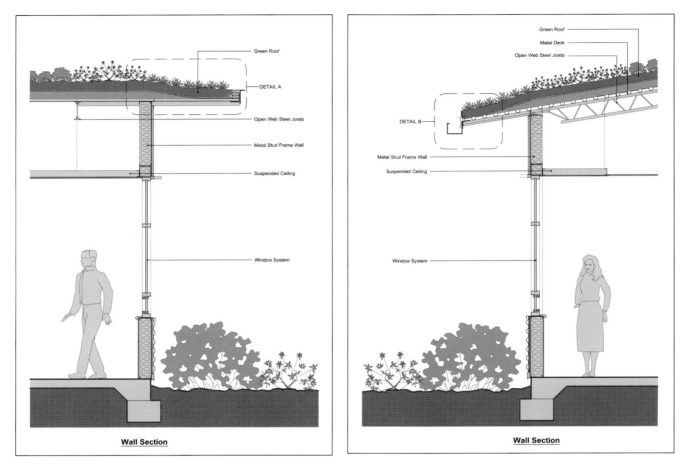

Green Roof

DETAIL A

Open Web Steel Joists

Metal Stud Frame Wall

Suspended Ceiling

Window System

Wall Section

Green Roof

Metal Deck

Open Web Steel Joists

DETAIL B

Metal Stud Frame Wall

Suspended Ceiling

Window System

Wall Section

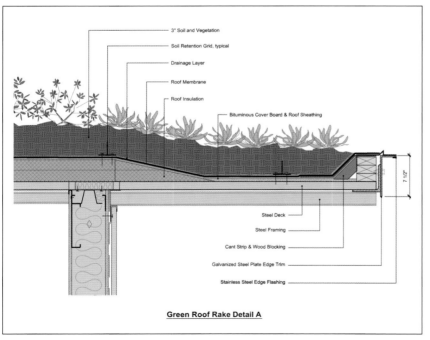

3" Soil and Vegetation

Soil Retention Grid, typical

Drainage Layer

Roof Membrane

Roof Insulation

Bituminous Cover Board & Roof Sheathing

7 1/2"

Steel Deck

Steel Framing

Cant Strip & Wood Blocking

Galvanized Steel Plate Edge Trim

Stainless Steel Edge Flashing

Green Roof Rake Detail A

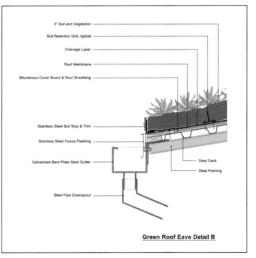

3" Soil and Vegetation

Soil Retention Grid, typical

Drainage Layer

Roof Membrane

Bituminous Cover Board & Roof Sheathing

Stainless Steel Soil Stop & Trim

Stainless Steel Fascia Flashing

Galvanized Bent Plate Steel Gutter

Steel Deck

Steel Framing

Steel Pipe Downspout

Green Roof Eave Detail B

5-77, 5-78, 5-79, 5-80. Typical cross sections of the green roof at the Clean Water Services Field Yard in Beaverton, Oregon. (Courtesy of PIVOT Architecture)

5-81, 5-82. At the Beaverton facility, pavements and walks, such as the main drive into the property and the sidewalk in front of the building, are designed to direct storm water for reabsorbtion by the vegetation or bioswales.

main highway and will eventually connect to future areas within the site. The green street has no curbs, so that water sheet flows across the pavement into swales, where it flows slowly through gravel planted with native plant materials whose root systems draw up water (Figs. 5-81 and 5-82). The only piping on the site connects the swales on either side of the pavement. The City of Beaverton demonstrated considerable flexibility in approving many components that were not part of the city code (such as some variances on porous pavements), establishing precedents that would make it easier for similar projects to move forward. The code previously required impervious pavements, but the revised code allows for porous pavements that let water drain directly through them. Porous pavement was planned for all pavements, but was implemented only on the employee parking lot because its coarse texture requires an adjustment for people used to consistently smooth concrete or asphalt pavements.

The ecoroof covers 8,200 square feet (761.8 m^2) of sloping roof with a pitch of one in six (or 16.6 per cent) (see Fig. 87). The most highly visible portion of the building was chosen for the eco-roof, so that it would be seen by passersby as well as visitors. The roof is drained both by gutters and scuppers, each of which creates miniature, free-falling waterfalls onto gravel areas on the ground. These areas are developed into separate scupper gardens, which slow the flow of the water, cool it, remove some sediments, and absorb most of the storm water before it reaches bioswales.

Green roof

The design team selected a torched down bitumen (Soprema) over rigid insulation and a steel roof deck. The steel deck is supported by open web steel joists and beams. Baffles on the sloping roof help to hold the growing medium in place (Figs. 5-77, 5-78, 5-79, and 5-80).

The total dead load used for the design, including the steel deck, was 45 pounds per

5-83. A scupper drain from the green roof empties into a "scupper garden" below.

5-84. The parking lots drain to absorptive swales planted with water-loving but drought-tolerant materials.

square foot (219.7 km²). Of this, approximately 30 pounds per square foot (146.5 kg/m²) was allocated to the dead weight of the ecoroof, with the assumption that the growing medium is saturated.

The growing medium is 3–4 inches (7.6–10.2 cm) in depth, and consists of 30 percent sandy loam, 15 percent compost, 25 percent pumice, 15 percent coir (a coconut husk byproduct), and 15 percent perlite.

Other features

During the construction phase of this project, many techniques were used to prevent erosion, control sediments, and monitor performance. The general contractor was chosen in part for its corporate policy of protecting the environment. Monitoring erosion during construction was routine. They also constructed settling basins, placed gravel cover over most of the site, added organic flocculents to ponds to speed the settling process, installed erosion membranes, and built a series of swales and a filter dam.

The long-term goals of this project were not only to slow the rate of runoff, but also to demonstrate innovative techniques by allowing runoff to percolate into the soil, cool it, and treat it before it leaves the site. In the sixty-vehicle employee parking lot, storm water runoff is minimized because of the porous concrete pavements. For example, a glass of water poured onto the pavement immediately disappears into the subgrade, which is an 18-inch-thick layer of compacted rock (Fig. 5-85). The rock acts as a subbase for the pavement and also serves as an underdrain system—a mechanism that is required because most of the site contains clay soils, which absorb water poorly. Areas on the site, for the storage of materials are paved with reinforced gravel, which, like the porous concrete, allows a considerable amount of percolation. On the walkways, paver blocks were set over a porous subbase of almost two feet of sand (22 inches; 56 cm), and then, in ascending order, crushed rock and ballast rock, plus a layer of geotextile fabric.

There are almost no storm drainage pipes on the site because all water drains along the surface to ditches or swales. These are wide and vegetated, so much of the water is cooled, filtered, and absorbed by a diverse palette of native plants or pervious materials. At the rear of the property is a much larger bioswale, or water quality swale, 50 feet (15.2 m) wide by 600 feet (182.9 m) long, which receives filtered water from the other, smaller bioswales. In this water quality swale, sediments such as silt are filtered out. Meanders and piles of wood debris provide habitat for animals. The Clean Water Services facility has only one catch basin on the entire site, whereas in standard developments most storm water routinely drains to catch basins and is then piped off site. This single catch basin is required by code so that water

5-85. When water is poured onto the porous employee parking lot at Beaverton, there is no runoff, as the water goes directly through the pavement, which is coarser than standard asphalt pavement.

5-86. At the rear of the property is a large bio-swale engineered to absorb excess water from the site and drain to an adjacent stream, but it is also set with old logs and new vegetation to provide habitat for animals.

CLEAN WATER SERVICES FIELD YARD, ORIGINAL PLANT LIST

Achillea millefolium	Yarrow	4 inch (10.1 cm) pot
Coreopsis auriculata 'Nana'	Dwarf coreopsis	4 inch (10.1 cm) pot
Crocus vernus	Dutch crocus	bulbs
Lavendula angustifolia	Lavender	4 inch (10.1 cm) pot
Muscari armenaiacum	Grape hyacinth	bulbs
Sedum species	Stonecrop species	cuttings
Thymus species	Creeping thyme species	4 inch (10.1 cm) pot
Veronica prostrate	Speedwell	4 inch (10.1 cm) pot
Verbena species	Verbena	4 inch (10.1 cm) pot

CLEAN WATER SERVICES FIELD YARD, REVISED PLANT LIST

Achillea 'Paprika' (1,315)	Paprika yarrow
Delosperma cooperii (1,638)	Ice plant
Festuca ovina (116)	Blue fescue
Isotorna fluviatilis (pratia pedunculata) (822)	Blue star creeper
Sedum kamtschaticum (1,348)	Stonecrop
Sedum 'Voodoo' (772)	Voodoo stonecrop

draining from the rear parking lot is filtered through an oil/water separator, which collects any oil leaking from vehicles and filters out water, before draining into the water quality swale.

Planting and irrigation

A mixture of sedum, wildflowers, and ground covers was planted in August 2003, toward the end of the region's typically dry summers, at variable spacings about 6–12 inches (15.2–30.5 cm) on center. The main selection considerations centered on drought tolerance, seasonal color, foliage contrast, and low maintenance.

Temporary irrigation was used during the initial planting period. The north-facing orientation was anticipated to increase water retention, compared to a south-facing roof, for example, where loss through evaporation would be much higher.

Bowles reports that about two-thirds of the roof was re-planted. "The original plant selection included plants that stayed in 'clumps' and didn't spread out. This resulted in a lot of bare growing medium that was prone to letting weeds get started and was not stable. If we had not replanted, we would have had to add about one inch of the growing medium. We also had quite a problem with moss in the open areas. We removed these plants and put in a different growing medium that would be more resistant to moss. We replanted with varieties that would spread out and give complete coverage. That work was completed in April 2007. We now have a problem with grasses taking over. It turns out the supplier of the soil had mistakenly put grass seed in the growing medium. That supplier will be paying for a crew to come out and hand pull all the grass, then he will spray the roof to prevent any further grass problems."[39]

Another unexpected problem was that the irrigation system had to be replaced. The original was a drip system installed under the growing medium so that it wouldn't be visible. However, there were two difficulties. It was very hard to adjust the system, because the roof slopes quite a bit, so there is a large pressure difference between the top and bottom. The sec-

5-87. A view of the green roof at the Clean Water Services Field Yard just after the initial planting installation. (Courtesy of PIVOT Architecture)

ond problem was that the connections started to separate, and it was difficult to locate the breaks. The irrigation system was removed in 2006, and standard above-ground sprinklers were installed in 2007, with no problems reported thus far.

Post-planting and maintenance

Bowles notes that "other than the replanting described above, we have had very little maintenance. We still have the irrigation system on the roof, and we use it during the hot and dry periods of the summer. One of our original concerns was the roof structure, such as developing leaks. We are happy to report we have had no problems at all with the structure. The bottom line is that we are very happy with our decision to install the green roof. It continues to get attention and draw people to our facility where they then also see all the other water quality features we are using. We have had our share of trouble with the roof, and ultimately decided to replant as described above. If we had originally chosen plants that spread out, we would have avoided all the problems."[40]

North Beach Place, San Francisco, CA

DESIGN TEAM
Landscape architect: PGAdesign, Inc., Cathy Garrett, Principal
Architect: Paul Barnhart, Barnhart Associates Architects
Associate architect: Serena Trachta, Full Circle Design Group
Waterproofing consultant: Ken Klein, Simpson, Gumpertz & Heger
Structural engineer: Amir Kazemi, FBA Structural

Context and concept

North Beach Place is a mixed-use project in San Francisco, developed by BRIDGE Housing Corporation on land owned by the San Francisco Housing Authority. The success of this new development rested in large part on its 2-acre (0.8 ha) intensive green roof, designed by PGAdesign, Inc. (PGA), to unify the new development and create an oasis for its occupants within its urban setting.[41]

5-88. A view of the North Beach Place complex site, in the heart of San Francisco, at night. (Courtesy of David Goldberg)

As a result of a long planning process in which **BRIDGE** was a key participant, the City of San Francisco decided to replace existing public housing with a mixed-use commercial and residential development that would relate well to the city's historic North Beach neighborhood. The new North Beach Place replaces a two-block 1960s public housing project with a program that includes under-building parking, street-level shops, and 341 affordable apartments for families and seniors. The site measures about 300 by 850 feet (91.4 by 259.1 m) curb to curb, or about 5.8 acres (2.3 ha), including sidewalks.

Because the new development is sited where the residential section of North Beach transitions to commercial, hotel, and other tourist-oriented areas, creating retail spaces for the residential community (rather than the already well-served tourists) established North Beach Place as a firm stronghold of the neighborhood's residential landscape. **BRIDGE** determined that the housing would be primarily family-oriented, with one somewhat autonomous Senior Center that includes apartments above the community facilities.

Given that San Francisco real estate is among the most expensive in the United States and is in critically short supply—particularly for affordable housing—**BRIDGE** understood the need to maximize the number of units. Yet, consistent with their values, **BRIDGE** refused to maximize density at the expense of open space for residents. They championed the green roof as a critically important element of the project. Cathy Garrett noted, "I think the project benefited significantly from a special chemistry that formed between the developer, end-users, design team and the City. The result is a design that's equally respectful of the neighborhood, the residents and the environment."[42]

Layout

To accommodate the density of units appropriate for the neighborhood and consistent with BRIDGE's development goals, the project was intended from the outset to be built to the property lines facing Bay, Mason, Francisco, and Taylor Streets and Columbus Avenue. The final density achieved was 77.1 residential units per acre (190.4 units/ha) with an average unit size of 907 square feet (84.3 m²). Despite the relatively small unit size and high density, the development looks and feels remarkably spacious. "By putting parking under the building, we created a large podium roof deck that presented an ideal open space opportunity," explains Garrett.[43] The space below the 2-acre (0.8 ha) roof garden is predominantly parking; one corner of the roof garden is above retail space. The structural slab is the ceiling of the parking garage and supports the green roof.

The four-story residential development is sited on a hill, and Barnhart Associates Architects (BAA) designed the buildings to follow the slope, so the structures read as a series of varied stepped masses. The Senior Center is a four-story building on grade (designed by associate architect Full Circle Design Group [FCDG]), and the residential units are located on the three stories above ground-floor retail spaces. In cases where there is no retail at street level, residential units occupy all four floors. The neighborhood's demographics gave the landscape design its initial direction. Children's play areas needed to be provided because the neighborhood has little child-oriented open space, and ground-floor retail made sense for this highly walkable part of the city.

Interior buildings were sited to set the stage for a free-flowing landscape design. Broader spaces between the buildings were dedicated to community uses, and narrower spaces were reserved either for circulation or private patios. The architect addressed the neighborhood context by giving the building elevations significant articulation.

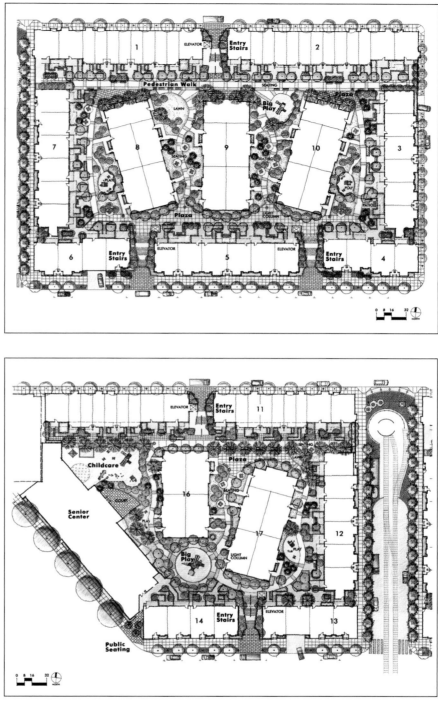

Green roof

A major innovation of this project was the development of a "set-down-slab" that allowed for the creation of inviting open space for residents. On most roof gardens, the structural slab (also called the podium) dictates the geometry of the surface (or topping) slab; normally the topping slab is close in elevation and generally a uniform height above the structural slab. However, at

5-90, 5-91. Plan views of the two adjoining areas of the site of North Beach Place. Each building labeled on these two plans is visible in the aerial view opposite. (Plans by PGAdesign Inc.)

North Beach Place, the project architect designed a 13-1/2 inch (34.3 cm) step-down of the structural slab below the elevation of the threshold of most first floor apartment units. This enabled the landscape architects to minimize the number of penetrations through the structural slab, because the irrigation and drainage lines ran through the set-down void. It also provided an increased depth for growing media, which enabled them to plant a greater variety of plants. Pedestrians do not walk on the set-down structural slab; rather, they walk on the surface-level paths, which are largely independent of the underlying structural slab. The step-down structural slab significantly reduced the number and height of planting walls, since more than a foot of the height of the planting depth is artfully hidden (Figs. 5-93 and 5-94).

"Think of it as a layer cake with two scenarios," Garrett explained about the two typical cross-sections. "The first, in planting areas, has the structural slab as the bottom, topped by a waterproof membrane and drainage system. Next is the base layer of soil without organics, then the top layer of soil with organics, and finally the planting, which acts as the icing. In the second scenario, located at paved areas, the structural slab is at the bottom; above which is the waterproof membrane and drainage system. Here, the filling is structural foam and the topping is concrete paving."[44]

The on-structure growing media mixes were developed and specified by PGA. Two special lightweight mixes were utilized for the growing media of the green roof. An organic mix was installed to a depth of approximately 18 inches (45.7 cm), with a nonorganic mix used as a base layer in the planters to support the organic mix. Both soil mixes were designed to be quick draining as well as to hold essential nutrients and water in the growing medium. Project-wide, growing media depths range from 9 to 36 inches (22.9 to 91.4 cm).

The growing medium consisted of 35 percent graded sand, 35 percent expanded shale, 20 percent fir bark, and 10 percent sphagnum

5-92, 5-93. Graceful walk alignments at North Beach Place are achieved with fluid forms. (Top, courtesy of PGAdesign Inc., Bottom, courtesy of David Goldberg).

peat moss. Large-grained sand was specified to ensure that water would flow freely through the filter fabric; the shale aids in water retention and gives structural stability to the mix. The fir bark was .25 to .125 inch (6.35 to 3.18 mm) in size with no fines that could clog the pores of the filter fabric, and the sphagnum peat moss served as another organic additive. Limiting the total organic composition to 30 percent resulted in a mix that will provide stability over time because less breakdown will occur than would with a more typical soil high in organics. The layered composition also limits the potential for anaerobic exchange at greater plant depths.

The typical depths for planting are suitable for each general type of plant material. Medium-size trees were planted in soil with a minimum depth of 36 inches (91.4 cm); any greater depth would have required enlargement of structural systems. Small trees were planted in soil 30 inches (76.2 cm) deep, and most shrubs were set in 24 inches (61.0 cm), though at times the depth was as little as 18 inches (45.7 cm). The lawns range from the minimum 9 inches (22.9 cm) to the preferred depth of 12 inches (30.5 cm).

The waterproofing membrane is a self-adhered sheet 60-mil (0.06 in or 1.5 mm) thick bituthene 4000, with a fluid, applied 60-mil (0.06 in or 1.5 mm) primer system (Grace Construction Products). Two layers of drain mat are a 1-inch (2.54 cm) Versicell and a .375-inch (9.5 mm) thick mat (Miradrain). Plenty of cleanouts (access points for accessing the pipes) for the drain system were included in planters and where planter drains connected to pavement drains, thereby allowing the entire system to be cleaned, monitored, and kept in good working order.

The layers developed by the waterproofing consultant (Simpson, Gumpertz & Heger) and associate architect (FCDG) include a structural slab, fluid-applied waterproof membrane, sheet membrane, protection board, 3/8-inch drain mat with integral filter fabric, 2-inch concrete protection slab, 1-inch drain mat, filter fabric, and plantings.

The structural slab itself comprised a series of inverted pyramids that allow the slab to drain. Where paved, the surface reflects the same inverted-pyramid shape even though the surface does not strictly follow the slopes estab-

lished by the structural slab. Entries at interior buildings, which lead to upper residential units, are higher than those that directly access the podium level, creating further opportunities for paved surface undulation.

Unlike drainage on the natural ground plane where water may run off the site, the complex podium of a roof garden is a closed environment, so water needs to be completely contained within the podium, and runoff directed appropriately. At North Beach Place, there were a large number of finish grades that had to be accommodated within a tight geometry. In order to avoid slopes that would be too steep, the configuration of the structural slab required that the low points of the inverted pyramids could only be several inches deeper than the high points along the ridge lines of the pyramids. Over the entire site, the elevation range for the paving is 14.5 inches (36.8 cm), with the lowest point located at one of the drains and the highest point at the surface of one of the play areas. The elevation range for the surface of planting areas is 27.5 inches (69.9 cm). This depth added to the set-down slab represents the overall maximum planting depth of 41 inches (104.1 cm). Pedestrian circulation occurs in many directions, so slopes steeper than two per cent had to be limited, so as to not be experienced as uncomfortable cross slopes. Such slopes only occur where the direction of circulation is contained, and then only to a 4.9 percent maximum slope.

5-94. A view of North Beach Place during construction. The amount of elevation change necessary to bring finish grade flush with the walks is clearly visible. A planter to accommodate a tree is also in place at this early stage of construction. (Courtesy of PGAdesign Inc.)

Because the interior buildings are not sited in a rectilinear organization, the landscape is free flowing; by contrast, the slab joint that addresses concrete shrinkage in the post-tensioned structural slab forms a straight line and cuts through the middle of the project on the east block. The *slab joint* is a large (approximately 6 inches or 15.2 cm) joint with flexible bellows in between, which cuts through the middle of the garden in a straight line. Garrett explains, "The layout of the roof garden is curvilinear, which meant that we wanted to cross the slab joint at multiple places with planters, lawns, irrigation lines as well as planting. In the end we worked out a way to have the free flowing design and the slab joint." These various design elements disguise the slab joint.[45]

The design team focused on the sustainable features of the roof, paying particular attention to water conservation and minimizing peak velocities of unfiltered storm water. The project's green roof releases rainwater to the city's storm water system more slowly than a traditional paved or other roof surface. Rock packs were installed at pavement drains and are joined by pipes that drain planters—the connection occurring in the foot-deep space between the drain at the pavement surface and the point of drain penetration through the structural slab. This rock pack, composed of drain rock surrounding the perforated drain and perforated pipe collar wrapped in filter fabric, provides an additional layer of filtration, cleaning the water before it enters the city's drain system. And although the total lawn area had to be limited to conserve irrigation water, individual lawns were strategically placed to provide children with easy access and thus ensure the greatest possible use.

The roof includes a series of courtyards of various sizes and shapes that flow into one another and provide stimulating outdoor opportunities for community gatherings and resident relaxation. These courtyards were designed for accessibility to all residents. Paths,

5-95, 5-96. North Beach Place includes lawn areas both for individual buildings and more public settings. Retaining walls double as seat walls in many areas, making the use of space as efficient as possible. (Top, courtesy of PGAdesign Inc. Bottom, courtesy of David Goldberg)

5-97, 5-98. Two different play areas at North Beach Place: each has a clear spatial definition while allowing for parental supervision and pedestrian access. (Top, courtesy of PGAdesign Inc. Bottom, courtesy of David Goldberg)

NORTH BEACH PLACE PLANT LIST

TREES

Acer rubrum 'Red Sunset'	Red sunset red maple
Acer circinatum	Vine maple
Arbutus x 'Marina'	Marina strawberry tree
Gingko biloba 'Fairmount'	Fairmount gingko
Malus floribunda 'Harvest Gold'	Harvest gold crabapple
Malus x 'Red Jewel'	Red jewel crabapple
Pittosporum undulatum	Victorian box
Podocarpus gracilior	African fern pine
Podocarpus macrophyllus	Buddhist pine
Tristania laurina	Small-leaved trustania
Ulmus parvifolia	Chinese elm
Zelkova serrata 'Green Vase'	Green vase zelkova

SHRUBS AND PERENNIALS

Abelia x grandiflora 'Prostrata'	Dwarf abelia
Agapanthus 'Lily of the Nile'	Lily of the Nile agapanthus
Agapanthus 'Peter Pan'	Peter Pan agapanthus
Agapanthus 'Tinkerbell'	Tinkerbell agapanthus
Asparagus densiflorus 'Sprenger'	Sprenger asparagus fern
Asplenium bulbiferum	Mother fern
Aucuba japonica 'Nana'	Dwarf Japanese aucuba
Choisya ternata	Mexican orange blossom
Cistus skanbergii	Rock rose
Clivia miniata	Kaffir lily
Coleonema pulchrum	Breath of heaven
Coprosma 'Coppershine'	Coppershine coprosma
Coprosma 'Marble Queen'	Marble queen coprosma
Correa 'Dusky Bells'	Dusky bells correa
Disksonia antartica	Tasmanium tree fern
Dietes vegeta	Fortnight lily
Euryops pectinatus 'Viridis'	Green leaved euryops
Hebe 'Patty's Purple'	Patty's purple hebe
Hemerocallis 'Stella de Oro'	Stella de oro daylily
Hemerocallis 'Lemon Drop'	Lemon Drop daylily
Kniphofia 'Bressingham Comet'	Bressingham Comet dwarf torch lily
Kniphofia 'Little Maid'	Little Maid dwarf yellow torch lily
Lantana 'Patriot Cowboy'	Patriot cowboy lantana
Lavandula angustifolia 'Hidcote'	Hidcote English lavender
Lavandula stoechas 'Otto Quast'	Otto Quast Spanish lavender
Leucothoe axillaries	Coast leucothoe
Mahonia 'Golden Abundance'	Golden abundance Oregon grape
Myrtis communis 'Compacta'	Dwarf myrtle
Nandina domestica 'Nana'	Dwarf heavenly bamboo
Osmanthus delavayi	Osmanthus or tea olive
Pennisetum setaceum	Fountain grass
Philodendron x 'Xanadu'	Xanadu philodendron
Phormium cookianum	Dwarf mountain flax
Pittosporum tobira 'Wheeler's Dwarf'	Wheeler's dwarf pittosporum
Polystichum minitum	Sword fern
Punica granatum 'Nana'	Dwarf pomegranate
Rhododendron x 'Cristo Rey'	Cristo rey rhododendron
Rhododendron 'Snow Lady'	Snow lady rhododendron
Rosmarinus 'Huntington Carpet'	Huntington carpet creeping rosemary
Ruscus hypoglossum	Butcher's broom
Sarcococca hookerana humilis	Sweet box
Stipa tenuissima	Feather grass
Woodwardia fimibriata	Chain fern

courtyards, and patios comply with both the Americans with Disabilities Act and the rigorous City of San Francisco's Mayor's Office on Disability requirements. This intensive roof garden offers five play areas, each specifically geared to children of a different age group (Figs. 5-97 and 5-98).

A subtle integration of accessible surfaces was achieved by a variety of techniques. Terrace seating at the east block features seating "drums" that match the elevations of the concrete walls, and are integrated in a way that allow a wheelchair-bound person to sit comfortably with others The result is fully code-compliant without appearing stiff or merely utilitarian.

Planting and irrigation

Automatic irrigation was required, due to California's climate and typically shallow soils. The innovative set-down slab facilitated many aspects of the irrigation system's installation. Pipe could be run in the structural foam between the topping slab and the structural slab or directly in planter areas, reducing the number of penetrations needed for irrigation. Particular emphasis was given to increasing the number of irrigation circuits and grouping circuits of similar aspect to provide maximum watering control, and the head layout eliminates overspray onto pavements. Water application rates are kept low, not only to conserve water but also to provide the most suitable amount of water to the shallow root zones inherent to on-structure planting. Although heavy-duty materials and equipment are used, they are completely screened from view.

Walkways set above the structural slab allow a variety of walkway elevations as well as planters with more soil than is visually apparent. The increase in overall soil depth allowed the integration of a rich palette of plants, including a dozen tree species complemented by sixty other plant varieties. The set-down slab allowed for—and even promoted—lower planter wall heights, resulting in a parklike, on-structure garden instead of a courtyard dominated by walls with limited greenery. Almost half of the entire roof is planted.

California's climate permits planting during much of the year, so the work was bid and planted as the construction schedule allowed. Because the planting depths allow for an

5-99. At North Beach Place the mounding of a large lawn area within the green roof accommodates the sizable depth required for the root ball of a major tree. (Courtesy of PGAdesign Inc.)

unusually full range of plant selection, the palette is expansive and diverse, creating a range of habitat potential.[46]

Post-planting and maintenance

After completion of the installation of the green roof, PGA created a maintenance manual for the owner and landscape maintenance contractor. There was a one-year maintenance period, followed by a full-year warranty period for the trees and a six-month warranty period for all other plants. On the first anniversary of project completion, PGA met with the architects, representatives from the building manager (the John Stewart Company) and BRIDGE, and the landscape maintenance contractor to review site

NORTH BEACH PLACE PLANT LIST

VINES

Campsis grandiflora 'Morning Calm'	Morning Calm Chinese trumpet creeper
Clematis armandii	Clematis
Clytostoma callistegioides	Violet trumpet vine
Hardenbergia violacaea	Lilac vine
Wisteria sinensis	Wisteria

GROUND COVERS

Aspidistra eliator	Cast iron plant
Butera cordata	Bacopa
Convolvulus mauritanicus	Ground morning glory
Cotoneaster 'Lowfast'	Lowfast cotoneaster
Dymondia margaritas	Silver carpet
Heuchera 'Bressingham Hybrids'	Coral bells hybrids pink and white
Iberis sempervirens	Evergreen candytuff
Lamium maculatum	Dead nettle
Liriope muscari 'Big Blue'	Big blue liriope
Liriope 'Silver Dragon'	Silver dragon liriope
Plectranthus cliatus	Spur flower
Polygonum capitatum	Knotweed

5-100, 5-101, 5-102. A view of the completed housing area at North Beach Place. The bottom image shows a trolley turnaround, the public face of the residential complex, and a popular destination for tourists. (Top and bottom, courtesy of David Goldberg. Middle, courtesy of PGAdesign Inc.)

issues. They reviewed procedures for regular maintenance, with particular emphasis on soil fertility testing and appropriate treatment with organics and/or fertilizers, root pruning, canopy pruning, planter drains, top dressing of soil, mulch, and irrigation. North Beach Place's green roof literally provides a park at the doorstep of every residence and is an important community resource and neighborhood focal point. One of San Francisco's most popular cable car routes terminates at North Beach Place (Fig. 5-102). In the past, tourists would leave the cable cars and immediately head for Fisherman's Wharf, a few blocks to the north, walking between partially vacant, worn, and at times unsafe public housing. Now many remain in the immediate neighborhood to explore, shop, and enjoy the ambiance of one of San Francisco's most colorful and historic areas before moving on to other attractions.

The project enjoys 100 percent occupancy, and residents are justifiably proud of their home. North Beach Place has turned what was once a scar on the city's visage into a dynamic and attractive spot where tourists and residents of all income levels come together in an unique and cohesive urban environment.

DESIGN TEAM
Project landscape architect: Terry Guen
   Design Associates
Landscape architect: Gustafson Guthrie
   Nichol
Landscape and perennial design: Piet Oudolf
Conceptual design: Robert Israel

Context and concept

Millennium Park is a large intensive green roof project built over old railroad yards in Chicago. This 24.5 acre (9.9 ha) public park was dedicated on July 16, 2004 as a crowning civic achievement in the city, part of Mayor Richard Daley's fifteen-year quest to "green" an industrial metropolis and develop cultural arts. The green roof construction furthered Daniel Burnham's 1908 plan for the 320-acre (129.5 ha) Grant Park by completing the historic park's northwest corner and consequently stabilizing and stimulating new economic growth at this edge of Chicago's downtown.[47]

City agencies and a private donor group, Millennium Park, Inc., partnered to champion and direct this vision as well as raise the necessary $480 million. This project probably could not have occurred anywhere else but in Chicago, one of the centers of American architecture, with its tradition of major achievements in which the talents of many great designers are harnessed in order to achieve civic monuments. At least as much coordination and cooperation was required for Millennium Park as for the World's Columbian Exposition of 1893, a fair that brought glamor and publicity to the city at an important point in its history.[48] Ed Uhlir played a key role in this project; he shepherded Millennium Park through numerous design and budget reviews, contentious hearings, and scheduling conflicts. Terry Guen, the project landscape architect, describes his contribution: "Ed Uhlir was appointed by Mayor Daley to oversee the Lakefront Millennium Park Project as a Special Assistant to the Mayor and Director of the Project. Ed coordinated the efforts of the donor group, Millennium Park, Inc., and various City agencies—the Public Building Commission, Department of Transportation, Chicago Park District, Department of Cultural Affairs, Department of General Services—as well as

5-103. Except for this view underneath the railroad bridge, it is difficult to tell that Millennium Park is an intensive green roof garden.

scores of consultants, artists, engineers providing design services. Ed directed the successful composition of art within the garden, and design of structural and hardscape construction which permanently supports the full-scale green roof installation. He is the pivotal figure in both the Park's conception and construction."[49]

As with the Columbian Exposition, a competition was staged to raise the design repute of Millennium Park, as well as to secure a highly original design suited to the extraordinary loca-

tion. Although most of the park's landscape was designed by the city's design team, the 3-acre (1.2 ha) Lurie Garden site was the subject of an international design competition held in 2000.[50] Sixteen designers were invited to submit proposals for the complex garden that was taking shape, which had to link to Grant Park, accommodate major art and music facilities, provide sufficient space for thousands of visitors, and display plants year round. Eventually there were eleven submissions. The winning entry was the "Shoulder Garden." This design became the backbone for the layout of the entire park.

The overall project objective was to create a free cultural venue for Chicagoans and tourists with a new, state-of-the-art outdoor music facility. The secondary goal was to remove or cover the unsightly train terminal, railway lines, and an 800-space surface parking lot that occupied this prominent location in Chicago's front yard. Transformation of the underutilized rail yard and deteriorated underground parking facility into Millennium Park required the cooperation of city agencies, the donor group (the philanthropists who gave funds), artists, landscape architects, architects, engineers, construction managers, and contractors; it took six years (1998–2004) to complete. The landscape architect of record was responsible for all the construction documents for the various gardens, allées, and components of the park, coordinated with all the other design principals, and was responsible for site inspections while the work was under construction.[51]

The design of the new park has transformed the physical and economic vitality of the location. While matching the context of the historic Michigan Avenue frontage, the park comfortably integrates cutting-edge technology and art into a multilevel, contemporary, and highly usable public space. The park holds many now renowned works of architecture, fountains, sculpture, and botanic garden spaces, as well as grand performance facilities, restaurants, and a skating rink. The green roof component covers two new subterranean parking garages with 4,000 spaces, a multimodal transit center that includes a bridge over the existing railroad lines

5-104, 5-105. Two views of the construction of the Jay Pritzker Pavilion by architect Frank Gehry at Millennium Park.

5-106. An aerial view of Millennium Park shows its size and scale. (Courtesy of Millennium Park)

5-107. A view of the Lurie Garden and Jay Pritzker Pavilion at Millennium Park. (Courtesy of Mark Tomaras and Millennium Park)

and station, and a 1,525-seat indoor performance theater.[52]

Layout

The layout of the park connects pedestrian circulation from the city blocks of Michigan Avenue to two walkways lined with formal double rows of pear trees that bloom white in the spring (Fig. 5-106). Separate "rooms" defined by allées of elm, maple, crabapple, and hawthorn trees provide space for the Wrigley Square fountain and peristyle, the McCormick Tribune Skating Rink/Dining Terrace at the Park Grill, and the Crown Fountain, whose 50-

LURIE GARDEN, MILLENNIUM PARK, PLANT LIST [53]

TREES

Cercis Canadensis	Redbud – native
Prunus sargentii	Sargent's cherry
Prunus subhirtella 'Autumnalis'	Flowering cherry
Quercus macrocarpa x bicolor 'Schuettii'	Schuetti burr oak
Robinia pseudoacacia 'Chicago Blues'	Chicago Blues black locust

SHRUBS

Buxus micorphylla v. koreana 'Wintergreen'	Wintergreen boxwood
Caryopteris x clandonensis 'Black Knight'	Black Knight bluebeard
Euonymus alatus 'Compacta'	Dwarf burning bush
Paeonia suffruticosa 'Renkaku'	Renkaku tree peony
Perovskia 'Little Spire'	Little Spire russian sage
Syringa meyeri 'Palibin'	Palibin lilac
Taxus cuspidata 'Capitata'	Capitata Japanese yew
Taxus cuspidata 'Dwarf Bright Gold'	Dwarf Bright Gold Japanese yew
Taxus x media 'Hicksii'	Hick's yew
Vitex agnus castus	Chaste tree

SHOULDER HEDGE

Carpinus betulus 'Fastigiata'	Upright hornbeam
Fagus sylvatica	European beech
Thuja occidentalis 'Nigra'	Nigra arborvitae
Thuja occidentalis 'Wintergreen'	Wintergreen arborvitae
Thuja occidentalis 'Pyramidalis'	Pyramidal arborvitae
Thuja occidentalis 'Brabant'	Brabant arborvitae
Thuja standishii x plicata 'Spring Grove'	Spring grove arborvitae

GRASSES AND SEDGES

Briza media	Quaking grass
Calamagrostis x acutiflora 'Karl Foerster'	Karl Foerster feather reed grass
Calamagrostis brachytricha	Korean feather reed grass
Carex muskingumensis	Palm sedge – native
Chasmanthium latifolium	Northern sea oats – native
Deschampsia caespitosa 'Goldstaub'	Goldstaub tufted hair grass – native
Eragrostis spectabilis	Purple love grass – native
Hakenochloa macra	Hakone grass
Miscanthus sinensis 'Malepartus'	Malepartus common eulalia grass
Molinia caerulea 'Dauerstrahl'	Dauerstrahl moor grass
Molinia caerulea 'Moorflamme'	Moorflamme moor flame grass
Molinia litoralis 'Transparent'	Transparent moor grass
Panicum virgatum 'Shenandoah'	Shenandoah red switch grass – native
Pennisetum alopecuroides 'Cassian'	Cassian fountain grass
Schizachyrium scoparium 'The Blues'	The Blues little bluestem – native
Sesleria autumnalis	Moor grass
Sorghastrum nutans 'Sioux Blue'	Sioux Blue indian grass – native
Sporobolus heterolepis	Prairie dropseed – native

PERENNIALS

Achillea 'Credo'	Credo yarrow
Achillea 'Walther Funcke'	Walther Funcke yarrow
Actaea simplex 'James Compton'	James Compton bugbane
Agastache 'Blue Fortune'	Blue Fortune giant hyssop
Allium 'Summer Beauty'	Summer Beauty ornamental onion
Amorpha canescens	Leadplant – native
Amsonia hubrichtii	Arkansas blue star – native
Amsonia tabernaemontana v. salicifolia	Willowleaf blue star
Anemone hupehensis 'Preacox'	Preacox japanese anemone
Anemone hupehensis 'Splendens'	Splendens japanese anemone
Anemone leveillei	Windflower
Aruncus 'Horatio'	Horatio goatsbeard
Asclepias incarnata	Swamp milkweed – native
Asclepias tuberosa	Butterfly weed – native
Aster ericoides 'Blue Star'	Blue Star aster – native
Aster 'October Skies'	October Skies aster
Aster divaricatus	White wood aster – native
Aster lateriflorus 'Horizontalis'	Horizontalis calico aster – native
Aster novae-angliae 'Violetta'	Violetta new England aster – native
Aster oblongifolius 'October Skies'	Oblong October skies aster – native
Astilbe chinensis v. taquetii	'Purpurlanze' Purple lance astilbe
Astrantia major 'Claret'	Claret masterwort
Astrantia major 'Roma'	Roma masterwort
Baptisia leucantha	Wild white indigo – native
Baptisia 'Purple Smoke'	Purple Smoke hybrid wild indigo
Calamintha nepeta subsp. nepeta	Calamint
Campanula glomerata 'Caroline'	Caroline clustered bellflower
Clematis heracleifolia 'China Purple'	China Purple bushy clematis
Dalea purpurea	Purple prairie clover – native
Digitalis ferruginea	Rusty foxglove
Dodecatheon 'Aphrodite'	Aphrodite shooting star – native
Echinacea pallida	Pale coneflower – native
Echinacea purpurea 'Green Edge'	Green Edge coneflower – native
Echinacea purpurea 'Rubinglow'	Rubinglow coneflower – native
Echinacea tennesseensis	Tennessee coneflower – native
Echinacea 'Orange Meadowbrite'	Orange Meadowbrite coneflower
Echinacea 'Sunset'	Sunset coneflower
Echinops bannaticus 'Blue Glow'	Blue Glow globe thistle
Epimedium x versicolor 'Sulphureum'	Sulphureum bishop's hat
Epimedium grandiflorum 'Lilafee'	Lilafee longspur barrenwort
Eryngium bourgatii	Mediterranean Sea holly
Eryngium yuccifolium	Rattlesnake master – native
Eupatorium maculatum 'Gateway'	Gateway joe Pye weed – native
Eupatorium maculatum 'Purple Bush'	Purple Bush joe Pye weed – native
Filipendula rubra 'Venusta Magnifica'	Venusta Magnifica queen of the prairie – native
Gentiana andrewsii	Gentian – native
Geum rivale 'Flames of Passion'	Flames of Passion avens

Geum triflorum	Prairie smoke – native
Geranium x cantabrigiense 'Karmina'	Karmina cranesbill
Geranium 'Dilys'	Dilys cranesbill
Geranium phaeum v. album	White dusky cranesbill
Geranium sanguineum 'Max Frei'	Max Frei cranesbill
Geranium x oxonianum 'Claridge Druce'	Claridge Druce cranesbill
Geranium soboliferum	Cranesbill – native
Gillenia trifoliata	Bowman's root – native
Helenium 'Rubinzwerg'	Rubinzwerg sneezeweed or Helen's flower
Helleborus orientalis	Lenten rose
Hemerocallis 'Gentle Shepherd'	Gentle Shepherd daylily
Hemerocallis 'Chicago Apache'	Chicago Apache daylily
Heuchera 'Palace Purple'	Palace Purple coral flower
Hosta 'Blue Angel'	Blue Angel plantain lily
Hosta 'Halcyon'	Halcyon plantain lily
Hosta 'White Triumphator'	White Triumphator plantain lily
Inula magnifica 'Sonnestrahl'	Sonnestrahl fleabane
Jeffersonia diphylla	Twinleaf – native
Kalimeris incisa	Cast-iron plant
Knautia macedonica	Knautia
Liatris spicata	Blazing star – native
Liatris spicata 'Alba'	White blazing star – native
Limonium latifolium	Sea lavender
Lythrum alatum	Loosestrife – native
Mertensia virginica	Virginia bluebells – native
Mondarda didyma 'Scorpion'	Scorpion bee-balm
Origanum vulgare 'Herrenhausen'	Herrenhausen oregano
Paeonia lactiflora 'Jan Van Leeuwen'	Jan Van Leeuwen peony
Persicaria amplexicaulis 'Firedance'	Firedance knotweed
Persicaria polymorpha	White dragon knotweed
Phlomis tuberosa 'Amazone'	Amazone phlomis or Jerusalem sage
Phlox paniculata 'Blue Paradise'	Blue Paradise garden phlox – native
Phlox maculata 'Delta'	Delta wild sweet William – native
Polystichum setiferum 'Herrenhausen'	Herrenhausen soft shield fern
Potentilla nepalensis	Nepal cinquefoil
Rodgersia pinnata 'Superba'	Superba featherleaf rodgersia
Ruellia humilis	Wild petunia – native
Salvia x sylvestris 'Blue Hill'	Blue Hill meadow sage
Salvia x sylvestris 'Dear Anja'	Dear Anja meadow sage
Salvia x sylvestris 'May Night'	May Night meadow sage
Salvia x sylvestris 'Amethyst'	Amethyst meadow sage
Salvia x sylvestirs 'Rugen'	Rugen meadow sage
Salvia x sylvestris 'Wesuwe'	Wesuwe meadow sage
Salvia verticillata 'Purple Rain'	Purple Rain meadow sage

Salvia pratensis 'Pink Delight'	Pink Delight meadow sage
Sanguisorba menziesii	Burnet – native
Sanguisorba canadensis 'Red Thunder'	Red Thunder Canadian burnet
Saponaria x lempergii 'Max Frei'	Max Frei soapwort
Scutellaria incana	Skullcap – native
Sedum x hybrida 'Bertram Anderson'	Bertram Anderson stonecrop – native
Sedum 'Sunkissed'	Sunkissed stonecrop
Sedum 'Bronco'	Bronco stonecrop
Sedum telephium 'Matrona'	Matrona stonecrop
Silphium laciniatum	Compass plant – native
Smilacina racemosa	False Solomon's Seal – native
Stachys officinalis 'Hummelo'	Hummelo betony or hedgenettle
Stachys officinalis 'Rosea'	Rosea betony or hedgenettle
Thalictrum delavayi 'Elin'	Elin meadow rue
Tradescantia 'Concord Grape'	Concord Grape spiderwort – native
Tricyrtis formosana	Toad Lily
Tricyrtis x 'Tojen'	Tojen toad lily
Trifolium rubens	Clover
Veronica longifolia 'Pink Damask'	Pink Damask speedwell
Veronica spicata 'Giles Van Hees'	Giles Van Hees speedwell
Veronica longifolia 'Lila Karina'	Lila Karina speedwell
Veronicastrum virginicum 'Rosea'	Rosea culver's root - native
Veronicastrum virginicum 'Fascination'	Fascination culver's root - native
Veronicastrum virginicum 'Temptation'	Temptation culver's root – native
Veronicastrum virginicum 'Diane'	Diane culver's root – native
Zizia aurea	Golden Alexander – native

BULBS

Allium christophii	Garlic
Allium atropurpureum	Garlic
Allium sphaerocephalon 'Drumstick Allium'	Garlic
Allium aflatunense 'Purple Sensation'	Garlic
Camassia leichtlinii 'Blue Danube'	Blue Danube quamash
Camassia cusickii	Cusick's camus or Cusick quamash
Crocus vernus	Crocus
Crocus sieberi sp. 'Firefly'	Firefly crocus
Crocus pulchellus 'Zephyr'	Zephyr fall crocus
Colchicum speciosa	Fall
Tulipa hageri 'Splendens'	Splendens tulip
Tulipa bakeri 'Lilac Wonder'	Lilac Wonder tulip
Tulipa pulchella v. albocaerulea	Tulip
Tulipa aucheriana	Tulip
Tulipa 'Spring Green'	Spring Green tulip

foot-high (152 m) video towers project a thousand faces of Chicagoans. In the center of the park, on top of the restaurant roof, sits the 110-ton (99,790.3 kg) *Cloud Gate* silver bean sculpture, reflecting the lakefront, city, sky, and visitors. By British artist Anish Kapoor, the elliptical sculpture is constructed of polished stainless steel plates. A 12-foot (3.7 m)-high gate underneath the curve of the bean allows visitors to touch the surface and see a magical reflection of their image (Figs. 5-109 and 5-110).[54]

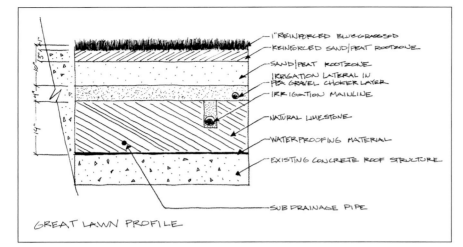

GREAT LAWN PROFILE

- 1" REINFORCED BLUEGRASSOD
- REINFORCED SAND/PEAT ROOTZONE
- SAND/PEAT ROOTZONE
- IRRIGATION LATERAL IN PEA GRAVEL CHOKER LAYER
- IRRIGATION MAINLINE
- NATURAL LIMESTONE
- WATERPROOFING MATERIAL
- EXISTING CONCRETE ROOF STRUCTURE
- SUB DRAINAGE PIPE

The centerpiece of the park is the Pritzker Pavilion and BP Pedestrian Bridge, constructed of enormous sculptural plates of curvilinear stainless steel. The 4,000-seat pavilion is home to the Grant Park Music Festival, which provides free performances throughout the summer. The pavilion is backdrop to the 7,000-seat great lawn—a 95,000-square-foot (8,825.8 m²) reinforced natural turf lawn, spanned by a grand steel trellis, which holds lighting and a state-of-the-art sound system. Designed for recovery from heavy use, thanks to emerging "turf technology," the great lawn includes a layered high-performance drainage system.[55]

Green roof

Because the structural deck was designed to support 4 feet (1.2 m) of growing medium, the planting is not limited by the pattern of the structural columns below. The growing medium for most park areas is a natural, locally available sandy loam or a blended soil based on the sandy loam mix. The end result is varying profiles of growing medium and drainage ranging from 8 inches (20.3 cm) to 4 feet (1.2 m) deep. This gives a lot of flexibility to the layout of major design elements, including the placement of large shade trees.

The entire 24.5-acre (9.9 ha) deck was waterproofed with a hot-applied rubberized membrane system. Styrofoam fill was used to create landforms that did not exceed the designed load capacity. Below the green roof, the parking areas provide direct pedestrian connections to the theater and restaurants. Two reinforced concrete cast-in-place garages support most of the roof deck, and a combination of steel structure and precast concrete structural tees spans the railroad tracks.[56]

The Pritzker Pavilion's open-air seating is a significant part of the experience it was designed to provide, with stars overhead and the

5-108. The cross section of the great lawn at Millennium Park shows how its depth and the materials of the various layers allow it to withstand a great deal of pedestrian traffic and associated loads. (Courtesy of Terry Guen Design Associates)

5-109, 5-110. Two views of the *Cloud Gate* silver bean sculpture by Anish Kapoor. (Middle: courtesy of City of Chicago and Walter Mitchell, bottom courtesy of Terry Guen Design Associates)

city's skyline as a backdrop. In the event of rain, the great lawn under the trellis has underlying layers of sand and gravel that allow water to drain quickly. Concerts and performances in the pavilion are held rain or shine.

The large lawn areas in other parts of the park, designed to accommodate thousands of visitors for concerts and other events, are modeled after fields used for professional sports. The lawns feature a thick cross-section of well-drained gravel and sands, peat, and root zone reinforcement to protect the turf from heavy traffic.[57]

Planting and irrigation

The Lurie Garden is a 2.5-acre (1.0 ha) botanic garden featuring the grand "Shoulder Garden" of mixed arborvitae, beech, and hornbeam trees. The hedge, a major feature, visually separates the garden from the active public areas of the park and shelters the 26,000 perennial plants of 140 varieties that constitute a vignette of the presettlement Midwest landscape with blended sweeps of flowering plants and grasses. The planting in the Lurie Garden is a carefully developed blend of prairie plants, 60 percent of which are native to Illinois, with hardy introduced or non-native materials that have "native" qualities.

"Implementing a roof garden of this size," landscape designer Terry Guen explains, "was about constructing and installing an ecological system from scratch. It was not just the placement of grown plant material, but the design had to be informed by how the public in today's world interacts with and uses a public space." At the same time, this is not a "habitat restoration, in which the approach is to cultivate diversity, and over time, the eventual perpetuation as a root and seed mass develops. By contrast, although this is conceived as an ecosystem, it is designed to be naturalistic, yet feature displays and interactions of color, texture and foliage."[58]

The overall garden, designed by Gustafson Guthrie Nichol, is divided between light and dark plates, separated by the hedge. The dark plate, which represents Chicago's history, consists of shade-loving plant material that includes a combination of trees called Cloud Grove. With time, these trees will provide a shade canopy for the plants. The light plate, which represents the city's future, contains sun-loving perennials. These plants thrive in the heat and the sun. No trees are planted in the light plate.

The Lurie Garden is the most intensively planted area in the park. Its purpose, in Guen's words, is "to put people into the middle of an impressionist painting, to immerse the visitor into art itself."[59] She explains, "All of the plants for the Lurie Garden grow well together in a garden setting with similar cultural and maintenance requirements. The plantings create a dramatic and naturalistic feel and a specific aesthetic effect." The use of native plants is unique, and as emphasized by the Lurie Garden, the designers chose plants proven to be botanically ornamental in order to foster a growing local interest in gardening in general, and the use of native plants. The Lurie Garden demonstrates how they are used and serves as a resource for seeing them first hand. It is proof that "natives can contribute aesthetically in this important garden but with an expectation quite different from naturalistic restoration type native plant uses."[60] Strong forms and careful massing of shrubs and perennials give separation from the other spaces while also inspiring an appreciation of nature. No annuals are included in the palette. Many migratory birds from the Great Lakes flyway are now using the garden as a stopover point. It is also a popular place for weekday lunches and sitting quietly.

A "marbleized appearance" was desired by Dudolf, so Guen selected plants that would fulfil that request: "Dawn redwood would never be happy in a hedge, but hornbeam would."[61] Even though the hedge materials are planted quite close together, it is anticipated that it will take about ten years before the shoulder hedge is completely solid to its full height. The armature structure, within which it is planted, is permanent and will not be removed.

Post-planting and maintenance

The Lurie Garden has a separate maintenance endowment, so a gardener is employed specifically to work with the designer to maintain the garden year-round. (The balance of the site is maintained independently either through the City of Chicago or a contract with the park district. Millennium Park is the only park owned by the City of Chicago instead of the park district.) Economic stimulation of area real estate includes seven adjacent condominium developments, which directly attribute their success to the construction of the park. For example, in 2005, an additional 3 to 4 million park tourism visits to the city translated into a major financial benefit for the city. This project is proof that an innovative public–private funded partnership can spearhead a major public works construction project and achieve a product that serves as public open space, and provides an unprecedented center for world-class art, music, architecture, and landscape architecture. Millennium Park also proves that carefully conceived urban centers can be redesigned with green roofs, changing key locations of civic blight into cultural and economic amenities, and generators of urban pride.[62]

Winnipeg Mountain Equipment Co-op, Winnipeg, Manitoba, Canada

DESIGN TEAM

Architect: Prairie Architects, Dudley Thompson

Mechanical engineer: Faraci Engineering, Ed Faraci

Electrical engineer: MCW/Age Engineering, Elliot Garfinkel

Structural engineer: Wolfrom Engineering, Dan Wolfrom

Construction manager: Milestone Project Management, Gerry Humphreys

Scientist and project manager: Richard Kula

Horticultural consultant: Prairie Habitats, Inc., John Morgan

5-111. View of the Winnipeg Mountain Equipment Co-op building with its two separate roofs and tall shade structures, symbolizing trees, at the entrance. Only the lower building has a green roof.

Context and concept

Downtown Winnipeg includes areas of dynamic urban design and renewal juxtaposed with economically depressed areas with potential for development. The Winnipeg Mountain Equipment Co-op building, in the midst of this rapidly evolving district of shopping areas, entertainment and dining, planned for the expansion of its existing facility.[63]

Richard Kula, a scientist residing in Winnipeg, was the project manager and consulting scientist for the design team. The team recognized that in reusing their existing site, there was limited room at the footprint level for usable outdoor space. A green roof was conceived as a feasible solution. They planned to apply for LEED certification, so the green roof became one of many components that had to be carefully documented to comply with LEED criteria. The project earned a gold certification by the U.S. Green Building Council.

Originally, there were three buildings on the site, located at the intersection of major streets in downtown Winnipeg. Only one building was in robust condition. However, most of the existing building materials, such as Douglas fir and brick, were reusable. The wall between two of the existing buildings was in good condition, and it was sawn open in a few locations to allow circulation between different areas of the new store. Over 300,000 bricks were reclaimed, some for paving but most for walls and typical building construction. By the end of the construction process, the design team was able to verify that 97 percent of the materials were reused. As a result, the total cost of the building averaged $87 per square foot (Canadian) or $936/m², a savings of 50 percent over the cost of a new retail facility in Winnipeg.

The cooperative is a membership organization, that is, customers can purchase memberships that enable them to buy merchandise at a discount. Typical of many retail establishments, facilities such as showers, restrooms, and rest areas were planned for the employees. The design team conceived of these employee-only features as an opportunity to incorporate energy efficient and sustainable design.

Layout

The new building is three stories tall with a green roof two stories up, and a conventional roof on the third story, which continues upward on the other side of the party wall. The green roof is easily accessible by elevator and stairs within the building. Shade structures act as unifying features. There are three at street level, sculptured to resemble trees, enhancing the entrance; another, more conventional in shape, is positioned on the green roof, providing some shade over pavements and plantings (Fig. 5-111).

To passerby, the shade structures at the entrance and on the green roof might appear to be primarily aesthetic; however, the design team actually used them as cooling devices. The shading coefficient of three galvanized "trees" at street

5-112, 5-113. The green roof at the Mountain Co-op soon after planting (*top*) and after establishment. A shade structure is set over the parapet wall and adjacent seating area.

level would be required to provide the equivalent shading of the shade structure over the green roof. A third shade structure is placed on the conventional roof as an aesthetic component.

Green roof

The design team chose the Soprema green roof system, which combines a root-inhibiting membrane with a drainage mat. The total area of the green roof is 4,294 square feet (398.9 m²), of which 2,882 square feet (267.7 m²) are the plantings and 1,412 square feet (131.2 m²) are for paths and gravel. A conventional membrane was used on the third floor roof.

Another design detail of the green roof is that the parapets are wrapped with galvanized aluminum. This reflects as much light as possible, and reduces the amount of heat absorbed, thus reducing the cooling needs of the entire building.

Curbed paths, constructed of concrete pavers, provide access around the perimeter and against the parapet of the green roof. Gravel is used as infill between pavers and in odd-shaped areas. This material provides drainage, and also circumvents the need to cut pavers in irregular shapes. The path is slightly pitched toward the gravel to facilitate drainage, and drainage occurs between the individual pavers as well. The curbs themselves are a non-combustible composite material made of tires, metal scraps, shopping bags, and other recyclable materials compressed with a binder (Figs. 5-115, 5-116, and 5-117). Several portable benches are located in a central paved area under the canopy of the shade structure (Fig. 5-112).

The goal was to recreate a natural prairie system, whose soils tend to hold substantial moisture, so significant clay content was included in the growing medium. It was applied to a uniform thickness of 8 inches (20.3 cm) and consists of a mixture of one-third clay, one-third peat and one-third pumice. The growing medium and the filter cloth remove and collect suspended sediments within the rainwater.

Other features

The design team sought to draw energy for irrigation and cooling from solar panels. Even though electricity in the province of Manitoba is relatively cheap, it was still deemed reasonable to incorporate some energy-efficient solar technologies. Cooperative cooling from the green roof produces "sweating," which reduces the heating load through evaporation and thus the need for air conditioning. At the peak of summer, in July, a total of 43 million British Thermal Units (BTUs) of cooling energy are generated, the equivalent of 30 kilowatts, or about one third of the total required for cooling the entire building.

Because the design team made every effort to comply with principles of sustainable design while applying for a LEED certification, there are many unusual features of the building that are examples of these two goals. Whenever possible, the fittings, components, and furnishings are energy efficient yet comfortable. For example, no volatile organic compounds were permitted. A radiant heating system is used throughout the building. The toilets in public areas are dual flush (Caroma), meaning that there are two buttons; one results in a 1.6-gallon flush (6.1 L), and the other (for liquid-only waste) is only a .8 gallon flush (3.0 L).

In the employee-only areas there are composting toilets (Clivus multrum) that gradually turn all waste into a recycled compost product. All co-op employees and members are encouraged to use the composting toilet just once per shift or during rainy periods, to reduce the impact of combined sewage overflows to the local rivers. Because rainwater is collected on the roofs, more water is available for flushing during periods of rainfall. It is expected that within three to four years the clivus multrum toilets can be "harvested" of compost from solid wastes. By contrast, liquid waste is harvested right away. It is pumped as a nitrogen-rich gray water, or compost "tea" fertilizer, to the green roof, where it mixes with the irrigation water.

The faucets and showerheads (Bricor) reduce water consumption by 72 percent. These operate by the Venturi effect, whereby pressurized water is mixed with air and generates turbulence, which gives the texture of a lot of water without a great deal of flow. Therefore, someone using either the faucet or shower would have little sense of such a significant reduction in water usage.

Many of the rooms that are not in continuous use have occupancy-sensored lights; that is, when someone enters the room by opening a door, the

lights turn on. If no movement is sensed after a certain period of time, the lights turn off, saving significant electricity and light bulbs.

The top floor of the building is leased to the Manitoba Eco-Network, an environmental consortium. Although there is ready access to the top floor via stairs and elevator, there is limited accessibility because people would have to go through the Eco-Network space in order to reach the green roof. However, the Manitoba Eco-Network provides green building educational tours to interested customers and employees of the co-op, as well as the general public.

LEED process

The co-op building was one of the first in Manitoba in which the LEED process was used. Now the LEED certification process is mandatory in Manitoba on all projects in which government funds are used; the approximate total budget for government funded construction projects in 2007 was four billion Canadian dollars. Because LEED certification is gaining such importance, a discussion of the specific credits granted for this project is warranted. In the LEED process the green roof contributed directly to earning six credits and indirectly to earning one credit in association with other sus-

tainable building elements. As many as fifteen credits are awarded for compliance with all requirements.[64]

The project earned four Sustainable Site credits: one credit for reduced site disturbance; two for storm water management; and one additional credit for the reduction of the heat island on the roof. Since most existing construction materials were reused on site, there was a significant reduction in site disturbance. All storm water is captured on the roof by gutters and collected in rainwater tanks. The reflective aluminum covers on the parapets, the green roof plantings, and the treatment of the conventional roof, a "cool" roof, all contribute to reduction of building temperatures.

The green roof earned two Water Efficiency credits and supported the achievement of one additional credit in this category. A storm water capture system to collect runoff from gutters and roofs reduces the storm water discharge from the site. The captured storm water is used exclusively to irrigate the green roof. An irrigation pump powered by a photovoltaic cell was coordinated so that the generation of electricity increased in direct proportion to the solar radiation received by the green roof (Figure 5-114). The green roof contributed indirectly to one credit for innovative wastewater technologies because the growing medium receives the solid and liquid by-products of the composting toilets within the building. The nitrogen-rich composting "tea" was incorporated into the storm water irrigation system. The tea is also rich in phosphorus, a nutrient for the green roof plants. The green roof serves both to treat the gray water and reduce the production of wastewater from the building.

There were no LEED credits for the energy efficiency of the green roof. Methods of measuring and verifying energy benefits of the green roof made it too difficult to incorporate such data into the energy model of the building. However, methods of measuring energy and creating scientific models will continue to advance, so that the energy related benefits of a green roof will be easier to establish.

An innovation in design credit was awarded for exemplary water use reduction, but this was a project-wide application, rather than just for the green roof. However, more innovative use of the green roof infrastructure, for example, to save potable water by substituting storm water for water in toilet flushing and other functions, could easily result in considerable LEED credits for future green roof designs.

Plant materials and irrigation

Consistent with the native environment around Winnipeg, the plant palette included twenty-six prairie species. Some are expected to grow better than others so that, in time, an evolving plant community will emerge on the roof, even if it does not consist of as many species as the original plantings. All plant materials were planted as small plugs because the size of the green roof, about 3,000 square feet (278.7 m²),

5-115, 5-116, 5-117. At the Mountain Co-op green roof, pavements, edges, and the walks adjacent to the parapet allow access for maintenance.

228

was limited. Volunteers assisted in the planting process.

The design team considered establishing food production on the green roof, but research indicated that considerably more maintenance would be required than for prairie-type plantings, which are adapted to long periods of drought, as well as fire and flood. In addition, there was some concern that the growing medium required for food production, which requires a greater amount of clay in the soil, could create too much weight.

The plant list on this page was provided by Prairie Habitats, Inc. and includes the specific quantities of each plant. The planting was done in the fall of 2004 with the assistance of volunteers. A mixture of grasses and wildflowers was used, to simulate a prairie landscape. Most require full sun, but some do well in partial shade. All plants were in 2.5 x 2.5 x 4-inch (6.4 x 6.4 x 10.2 cm) containers.[65]

In addition to the contained plants, a 10-pound seed mix of native prairie wildflower and grasses was broadcast over the entire green roof planting area. These seeds were collected from various remnants of Manitoba's native prairie or from seed plots originally started from local seed. All the plants are propagated from this seed. The final seed mix was composed of Little Bluestem Mix, which consists of eighty-five percent Little Bluestem grass mixed with many other species, as shown in the first group of plants in the second list. For this specific project, additional grasses were added (see the second list).

The irrigation system is on the surface and will be phased out once the plantings become established. A photovoltaic unit 3 feet square (0.28 m²) generates as much as 150 watts of electricity per hour, which is used to power a ¾ horsepower pump, carefully sized and specified by the project engineer to provide the maximum output in proportion to the anticipated power output of the photovoltaics. The system can provide up to 5,000 gallons (18,927 L) of water per month. Sensors in the photovoltaic system provide water in proportion to the intensity of the sun; when the sun is brighter and more intense, more water will be delivered.

On the roof are two 1,250-gallon (4,732 L) rainwater tanks, with the potential for double

---

WINNIPEG MOUNTAIN EQUIPMENT CO-OP PLANT LIST

Anemone patens (5)	Prairie crocus
Anemone virginiana (57)	Woodland anemone
Aquilegia Canadensis (5)	Wild columbine
Aster laevis (50)	Smooth aster
Aster ptarmicoides (43)	Upland white aster
Aster sericens (11)	Western silvery aster
Astragalus crassicarpus (2)	Ground plum
Beckmannia syzigachne (45)	Slough grass
Fragria virginiana (28)	Wild strawberry
Gaillardia aristata (15)	Gaillardia
Geum triflorum (10)	Three flowered avens
Heirochloe odorata (50)	Sweet grass
Heliopsis helianthoides (16)	Rough false sunflower
Iris versicolor (50)	Wild iris
Muhlenbergia glomerata (10)	Bog muhly
Opuntia fragilis (10)	Prickly pear cactus
Potentilla arguta (61)	White cinquefoil
Ratibida columnifera (37)	Yellow coneflower
Rosa woodsii (15)	Wild rose
Solidago rigida (20)	Stiff goldenrod
Solidago nemoralis (30)	Showy goldenrod
Thalictrum dasycarpum (10)	Tall meadow rue
Verbena hastate (4)	Blue vervain
Zizia aurea (4)	Golden Alexander

WINNIPEG MOUNTAIN EQUIPMENT CO-OP 2ND PLANT LIST

Achillea millefolium	Yarrow
Agropyron subsecundum	Awned wheatgrass
Anemone cylindrica	Long-fruited anemone
Anemone multifida	Cut-leaved anemone
Bouteloua gracilis	Blue grama
Campanula rotundifolia	Harebell
Dalea candida	White prairie clover
Erigeron annuus	Daisy fleabane
Galium boreale	Northern bedstraw
Heterotheca villosa	Hairy golden aster
Koeleria macrantha	June grass
Monarda didyma	Bergamot
Ratibiba pinnata	Yellow coneflower
Rudbeckia hirta	Black-eyed Susan
Schizachyrium scoparium (85%)	Little bluestem
Solidago missouriensis	Low goldenrod
Thalictrum venulosum	Veiny meadow-rue
Trifolium pratense	Purple clover
Adropogon gerardii	Big bluestem
Agrostis hiemalis	Hair grass
Elymus Canadensis	Canada wild rye
Sorghastrum nutans	Indian grass

this volume if necessary. Rainwater is captured both from the green roof and conventional roof. The tanks are additional sources for irrigation water. The total amount of stormwater generated is about 60,000 gallons (227,125 L) per year on the conventional and green roofs combined. Kula reports, "The tanks are sized for about twice the maximum recorded rainfall so it is our expectation that we capture essentially all of the rainwater that falls in the site. However there are times that we expect our capacity will not handle the storm water during times of continued intense rainfall. So we have a failsafe gravity overflow to the storm drain."[66]

Post-planting and maintenance
The installation is being evaluated by volunteers from Manitoba Eco-Network. Prairie Habitats consults on the planting and maintenance and reported that "no special problems were encountered in maintenance," except that the growing medium "compacted to about half of what it was supposed to be, giving reduced room for the deep prairie plant root systems." This may account for the observation that species native to wet environments do better in the planting area.[67] The amount of clay in the substrate also may be a factor. The plants appeared to be nitrogen-deficient, requiring further research. The prickly pear cactus and avens have barely survived. The plants that have done best are yarrow, wild strawberry, sweet grass, slough grass, hair grass, veiny meadow rue, wild columbine, black-eyed Susan, gaillardia, harebell, and Canadian wild rye. The big grasses (big bluestem and Indian grass) germinated very well from seed but have neither grown tall nor matured.

Planted with native prairie species that might attract insects and birds, the modestly-sized green roof is substantial enough to create habitat. Because the plants are on the roof, they are protected from street-level air pollution, and visiting birds are protected from predators. The educational function of the green roof is also important; exhibits and guides explain that the plantings represent the densest concentration of threatened and endangered native prairie plants in Manitoba.

The Monica and Charles A. Heimbold Jr. Visual Arts Center, Sarah Lawrence College, Bronxville, NY

DESIGN TEAM
Landscape architects: Nicholas Quennell, partner-in-charge, Quennell Rothschild & Partners; Mark Bunnell, project manager
Architect: Susan T. Rodriguez, principal-in-charge, Polshek Partnership Architects
Structural engineer: Severud Associates
MEP engineer: Altieri Sebor Wieber
Client representative: Daedalus Projects, Inc.: Richard Marks, Shane Nolan
Construction manager: F.J. Sciame Co., Inc.

Context and concept
The new Monica and Charles A. Heimbold Jr. Visual Arts center (Heimbold Center for short) provides a dynamic interdisciplinary environment for the visual arts at Sarah Lawrence College, a progressive liberal arts institution whose bucolic campus is about 15 miles (24.2 km) north of New York City. Although visual elements have always been integral to the college's curriculum, over time the various program disciplines were dispersed across the campus, in often inadequate spaces. The design team felt that the college's dual objectives for this building—strengthening the arts curriculum and forging a new educational direction in the arts—could be achieved only through the creation of a unified environment that would foster an intensive and creative dialogue between students and faculty. In addition, the college sought a leadership role in sustainable design.[68]

The site for the building had been determined by a previous campus master plan, but the program for the building was more complex than originally thought. The architect's solution was to locate functions not requiring significant daylight in a below-grade area. The green roof evolved from the LEED process, and the architect determined that a substantial portion of the building program could be underground, allowing a green roof.

Layout
Sarah Lawrence's campus is characterized by undulating topography, dramatic rock outcroppings, and dense foliage. The Heimbold Center

occupies a prominent site adjacent to the president's house, a two-story fieldstone structure dating from the early twentieth century. The new building is integrated into the topography of the existing hilltop: on the south a stepped, grass-covered rooftop reduces the overall impact of the building on the natural environment. The resulting landscaped space is a new outdoor public focal point for the campus.

To promote engagement with the building, encourage movement through it, and ultimately afford all students visual access to the creative process, the design for this 60,000 square-foot (5.574 m²) building incorporates preexisting patterns of pedestrian movement between classroom facilities on the campus and dormitories to its west. Moreover, as the building emerges from the ground plane and its stone base, glass is employed as the primary material, affording visual transparency and maximizing indoor daylight. Integration between the indoor and outdoor space is achieved by means of glass garage-type doors, which open to the landscaped terrace from studios, critique spaces, and a café.

On the interior, teaching and exhibit spaces are integrated into the network of circulation and movement. Although the studio spaces for painting, drawing, sculpture, printmaking, photography, film/new media, art history, and visual culture are specific to each discipline, production spaces are accessible to all students. General critique spaces, seminar rooms, and technology clusters are interspersed throughout the building.

Green roof

The green roof is an intensive system composed entirely of terraced lawn panels, integrated seamlessly with the surrounding landscape. The lawn panels, which are separated by stone retaining walls, serve as open space, outdoor classrooms, and audience seating for outdoor film screenings and other events. Below the green roof are mechanical, storage, workshop,

5-118. The substantial green area of the terraces at the Heimbold Center at Sarah Lawrence College sets a foreground for the building and is fully utilized. (Courtesy of Steven Turner for Polshek Partnership)

5-119. The terraces at the Heimbold Center can be clearly seen as they step down over the underground portion of the building while linking spaces on either side. (Courtesy of Polshek Partnership)

5-120. Broad spaces between adjacent buildings at the Sarah Lawrence campus maintain a feeling of spaciousness. (Courtesy of Polshek Partnership)

5-121. Comfortable use of the space by students. (Courtesy of Polshek Partnership)

and other utility spaces. The roof comprises three levels of terraces plus a stage area covering a total of approximately 10,000 square feet (929 m^2).

The composition of the green roof layers was an integrated system (Hydrotech), and the growing medium is a mixture of three components: 75 percent .375-inch (9.5 mm) expanded slate aggregate (PermaTill Stalite), 20 percent typical root zone sand (USGA), and 5 percent typical local humus.

Other features

From the start, fundamental principles of sustainable design relating to siting, solar orientation, material selection, daylighting, and mechanical systems informed the design process and were integrated into the overall conceptual design. The project is characterized by an extraordinary level of detail resolution, inventive integration of natural light, and exploration of innovative materials, technologies, and systems. Exemplary are a recycled glazing system, which defines the painting studios' northern exposure, and a central skylit gallery, which forms a two-story light-filled focal point for the building. Inspiration for the building's primary materials—fieldstone, cedar, channel glass, and zinc—was found in the campus's rich landscape and historic architecture. Quarrying the stone near the site continued the college's history of utilizing local fieldstone in the construction of its buildings and contributed to the project's twenty-nine LEED points, a "certified" rating. LEED points were also awarded for water-efficient landscaping; the amount of water use was reduced and irrigation is extremely efficient.

Planting and irrigation

The lawn was seeded (or sod was placed) and is composed of 80 percent tall fescue, 10 percent blue grass, and 10 percent perennial ryegrass. Planting occurred during June and July 2004. The irrigation system is a standard 6-inch (15.2 cm) pop-up sprinkler system (Rain Bird).

Post-planting and maintenance

Maintenance consists of standard mowing, fertilization, and irrigation, as would be required on any high-use public lawn. There have been no significant problems since its opening.

California Academy of Sciences, Golden Gate Park, San Francisco, CA

DESIGN TEAM
Architect: Renzo Piano Building Workshop, Genoa and Paris
Collaborating architect: Stantec Architecture, formerly Chong Partners Architecture, San Francisco
Green roof consultant: Paul Kephart, Rana Creek
Landscape architect: SWA Group, Sausalito, California
Structural, mechanical, electrical, acoustical, plumbing, fire safety engineering, and LEED consultant: Ove Arup & Partners, San Francisco
Civil engineer: Rutherford & Chekene, Oakland, California

Context and concept

The new California Academy of Sciences, scheduled to open in 2008, begins with a natural disaster that led to a decision to rebuild the academy, which was founded in 1853 and housed in twelve buildings in Golden Gate Park, dating from 1916. The 1989 Loma Prieta earthquake caused serious structural damage. The Board of Trustees decided in the spring of 2000 to build anew.[69]

Underneath one undulating "living" roof of native plants, aquarium, planetarium, and public exhibit spaces are distinct yet interconnected forms. The same roof encompasses the research departments and the storage of the more than eighteen million specimens, which are the basis for scientific research. Architect Renzo Piano said that he wanted to cut a piece of Golden Gate Park and lift it 35 feet (10.7 m) into the air, like a flying carpet, but no element is higher than any part of the previous buildings, so the academy tends to blend into the park.[70] Compared to the formerly spread-out campus, the more compact arrangement of new facilities returns an additional acre (0.4 ha) of land to Golden Gate Park.

As a model of sustainable design, the new academy will embody the mission statement of the institution. Throughout the integrated design is an emphasis on water and energy efficiency, natural light, natural ventilation, indoor environmental quality, and sustainable site

management. Recycled building materials are incorporated where possible, and native plant materials are used not only on the green roof but also in the surrounding landscape. The academy intends to achieve a platinum LEED rating, which would be a first for this type of project.

Layout

A beautifully scaled piazza, partially covered with glass, is the central space of the complex. The undulating domed green roof reflects the exhibits below: the Steinhart Aquarium entrance and two 90-foot (27.4 m) diameter spheres, one a planetarium seating three hundred and the other a three-level living rain forest exhibit. The green roof will measure approximately 520 by 250 feet (158.5 by 76.2 m) or 130,000 square feet (12,077 m²) or almost 3 acres (1.2 ha) and be visible to the public from an observation deck, accessible via stairs and elevators.

African Hall, one of the four rectangular volumes under the green roof, features Beaux-Arts–style rooms and will be restored. Some historic features of the earlier architecture, such as the barrel-vaulted ceiling of the Steinhart Arch and the Swamp Tank, will be recalled in the new architecture. A very large aquarium is located under the main floor. Large tanks are visible on the main floor and receive daylight in the aquarium level.

Green roof

The architectural form of the green roof is constructed with steel and concrete. There is an almost 40-foot (12.2 m) elevation change between the lowest and highest points. Even so, most of the layers are typical for a green roof. The top layer will be vegetation, and the slopes on the dome, which can be at an angle as high as 40 percent, call for a soil retention system made with an interlocking gabion grid. In between the gabions, the built-up section of the green roof contains (from the top layer down)

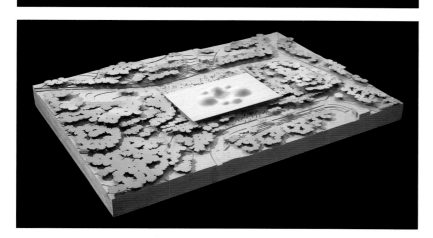

5-122, 5-123, 5-124, 5-125. A rendering, a computer model and two architectural models demonstrate how the green roof at the California Academy of Sciences will appear to float above the building like a magic carpet. (Second from bottom: photo by Stefano Goldberg © Publifoto; all courtesy of Renzo Piano Building Workshop)

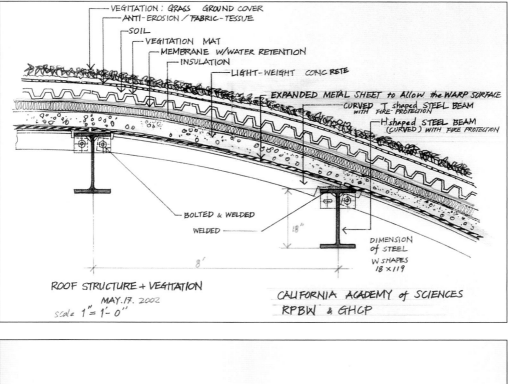

VEGITATION: GRASS GROUND COVER
ANTI-EROSION / FABRIC-TESSUE
SOIL
VEGITATION MAT
MEMBRANE w/WATER RETENTION
INSULATION
LIGHT-WEIGHT CONCRETE
EXPANDED METAL SHEET to ALLOW the WARP SURFACE
CURVED T shaped STEEL BEAM with FIRE PROTECTION
H shaped STEEL BEAM (CURVED) WITH FIRE PROTECTION

BOLTED & WELDED
WELDED
18"
DIMENSION of STEEL W SHAPES 18 x 119
8'

ROOF STRUCTURE + VEGITATION
MAY. 17. 2002
scale 1" = 1'- 0"

CALIFORNIA ACADEMY of SCIENCES
RPBW & GHCP

5-126, 5-127. A section showing the green roof layers at the California Academy of Sciences and a design section showing the green roof forms. The steep slopes are apparent. (both courtesy of Renzo Piano Building Workshop; bottom photo by Stefano Goldberg © Publifoto)

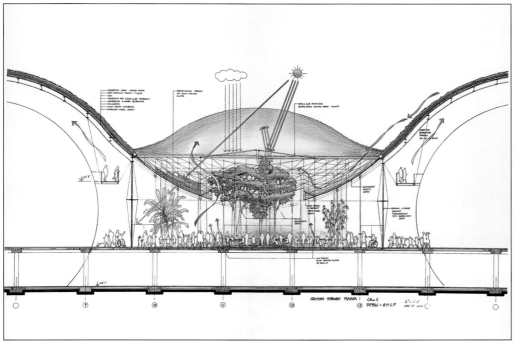

the growing medium, vegetation mat, and drainage membrane with water retention and insulation. The gabions will also be used for capturing surface water runoff and directing water towards perimeter drainage systems.

The lightweight growing medium when saturated weighs only 31 to 36 pounds per square foot (151.3 to 175.8 kg/m²)—quite low compared to standard loam soils, which can weigh three times as much. The consultant for the green roof, Paul Kephart, believes that failures occur as a result of poor drainage more than any other factor, so having the right approximation of coarse-to-fine substrate material is also important. A growing medium composed primarily of pumice dried up and blew away in early mock-up tests. The current growing medium being tested is a local volcanic material with 55 percent mineral component, and coconut coir as an organic, sustainable replacement for

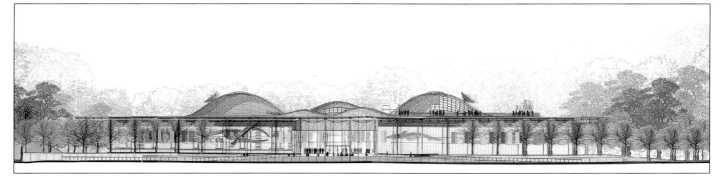

5-128. An elevation of the complex of buildings at the California Academy of Sciences with the unifying green roof. (Courtesy of Renzo Piano Building Workshop)

peat moss. Coconut coir is long fiber extracted from the husk of the nut. The specified plants are being grown to maturity in a nursery in coconut fiber trays, approximately 2 feet square (.19 m²), which will be placed directly on the green roof for ease of installation and will decompose, allowing the roots to expand and create a strong vegetative layer that bonds to the roof.[71]

5-129. A mock-up planter is built at the same slope as the future design and displays to the public the types of plant materials that will be established on the green roof. (Courtesy of Renzo Piano Building Workshop)

The waterproofing will be a monolithic hot rubberized asphalt application, with a root barrier cap sheet providing additional protection. A reservoir-type drain board allows retention of water within egg-crate-like structures and the drainage of excess water through pinholes into the building storm drainage system. The amount of retained moisture will vary a great deal depending on weather conditions, seasonal fluctuations, and plant growth patterns. The drainboard retains a quarter cup of water per square foot (2.54 L/m²), and can drain as much as 350 gallons of water per square foot (14,261 L/m²) per hour, so it has the capacity to handle large, sudden rain events. As the plant roots grow, they will fill the growing medium, so less water will penetrate through it to the drainboard.

Through the green roof components that use, store, and absorb water, it is estimated that the storm water runoff from the new academy will be reduced by at least half, or about 2 million gallons, annually.[72] Runoff from the roof and on site is directed into underground recharge chambers adjacent to the building. A subsurface irrigation system will be installed on the green roof, because particularly on steep slopes, it is the most efficient way to distribute water to the plantings, with minimal loss from runoff and evaporation. An 18,000-gallon (68,137 L) recharge chamber will release collected water back into the aquifer on the site, and also supply irrigation water for use during the driest summer months and other periods, as needed, particularly while the plantings are becoming established.

Other features

The edge of the green roof is a steel structure with 60,000 photovoltaic cells embedded in glass panels. It is anticipated that these panels will provide approximately 213,000 kilowatts of energy annually, about 5 percent of the academy's energy needs. The exhibit space is naturally ventilated by the geometry of the undulating roof. Warm air flows upwards through the top of the roof to prevent overheating of the interior environment. A radiant heating and cooling system will be installed for supplemental thermal comfort. Retractable rolling fabric screens are incorporated in the façades and the glass roof of the piazza for solar, weather, and even acoustic protection. The academy will feature operable windows, and most interior spaces will receive daylight and give views toward the park.

Planting and irrigation

There were many concerns about the range and types of plants that would be planted on the green roof. Many species of forbs and grasses were surveyed for performance and for attractive appearance all year without irrigation, fertilizer, and maintenance. Sudden, substantial rains followed by droughts typify San Francisco's climate. Plants that survive in this environment often go into a long dormancy period during dry weather.

Using mock-ups of different sections of the proposed green roof that matched the slope conditions of the design and the four solar orientations of the final domed shape of the green roof, with a maximum root depth of 6 to 8 inches (15.2 to 20.3 cm), the green roof consultant selected twenty-four species in 2003. The medium was in very-well-drained soil composed of lightweight pumice with some organic matter, and although the the plants received torrential rains almost immediately—8 inches (20.3 m) of rain in a 36-hour period—the growing medium held together well. The relative location of each species

5-130, 5-131, 5-132. Three views of a mock-up of a portion of the green roof at the California Academy of Sciences from initial construction through full growth of the plant materials. In the bottom image the outline of the gabion infrastructure initially installed can be observed barely showing through the dense vegetative growth. (Courtesy of Renzo Piano Building Workshop)

CALIFORNIA ACADEMY OF SCIENCES PLANT LIST		
*Armeria maritime	Sea thrift	High on the roof
Carex panza	Sand sedge	Low
Festuca rubra	Red fescue	Low
*Frageria chiloensis	Beach strawberry	Medium
*Prunella vulgare	Self heal	Medium
*Sedum spathilifolium	Stonecrop	High
Stachy bullata	Hedge nettle	Medium to high

within the green roof was another consideration because those plants growing higher up would receive less moisture and different amounts of solar radiation than those toward the middle and bottom of the slope. In May 2003, after evaluating the condition of the test plantings, the list was narrowed to the seven most successful plants, and finally to the four species starred in the above plant list.[73]

These plants are remarkably tough. *Carex panza*, for example, can live up to one thousand years as an individual plant; it could outlive the building itself. The sedum is a host for the passion blue butterfly larva; the other three finalists have unique characteristics that make them desirable as well as adaptable within a commu-

nity of plants. However, the plantings will not be limited to these species. During the growing season, the planted roof will be seeded with annual wildflowers to contrast with, and complement, the previously planted species. An important principle of this green roof planting is that it should not increase the biomass. The ecological approach is to select plants for adaptation and performance rather than just aesthetics.

Kephart explains: "I demonstrated those plant materials in a series of mockups that allowed for the life cycle to occur. The other members of the design team, even though they are dedicated to dissemination and exploration of natural world, were primarily concerned with public perception about the appearance of the landscape. And it was the amenity and adornment parameters that ended us with the final selections of four diminuitive plants, they are good plants, they do provide habitat, but they behave themselves, and they get along together like kindergartners."[74]

Included in the plant list are both wind- and sun-adaptive plants. Some volunteer plants will take root as a result of windblown seeds or deposition from birds, but they can be weeded out, depending on what they are and whether they

5-133. The California Academy of Sciences under construction, with the green roof dome taking shape. (Photo by Jon McNeal; courtesy of Renzo Piano Building Workshop)

5-134. The North elevation of the Academy, which will be the main public entrance. (Courtesy of Kang Kiang at Stantec Architecture, formerly Chong Partners Architecture, San Francisco)

5-135. The piazza is directly below the large concave shape. The circular skylights provide natural ventilation into and exhaust from the exhibit halls below. (Courtesy of Kang Kiang at Stantec Architecture, formerly Chong Partners Architecture, San Francisco)

5-136. Bands of gabions keep the biotrays stable while also receiving storm water runoff during heavy rains. Metal mesh covers the mechanical intake point in the roof. (Courtesy of Kang Kiang at Stantec Architecture, formerly Chong Partners Architecture, San Francisco)

5-137. The yellow blooming plant is a wildflower, *Layia platyglossa* (Tidy tips). (Courtesy of Kang Kiang at Stantec Architecture, formerly Chong Partners Architecture, San Francisco)

are deemed appropriate for the roof ecosystem. The diversity of the final four plant species selected will make the combination of plantings biologically more stable, that is, less prone to pathogens, disease, and seasonal fluctuations. The plants will form a continuous mat of vegetation on the roof, just as they form a continuous root mass below the surface. The entire growing medium will be inoculated with microrhize as well. It is anticipated that microorganisms and insects will help maintain aeration of the soil.

Post-planting and maintenance

Maintenance will be minimal. In part this is a necessity, based on the steepness of some areas of the domed green roof, which would make access difficult. The green roof will not accom-modate visitors for safety and maintenance reasons, but interpretive materials will be available on the viewing deck. Studies are currently being conducted to test the use of cameras, focused on plants of interest or other special features, to provide visitors with a close-up look at the habitat. The green roof will serve many educational functions, such as informing the public about San Francisco's climate, native and invasive species, birds, butterflies, and insects, as well as the unique aspects of this particular installation. Stormwater runoff and retention, temperatures, and other variables will also likely be monitored.

Top left: 5-138. Green roof under construction at the California Academy of Sciences in February 2006. (Photo by Jon McNeal, courtesy of Renzo Piano Building Workshop)

5-139, 5-140, 5-141. Installation of the planter trays in May 2007, with special precautions to stabilize them on the steeply sloping roof. (Photo by Jon McNeal, courtesy of Renzo Piano Building Workshop)

CHAPTER SIX
Trends

The previous chapters have presented an overview of green roof projects in Europe and detailed case studies in North America. What directions may green roof design take in the future?

Contemporary design, critics contend, has become homogenous. A subdivision layout in Las Vegas may resemble one in Los Angeles, Atlanta, Boston, Dallas, or even Shanghai. An industrial park in Calgary, Alberta, may look like one in Louisville, Kentucky. A giant shopping mall in Edmonton, Alberta, could be mistaken for one in Minneapolis or Chicago. With franchises for Starbucks, McDonalds, and Dunkin Donuts spread across the globe, prefabricated and predetermined architectural components and landscape vocabularies are becoming the norm, rather than the exception.

Green roof design could fall victim to this same defect, yet nature may offer an alternative. Although construction materials and installation techniques are similar regardless of location, different climates and economies require different choices of substrates and plant materials. Copycat approaches may not work; for example, installations in Japan based on European models have failed because they did not respond to the unique aspects of the Japanese climate. In Tokyo, during the summer there may be rain on a daily basis, followed by long periods of dry weather. Early attempts to install green roofs used sedums, but these plant materials sometimes rotted because they are not comfortable being kept wet for long periods. In time the Japanese will find substrates drawn from local sources, as well as a range of plant material adaptable to their variable climates. The result will be a green roof vocabulary with its own aesthetic. As discussed in Chapter One, the Japanese have pioneered innovations in living walls.

The following discussion examines groups of projects with common themes in order to demonstrate the breadth of contemporary practice and draw some conclusions about it. Vernacular designs which incorporate green roof techniques serendipitously, despite isolation from modern practice, are presented first. Then, traditional designs are presented, based on established modern practice. Traditional design will no doubt continue to flourish, in much the same way that the continual reinven- tion of classical style remains popular in residential architecture and other types of projects.

In an increasingly urban environment, the spaces between buildings, as well as overlooked entrances, are being rediscovered, reinterpreted, and given design emphasis. There are also some notable projects in which major institutions followed a sustainable design approach from the beginning of the design process. And green roof technology offers opportunities to small-scale homeowners and community organizations to enhance their environments within reasonable budgets.

The chapter profiles some of the specialists emerging in the green roof industry. Hybrid designs are also presented, in which modern roof gardens are created through a merger of traditional and contemporary techniques. Complete plant lists are provided for some projects; for others, particular plant materials are highlighted. The chapter concludes with a summary of predictions about green roof design.

Vernacular Designs

Some designers emphasize the vernacular —that is, the indigenous qualities and materials of a particular location that give it a unique flavor. Three examples are: the pedestrian Bridge of Flowers in Shelburne Falls, MA, where an ordinary bridge over the town's main river was transformed into a sensory experience; Square Viger in Montreal, Quebec, in which an urban renewal project was taken over by local artists; and the studio roof garden space of RockWerks in Brooklyn, New York, where a sculptor used leftover materials scavenged from many sources to create an intimate garden. In some ways all three examples might be thought of as green roofs by accident.

The Bridge of Flowers, Shelburne Falls, MA[1]

The Bridge of Flowers across the Deerfield River is now a gateway to the town of Shelburne Falls, and a precursor of green roof design in America. The 400-foot-long by 15-foot-wide (122.0 x 4.6 m) bridge, with its five graceful concrete arches, was originally built in 1908 to carry trolleys between Shelburne and the adjacent town of Buckland. The bridge was abandoned in 1928, when the trolley ceased to

Top left:
6-1. The Bridge of Flowers in Shelburne Falls is planted for its full length across the river.

Left:
6-2. The main vehicular bridge across the river also includes a sidewalk so that visitors can take a loop walk from one bridge to another.

Above:
6-3. Trees are planted over the structural supports for the bridge at the base of each arch, where there is both a greater loading capacity and also a greater planting depth.

run. In 1929, just fifteen years after the construction of the Moos Lake Water Filtration Plant in Zurich, Mr. and Mrs. Walter Burnham began raising awareness to renovate the bridge, and transform it from urban eyesore to country-like flower garden. Because of its original purpose, there was adequate structural support to develop a pedestrian walk down the center, with symmetrical garden beds on either side. The soil depth over each arch varies from approximately 2.5 feet (0.76 m) over the top of each arch to as much as 9 feet (2.7 m) over the low points. As a result, this roof garden accommodates trees and shrubs in the deeper beds and a wide range of perennials—as many as 500 species altogether.

The Shelburne Falls Women's Club created the Bridge of Flowers Committee to maintain and continue plantings for the garden. Maintenance is carried out by volunteers and part-time gardeners funded by donations and memorial gifts. Many of the plant materials have identifying name tags. The popularity of this park has led to the development of additional gardens, such as a memorial garden adjacent to one end of the walk, and additional tourist attractions.

Square Viger, Montreal, Quebec

Square Viger's green roofs are the result of chance. Built in the late nineteenth century, the lower floors of the grand hotel Place Viger, which faced the Avenue Viger, were used as a major railway station. Hotel guests and travelers could enjoy the nearby gardens which stretched along several blocks adjacent to the hotel. However, following the Great Depres-

sion, the hotel closed, and the commercial district relocated. The building was used for office space; most of the gardens were destroyed in the process of tunneling for a new highway, leaving only an eccentric concrete plaza with pools and some sculptural elements, such as highway bridge supports, with plantings in them instead of roadbeds. A public space was completed by Charles Daudelin in 1983.

Left:
6-4. Place Viger includes large reinforced concrete forms in which a riotous growth of plants flourishes.

Below left:
6-5, 6-6. At Place Viger, a large water feature with a map of Montreal is decorated by artist Rose-Marie E. Goulet with landscape images. Her installation is titled "Nos frontiera, our borders."

Below:
6-7. Rose-Marie E. Goulet sits below one of the structural beams for the park. (Courtesy of the artist)

Structures, such as elements of an abandoned interchange one to two stories tall, punctuate the plaza. Originally irrigated when they were first planted, these areas have been abandoned, yet luxuriant vegetation abounds. An interconnected series of wide channels and pools, one with a large waterfall, masks the noise from adjacent streets and the highway below. Visitors wandering through the square appreciate the shade and shelter offered by the massive overhead structures, which appear to be remnants of a roof garden left unfinished, or one that, once implemented, was left to its own devices. The most common plants are Virginia creeper (*Parthenocissus quinquefolia*) and Boston ivy (*Parthenocissus tricuspidata*). Their rapacious growth over and through many of the concrete columns and structures provides a respite from an otherwise depressing environment.

Since 2001, various independent artist groups, such as Dare–Dare, have installed temporary art in an effort to humanize the space and make it more comfortable.[2] They have met some degree of success, although often their works have been vandalized soon after installation. The starkness of the reinforced concrete forms is offset by the richness of the hanging vegetation and the human scale suggested by the art works. Plans are being made to reclaim and renovate the entire park. One section was already spruced up as a major venue for the Gay Games, held in Montreal in the summer of 2006.[3]

Brooklyn RockWerks, Brooklyn, NY[4]

Adam Distenfeld is a sculptor whose home and business studio, called Rockwerks, is located in the neighborhood of Bushwick in Brooklyn. Using scavenged materials—wood, metal, rock—his sculpture involves drilling into large boulders to transform them into water features. He works on the ground floor of an old industrial building and lives on the second floor, where an irregularly shaped wooden deck squeezes between the eccentric geometry of the edges of his building and adjacent warehousing. On the deck he and his partner grow vegetables, flowers, and decorative perennials in a series of makeshift planters, precursors of the modular, prefabricated units of a green roof. These urban pioneers humanize an industrial landscape with their roof garden.

Traditional Designs

A strong market for the traditional still exists in residential design. In roof gardens, the same long-established methods of constructing structurally reinforced roofs that provide space for outdoor rooms with large planters, varied pavements, and water features will no doubt continue when budgets are large, and the client favors this style. Three notable examples are the roof gardens that wrap around the upper floors of the Hilton Hotel in Montreal, Quebec; the spectacular park built over a waste water treatment plant along the Hudson River in Harlem, New York; and an intimate residential roof garden about six miles (9.7 km) downriver in the heart of Chelsea, a vibrant residential neighborhood.

6-8. A roof garden at Brooklyn RockWerks assembled from vernacular materials scavenged from various locations. This is a popular approach in densely populated urban environments where a lot of material is thrown away for others to use.

Hilton Hotel, Montreal, Canada[5]

The Hilton Hotel commands almost an entire square block in downtown Montreal. On the upper floors are a series of spectacular roof gardens that draw guests outside and encourage them to walk a perimeter route through a well-modulated sequence of garden spaces, including contemplative areas and others with waterfalls and pools. Narrow passageways alternate with broader gardens, whose boundaries

6-9. Water features at the Montreal Hilton include large pools, a continuous trough of moving water that follows the circumference of the gardens, and a large swimming pool.

Right and opposite:
6-10, 6-11. The gardens at the Montreal Hilton consist of spectacular compositions of stone masonry, water features, walks, and plantings that permit visitors to walk around the entire building.

(All images of this project are by the author; courtesy of Hilton Montréal Bonaventure)

6-12. Although built on a grand scale, some quiet areas of the Montreal Hilton roof garden have the intimacy of a Japanese garden.

Riverbank State Park, Harlem, NY[6]

The Hilton Hotel's exclusive gardens are the province only of hotel guests and occasional visitors; by contrast, the spaces built over the Harlem Water Treatment Plant are designated as a public park. Riverbank State Park, as it is called, opened in the spring of 1993, and covers 28 acres (11.3 ha) along a half-mile-long stretch (0.8 km) of the Hudson River. These huge gardens—the crown atop a large sewage treatment plant abutting the river—include: an outdoor 400-meter track with bleachers; three swimming pools, including one of Olympic dimensions; an ice and roller skating rink; basketball, handball, and tennis courts; picnicking areas; a 1000-seat theater, and an art gallery. Playgrounds and promenades for pedestrians, vehicles, and bicycles complete the park's recreational facilities.

The park was built to offset opposition to the location of a sewage treatment plant in Harlem, where political clout was insufficient to counter it. It took twenty-five years of planning and design and many consultants for the state to put a park on top of a sewage treatment plant. The architect and landscape architect of record are Richard Dattner and Howard Abel, respectively, both of New York City.[7]

The roof garden over the sewage treatment plant is typically 4 feet (1.2 m) deep because the live load limits were 400 pounds per square foot (1,953.0 kg/m^2). A lightweight topsoil mix was used to that full depth where trees are planted; and where trees were not part of the program, 2 feet (0.6 m) of the soil mix was placed over an equal depth of Styrofoam. For the entire park, about 6 million board feet (14,158.4 m^3) of Styrofoam were required. Among the plantings were over seven hundred trees. There is a typical irrigation system with pop-up sprinklers and sprayheads, with a back-up system that can desalinate the river water if necessary.[8]

Seventeen smokestacks poke through and soar above the roof garden. Vehicular and pedestrian routes extend over the West Side Highway and connect the park to the adjacent neighborhood of Harlem. Although depressed in relation to the park and effectively screened, the highway is a barrier that may prevent the park from being more integrated into the neighborhood.

Millions of dollars in additional funding have

are disguised by both skillful use of geometry and strategic placement of vegetation. There is a complete sense of separation from the often hectic and noisy hotel. This garden remains an elegant example of what is possible when the structural design of a roof is unencumbered by major budgetary restraints. Despite a more budget-conscious, conservation-oriented world, the luxuriant garden, whether on a rooftop or a grand estate, is a longstanding tradition of landscape architecture, and will no doubt continue. The gardens wrapping around the Hilton are meticulously maintained. They suggest an Eden in the sky.

6-13: An aerial view of Riverbank State Park reveals its grandiose scale. (Courtesy of Philip Caravalho, photographer and Abelie Bainnson Butz, LLP)

6-14. Riverbank State Park features an amphitheater near the Hudson River. The sewage treatment plant is visible in the background, and many other recreational facilities are on top of it. The George Washington Bridge completes the view.

6-15. An esplanade at Riverbank State Park extends the full length of the park along the edge of the river, and affords spectacular views.

6-16. Among the many recreational facilities at Riverbank State Park are a full-size track. The smokestacks for the sewage plant are in the background.

been invested to control odors. Soon after the park opened, people complained about smelling sewage in the swimming pools and at major construction joints between facilities. Although these problems have been ameliorated, occasional wafts of odor still escape, no doubt reminding park users of the behemoth underneath them.

6-17. The landscape at Riverbank State Park has a monumental character. Major features are separated by significant elevation changes.

Roof Garden, Chelsea, NY, NY[9]

Traditional techniques in a modern guise need not only be applied at large sites. Roof gardens are still built for individual apartments on challenging sites, such as this one designed in Chelsea, a neighborhood in Manhattan, by Robert Martin, a wood craftsman, and Dean Anderson, a metal fabricator. The client sought an outdoor space over a sloping roof 32.7 feet (10.0 m) long by 20 feet (6.1 m) wide. Not wanting to be observed from surrounding apartments, the client also requested privacy. Over a roof that slopes 25 inches (63.5 cm) over its total length or 6.4 percent, the designers built a series of level wooden platforms with a connecting flat walk of wood decking connecting back to the entrance. A wood and steel infrastructure, like the framing for a typical deck, supports the substantial weight of all the roof garden elements. The edges of the walk are flanked by a planter about 8 feet long by 4 feet wide by 1 foot deep (2.4 x 1.2 x .3 m) and a quiet pool for aquatic plants of matching dimensions with the same sturdy construction. In order to comply with code requirements forbidding the creation of a new room on the roof (which is defined by the percentage of cover provided), the designers provided privacy and enclosure by installing stainless steel overhead structures measuring 7.3 feet (2.2 m) which provided a frame for retractable awnings, and guardrail panels 42 inches (1.07 m) high, with just enough density to satisfy the building code. Utilities, as with pavers-on-pedestal systems, are carried underneath the deck. The planters and water feature are fitted with bituthene liners which protect the wood, while holding in the water for the pool and the planting soil. The clients installed a lightweight loamy topsoil and the plantings. The luxuriant growth, particularly of vines, such as sweet potato (*ipomea* sp), reinforces the sense of enclosure achieved by the elegant structure.

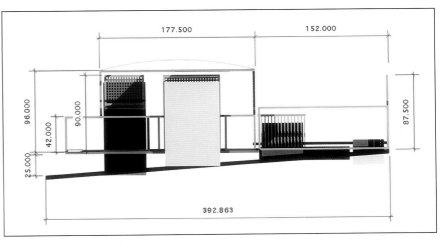

6-18, 6-19. A design elevation for this Chelsea roof garden shows the dimensions and locations of major features. The roof is 392.86 inches (10 m) long. The height of the structure is 96 inches (2.4 m). The deck absorbs an elevation change of 25 inches (0.6 m). As construction began, the perimeter enclosure and the support structure to create a flat space took shape. (Courtesy of Robert Martin Designs and SuperSquare)

Above and right:
6-20 and 6-21. The completed roof garden features graceful stainless steel forms, a range of plants, and a water garden. (Courtesy of Robert Martin Designs)

Below left:
6-22. The simple yet elegant design of the guardrail and the luxuriant vegetation create an oasis of privacy in the midst of a dense urban environment of high-rise buildings. (Courtesy of Robert Martin Designs)

Below right:
6-23. The main deck and its sculptural enclosures create a striking environment. (Courtesy of Robert Martin Designs)

Spaces Between Buildings, Entrances, Accents

In most cities the best available land is taken for development, so attention focuses on the spaces between buildings, or small leftover spaces, previously overlooked, that still provide design potential. At Sniffen Court in New York City, for example, a family developed a series of gardens in previously abandoned spaces and thereby helped to link several buildings and living areas. In a high-rise building on Manhattan's Upper East Side, two tenants renting an apartment created their own roof garden (including space for their pet rabbit). At the main entrance to the Brooklyn Botanic Garden, visitors are welcomed through a gateway formed by small twin buildings with green roofs. Two final examples are in Vancouver, British Columbia, where in one case, a space between buildings was transformed into a serene courtyard welcoming visitors to adjacent cultural and religious institutions, and in the other, a series of spaces, including a roof garden, animate a residence for addicts.

Sniffen Court, NY, NY[10]

Ed and Frances Barlow purchased a historic carriage house dating from the mid-nineteenth century in Sniffen Court, a gated alley in the Murray Hill neighborhood of New York City. Five carriage houses face the narrow alley on either side, and their rear yards are small spaces between the narrow property lines and the rear yards of adjacent buildings. The client's house, 50 feet long by 20 feet wide (15.2 m x 6.1 m), backed up to an illegal storage shed tacked onto the rear of a building facing Third Avenue. Wanting to provide additional space for family members' apartments and to expand their space, the client also purchased the Third Avenue building.

6-24. The residence at Sniffen Court has roof gardens on different levels of two adjacent buildings with an at-grade courtyard garden in between. Tall Ailanthus trees contribute to a multilayered effect.

6-25. The view from the roof garden in Sniffen Court reveals a private garden in an abandoned restaurant storage area. Stone work is by Bruce O'Brien. (Courtesy of Higher Ground Horticulture)

PLANTING PLAN - FRANCES HILL & ED BARLOW RESIDENCE

The existing spaces between these buildings consisted of unsightly pavements, debris and barriers in the midst of a few large ailanthus trees.[11] As the landscape architect, I sought to make the proverbial silk purse from a sow's ear. The removal of the shed revealed a huge slab of bluestone flooring, most of which was unfortunately demolished before it could be salvaged for use on site. Off the kitchen/dining space of the Sniffen Court building, a wood deck was added which projected into the rear space. The deck steps led down to existing grade, which was aerated and transformed into an irregularly shaped garden. In excavating for the footings for the deck, schist was uncovered; slabs of it were used to build dry-laid stone walls to retain earth for plantings. A spiral staircase was installed in one corner to lead up to the first-story roof of the Third Avenue building, which became a roof garden shared by the tenants of this building and the Sniffen Court owners. Bluestone steppingstones and an informal, intimate sitting area were situated below the deck. A narrow alley connecting to the rear entrance of the Third Avenue building was paved with alternating patterns of salvaged schist stones and gravels together with some slate pavers remaining from pavements used for other roof garden spaces on the residence. A steel and wood gate terminates this walk. A tiered water feature built into the rear wall of Third Avenue building masks street noise and adds a focus so that the owners sitting on the wood deck have a splendid view, framed by plantings, of the waterfall from the top level down into a semicircular pool. Throughout the garden, organic forms and plant materials merge with the rectilinear architectural elements.

The various roof garden spaces on the Sniffen Court residence and the Third Avenue building are paved with grids of square slate or bluestone on a pedestal system. The existing roofs of both structures were reinforced to support additional weight. The pedestals are

6-26. A plan view of the garden spaces at Sniffen Court and the gardens between the two buildings. (Courtesy of Madison Cox Design and the author)

6-27. At the Sniffen Court residence, a view from the basement-level kitchen, which connects to a wood deck linking the at-grade and roof gardens.

adjusted to different heights to absorb the grade changes on the pitched roof, so that the resulting pavement is flat. Utility lines for irrigation and lighting run underneath the pavers, and water drains unimpeded from the roof to existing gutters and drains. Wood planters and the owner's terra cotta and ceramic containers are planted with hardy materials and supplied by a drip irrigation system. Landscape lighting illuminates key trees and architectural elements in the evening. Simple steel handrails frame the Third Avenue building's roof garden and protect the edge of the Sniffen Court wood deck. Lattice panels disguise the underside of the deck.

The major ailanthus trees were saved; the deck and the garden were built around them. These trees give an appropriately scaled ceiling to a space four stories tall. Other trees planted at grade include American dogwood, amelanchier, and a stewartia. Materials in planters include hollies and viburnums. A diverse array of shrubs and groundcovers have thrived in the low light, including Japanese andromeda, periwinkle, aucuba, and bulbs. Several large clumps of English ivy (salvaged from old estates being cleared for construction) were transplanted into the garden to give an immediate effect of cloaking the tall masonry walls on one side of the site. The various levels of the garden create an oasis in the midst of the surrounding buildings. Mark Davies of Higher Ground Horticulture, originally hired to do the planting installation, has maintained it over the years, contributing such design touches as an espaliered witch hazel (*Hammamelis virginiana*) on the lower roof garden, and the use of Christmas rose (*Helleborus niger*,) and lenten rose (*Helleborus orientalis*) which flourish in the shade, in the at-grade garden.[12]

Almost all of the plant materials used in the at-grade garden would be suitable on a roof garden, if planted at a small enough size. Over time, some plants have been replaced, based on availability and which plants adapted best to the shady conditions.

SNIFFEN COURT PLANT LIST

AT-GRADE GARDEN

Amelanchier canadensis	Amelanchier or shadblow
Aucuba japonica v.'Golddust'	Variegated Japanese acuba
Aucuba japonica v. 'Picturata'	Variegated Japanese aucuba
Aucuba japonica nana	Dwarf Japanese aucuba
Cornus florida	Flowering dogwood
Crocus sp.	Crocus
Hedera helix	English ivy
Helleborus niger	Christmas rose
Helleborus orientalis	Lenten rose
Narcissus sp	Daffodils
Hydrangea petiolaris	Climbing hydrangea
Pieris japonica	Japanese andromeda
Stewartia koreana	Stewartia
Tulipa sp.	Tulips
Vinca minor	Periwinkle

ROOF GARDENS

Hammamelis virginiana	Witch hazel (espalier)
Hydrangea quercifolia	Oakleaf hydrangea
Ilex verticillata	Winterberry
Magnolia stellata	Star magnolia
Malus floribunda	Japanese flowering crabapple
Tulipa sp.	Tulips
Viburnum plicatum v. tomentosum	Doublefile viburnum
Vinca minor	Periwinkle

NOTE: Annuals are added in the planters for seasonal color and texture.

6-28. The bedroom roof terrace at Sniffen Court has pavement of slate tiles and two elegant trained Japanese crabapples.

APARTMENT ROOF GARDEN PLANT LIST[14]

Acer x freemanii 'Jeffersred'	Jeffer's red maple
Aster x frikartii 'Monch'	Monch asters (Michaelmas daisy)
Buxus 'Chicagoland Green'	Chicagoland green boxwood
Ipomoea alba	Moonvine, morning glory (annual)
Malus sp. 'Prairifire'	Prairifire crabapple
Narcissus sp.	Daffodils
Syringa Meyeri palibin	Palabin dwarf Korean lilac
Thuja occidentalis 'Smaragd'	Smaragd emerald green arborvitae

NOTE: Seasonal bulbs within the aster planter vary each year (usually a single type of tulip)

6-29, 6-30. A planter of asters acts as a pivot point for geometric forms in this roof garden on the Upper East Side of Manhattan.

Apartment Roof Garden, NY, NY[13]

Manhattan's Upper East Side is a dense neighborhood of high-rise residential buildings, bustling commercial streets, and museums; roof gardens are common. However, it is unusual for a rental tenant to partner with an owner to develop a roof garden for mutual benefit. Usually the cost would be prohibitive; neither would want to foot the bill. However, in a serendipitous situation, two architects (names withheld) did just that, gaining permission from their landlord to take advantage of their fifteenth-floor apartment and its adjacent outdoor terrace and rebuild it completely. The building owner re-roofed and put in a concrete paver system on pedestals. Then, as one of the architects explains, "we had planter and pool boxes built out of marine-grade plywood and plexiglass, which were sized to align with the paver grid and be movable, should any roof work need to be done in the future."

Their design emphasizes a gracious connection between indoors and out. The simple geometric layout of pavers on pedestals is understated yet unifying. Perimeter plantings along the parapet provide a clean backdrop for freestanding planters. A simple rectilinear pool is the centerpiece of two outdoor rooms. There is storage space for garden tools, and seating for entertainment and relaxation. The plantings are both permanent and seasonal.

Brooklyn Botanic Garden, Brooklyn, NY[15]

At the Brooklyn Botanic Garden, an interconnected collection of diverse gardens covering 52 acres (21.0 ha) near the Brooklyn Museum, the entrance features a green roof completed in 2006. Designed by the Polshek Partnership Architects, LLP, two small admission buildings flanking the entrance are cloaked with a steeply sloped planting of bulbs, groundcover, and ferns as developed by the Garden's horticulture staff. The palette of ferns changes at the lower ends of the plantings where more moisture collects as it drains; at the bottom, some of the plantings blend into those on the adjacent at-grade gardens. The green roofs welcome visitors and educate them about the Garden. The ferns were chosen as an example for Garden visitors to demonstrate plants that are adaptable to dry or damp shady areas, typical of the conditions that homeowners might experience in Brooklyn and other similar environments. The ferns on the berms are evergreen/semi-evergreen, while the ferns at grade are deciduous.

Since more water collects towards the downhill side of the green roof, ferns that prefer a more moist environment (cinnamon fern and ostrich fern, *Osmunda cinnamonea* and *Matteuccia struthiopteris* respectively), are planted there and transition directly into groups of the same species planted at grade. On the higher reaches of the green roof is Christmas fern

Top:
6-31. From inside the Brooklyn Botanic garden the twin green roof mounds help give enclosure and separation from the street.

Above and left:
6-32, 6-33. The twin green-roofed entrance buildings form a gateway from Eastern Parkway into the Brooklyn Botanic Garden. The green roofs are not entirely visible until visitors are inside.

(*Polysthichum acrostichoides*), a native evergreen fern which likes drier, well drained soil. The roof slopes between the Christmas and deciduous ferns are planted with *Polystichum polyblepharum* or Japanese tassel fern. The effect from a distance is not of three distinct textures, but of a continuous sweep of fronds. Similarly, in the spring, there is a continuous carpet of daffodils, extending up from the ground level to the top of each green roof, although the slightly different microclimates of each green roof (one is more shaded than the other) affect the density of growth and the time of bloom.

Most plants are labeled for the benefit of visitors, who can gain an appreciation not only of the effectiveness of the green roof in containing the edge of the gardens, but also a whole collection of plant materials.

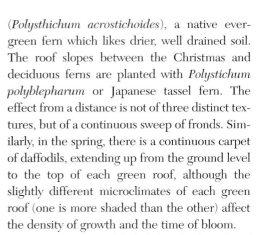

6-34, 6-35. In early spring daffodils are prominent atop the green roofs at the Brooklyn Botanic Garden, but are gradually replaced by a solid carpet of ferns which blend into adjacent plantings in the garden.

Cathedral Place and the Portland Hotel, Vancouver, BC, Canada[16]

The two projects described here, designed by landscape architect Cornelia Oberlander, although small in area, are remarkable in the sense of how large an impact they have on their surroundings, and the people who use the spaces. Both of these roof gardens, one a public open space, the other a series of private gardens within a residential center, dramatize how much a modicum of thoughtful environmental design can contribute to a larger context, and also spur additional contributions.

Cathedral Place, built in 1987–91, only a block from one end of Robson Square (described in Chapter Five), is centered between office buildings and a major church in downtown Vancouver. A crisp rectilinear circulation pattern of paved walks bounds three sides, with entrances into the two opposite buildings, Cathedral Place Tower and the two-story former home of the Canadian Craft Museum, and an overlook to the Christ Church Cathedral. A concept was developed to respect the Gothic-style cathedral and derive from it the notion of a medieval cloister garden. Contributing to the unity of this space are its architectural and landscape architectural details, which draw upon the vocabulary of the other buildings, so that every-

6-36. One of the entrances to Cathedral Place recalls the architecture of the adjacent church.

6-37. The main quality of Cathedral Place is the serenity of its fine lawn and surroundings.

thing feels both comfortable and anchored. A traditional approach was taken in planting flowering trees, groundcovers, and a vine-covered pergola. Perhaps the most compelling element is the elegant lawn, which gives warmth and tranquility in the midst of an urban environment, a lively mix of office retail, commercial, and institutional facilities. This garden was not conceived of as an environmental green roof in the sense of holding storm water runoff or filtering pollutants from the air, yet it provides a calm oasis within the city. The depth of the growing medium, a lightweight soil mix, is about a foot (30.5 cm) with underground parking beneath the square.

The Portland Hotel in Vancouver, also not far from Robson Square, is unique in that, unlike

Above:
6-38, 6-39. The Japanese holly hedges at Cathedral Place are clipped and concentrically stacked in an architectonic fashion.

Left:
6-40. Details at Cathedral Place are crisp and clean, such as the consistent treatment of each honey locust.

CATHEDRAL PLACE PLANT LIST

Buxus sempervirens	Boxwood
Malus floribunda	Japanese flowering crabapple
Platanus x acerifolia	London plane tree
Tulipa sp.	White tulips
Seasonal plantings, vines	
A shade tolerant lawn mix	

most residential facilities throughout Canada and the United States, an addict seeking housing does not need to give up his or her particular addiction in order to live within a safe environment. Instead, it is the policy at the Portland Hotel that providing a safe environment and a network of social services will encourage the addict to seek the support necessary to quit. A person admitted to the center may remain as long as necessary to demonstrate a strong possibility of re-integration into society.

The roof garden and other planted spaces in the building's interior courtyards reinforce the welcoming environment by providing public spaces for congregation and semi-private places for contemplation. Substantial planters hold sizable plant materials, such as large vines, shrubs, and trees, while not being so large as to block views or inhibit community interaction. The growing medium is the same used on the Vancouver library roof: one-third Humus Builder (a compost); one-third washed sand; and one-third pumice. For plantings on grade a more standard soil was used, called Pro-Mix, from a garden products company in Aldergrove, British Columbia. Screen plantings give privacy, and additional plantings in front of them add fanciful touches. The roof garden is nevertheless an intensive green roof in which a limited amount of space is transformed into a welcoming signature for the diverse residents of the center.

PORTLAND HOTEL PLANT LIST

TREES

Robinia pseudoacacia (1)	Black locust
Malus 'Wijeck' (16)	Spindle apple tree
Thuja occidentalis 'Smaragd' (27)	Smaragd cedar or arborvitae

SHRUBS

Pinus mugo pumilio (4)	Dwarf mugho pine
Ribes sanguineum (1)	Red flowering currant
Rosa nutkana (3)	Nootka rose
Rubus sp. inermis (3)	Thornless blackberry
Salix purpurea 'Green Dicks'	Green Dicks willow
Vaccinium Cor. 'Northblue'	Semi-dwarf blueberry

GROUNDCOVER

Arctostaphylos uva ursi (50)	Kinnikinnick or bearberry
Dodecatheon spp. (50)	Shooting star
Fragaria virginiana (390)	Wild strawberry
Hernaria glabra (450)	Green carpet
Lillium columbianum (50)	Tiger lily
Maianthemum dilatatum (30)	False lily of the valley
Viola adunca (50)	Early blue violet

FERNS

Blechnum spicant (20)	Deer Fern
Polystichum munitum (30)	Western Sword Fern

VINES

Aristolochia durior (2)	Dutchman's pipe
Clematis armandii 'Snowdrift' (2)	Snowdrift evergreen clematis
Clematis montana 'Alba' (2)	Alba May flowering clematis
Clematis paniculata (2)	Summer flowering clematis
Lonicera cilliosa (2)	Western trumpet honeysuckle

6-41. The ground-floor courtyard at the Portland Hotel provides a comfortable seating space; the edge of the roof garden is visible at the right.

Above:
6-42. Lush vines cover the wall of the staircase leading to the roof garden at the Portland Hotel.

Above right and right:
6-43, 6-44. In spite of the bleak surroundings and limited choices in plant materials, the Portland Hotel roof garden is still a comfortable space.

Sustainable Design

Perhaps green roofs will soon be acknowledged as one of many sustainable design techniques and technologies to consider for new buildings and renovations of existing buildings. As energy costs for coal and oil continue to climb, photovoltaic cells and wind-powered turbines will become more widely used and appreciated. Indeed, many aspects of sustainable design will be used more widely in standard architecture and landscape architecture practice. The William J. Clinton Presidential Center and Park and the Heifer International World Headquarters are on adjacent sites in Little Rock, Arkansas. Both designs are ambitious demonstrations of sustainable design practices that include green roofs and reveal the myriad ways that sustainability can influence the aesthetics and architecture of major facilities.

William J. Clinton Presidential Center and Park, Little Rock, AR[17]

The main building of the Clinton Library is set perpendicular to the Arkansas River. The Heifer International building, by contrast, is set farther back, more or less parallel to the river, so that from almost anywhere within the building, there are views to it.

Stirred on by President Clinton's desire for an energy-efficient building as well as one filled with a lot of light, the design team—the Polshek Partnership Architects; George Hargreaves, landscape architect, and Mr. Clinton —decided to aim for LEED certification; a silver rating was achieved. Siting the main library building on a north site axis resulted in maximum exposures to the west and east, which bathes different sides of the building in light in the morning and afternoon. The adjacent Archives Building carries extensive solar panels. A former railroad depot was renovated to become an education center, the third building of the complex. Despite extensive reshaping and recontouring of the land near the river to create parking for all three buildings and pedestrian links to downtown Little Rock, no wetlands were filled in during construction. Strong pedestrian links were established via a network of walks, affording continuous views of the river, and connecting to downtown Little Rock.

The architects used recycled materials and materials from nearby sources in the library and archives buildings whenever possible. For example, the second floor of the library uses bamboo, a fast-growing and easily regenerated plant. Much of the ceiling incorporates recycled aluminum, most of which comes from beverage cans. Most of the stone used in the building,

6-45. A birds-eye perspective of the William J. Clinton Presidential Center shows it perpendicular to the Arkansas River with a hint of the green roof over one section of the building. (Courtesy of the Clinton Foundation and the Polshek Partnership)

limestone and marble, came from quarries in the adjacent state of Tennessee. During building and construction, as well as on-going maintenance, the Clinton Center utilized recycled content materials, such as concrete, steel, insulations, ceiling tiles, wallboard, and carpet. These materials are durable and provide for easy maintenance and replacement. In addition, environmentally-friendly paints and sealants were used. Overall, 50 percent of the materials used in construction were from this region.

In order to allow a green roof to be added at a future date, the architects specified structural loads and a waterproofing membrane (American Hydrotech) consistent with an intensive green roof. The waterproofing membrane, as well as glass and stainless steel handrails, was installed so that an accessible green roof could be added without major construction changes. The roof is almost flat, but slight variations in the thickness of the waterproofing layer allow water to drain towards scuppers. A final green roof design was selected for implementation in June 2007.

The green roof design (Tremco) covers 17,500 square feet (1,625.8 m²) and includes both an extensive green roof with visual interest as well as an intensive green roof with planters and pedestrian amenities, used for parties and special events. Access for construction is through elevators and stairwells that serve the roof level, although some materials, such as the substrate, are hoisted. The original construction of the roof of the building included large areas covered with a white rock ballast, which was removed as a preliminary step towards the construction of the green roof. The extensive green roof has a growing medium 4 inches (10.2 cm) deep. The intensive green roof has a growing medium with a variable depth of 8 inches (20.3 cm) or more. The planting palette features a plant community associated with the environs of the Arkansas River, and includes native grasses and perennials that will create a rich tapestry on the roof. Maintenance is by a partnership of the landscape contractor and volunteer master gardeners.[18]

6-46, 6-47, 6-48. The end of the library building approaches the edge of the Arkansas River. A pedestrian walk system will extend over the nearby railroad bridge. The railroad bridge will bring pedestrians across the river. (These and all subsequent images of this project are by the author; courtesy of the Clinton Foundation and the Polshek Partnership.)

The photovoltaics installed during the original construction will remain in their current location on the roof of the archives building, where they have been quite effective. However, additional solar panels may be installed at a later date in some portion of the new green roof, since it is expected that the green roof will moderate extreme temperatures, and make photovoltaics within it operate more efficiently. On sunny days, the existing 306 photovoltaic solar panels provide between 30 and 40 percent of the center's electrical needs, or about 3 to 4 percent of the center's annual needs.

To protect against the intense afternoon sun, the entire western side of the building features fritted glass, treated to prevent ultraviolet light from entering the building and reducing heat gain by as much as half. Like many residential buildings throughout the south, the Clinton Library has a veranda or porch, detailed in a modern architectural style, which shades the building. All appliances and light fixtures have high energy-efficiency ratings. There is also a radiant floor with a 10-mile-long (16.1 km) coil

---

CLINTON LIBRARY PLANT LIST[19]

STREET TREES

Quercus borealis	Northern red oak
Ulmus parvifolia	Lacebark elm
Nyssa sylvatica	Black gum, tupelo, sourgum

EAST SIDE OF THE PARK

Liriodendron tulipifera	Tulip tree or yellow poplar
Magnolia grandiflora	Southern magnolia
Magnolia virginiana	Sweetbay magnolia
Quercus lyrata	Highbeam overcup oak
Quercus nigra	Water oak
Quercus nuttallii	High Point Nutall oak
Vaccinium arboreum	Farkleberry, sparkleberry, tree huckleberry

RIVER'S EDGE

Acer rubrum	Red maple
Ilex opaca	American holly
Populus deltoides	Cottonwood
Salix exigua	Sandbar willow
Betula nigra	River birch

6-49. View of the former train depot, renovated into a learning center as part of the complex.

for heating and cooling. As a result of all of these features, the Clinton Center uses 34 percent less energy than comparable "code compliant buildings" and uses over 23 percent less potable water.

Landscape architect George Hargreaves selected for the site many native and introduced species of trees that create sequential views, enclose outdoor rooms, screen and separate major functions, and form allées in pedestrian areas and along streets. The landscape is designed to reduce heat zones by careful placement of masses of trees, often perpendicular to the river, to direct breezes.

The total cost of the three buildings and park at the time of writing is $167 million, all in private funds.

Above:
6-50. An end view of the Clinton library with one of the garden spaces by landscape architect George Hargreaves in the foreground.

Left:
6-51. The solar panels on top of the archive building (immediately adjacent to the library). The Heifer International building is under construction in the background.

Heifer International's World Headquarters, Little Rock, AR[20]

Heifer International, founded in 1944, is a non-profit, non-denominational humanitarian organization dedicated to the stewardship of the earth and ending world hunger. Heifer International's Learning Centers in Arkansas, California, and Massachusetts offer hands-on educational experiences with farm animals, construction, and agroecology.

When the organization began to plan for its international headquarters building in Little Rock, Arkansas, the design team—Polk Stanley Rowland Curzon Porter, architects, and Larson Burns Smith, landscape architects—sought to build green, to reflect the organization's goals and programs. Heifer's founder, Dan West, emphasized that "the important decisions were made where people sat in a circle, facing each other as equals." The Heifer International approach is to spread sustainable design through "concentric rings of influence," like the rings formed when a pebble is dropped in a quiet pool of water, a concept adopted to the design for the organization's complex of buildings. Concentric rings define first the arrival plaza, then a pedestrian movement zone, then the pattern of use for water for the buildings, and finally the building itself. The riverfront park, developed as part of the presidential

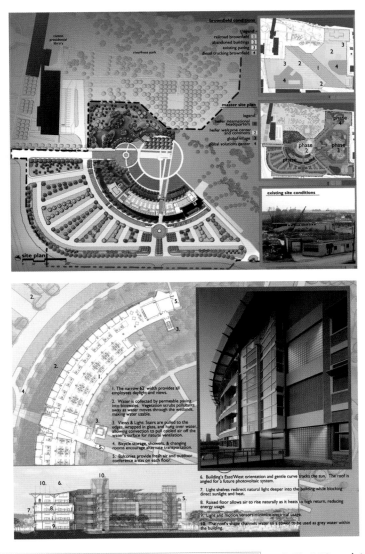

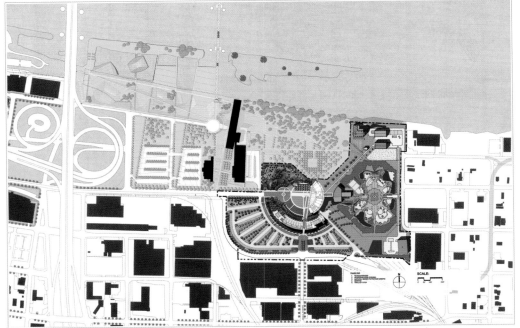

6-52, 6-53, and 6-54. A site plan of the Heifer International campus shows the concentric forms of the main building and future phases of work; the site plan shows the complete campus, which wraps around the rear of the Clinton Center. The plan, perspective, and section/elevation reveal key elements of the building, and highlight LEED compliance. (Courtesy of Polk Stanley Rowland Curzon Porter, Architects)

library, blends into the Heifer property, allowing both projects to share a large green space.

Like the Clinton Center, the design team sought a certification from LEED; in 2007, a gold certification was earned. In setting a gold LEED standard as part of the building program, the design team sought not only to express Heifer's core mission within the architecture of sustainable design, but also to achieve practical results. "Our overall goal for payback of any added cost to the building was generally in the range of 10 years," explained architect Reese Rowland. Because the life of

Top:
6-55, 6-56. Two views from the Heifer building, the first soon after completion of construction, the second after the landscape was established. (Courtesy of Timothy Hursley)

Middle and left:
6-57, 6-58, 6-59. The use of water at the Heifer building. (Middle two images courtesy of Timothy Hursley. Bottom left, courtesy of Larson Burns Smith, Landscape Architects)

Above:
6-60, 6-61. Two interior views of the Heifer International building. The interior is spacious and light-filled. (Courtesy of Timothy Hursley)

Left:
6-62. The unusual exterior claddings of the Heifer International building. (Courtesy of Timothy Hursley)

HEIFER INTERNATIONAL PLANT LIST[23]

TREES

Betula nigra 'Heritage'	Heritage river birch
Liriodendron tulipifera 'Arnold'	Arnold tulip popular
Magnolia virginiana 'Australis'	Australis sweetbay magnolia
Nyssa sylvatica 'Sylvatica'	Sylvatica black gum
Quercus lyrata 'Highbeam'	Highbeam overcup oak
Taxodium distichum 'Shawnee Brave'	Shawnee Brave bald cypress
Ulmus americana 'Creole Queen'	Creole Queen American elm

SHRUBS, VINES AND FERNS

Callicarpa americana	American beautyberry
Dryopteris marginalis	Wood fern
Fothergilla gardenia 'Mt. Airy'	Mt. Airy dwarf fothergilla
Hypericum frondosum 'Sunburst'	Sunburst St. Johnswort
Lonicera sempervirens	Coral honeysuckle

GRASSES

Buchloe dactyloides	Buffalo grass
Chasmanthium latifolium	Inland seaoats
Muhlenbergia capillaries 'Regal Mist'	Regal Mist gulf muhly grass
Schizachyrium scoparium 'frequens'	Frequens little bluestem
Sorghastrum nutans 'Blacklands'	Blacklands Indian grass

AQUATICS

Acorus americanus	Sweet Flag
Iris fulva	Copper Iris
Iris virginica	Blue flag iris
Juncus effusus	Soft rush
Osmunda cinnamomea	Cinnamon fern
Peltandra virginica	Arrow arum
Pontederia cordata	Blue pickerel rush
Saururus cernuus	Lizard's tail
Thalia dealbata	Thalia

PERENNIALS AND FORBS

Aphanostephus sp.	Lazy daisy
Asclepias tuberosa	Butterfly weed
Cassia fasciculate	Partridge pea
Castilleja indivisa	Indian paintbrush
Coreopsis lanceolata	Lanceleaf coreopsis or tickweed
Coreopsis tinctoria	Plains coreopsis or tickweed
Dracopis amplexicaulis	Clasping coneflower
Echinacea purpurea	Purple coneflower
Helianthus maximiliani	Maximilian sunflower
Liatris pycnostachya	Dense blazing star
Liatris spicata	Gayfeather
Lobelia cardinalis	Cardinal flower
Lobelia siphilitica	Great blue lobelia
Monarda citriodora	Lemon mint
Physostegia intermedia	Spring obedient plant
Ratibida columnifera	Mexican hat
Rudbeckia hirta	Rudbeckia
Rudbeckia maxima	Swamp coneflower
Salvia azura	Pitcher sage
Tradescantia occidentalis	Virginia spiderwort

the building may be at least ten times that, the potential savings would be quite significant, allowing investment in funds for other Heifer International functions. The architect's research showed that the cost increase for a sustainable building over the cost of a conventional building would be about 23 percent. However, after only a short time in operation, energy savings for the Heifer International Headquarters Building compared to conventional buildings are averaging between 35 percent to 50 percent. These results will help Heifer continue its mission to provide education about sustainable design.[21]

The four-story, curving structure faces a rolling landscape with prominent views of the Arkansas River. Since the building is only 62 feet (18.9 m) wide and set in an east-to-west orientation, sunlight easily penetrates the full depth. All parking is to the side or at the rear, with gravel spaces to allow for percolation of rainwater and to minimize runoff. Much of the brick used for the circular entry and sidewalks around the building is recycled material salvaged from the brownfields by Heifer employees. From the gravel parking spaces in the rear of the building, water is directed through sand filters and collected into bioswales, which, in turn, direct the filtered water to either an engineered retention pond with a filtering mechanism, or newly created wetlands that surround the building, almost like a narrow moat, but without steep sides. The wetlands are planted with plants such as pussy willow that naturally filter impurities from the water. The wetlands do not overflow, because excess water is drained underground to retention ponds. Some of the vegetation used in the wetlands was chosen specifically for its filtering characteristics.[22]

The planting palette emphasizes natives and groups plants in a naturalistic approach. Each layer of the plant community is anticipated, from shade trees to fill the upper canopy, smaller trees and shrubs for the mid-range height down to perennials for groundcovers. Some horticultural varieties of native species are used, such as Creole Queen American elm, selected because they are hardier than the standard species.

Many energy-saving materials and construction techniques were used. Most of the steel used for reinforcement is recycled, and all countertops, bathroom stalls, and carpets are made of recycled materials. As with the Clinton Center, the wood floors are bamboo. Local materials were used whenever possible to cut down on transportation costs and fuel usage. The insulation throughout the building is made from locally grown cotton and soybeans. The exterior stone veneer is Arkansas limestone. The top floor's ceilings are Mississippi delta pine. Finally, the building features raised flooring sections that improve ventilation and make the heating and cooling process more efficient.

The remaining buildings under construction at Heifer International at the time of writing are a Welcome Center Pavilion and the Global Village. The Welcome Center, to be completed in 2008 by the same architect, Polk Stanley Rowland Curzon Porter, of Little Rock, will contain facilities for educating the public, such as exhibit space, a gift shop, meeting and seminar rooms, and a dining room. A green roof will cover about half of the building. The design team has selected a modular system (Green Grid) because they may add to the total coverage over time.[24] The building materials, methods of construction, and site planning will demonstrate the same environmental development strategies as the main headquarters building. This building will also serve as the gateway to the Global Village, an interactive environment educating visitors about the cultures of the eight countries where Heifer International has operations and programs.

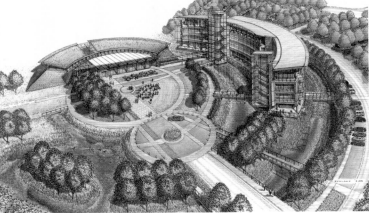

6-63. Luxuriant vegetation including flowering perennials abounds in the bioswale adjacent to the Heifer International building. (Courtesy of Larson Burns Smith, Landscape Architects)

6-64, 6-65. Two renderings showing the proposed green roof on the Welcome Center Pavilion at the Heifer International campus. The second concept dates from six months later and shows how far the planning has evolved. (Courtesy of Polk Stanley Rowland Curzon Porter, Architects)

6-66. The view towards lower Manhattan from the roof of this 4-story brownstone in Brooklyn.

6-67. The decking provides a comfortable walking surface and the modular green roof units are fit against the decking and against one another. In the background, the hatch is open, allowing access to and from the building floors below.

Homeowners and Community Organizations

As the industry branches into more specialized areas, there will be a significant market in green roofs for individual homeowners, for both new residences and as components that can be added to existing residences. Community organizations may well take on an educational role in explaining and training the public about the advantages of green roofs.

Jeff Heehs, Brooklyn, NY[25]

Jeff Heehs, a homeowner in the Park Slope neighborhood of Brooklyn, provides a good example of private sector participation in the green roof market. He has gradually installed a modular system on about half of the roof of his brownstone (a traditional residence constructed typically of dark sandstone from upstate New York); as he sees fit, he can expand it. Some of the green roof materials were carried up through all three stories of his residence, and the balance was hoisted. A self-sealing asphaltic cold rubber roofing material with a thirty year warranty was installed first; it was painted with an aluminum colored exterior asphaltic paint (Karnak). Aluminum particles suspended in the mineral oil of this paint give it reflective qualities when it dries, thus reducing the heat absorbed by the building.

Heehs used a system of modular planters (Green Grid) 4 by 4 feet (1.2 x 1.2 m) and 2 by 4 feet (0.6 x 1.2 m) by 6 inches (15.2 cm) deep. The planting medium is 50 percent expanded slate (Stalite) shipped from Salisbury, North Carolina, 15 percent perlite, 15 percent vermiculite and 20 percent compost from a local parks department source. This mixture weighs approximately 22 pounds per square foot (107 kg/m^2) when dry and 28 pounds per square foot (136.7 kg/m^2) when wet. A layer of filter fabric spread at the bottom of the modular units prevents fine particles from clogging the built-in system. Components for drip irrigation (Berry Hill Irrigation Inc.) provide water. The system is connected to a hose bib on the roof with a small backflow preventer and a filter (Orbit). A solid feed line connects to the polypipes, or drip tapes, to which emitters are attached, from which droplets of water emerge. The junction for the entire system is positioned at a low

6-68. Kitchen herbs being grown in modular green roof units.

point, so that the system can be drained manually when necessary.

The palette of plant material is not exotic but would certainly qualify as eclectic. Heehs also experimented with growing vegetables, with considerable success. The advantage of this system is that he has organized the green grids in an efficient and easily reached layout; if one plant struggles or dies, he can easily try another. He has occasionally used a fish emulsion fertilizer, 3-3-3 formula, for the vegetables.

The green roof has resulted in a significant reduction in heat buildup in the upper floors of the building. There has been a significant decrease in air conditioning and heating costs.

JEFF HEEHS PLANT LIST	
Allium 'Nutane'	Nutane circle plant
Rumex sanguineus	Bloody dock
Sedum 'Bertram Anderson'	Bertram Anderson stonecrop
Sedum mysteriosum	Contrasting sedum
Sempervivum tectorum	Hens and chicks
Thymus sp.	Lemon thyme

Sustainable South Bronx, Bronx, NY[26]

The use of a flexible, expandable green roof has similar applications for a larger organization, such as Sustainable South Bronx, which was founded in 2001 by Majora Carter, a native of the Hunts Point community in New York City. Sustainable South Bronx also happens to be located in New York's poorest congressional district. As described in the organization's newsletter, Sustainable South Bronx "is dedicated to community-driven development that counters the legacy of environmental racism, supports environmental justice, and brings about the social, economic and environmental rebirth of the South Bronx."[27]

Housed in a portion of one floor of the historic American Banknote Building, a former mint which printed money during the heyday of this region, the organization has asserted a role for itself in community-development projects. There are eight full-time and two part-time employees. Some of the organization's projects include the development of a greenway with two waterfront parks, and planning and advocating for the decommissioning of the Sheridan Expressway (which currently connects the Bruckner and South Bronx expressways) as a member of the Southern Bronx River Watershed Alliance. These plans, if fully implemented, could improve the environment, increase recreational activities, and stimulate the economy of an economically depressed neighborhood where 17 percent of school-age children have asthma, a rate over twice the New York City average. The amount of open space is lower than that of most other neighborhoods, while there are many highly congested freeways, power plants, and industrial facilities that generate air pollution, with dense concentrations of particulate matter, which contributes to the asthma epidemic.

One of the most successful programs at Sustainable South Bronx is the Bronx Ecological Stewardship Training (BEST) Program, in which students from the community learn ecological restoration, tree pruning, green roof installation and maintenance, and gain certification in several of these areas. There is also training in cardio-pulmonary resuscitation (CPR) and inspection rules of the Occupation and Safety Health Administration. As of January 2007, 90 percent of the graduates of this

6-69. Sustainable South Bronx's green roof is on top of a massive masonry building, a former mint now used by a diverse group of community organizations.

6-70. The modular units for Sustainable South Bronx are laid out in a concentric pattern, with a range of depths and plant materials. (Courtesy of Sustainable South Bronx)

program have jobs, 85 percent in the field of ecological restoration.

It was a natural progression for Sustainable South Bronx to implement a green roof, because it provides an opportunity to advocate that the city adopt sustainable development policies and educate the community about the advantages of green roofs, while provide a setting for training in green roof design and maintenance and horticulture. Funding was provided by Con Edison, the Bronx Initiative for Energy and Environment, and the New York Community Trust Foundation. The green roof was installed in September 2005. The roof membrane is manufactured by Acrymax Technologies. The Green Grid technology was used, and Sustainable South Bronx worked with the manufacturer's representatives. The modules of the Green Grid system seemed the most practical, especially because New York City building owners frequently prefer the modules' mobility to a more complex system. Over a substantial area in the middle of the roof, they first established a cool roof of reflective fabric. Then a large U-shaped pattern of concentric Green Grid modules was placed down with tiered depths, 2– 4– and 8 inches, with buffer areas to allow people to walk by the parapets. Eight different plant mixes were tried in these modules of varying depth. All plants were brought to the roof in quart size (.25 l) containers. One half of the "U" was planted with natives and ecologically significant plants that might provide habitat. The other side includes readily available ornamental plants, with some vegetables in the center. Finally, some modules are left entirely free of plants in order to see what native plant materials might appear.

Susanne Boyle and Kathleen Bakewell, the landscape architects, reported, "The roof is doing well, but it has changed a bit. We lost some native plants during last year's (2006) heat waves and we are modifying the original layout a little bit."[28]

The extensive growing medium was 75 percent light-weight expanded shale, 15 percent leaf mold or comparable compost and 10 percent perlite or other lightweight additives. The intensive growing medium was 45–50 percent coarse expanded baked clay, 10–15 percent Canadian peat moss, 20–30 percent leaf compost, 5–10 percent horticultural vermiculite, and 10–15 percent coarse sand.

SUSTAINABLE SOUTH BRONX PLANT LIST[29]

8″ (20.3 CM) MODULES

PLANT MIX A

Aster novae-angliae (120)	New England aster
Echinacea purpurea (90)	Purple coneflower
Liatris spicata (90)	Blazing star
Schizachyrium scoparium (30)	Little bluestem

PLANT MIX B

Vaccinium angustifolium (65)	Lowbush blueberry

PLANT MIX C

Achillea x 'Moonshine' (120)	Moonshine yarrow
Echinacea purpurea 'Kim's Knee High' (90)	Purple coneflower
Liatris spicata (90)	Blazing star
Panicum virgatum (130)	Switch grass

PLANT MIX D

Juniperus procumbens 'Nana' (65)	Japanese garden juniper

VINES

Clematis virginiana L. (2)	Devil's darning needles
Clematis Montana 'Rubens' (4)	Anemone clematis

4″ (10.2 CM) MODULES

PLANT MIX E

Coreopsis lanceolota (40)	Lance leaved tickseed
Fragaria chiloensis (55)	Beach strawberry
Festuca rubra (40)	Creeping red fescue

PLANT MIX F

Coreopsis verticilata 'Moonbeam' (40)	Moonbeam tickseed
Thymus serphyllum 'Coccineum' (55)	Mother of thyme
Festuca ovina glauca (40)	Blue fescue

2″ (5.1 CM) MODULES

PLANT MIX G

Sedum acre (40)	Gold-moss stonecrop
Sedum cauticola (55)	Stonecrop
Sedum reflexum (40)	Jenny's stonecrop

PLANT MIX H

Sedum acre (40)	Gold-moss stonecrop
Sedum album (40)	White stonecrop
Sedum kamtschaticum (55)	Kamschatka sedum

"The green roof has become an educational asset for the BEST program and a teaching and advocacy tool," explains Rob Crauderueff, SSB's Program Coordinator for Sustainable Alternatives. Students from the BEST program and the Green Teens program, a high school program in which students learn about ecology, are also using SSB's green roof to study the adaptability of the various plant species to different depths of planting. Sustainable South Bronx continues to employ BEST graduates to install green roofs.

Specialists

Just as there is growth in green roof-related organizations, there is also a concomitant increase in specialists—contractors, designers, ecologists—who focus on different aspects of green roof design. The following individuals exemplify a welcome trend toward innovation in some particular aspect of green roof design.

Maintenance: Richard Heller, NY, NY[30]

Richard Heller, president of Greener by Design, focuses entirely on roof gardens, green roof installations, and green roof maintenance. The most common problem that his company encounters on green roofs is soil culture. Severe problems with both weed growth and plant growth may arise if there is too much organic matter in the growing medium, or if the organic matter is too rich or not mixed uniformly within the overall soil profile. Sedums, for example, may not adapt well to a rich soil, and if they are slow in covering the entire bed, weeds have an opportunity to become well established. Heller reports on one green roof project in which "there must have been a lot of settlement in the bags" used to bring the growing medium to the roof, "because when we pulled weeds up, it's not like pulling them from

a lawn, where they come up pretty easily, but there are balls of roots because they found a clump of organic matter and they grow around it instead of spreading out as they would in a lawn. The good news is that they keep coming out very easily. The bad news is that this will keep happening until all the big lumps of clods of organic matter come out." By contrast, he often plants sedums in soil mixes that are nutrient-poor, and even include a lot of sand and clay, a mixture that he would never use for a standard perennial bed, but that sedums love. Generally, the richer the soil mix, the more weeding is required.

Heller has planted several installations with modular green roof systems. He reports that the modular systems "might be a better product for owners because if you have to deal with a leak, it's easier to remove a section of green roof." However, in general he finds modular systems difficult because "you have to walk on the edges, and the modules are big and bulky. The only strength is that we were able to load all of the soil into the modules, and use them as soil bags, which saved a lot of labor" (See Figs. 1-7, 1-8, and 1-9). One concern he has about modular roof systems is their durability compared to layered systems that are spread down. He explains: "If you are putting in a brand new

6-71. Wood planks laid over the green roof at the Life Expression Chiropractic Center protect the plants while providing access for maintenance. (Courtesy of Roofscapes, Inc.)

roof, there's no sense in going modular. Theoretically, your roofer knows what he is doing, and he's doing a great job, and the protective matting helps, and the green roof will protect it, and so on. But I think for existing roofs, a modular system has huge advantages. But you're also talking about a prefabricated, preplanted system and the problem with some is that the modules are flimsy. I think after ten years of exposure to the sun, the walls might start breaking down, especially if people step on them,"—which they might have to do in order to access them for maintenance.

Heller cautions: "I think the whole movement in the green roof business in America to sell people instant green roofs is a huge mistake. It gives people the impression that they don't need to be maintained, it gives people the impression that anyone can take care of a green roof. When you get into green roofs, you have to have someone who knows what they are doing. You can't just roll out a pre-grown prefabricated matting with soil medium and plant on it, or slap in a pre-grown module and think that everything's going to be OK. It isn't going to happen." In his experience, most sedum green roofs require irrigation the first year, after which the irrigation can be removed or disconnected, but "most people leave the system in place in case there's an extreme drought, which hasn't happened yet, but you never know with the weather changes going on." On the other hand, although drip systems are quite popular, he feels that they do not work well unless the organic content of the growing medium is high. "Drip systems depend on organic soil. In organic soil, water will travel 5 inches (12.7 cm) on either side of the drip pipe. With 70 percent expanded shale, there's not movement of the water, because there's no organic matter for the water to travel through." Therefore, he prefers spray systems, particularly for sedum green roofs. He also finds that occasional light applications of organic fertilizers make a difference in plant growth; however, if there is little organic matter in the growing medium, then organic fertilizers such as "compost tea" have nothing on which to feed. "Compost tea is alive. It's great for getting soil culture going. If you don't have something in there for the soil culture to feed on, then the results may be poor. That's something we're still experimenting with."

Two other maintenance issues for green roofs are controlling soil acidity and establishing lawn. Heller says that it is essential to check the soil acidity annually and "amend the soil approximately every two to three years to bring the soil acidity down." Acid rain exacerbates the acidity of the growing medium. He therefore recommends regular testing of the growing medium for nutrients and acidity. Pelletized lime (which has been compressed so that it absorbs more acid per unit of volume compared to standard agricultural lime) is his preferred method for lowering the acidity of the growing medium.

Lawn is still a desirable and treasured amenity, even on a green roof. Green roof maintenance practices dictate how to establish an excellent lawn on a roof. A typical problem with lawns on roofs is that they gradually sink. Typically, Heller's solution is "to amend the soil with a lot of sand, something we knew that the soil wouldn't eat," and a layer of expanded slate (Solite) on the bottom. Adding a lot of inorganic matter helps because it does not decompose. He advises not to remove grass clippings, but instead use a mulching mower. He reports that there can still be problems with thatch, but generally, "if you're aerating once or twice a year, that will take care of it."

Jennifer Appel, Houston, TX[31]

The landscape architect Jennifer Appel practices design with an emphasis on sustainability. Her Web sites provide considerable information about green roof designs and various sustainable design and maintenance practices that she implements in her projects. She has developed and marketed compost tea and granular vitamin products for organic gardening. Compost tea is essentially liquid compost, with beneficial aerobic organisms—bacteria, fungi, amoeba, flagellates, ciliates, protozoa, and nematodes—which survive from the composting process. Organic granular vitamins are either added to the compost tea or spread over prepared beds like a fertilizer, to provide nutrients to the compost for better results. She recommends soil testing to determine the nutrient values and deficiencies of the existing soil followed by the application of compost tea and granular vitamins dissolved in water. Drenching in this way kick-starts the landscape, and helps

the soil absorb moisture, so that in subsequent severe weather events there is less likelihood for runoff because the rain water will percolate much better into the soil. Subsequent applications of both the compost tea and liquid vitamins can be made through the irrigation system. A dechlorinator is added to the irrigation system between the water source and the vitamin tank, since the active chlorine would kill all organisms indiscriminately. The active organisms in the compost attack common pests. For example, the nematodes are natural predators of fleas, grubs, and mosquitoes. The protozoa attack fire ants, a major pest in Texas. The composting organisms also digest thatch, which is turned into additional compost, and improve the ability of the soil to hold moisture. Weed growth is also retarded, so that over time, the result is a sustainable landscape free of any synthetic chemicals, pesticides or fertilizers.

The first green roof project in which Appel had a major role, the Humble Oil Marriott in downtown Houston, Texas, uses a weekly application of compost tea and vitamins. This extensive green roof was implemented in March 2003, with a growing medium of a variable depth of perlite and U.S. Postal Service "packing peanuts," which were covered with a layer of compost 2 to 6 inches (5.1 to 15.2 cm) thick. An rrigation system (Rainbird) with a vitamin tank applies a weekly feeding of compost and vitamins. Irrigation water is consistently applied, except during rainy weather, about two minutes per day. Since its implementation, all of the plantings have been monitored carefully. The largest materials, 1–inch (2.54 cm) caliper crape myrtles (*Lagerstroemia indica*) were as large as 4 inches (10.2 cm) in caliper by October 2004. Annual plants such as coleus, planted originally as 4-inch (10.2 cm) pots, had grown up to 9 feet (2.7 m) wide and 3 feet (0.9 m) tall.

The green roof system that Appel created in the Humble Oil facility and used in additional projects in the Houston metropolitan area is hydroponic. The growing medium is entirely

6-72. Mulch being applied at the Humble Oil Marriott in downtown Houston. (Courtesy of Jennifer Appel)

6-73, 6-74. The Humble Oil Marriott site with plantings well established. (Courtesy of Jennifer Appel)

inorganic and contains no nutrients, so its purpose is to provide a lightweight, permanent, and structurally sound base that supports the roots of the plantings. Weekly feeding of the plantings contributed to spectacular growth and flowering rates.

The approach used by Appel emphasizes an important lesson for all green roof designers.

Local conditions have a major impact on green roof design and results. Houston, for example, has a semitropical climate with intense heat, periods of heavy rain, and a chance of hurricane force winds. Therefore, it is essential to have growing media that accommodates twelve months of growth. Perlite, mined from diamond mines, is the growing medium she most recom-

6-75, 6-76. Two demonstration plots at the Rana Creek Nursery show sedum roof prototype and living roof prototypes, respectively. *Sedum acre aureum* is surrounded by *Sedum album var. murale* (top). A more diverse composition features *Penstemon heterophyllus* 'Blue Spring' with *Sedum* 'John Creech', *Semperviven tectorum* 'Sunset' & *Semperviven tectorum* 'Red Beauty', *Sedum* 'Borschi Sport', *Sedum* 'Blue Spruce' and *Sedum kamtschaticum* (bottom). (Courtesy of Rana Creek Nursery)

mends because it is the lightest in weight and also white in color. It absorbs the least amount of solar radiation, a critical factor to the health of plants in her locale, given that temperatures on a Houston green roof can easily reach 180° Fahrenheit (82° C) and high temperatures in the growing medium can stunt plant growth.

Appel's recommendation is to put a layer of compost twice a year on top of the structural media, which has no organic content. The compost can be blown onto the surface with a pump system. Although some other green roof designers use sand, she feels that it should be avoided, because it is quite heavy when wet and does not retain moisture. She also avoids the use of organic matter in the growing medium. Finally, her experience indicates that urea or ammonium nitrate fertilizers may cause a chemical reaction with some waterproofing membranes with disastrous results, and she recommends the use of compost tea and vitamin mixtures instead. Her success and her divergence from practices commonly followed elsewhere emphasizes how much remains to be learned and applied.

Paul Kephart, Rana Creek, Carmel Valley, CA[32]

Paul Kephart is director of Rana Creek, an environmental consulting firm located 19 miles (30.6 km) inland from the Pacific coast in the Carmel Valley of California. With some of its property set aside for research and development, considerable effort is given to studying specific indigenous, drought-tolerant plants, Mediterranean plants, and customized hybrid plants, as well as many grasses, because they are so common in the California landscape. The company has become an advocate of living architecture, in which "architecture and ecology take on a symbiotic relationship, incorporating vegetation into structural and architectural design." Kephart's efforts on the green roof design and implementation at The Gap, Inc. and the California Academy of Sciences are documented earlier in this book. Here, the focus is on his particular approach to and aesthetic of green roofs.

Paul Kephart is a trained biologist; he is also a registered contractor and horticultural expert, and therefore can both design sustainable systems and implement them. With his focus on ecological processes, it is inevitable that his

approach to green roofs and his expectations for the future of the green roof industry in North America are based on his concepts of habitat restoration. He believes that modern landscape design efforts should acknowledge some of the basic processes that define the natural world, of which humans are also a part. One of the most important is seasonality: "Landscapes are cyclic. We describe natural process in terms of its life cycle. We relate life cycle to buildings, and we relate life cycle to landscapes in terms of the plants. So healthy, sustainable plant communities or landscapes have new seedlings and regeneration so new generations are coming on." He embraces green roofs that incorporate plant communities that are permitted or encouraged to self-seed, regenerate, and decay, even if this means to the uneducated observer or visitor that the landscape at times is dead, ugly, or brown. What is a weed to a casual observer is, to him, a treasured emblem of nature.

Kephart is critical of landscape architects. "Landscape architecture professionals are critical of volunteer species, particularly thistles, clovers, and other genuses from Mediterranean and European and eastern Mediterranean origin. It is not necessarily that California's habitats are being invaded, it's just that there is an abundance of resources available that those species take advantage of. So it's not like a big takeover. Actually we're seeing an increase in biological diversity." Rather than limit plantings to a set palette of plant materials, he is more comfortable with establishing the parameters of the habitat, planting it, and then studying what species become established, even if many are volunteers that were not originally planted. Yet, some landscape architects, inured to a strict layout and vocabulary, may become uncomfortable with this approach.

His experience at The Gap, Inc. taught him a lesson about the aesthetics of green roofs. After an irrigation malfunction coupled with a severe drought seriously affected the original plantings, he was still quite pleased with what he found:

> From a biological diversity standpoint and regenerative standpoint, the roof has a greater number of species than than what was originally planted. There were thirty-

two more species than the planting mix that we provided. The more diverse landscape has wider appeal. Just as California perennial/annual climate changed to a more drastically arid one, the selection of green roof plants needs to reflect this. The Gap wanted the original plant material planted. And when I visited the roof and saw the enormous amount of diversity, flowering plants, some of the original grass matrix, and also natural regeneration of annual wildflowers that I had originally seeded ten years ago, which had reseeded every year, and had sustained their occupation on the roof for ten years relying just through annual seed production, when I saw this, I thought why should we do anything? My first recommendation was why don't we let the weeds coexist with the perennials that remained, and enjoy the diversity of the plants that were there. The Gap Corporation was not receptive to that. They wanted the grassy meadow look that we had originally started with. So, again, much of this work revolves around our perception of amenity and adornment, and doesn't seek to enjoy that element of change. We want landscapes that are objects. We want to cut the ribbon and walk away.[33]

Among Kephart's research efforts have been studies of a product from coconut fiber: coir. He feels that coir is a viable alternative to peat moss, which, at its current rate of extraction from bogs and other often sensitive locations, will not remain a sustainable industry; that is, the rate of extraction is much greater than the rate of renewal. "Coir fiber is a byproduct remaining after coconut husks have been processed for coir fiber, used primarily to make rope. The material is a mixture of short fibers and corky cellular materials. Comparative analyses with peat moss demonstrate that coconut coir has similar properties. It holds water, is long-lasting, has a high carbon exchange, and is pathogen free. (Pathogens are soil-born bacteria and disease.)"[34]

Kephart envisions a future in which green roofs are constructed of entirely sustainable products: "I want to turn our living roof industry on its sustainable ear and get people's attention that the products we are using are toxic, not sus-tainable. Some are well-intentioned, as some can be recycled. But I think we are entering a new era in the living roof industry where all products will be non-toxic, organic, or mostly organic and sustainable. And we won't rely on plastics or rubberized asphalt and I'll look towards products like coconut coir not only for drainage, but for bioremediation and water filtration, and I'll look for products that are soy based or latex-based for waterproofing. That revolution will really turn green roofs *green*."

Other Nurseries

Of course, Emory Knoll Farms (profiled in Chapter Three) is not the only grower and supplier of green roof plant materials. As the green roof industry continues to grow, companies that specialize in growing, supplying and shipping plant materials for green roofs will emerge. Six such companies are: Prairie Habitats Inc. in Argyle, Manitoba; RanaCreek Nursery in Carmel Valley, California; Native Plant Solutions in Winnipeg, Manitoba; Midwest Trading Horticultural Supplies, Inc. in Virgil, Illinois; Classic Groundcovers, in Athens, Georgia; and Midwest Groundcovers, in Glenn, Michigan. These companies are representative of many across the United States and Canada. The first three of the group often specialize in growing plant materials for the restoration of particular habitats, such as prairies. Therefore, they often have considerable supplies of seed for establishing new plantings as well as more standard nursery containers.

Prairie Habitats started in 1987 as a prairie restoration company, with the goal of conserving endangered native plants and the wildlife that depends upon them.[35] The company provided the plants and seed for the Winnipeg Mountain Co-op (profiled in Chapter Five). Because many green roof projects propose to create a native plant community, Prairie Habitats is becoming expert on which plants and combinations of plants and seeds perform best in different settings with different growing media. Indeed, it has more than twenty-five years of experience in wildlife conservation and natural habitat management. The company's services include the planting and development of native landscapes in both residential and commercial projects. Additionally, it provides services to schools in Manitoba that want to naturalize their grounds. In these school programs, Prairie Habitats partners with the Evergreen Foundation, a registered national Canadian charity founded in 1991, and educates schoolchildren about the importance of conservation. The outdoor areas of the schools that participate become conservation laboratories for the students and demonstration projects for the communities.

Rana Creek Wholesale Nursery specializes in native and Mediterranean plants that add ecological function and a sense of place to developed landscapes and open spaces.[36] Paul Kephart, the biologist profiled in the preceding section, is one of the principals of the company. He helped initiate the development of the nursery in response to the demand for plant materials suitable for restoration projects in the region and for green roof installations in Mediterranean climates (Figs. 6-75, 6-76). The plants are grown "organically without pesticides, herbicides or chemical fertilizers and are currently undergoing certification by the California Certification of Organic Farmers." Among the specialized collections of plant materials are native and ornamental grasses, turf-grass alternatives, sedums, other succulents, plants that attract hummingbirds, birds, and butterflies, and species of trees native in the region, such as Monterey pines, oaks, and fruit trees. They also contract to grow plant material for specific green roof or restoration projects. Specialists at the nursery provide consulting services in plant maintenance and restoration.

Native Plant Solutions was set up as a business by Ducks Unlimited Canada (DUC) (see Chapter Five).[37] The parent organization began seeding grasses throughout wetlands and native areas in 1976, using traditional forage mixtures. It quickly became apparent that native plant material would provide a long-lived, easily-managed alternative to introduced grasses on long-term plantings. Native Plant Solutions (NPS) is the accumulation of DUC's more than sixty-five years of waterfowl, wetland, and associated habitat work in Canada. When the price of commercial native grass seed skyrocketed in the 1980s because of demand from the new U.S. Conservation Reserve Program, DUC started experimenting with growing the grasses themselves. This, combined with growing demand from commercial clients, created the impetus for Native Plant Solutions to set itself up as a business that helps seed and maintain natural plantings.

There are many nurseries and suppliers across the United States and Canada that have been in business for years and have also sought to respond to the increasing demand for green roof materials, such as growing media and plants. Midwest Trading Horticultural Supplies, Inc. is a horticultural hardgoods ("nonplant") supplier headquartered in Virgil, Illinois, approximately fifty-five miles west of Chicago.[38] Among the green roof-related products they supply are hardwood and pine bark mulches, growing media, structural soil, composts as well as tools and supplies. The company has a state-of-the-art soil blending facility, quite useful for pre-mixing green roof growing media. Classic Groundcovers in Athens, Georgia is a wholesale nursery specializing in over 130 varieties of groundcovers, some of which are suitable for green roofs.[39] Plants are sold bare root, and in several pot sizes: 2.25 inch (5.7 cm), pint (0.47 L), and gallon size (3.79 L). Another supplier is Midwest Groundcovers, located on a 320-acre (129.5 ha) farm in Glenn, Michigan, where perennials, ornamental grasses, and many varieties of vinca and euonymus are grown.[40] In response to the growing demand for green roof plants, they recently installed a green roof on one of their shops.

Modern Roof Gardens as Hybrid Designs

Green roof techniques are becoming one of many different design strategies that respond to specific programs and problems, such as humanizing new construction projects and providing public space and private amenities. Green roof technology can be applied to sites that have not typically been associated with roof gardens, such as railroad tracks and waterfront piers. Nevertheless, these structures lend themselves to a layered construction that accommodates green roof technology quite well. One landscape architect whose work links traditional styles with new techniques is Signe Nielsen in New York City. Nielsen's diverse green roof designs demonstrate great potential for modern urban designs and landscapes. A range of her roof garden projects is profiled in the following section. There follows a description of landscape architect Randy Sharp's living wall at the Vancouver Aquarium. Finally, there are brief descriptions of two projects in which green roof technology is being applied to former train tracks: the High Line in New York City, and the Beltline in Atlanta.

Signe Nielsen, NY, NY[41]

Since 1978, Signe Nielsen of the firm Mathews Nielsen has practiced landscape architecture and urban design; she has collaborated with co-principal Kim Mathews since 1983. Nielsen has a diverse portfolio of public open space projects. It has been a natural transition for her to work on many roof garden projects, for both private and public clients, in order to extend the meaning of open space to the roofs of buildings.

A trend in her work on roof gardens has been to integrate green roof technology into the design of complex open space projects in New York City and other locations. She explains:

The genesis of doing this comes from two directions: as dwellers of urban environments, we have less and less open space for people to use, and roof tops are logical places for people to look. For many years, designers have been doing rooftops for peo-

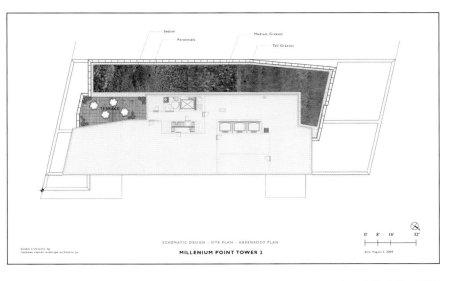

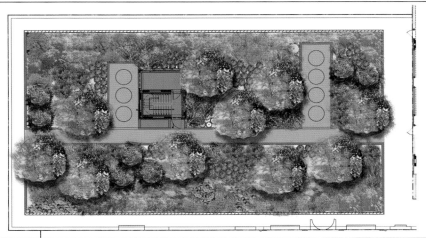

Above: 6-77, 6-78. Site plans for Millennium Point Tower, Site 2A, and Tribeca Green, Site 19B, at Battery Park City show the great variety of plant materials even for green roof designs. (Courtesy of Mathews Nielsen)

Left: 6-79. Millennium Point Tower, soon after planting in the summer of 2007, illustrating the limited space available for greening. (Courtesy of Mathews Nielsen)

ple to enjoy, whether it's to read a newspaper, barbecue, entertain, or even a form of recreation. More recently, larger buildings, corporations, warehouses and more unusual facilities have begun to look at green roofs as opportunities for their employees to have safe, protected, and maintainable and controllable space to go outside. Some of it is in order not to lose them to a more distant location. They can bring a sandwich outside, and not go very far, and therefore be more productive in the end.

So then come along these ideas of sustainability and greater awareness of some of our other very big urban problems beyond lack of available open space. It relates to our urban heat island, combined sewer overflows, and it relates to our periodic, not continuous, problem with water availability. Then, we began to look at how can anything that we do on a roof begin to serve two masters. That to me, is an interesting direction, because thus far, what I've seen coming from Europe and Japan, is a mandate to provide green roofs generally for heat island, as highest priority, secondly storm water, third for re-use of water, as part of a gray water system. I would say hierarchically, that's what I've seen. I would say, a fourth one, that's catching a lot of steam right now,

6-80. At Tribeca Green an undulating walk wanders through diverse green roof plantings. (Courtesy of Mathews Nielsen)

6-81, 6-82. These close-up images of green roof plant materials at Tribeca Green suggest the array of delightful textures and colors possible with a limited palette. (Courtesy of Mathews Nielsen)

is creating new habitat, particularly in Switzerland and England. But already there's a conflict because people who focus on creating the habitat don't want people, since people might dislodge nests or destroy the habitat of the animal. How do you provide space for people in the building, and at the same time provide habitat for species? I don't see an easy compromise on that.

Yet some of Nielsen's designs have incorporated that type of compromise. For the Battery Park City Authority (BPCA), in charge of urban development since 1968 in large landfill areas adjacent to the World Trade Center site, she has designed some unusual roof gardens. These designs meet the stringent requirement of the BPCA that 75 percent of the entire roof area of a residential building be green while still providing amenities for these residential owners. The designs for Site 2A, Millennium Towers, and Site 19B, Tribeca Green, reveal how green roof design has been integrated into the overall design of the roof (see Figs. 6-77 and 6-78).

The BPCA came up with their own guidelines, although Mathews Neilsen advised them during the process. Nielsen explains: "I actually tried to get them to separate the mechanical roof areas from private residential terraces, because there are people who buy an apartment for several million dollars with the expectation that they can use it. If you add 75 percent green area to a smaller terrace, you don't end up with usable space, merely a place for two chairs and a table. I tried to get them to relax that requirement, even if you could completely green the mechanical roof system, for example, you would still not have enough private usable open space at the terrace level." However, the BPCA held fast to the 75 percent standard.

Nonetheless, the designers achieved some effective results. "Site 2A, Millenium Towers, is interesting, because that's the one where we've failed to persuade the authority that we should allow people to occupy more than 25 percent of their roof. They say to us, for example, well, why don't you use grass? To me, grass is less sustainable than many other things that we could do, so I don't want to give them a surface material that generates more environmental problems than we are solving. Site 2A is kind of an interesting

MILLENINIUM POINT TOWER, SITE 2A PLANT LIST

STREET LEVEL PLANTERS

Allium Gladiator	Gladiator allium
Calluna vulgaris 'Sandy'	Sandy Scotch heather
Festuca filiformis	Hairy fescue
Paxistima canbyi	Paxistima
Pyrus calleryana 'Aristocrat'	Aristocrat pear

GREEN ROOF

Sedum album 'Murale'	Murale stonecrop
Sedum sexangular	Sexangular stonecrop
Sedum spurium 'Fuldglut'	Fluda Glow sedum

PRIVATE GREEN ROOF TERRACES

Allium schoenoprasm	Chives
Sedum album 'Murale'	Murale stonecrop
Sedum sexangular	Sexangular stonecrop
Sedum spurium 'Fuldglut'	Fulda Glow sedum
Talinum calycinum	Fameflower

show." The plantings are a groundcover that can be walked on but most pedestrian movement is on decking or paths of steppingstones, so that people "get the best of both worlds. We allow people to access it but still gave the authority their 75 percent green coverage."

By contrast, on Site 19B, the Tribeca Green project, private terraces are adjacent to or overlook distinct viewing areas that comprise an extensive, inaccessible green roof system. Some areas are raised up with Styrofoam to create potential for more diverse plant materials. A tall-grass prairie is followed by a medium-grass prairie and then a short-grass prairie, and then the design shifts into a straight extensive roof. There is a maintenance path and a stepped-back edge around the perimeter of the roof to allow for maintenance; however, the whole green roof is viewed from above, so that it is a visual amenity but not one that can be occupied. "It is an extensive roof, although we have a few areas we're building up in order to get trees, which is something else I like to try to include, that is, to not be so literal about what is intensive and what is extensive, and where possible, where we can get topographic change, to get enough soil depth for trees." Some apartments look straight out on the extensive green roof, whereas others look down on it from above, and the residents consider it an amenity,

TRIBECA GREEN, SITE 19B PLANT LIST

STREETSCAPE

Gleditsia triacanthos 'Skyline'	Skyline thornless honey locust
Tilia cordata 'Greenspire'	Greenspire little leaf linden

SEMI-INTENSIVE GREEN ROOF AREA

Allium senescens 'Glaucum'	German garlic
Betula nigra 'Heritage'	Heritage riverbirch
Carex flacca	Blue sedge
Caryopteris clandonensis 'First Choice'	First Choice blue mist shrub
Myrica pensylvanica	Bayberry
Pinus aristata	Bristlecone pine
Sporobolus heterolepsis	Prairie dropseed

INTENSIVE GREEN ROOF AREA

Sedum acre aureum	Goldmoss stonecrop
Sedum sexangulare	White stonecrop
Sedum spurium fuldaglut	Fuldaglut stonecrop
Sedum stenopetalum	Wormleaf stonecro

even though they cannot access it. (The maintenance path cannot by used by residents.) The plantings at BPCA respond to this issue to a degree in that residents appreciate the amenities of green space, even if most of it is inaccessible to them. Some carefully located decks and steppingstone paths allow just enough access to give the residents a sense of privacy and ownership, but the great balance of the green space is potential habitat for wildlife, particularly birds, insects and butterflies.

Perhaps the best example of Nielsen's diverse and flexible approach to green roof design is the Felissimo Headquarters in Kobe, Japan. The client is a mail-order company with a large warehouse, but it is located in the middle of an industrial area with a network of highways, without any readily accessible amenities. Mathews Nielsen provided a roof that is almost a full acre (0.4 ha) in size. It has a tennis court on it, and spreads over two levels in a well-mod-

ulated sequence of spaces that include places for people to have lunch, meetings, dances, and birthday parties. According to Nielsen, "It's a fully functioning roof garden, but it's in the middle of nowhere. It's a very big amenity. The design themes are that one is about the sea and one is about the mountains. You can see the sea in one direction, and the mountains in another direction." From the technical point of view, it is "a semi-intensive green roof, from the standpoint of soil depth." Yet, it is also a comprehensive and sophisticated design: "We pick up all the drainage, and use the collected water off the pavements to feed the planting. Another

Opposite: 6-83, 6-84. The lower level of Felissimo Heaquarters in Kobe, Japan, and a view of the ramping system. The mountains, one of the themes of the design, are visible in the background. (Courtesy of Mathews Nielsen)

Above: 6-85. The upper level of Felissimo: the wavy edge suggests the sea. (Courtesy of Mathews Nielsen)

FELISSIMO HEADQUARTERS PLANT LIST

HERB GARDEN ROOF

Arabis caucasia	Rockcress
Lavendula angustifolia 'Munstead'	Munstead lavender
Rosmarinus officinalis 'Prostratus'	Trailing rosemary
Salvia officinalis	Common sage
Thymus 'Creeping Lemon'	Creeping lemon thyme
Thymus pseudolanuginosus	Wooly thyme
Thymus serphyllum	Creeping thyme
Teucrium chamaedrys	Wall germander

TOP FLOOR ROOF

Abeliophyllum distichum	Korean abelialeaf
Caragana arborescens	Siberian pea shrub
Cytisus scoparius 'Goldfinch'	Goldfinch scotch broom
Exochorda x macrantha 'Bride'	Bride pearlbush
Genista tinctoria	Woodwaxen
Liriope muscari 'Variegata'	Variegated lily turf
Nepeta mussinii	Catmint
Ophiopogon japonicus	Green mondo grass
Philadelphus coronarius x lemoinei	Lemoine mock-orange
Santolina chamaecypaissus	Lavender cotton

idea was to use a light color paving that can be as effective as green in solving the heat island problem." With a high albedo, or reflectivity, this treatment minimizes the heat absorbed by the building. "This is a place where people can be, yet we also create habitat depending on what is planted. It is an example of a roof where you get a lot of environmental benefit and also an occupiable space for people."

Four other smaller examples in New York City include an herb garden for senior citizens at Battery Park City, a day-care center, a mixed dormitory and rental residential building near New York University, and some educational facilities for the Cooper Union. In all of these designs, the treatment of the green roof is integrated into the design of amenities for building users. The garden at the assisted living facility in Battery Park City emphasizes one of the two major populations for whom roofs are an important asset: people who are elderly or disabled, and young children. Nielsen explains: "For them, the proximity to bathrooms, or the length of time that they can be outside, either because of attention span issues or because of impairment reason, makes a roof top that is immediately accessible to an indoor environment and facilities a very logical adjacency." This roof garden is over the parking garage, the second floor of the building. Residents can come from the living room or the café to enjoy a pleasant outdoor environment. There is a fountain for sound, which also attenuates street noise. A helpful component for Alzheimer's patients is a loop path layout. This is a semi-intensive garden with a growing medium depth

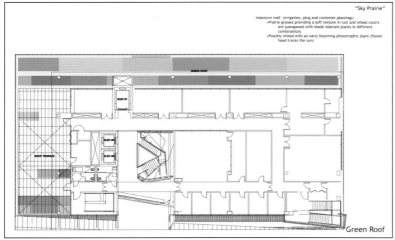

"Sky Prairie"

-Intensive roof- (irrigation, plug and container plantings)
•Prairie grasses providing a soft texture in rust and wheat colors are juxtaposed with shade tolerant plants in different combinations
•Possibly mixed with an early blooming phototropic plant (flower head tracks the sun)

Green Roof

6-86. This garden at the Hallmark Assisted Living features a circulation plan in a loop with a water feature and carefully selected plant materials. Among the people who use it are Alzheimer's patients. (Courtesy of Mathews Nielsen)

6-87. "Sky Prairie" is one of the concepts for the green roof at Cooper Union. (Courtesy of Mathews Nielsen)

Opposite:
6-88. The Day Care Center provides separate gathering points for children of different ages and interests. (Courtesy of Mathews Nielsen)

6-89. Armory Place features private terraces for residents. (Courtesy of Mathews Nielsen)

ARMORY BUILDING PLANT LIST

Second Floor Roof

TREES

Amelanchier Canadensis 'Robin Hill'	Robin Hill serviceberry

SHRUBS AND PERENNIALS

Aegopodium podagraria 'Variegatum'	Variegated goutweed
Cotoneaster salicifolia 'Repens'	Willowleaf cotoneaster
Hakenochloa macra 'Alba aurea'	Variegated hakone grass
Hypericum calycinum	Aaronsbeard st. johnswort
Hemerocallis 'Stella D'Oro'	Stella D'Oro daylily
Ilex crenata 'Helleri'	Heller Japanese holly
Leucothoe fontanesiana	Drooping leucothoe or dog hobble
Liriope muscari variegata	Variegated lily turf
Pachysandra terminalis	Pachysandra or Japanese spurge
Skimmia japonica	Japanese skimmia
Taxus x media 'Hicksii'	Hick's yew

Upper Roof

TREES

Betula nigra 'Heritage'	Heritage river birch

SHRUBS

Caryopteris clandonensis 'Heavenly Blue'	Caryopteris clandonensis 'Heavenly Blue'
Cytisus praecox	Warminster broom
Juniperus chinensis 'Torulosa'	Hollywood juniper
Phyllostachys Bissettii	David Bissett bamboo
Pleioblastus variegates	Variegated bamboo
Rosa 'Graham Thomas'	Graham Thomas rose

PERENNIALS

Artemisia ludoviciana	Wormwood
Campanula pyramidalis 'Alba'	White chimney bellflower
Campanula poscharskyana	Bellflower
Cerastium alpinum	Snow-in-summer
Hackenochloa macra	Hakone grass
Heuchera 'Mint Frost'	Mint Frost heuchera

ANNUALS

Coleus 'Black Magic'	Black Magic coleus
Heliotropum 'Alba'	White heliotrope
Ipomoea 'Margarita'	Ornamental sweet potato vine
Pennisetum alopecuroides	Rose fountain grass

tary school and high school. You don't want groups mixing together. With a limited amount of site area, what are you going to do? The roof becomes a viable alternative. There's a basketball court. We have actually what I call a social space, a place to hang out, to talk." Planters incorporated into a stepped area are tall enough so that kids can lean against them and form private areas, but still be visible to the administrators of the day-care center. The children are forced to be here, under supervision. So you use whatever space that you can find." This intensive roof garden sequesters the children while allowing them a considerable amount of privacy and a diversity of spaces in which to be themselves.

Half of the Armory building on Fourteenth Street in Manhattan is for graduate students from New York University, and the other half is rental housing. The Young Men's Christian Association (YMCA) is the major tenant for most of the nine-story building. There are two roof garden spaces: the ninth floor or top floor, the program for which was a party space on one side which residents could share and some private spaces as well; and over the swimming pool on the second floor, the program for which is an extensive, inaccessible green roof, views of which are provided to many of the private tenants of the building. The palette of plant materials is designed in swaths, or irregularly shaped concentric bands, because these masses are viewed from above, so that viewers see an interlocking pattern. About eight to ten species are used, 30 percent of which are evergreen. The diverse space on the ninth floor includes three different activities: private, building public and green roof. There are private terraces for residents, and an extensive roof area that helps to camouflage all the skylights and mechanical equipment. There is enough physical separation from the private terraces and planting, which are more intensive in nature, that the uses of the space are clear to the residents of the building.

Cooper Union, a college of design that students attend tuition-free, has plans for a new classroom building with several roof gardens. According to Nielsen: "This will be an extensive roof, visible from classrooms, and the terrace will be occupiable. Therefore, we are introducing themes of the green roof into occupiable space." This building will have a gray water system that will be used for irrigation of the plantings. Water

of about 12 inches (30.5 cm). The various plantings add some fragrance, some level of tactility, and familiarity for the residents. Trees are located directly over the structural columns for the parking garage.

Nielsen's roof garden for a day-care center had to address the need for separate areas for different-aged children. She explains: "On this space, we had kindergarteners, pre-K, elemen-

will also be collected from the roof on the story above, which has a high albedo surface and is not being planted. Each classroom would offer a different view. Some conceptual designs attempt to incorporate the nature of art and engineering into the green roof. The Doppler effect, for example, (the apparent change in frequency and wave length as a result of the relative motion of the source in relation to the observer) located by a physics or engineering classroom, would be represented by plant materials of different heights. Art education might be suggested by skillful modulation of the color of the plant materials. Another scheme suggests a sense of perspective, with plant materials of warm colors being near the viewers and cooler colored ones farther away. But again the overarching theme is "bringing a palette of plant material onto occupiable roof, so that you can see it and experience it out of doors."

Aquaquest Learning Centre, Vancouver Aquarium, Canada[42]

Among the specialties of Sharp & Diamond Landscape Architecture Inc. of Vancouver are designs for green roofs, living walls, green wall systems, and ecologically-based solutions to challenging problems. The firm collaborated with Stantec Architecture, architect Clive Grout, and Cobalt Engineering in the development of the Aquaquest Learning Centre in Stanley Park (by Frederick L. Olmsted) for the Vancouver Aquarium. The client sought not only to educate visitors about aquatic life, but also to teach them about green building design. The design team conceived of living walls as a sustainable method visible and palpable to visitors, who would be able to walk by the living wall, feel the vegetation, and even pick fruit and watch animals such as birds and squirrels interacting with the environment.

The green wall is adjacent to the bus arrival zone and main entrance, so the fern and wildflower-cloaked wall is a visitor's first impression of the green educational center. The eastern edge of the building resembles a cliff face or escarpment; therefore, the design team researched an ecosystem of plants representing a canyon wall. This plant community of ferns, wildflowers, and groundcovers withstands vertical exterior wall conditions and attracts insects, birds, and butterflies.

Installed in September 2006, the living wall of 538 square feet (50.0 m²) is made of 508 pre-vegetated panels containing plants and growing medium installed on a frame fastened into the building façade. The modular system (G-Sky Green Wall Panels) provides an entire exterior wall covered in plants. Installation, support systems, irrigation, replacement of modules, and maintenance are included in the complete wall system. A galvanized steel frame consists of vertical support rails spaced just under 12 inches (300 mm) apart and horizontal rails of 36-inch and 24-inch (900 mm and 600 mm) lengths to hold and support the wall panels. The concrete

6-90. At the Aquaquest Learning Centre at the Vancouver Aquarium, rainwater is collected off the rooftops (there is a small, accessible green roof with flowering crabapples) and stored in a cistern for irrigation of the living wall. (Courtesy of Randy Sharp)

6-91. The living wall features native West Coast wildflowers, strawberries, and groundcovers in modular panels by G-Sky. (Courtesy of Randy Sharp)

6-92. The green wall panels at the Aquaquest Learning Centre (G-Sky) are installed on a steel frame secured to the concrete wall. (Courtesy of Randy Sharp)

Species considered desirable by the landscape architects were tested carefully in green wall modules under greenhouse cultivation. Plants with clumping root systems were found to apply excessive pressure inside the green wall modules. Local sedums were rejected because the rubbery branches are tender and susceptible to breakage from the wind and daily handling by hundreds of visitors. Sharp & Diamond's original plant "wish list" of possible candidates included maidenhair fern, deer fern, wooly sunflower, coastal strawberry, alumroot, sword fern, Oregon stonecrop, and broadleaf stonecrop. Some of these West Coast-native plants were not available in time from local nurseries, were difficult to propagate, or did not perform well in the modules. It is challenging to develop a group of hardy plants that will not only simulate the plant community being re-created, but will have seasonal interest, and a variety of textures and colors.

The ferns and the strawberries are the dominant plants, complimented by wildflowers with spring and summer blossoms. Edible fruiting plants, such as strawberries and huckleberries, were placed lower on the wall within reach of the school children and wildlife such as birds and squirrels.

The pre-vegetated green wall panels provide an instant impact with an attractive variety of colors and seasonal texture. At the time of installation in September, the bleeding heart was very bushy, protruding 12 inches (30.5 cm) from the wall surface and creating a base relief in clumps. The spiny wood ferns show a brighter spring green color in contrast to the darker green licorice fern. The wintergreen, an Eastern hardy substitute for the native Oregon wintergreen, was placed on the upper crest of the wall in anticipation of its exposure to cold winter desiccating winds. Wintergreen leaves have a reddish tinge, especially during the fall and winter. The strawberry plants sent out runners with excessive growth that may shade some of the other plants. The bleeding heart blossomed until the end of October; however, it died back during a freeze in mid-November that exposed the panels, yet it resumed growth in the spring. The evergreen huckleberry, fringecup, and foamflower have grown slowly, but only a few plants of each species are planted on the living wall.

The pre-grown panels require a lead time of

wall is approximately 8 inches (200 mm) thick and made of a high-density concrete that contains waterproof admixtures. Zinc-planted steel fasteners with anchor bolts are secured almost 2 inches (50 mm) into the concrete wall. An outside frame and securing clasp hold the top and the sides of the frame to prevent lifting of the wall panels from the steel frame. The 11.9-inch-long by 11.9-inch-wide by 3.35-inch-deep (302 x 302 x 85 mm) panels are dark green plastic containers made of non-flammable polypropylene. The panel housing has securing hooks on the back to connect on a supporting frame and a guide groove on top for the drip irrigation line. The green wall is irrigated by rainwater collected from the roof and stored in an underground cistern. Each panel contains a proprietary growing medium, a peat block cut to the size of the panel with holes drilled in it for the plugs of plant materials, and encased in a non-woven, non-corrosive, non-flammable fabric. Either nine or thirteen plugs are installed in each panel.

six months prior to delivery for standard plants, or twelve to eighteen months where custom plants are required to allow for sourcing, seed collection, propagation and planting in the wall panels. The native plants were started as 1.4 by 2-inch (3.5 x 5.0 cm) plugs on a standard 72-unit starter tray in the green houses. After three to six months the plugs were transferred to the panels, which, like green roof modules, were pre-assembled with the growing medium, synthetic fabric, and strapping. The panels were grown horizontally until the date of shipment to the site. Another ten percent of the contract quantity, or about fifty additional panels, were planted in the greenhouse as potential replacements, and are held in the greenhouse as part of a maintenance contract.

Approximately 500 square feet (46.5 m²) of green wall panels can be installed in one day. At least one month prior to the installation of the wall, water supply and power supply for the automatic drip irrigation system are connected. The water supply must be active before the panels are delivered or installed. Filtration is a standard part of the irrigation system (G-Sky Drip). It includes a filter at the source of the irrigation to avoid clogging of the drip emitters. A standard fertilizer injector loop is required for the injection of liquid nutrients for the plants.

On the day of the installation, the steel frame was secured to the wall by drilling holes and attaching the anchor bolts. Meanwhile, the panels were loaded horizontally on trays and shipped in an enclosed plant delivery truck, similar to loaves of bread from a bakery, so they would not be crushed. The 508 panels were organized by species (one plant type per panel) and installed in horizontal rows starting at one end. The trays hook on to the frame and align vertically as columns in a grid pattern (Fig. 6-92). The irrigation system was installed, with one lateral drip line on top of each row, and two drip emitters per panel. Each dripline was attached to a vertical supply line that connected to the main supply at the far corner of the wall.

Each layer of the modular system was installed moving both vertically and horizontally across the wall, following the planting plan prepared by the landscape architect. The top row was capped off with two driplines for extra water to the top row of plants which are more exposed to winds and additional sunlight. A

AQUAQUEST LEARNING CENTRE PLANT LIST

Dicentra formosa	Pacific bleeding heart
Dryopteris expansa	Spiny wood fern
Fragaria vesca	Woodland strawberry
Gaultheria procumbens	Wintergreen (eastern Canada native)
Polypodium glycyrrhiza	Licorice fern
Tellima grandiflora	Fringecup
Tiarella trifoliata	Foamflower
Vaccinium ovatum	Evergreen huckleberry (blueberry)

stainless steel perforated outside frame on the top and the sides was added to secure the panels and for appearance. The excess water that flows through the panels drips onto a drainage bed comprised of river rock over a perforated PVC drain line. For other living wall applications, water can be collected at the bottom of the wall in a tray or gutter and re-circulated to the top of the wall or stored for reuse.

The growing medium in each panel was fully saturated once a day during the first week after installation. Thereafter, water was applied to maintain moisture without over-saturation. The living wall is monitored for plant performance during a variety of conditions including intensive rainfall, wind, snow and prolonged periods of freezing conditions. At the time of writing, none of the panels has required replacement, although the modular system is designed for easy removal and replacement of individual panels if necssary. The system allows for flexibility over time if the client wants to try different plant species.

Other innovations at the Aquarium include the use of seawater from the Pacific Ocean for the heat exchange system and a high-efficiency heat-pump chiller to heat the building, and in the summer to cool the building. Much of the roof of the new building is covered with a high-albedo, white TPO waterproof membrane. Rainwater is also collected for the freshwater fish tanks, flushing toilets and landscape irrigation.

The High Line, NY, NY[43]

The High Line is a disused, elevated railway on the west side of Manhattan. Built in the early 1930s and once used for shipping products to industries and warehouses, the railway declined in use following the development of the interstate highway system, as truck transport

6-93. The route of New York's Highline winds through Chelsea and provides a pedestrian walkway that connects many buildings.

6-94. An axonometric view of the proposed design of the Highline from Little West 12th Street to West 13th Street. (Courtesy of theHighline.org. Image created by Field Operations and Diller Scofidio + Renfro, courtesy of The City of New York, © 2004)

became more practical. The last train ran on the High Line in 1980. However, this steel and concrete structure is being rehabilitated into a new public open space as a result of a unique collaboration between community activists (led by Friends of the High Line), urban planners, and government officials.

The High Line consists of an elevated track almost 1.5 miles (2.4 km) long, stretching from West 34th Street south to Gansevoort Street. The tracks vary from 30 to 60 feet (9.1–18.3 m) wide and from 18 to 30 feet (5.5–9.1 m) above the streets. Over the course of twenty-five years of disuse, the existing tracks, with their typical layers of gravel ballast, have become a vernacular green roof, carpeted with a rich meadow of self-seeded species.

The competition-winning design by landscape architects Field Operations and architects Diller Scofidio + Renfro preserves the character of this emergent landscape, while creating a sustainable environment suitable for public use. Access points will be located every two to three blocks. A new walking surface of large-scale concrete planks meanders through a series of varying planted environments. Sections of rail track are preserved and incorporated into the plantings. The plantings, designed by Dutch horticul-

6-95. Rich vegetation has become established over many years on the abandoned Highline. (Courtesy of Joel Sternfield and © 2000 theHighline.org)

6-96. A proposed view of the Gansevoort Street entry looking north; the design similarities to a roof garden are apparent. (Courtesy of theHighline.org. Image created by Field Operations and Diller Scofidio + Renfro, courtesy of The City of New York, © 2004)

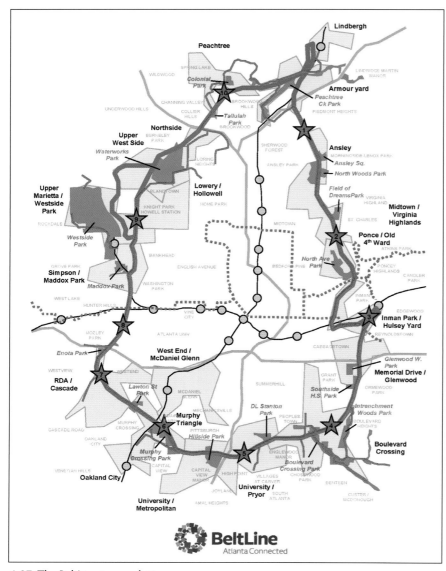

6-97. The BeltLine is an ambitious urban design project linking a large array of neighborhoods and transportation routes throughout the Atlanta region. (Courtesy of BeltLine.org)

turist Piet Oudolf, who also collaborated on the Lurie Garden at Millennium Park in Chicago, are composed of a grassland matrix interspersed with a variety of perennials, trees and shrubs, and utilize a new green-roof system built on top of the concrete structure. The design seeks "to create and preserve experiences of slowness, otherworldliness, and distractions," revealing the city around it in a new way.[44] The first segment of the High Line, from Gansevoort Street to 20th Street, opens to the public in 2008.

The BeltLine, Atlanta, GA[45]

An even more expansive project in earlier stages of development is the BeltLine in metropolitan Atlanta, Georgia. It would transform 22 miles (35.4 km) of existing, sometimes aban-

doned railroad right-of-way into a loop for pedestrians and bikers, and would link some of the old neighborhoods of the central city to newer, denser housing developments and other projects clustered around existing transit facilities. In addition, it would add eleven additional miles of spur trails to link other parks and attractions to the BeltLine area. Unlike the High Line, where the entire route is elevated, much of the route for the BeltLine is at grade or even depressed, yet some elevated portions, like trestles and bridges, would be treated with green roof technology. Its estimated cost is almost $3 billion (which includes the transit system, park land acquisition and development, development incentives, road improvements, subsidies for affordable housing for the workforce and the basic costs of construction), but because the project would weave together so many unique elements, forty parks, and forty-five neighborhoods into a vibrant whole, it has been embraced by almost everyone in the city, from neighborhood residents to developers, planners, and designers.

Conclusions

What can be anticipated as green roof design becomes more sophisticated and widespread?

An emerging aesthetic of multi-use facilities. Although green roofs will continue to be built for particular environmental functions, the aesthetic and environmental programs will merge. This will occur in response to public education, but also because roof spaces, particularly in urban areas, will become more valuable, and no longer single-purpose in scope. Both public and private clients will demand roof gardens with multiple functions. It is likely that definitions of what is beautiful or functional will also evolve. Just as green roofs are already referred to by some designers as ecoroofs or living roofs, in acknowledgment that they are not green all year long, people will appreciate that there is still beauty in a dormant landscape, whether primarily a community of perennials, such as prairie, or the graceful, sculptural forms of deciduous trees and shrubs in the fall and winter.

More competitive and practical technology required by law. Green roofs will become more practical for a variety of reasons. The technology will become more common and more competitive. Just as computers, with many more features and miniaturized components, are now available at a fraction of the cost of earlier models, economical green roof technology will advance. Different suppliers and manufacturers that have only recently become established in North America, after decades of innovation in Europe, will gradually respond with more materials and components better suited to the specific aspects of particular locations in Canada, Mexico and the United States. Local and regional governments will increasingly enact legal requirements to incorporate green roofs and other elements of sustainable design into new projects, and also into restorations and retrofits. Energy savings for cooling and heating, reductions in noise, reductions of storm water runoff to protect watersheds and water quality, and the implementation of amenities for the public will become mandated by law rather than something provided by the occasional forward-thinking developer or dedicated individual.

Growth of a regulatory function. Paralleling the growth of the industry will be concomitant growth in the training of green roof contractors and the testing and regulation of both the contractors and their installations. Organizations such as Green Roofs for Healthy Cities and Green Building Councils, as well as government agencies, will share these roles and develop courses for designers and contractors as well as certification procedures, so that seeking a green roof designer or green roof contractor will be as manageable a task as shopping for a kitchen designer or contractor. The LEED certification process will continue as a major recognition of sustainable design, but new programs may emerge as competitors.

At the same time, some could well argue that contractors do not have to take specialty tests to build anything else (waterproofing, windows, foundations, etc.). Many manufacturers require their installers to be certified by them to install their products, and this approach certainly will become more prevalent. Therefore, there may not be a need for a widely accepted certification process for the green roof industry. Once green roofs are more common, it will become apparent which contractors have a good track record, and green roof manufacturers/providers will be more careful about whom they license. The marketplace, not the government or independent organizations, will evolve to provide a more reliable product. Groups such as ASTM and possibly Green Roofs for Healthy Cities and Green Roofs.com can help by establishing standards, guidelines, and databases containing historical data on green roof installers. The installation of green roofs utilizes a variety of traditional skills, including roofing, horticulture, hydrology, architectural design, and hydraulics. Each of these occupations is already regulated, so green roof installation need not be viewed as a unique discipline requiring its own certification.[46]

Evolution of maintenance. Maintenance may evolve as well, as some contractors focus exclusively on green roof and roof garden installation and maintenance. Although we would like to think otherwise, there will never be maintenance-free gardens. Such innovations would defy the natural order. However, we can still anticipate machines and tools that will make maintenance an easier and more manageable task. Biological pest controls, fertilizer and conditioners will continue to be developed so that modern maintenance will have less impact on the environment.

Necessity of green roof design and sustainable design. Green roof design is rapidly evolving in North America from a novelty to a necessity, from an exotic new application at the leading edge of technology to something that will be ubiquitous and fundamental to modern sustainable design. As the design community, political leaders, and lay people are exposed to innovative approaches, it is vital to to educate and stimulate a dialogue.

The Jewish tradition teaches that there are four types of children (or perhaps four types of adult): the wise, the scornful, the confused, and the shy. The wise child might ask, "What are the statues and laws governing green roof design?" The scornful would challenge, "Why should I be interested in the subject at all—it has nothing to do with me?" The confused might ask, "What is green roof design all about?" and the shy child might lack the confidence to pose a question, yet still be curious. If the occasional green roof in the landscape is to yield to a tapestry of green roofs in a landscape of green roofs, then all of these questions, included the unvoiced ones, must be answered.[47]

NOTES

FOREWORD

1. Malcolm Wells, *Recovering America: a More Gentle Way to Build.* Malcolm Wells, 1999.

2. Banting, D., Doshi, H. et al. "Report on the Environmental Benefits and Cost of Green Roof Technology in the City of Toronto," Ryerson University. Published by the City of Toronto, 2005 Banting, Doug, Hiteshi Doshi, James Li, Paul Missios, Angela Au, Beth Anne Currie and Michael Verrati. Report on the Environmental Benefits and Costs of Green Roof Technology for the City of Toronto. Ryerson University, October, 2005.

3. Steven Peck and Angela Loder, "Green Roofs' Contribution to Smart Growth Implementation," presented at the Greening Rooftops for Sustainable Communities Conference, Portland, Oregon, June 2–4, 2004.

CHAPTER ONE

1. FLL. *Guidelines for the Planning, Execution and Upkeep of Green-Roof Sites.* Translated from the German, 1995 edition, p. 25.

2. Ibid.

3. Stephan Brenneisen, review comment, November 2006.

4. FLL.

5. Charlie Miller, Review of FLL Guidelines, November 12, 2006, and Steven Peck, review, Green Roofs for Healthy Cities, November 2006.

6. Charlie Miller, update on ASTM standards. See Chapter Three.

7. The GRHC website, www.greenroofs.org, includes many basic facts about green roofs.

8. Tom Liptan, Portland, Oregon, Bureau of Environmental Services, "Planning, Zoning and Financial Inventives for Ecoroofs in Portland, Oregon," GRHC Conference, Chicago, 2003.

9. Dusty Gedge, www.livingroofs.org.

10. Dunnett, Nigel and Noel Kingsbury. *Planting Green Roofs and Living Walls.* Portland, OR: Timber Press, 2004. Blanc, Patrick. *The Vertical Garden.* New York: W. W. Norton & Co, 2008.

11. Hohenadel, Kristin. "All His Rooms Are Living Rooms," *New York Times*, May 2, 2007, p. F1. Blanc, Patrick. *The Vertical Garden.* New York: W. W. Norton & Co, 2008.

12. I am grateful for information received from Randy Sharp on living walls and façade treatments, and for permission to draw freely from Randy Sharp, "Green Walls and Green Roof Gardens," paper presented at Greening Rooftops for Sustainable Communities, Minneapolis, Minnesota, April 29–May 1, 2007, and e-mail correspondence of July 2007. For more information on the Bio Lung, see www.expo2005.or.jp/en/venue/biolung and www.metro.tokyo.jp.

13. Charlie Miller, review comment, November 2006.

14. Stephan Brenneisen, review comment, November 2006.

15. Charlie Miller, review comment, November 2006.

16. Ibid.

17. Ibid.

18. Ibid.

19. Ibid.

20. Ibid.

21. Ibid.

22. Ibid.

23. Ibid.

24. Ching, Francis D.K. and Steven R. Winkel. *Building Codes Illustrated: Structural Provisions.* New York: John Wiley & Sons, 2003, p. 289.

25. Charlie Miller, review comments, November 2006, and www.leak-detection.com.

26. Charlie Miller, review comment, November 2006.

27. Green Roofs for Healthy Cities, www.greenroofs.org.

28. Mahatma Gandhi, quoted from exhibit at Brooklyn Museum. See also: www.gandhiinstitute.org. For a collection of general readings on sustainability, see *Sustainable Architecture White Papers.* Third ed. New York: Earth Pledge, 2000. See also Portland, Oregon's Green Building Policy ENB 901: www.portlandonline.com/auditor /index.cfm?&a=54355&c=deidf (includes definitions of sustainability and other terms relevant to green roofs).

29. Kellert, Stephen R. *Building for Life: Designing and Understanding the Human-Nature Connection.* Washington, D.C.: Island Press, 2005. Comment from Stephen R. Kellert, May 14, 2007.

30. Smuts, Jan Christiaan. *Holism and Evolution: the Original Approach to the Holistic Approach to Life.* Sanford Holst, ed. Sherman Oaks, California: Sierra Sunrise Publishing, 1999. p. 95.

31. "Whole Building Design" by Don Prowler, FAIA–Donald Prowler & Associates. Revised and updated by Stephanie Vierra–Steven Winter Associates, Inc. www.wbdg.org.

32. Enermodal Engineering is based in Kitchener, Ontario, and provides a full range of design services with an environmental perspective. For their description of the LEED process, and for additional information, go to www.enermodal.com /Canadian/leed_explained.html.

33. I appreciate the review of the section on LEED by Richard Kuhla, a Canadian scientist and the first accredited professional under the U.S. Green Building Council's LEED Green Building Certification Program.

CHAPTER TWO

1. Halprin, Lawrence. *The RSVP Cycles: Creative Processes in the Human Environment.* New York: George Braziller, 1969, p. 2.

2. "Whole Building Design" by Don Prowler, FAIA–Donald Prowler & Associates. Revised and updated by Stephanie Vierra of Steven Winter Associates, Inc. www.wbdg.org

3. "Oral History of Stuart Earl Cohen," interviewed by Betty J. Blum, compiled under the auspices of the Chicago Architects Oral History

Project, The Ernest R. Graham Study Center for Architectural Drawings, Department of Architecture, The Art Institute of Chicago, 2000, pp. 22–23.

4. Charlie Miller, review comment, November 2006.

5. Stephan Brenneisen, review comment, November 2006. See also Chapter Four.

6. Life-Cycle Cost Analysis (LCCA) by Sieglinde Fuller, National Institute of Standards and Technology, www.wbdg.org.

7. Green Roofs for Healthy Cities, www.greenroofs.org, and Stephen Peck, review comment, November 2006.

8. See City of Portland, Oregon, Office of Sustainable Development, at www.portlandonline.com/osd/index.cfm?a=bfdbdj&c=ebgcf. See also the British Columbia Institute of Technology's Centre for the Advancement of Green Roof Technology, at www.commons.bcit.ca/greenroof/publications/2006_regulations.pdf.

9. "Case Studies of Green Roof Regulations in North America," 2006, p. 5–6. City of Chicago Zoning Ordinance 17-4-1015. See www.commons.bcit.ca/greenroof/publications.html

10. "Case Studies of Green Roof Regulations in North America," 2006, p. 7-8. See also greenroofs.org website on the achievements of Councillor Joe Pantalone in helping to plan green roof incentives in Toronto.

11. Web site of the City of Portland, Oregon; Greenroof Case Studies of Green Roof Regulations in North America 2006; April 28, 2006; 11:00 AM/C; City of Chicago Zoning Ordinance 17-4-1015; Resolution No. 36310 adopted by Portland, Oregon, City Council, April 27, 2005

12. "Proposing Advancements in Safety, Savings, and Innovation: The Evolution of New York City's Building Code" (Draft report of April 25, 2007). www.home2.nyc.gov/html/dob/downloads/pdf/mc_report.pdf.

13. Cantor, Steven L. *Handbook of Landscape Architecture Construction.* Maurice Nelischer, ed., Washington, D.C.: Landscape Architecture Foundation, 1985, p. 224.

14. "Whole Building Design" by Don Prowler, FAIA, Donald Prowler & Associates. Revised and updated by Stephanie Vierra, Steven Winter Associates, Inc. www.wbdg.org.

CHAPTER THREE

1. Ed Snodgrass, e-mail comment, October 2, 2006.

2. Ibid.

3. Mark Davies, Higher Ground Horticulture, New York City, NY. Review comments on plant lists, November 2006.

4. Table based on author's experience and review comments by Mark Davies.

5. This section is based substantially on a site visit and interview with Ed Snodgrass and Ed Shepley on May 8, 2005 and e-mail comments received on June 2, 2005.

6. Charlie Miller has made numerous improvements on this section on irrigation. See also Pete

Melby, *Simplified Site irrigation Design* (New York: Van Nostrand Reinhold, 1995): p.167.

7. Cantor, Steven L. *Handbook of Landscape Architecture Construction.* Maurice Nelischer, ed. Washington, D.C., 1985: p.224–225.

8. Charlie Miller, review comment, November 2006.

9. Ibid.

10. Charlie Miller, review comment, and www.roofmeadow.com/technical/astm.shtml. See also www.astm.org.

11. Extracted with permission from E2396, E2397, E2398, E2399, E2400, and E2114, copyright ASTM International, 100 Barr Harbor Drive, West Conshohocken, PA 19428. A copy of the complete standards may be purchased from ASTM International, phone: 610-832-9585, fax: 610-832-9555, e-mail: service@astm.org, Web site: www.astm.org.

12. See www.astm.org.

13. Charlie Miller, review comment, November 2006.

CHAPTER FOUR

1. Comments from Stephan Brenneisen, October 6, 2006.

2. *Encyclopedia of Modern Architecture.* Gerd Hatje, ed. New York: Harry N. Abrams, Inc., 1964, p. 19, p.169-176.

3. Review comments from Stephan Brenneisen, September 12 and October 2, 2006. See also the Web sites www.hundertwasserhaus.at. and www.escapeartist.com/OREQ16/Vienna.html.

4. London Climate Change Partnership. "Adapting to climate change: Lessons for London." Greater London Authority: London. July, 2006, p. 64–68. See also "Green Roof Policy: Tools for Encouraging Sustainable Design, 2004," by Goya Ngan.

5. The author received much information on green roofs in and around Basel, Switzerland, during a two day tour sponsored by the International Green Roofs Association, and led by Nathalie Baumann, Paul Early, and Dusty Gedge in September 2005. The sites visited included Moos Lake, the Zurich train station, University Hospital, Organic Farm, Warehouse and Garden Center, Exhibition Hall #1 in Basel, and the Cave architecture of Peter Vetsch. Handouts of summary information about each project were often distributed, and I quote from some of these documents.

6. Landolt, Elias. "Orchideen-Wiesen in Wollishofen (AZuruch)—ein erstaunliches Relikt aus dem Anfang des 20, Jahrhunderts." *Vierteljahrsschrift der Natufforschenden Gesellschaft in Zurich,* Jahrgang 146, Heft 2–3, September 2001, p. 42–52.

7. Ibid.

8. Comment from Stephan Brenneisen, October 6, 2006.

9. Dr. Regula Boesch, associated with the design of this green roof, reviewed the text and provided comments on March 1, 2006.

10. Ibid.

11. One of the patients walking comfortably in

the landscaped grounds made this comment in September, 2005.

12. Review comment by Stephan Brenneisen, September 12, 2006.

13. Ibid.

14. Interview, Stephan Brenneisen, September 2005.

15. Baumann, Nathalie. "Naturschutz auf dem Dach: Bodenbrutende Vogel auf Flacdachern." Presented at the World Green Roof Congress, September, 15–16, 2005, Basel, Switzerland, and interview with Nathalie Baumann, September 2005, Basel.

16. Interview with Nathalie Baumann, September 2005, Basel.

17. A great deal of information was made available to me on the green roofs tour by the three experts referenced earlier, and they are the source for much of this text.

18. Mr. Gemperle provided a tour of the entire facility to a group of us on the green roof tour, which included not only seeing each green roof, but sampling refreshments within the gazebo structure overlooking a future bocce court.

19. Vetsch, Peter. "Earth Houses—Living Under the Ground." Paper presented at the proceedings of the World Green Roof Congress, September 15-16, 2005, Basel, Switzerland. I am grateful for Mr. Vetsch's permission to draw freely from this paper and appreciate his subsequent comments.

20. Sources for this section are an interview with Heidrun Eckert, September 2005 in Basel, and her paper, "MAG Gesilingen—A Public Park on a Private Shopping Mall in Germany," presented at the Washington, DC Conference of Green Roofs for Healthy Cities, May 2005. I am grateful for permission to draw from these sources freely.

21. Please note the following more technical information about the ZinCo system: For the intensive green roof, the protection and retention mat ISM 50 was used, with drainage element Floradrain FD40 and filter sheet SF. The extensive green roof system is constructed with the protection and retention mat SSM45, the drainage element Floradrain FD40 and the filter sheet SF. The Floradrain system permitted a drainage layer to be installed underneath the entire green roof system—without regard to whether it was extensive or intensive—and to provide for continuous drainage over the whole system, without the use of additional drainage elements at the edge of the roof for its entire perimeter.

22. I was referred to this project by the artist Joseph Dunn of New York City. I subsequently received information from the Web site www.adler-thermae.com and e-mail correspondence with Claudia Zancolli, the PR representative at the spa, and the architects Hugo and Hanspeter Demetz.

23. I am grateful for permission to draw freely from Marten Setterblad and Annika Kruuse, "Design and Biodiversity: A Brown Field Roof in Malmo, Sweden," a paper presented at the World Green Roof Congress, Basel, Switzerland, September 15–16, 2005. Additional review comments were received and incorporated on September 14, 2006.

24. I am grateful for permission to draw freely from Tobias Emilsson's "Vegetated roofs in Sweden: Green Revolution or Green Image?" a paper presented at the World Green Roof Congress, Basel, Switzerland, September 15–16, 2005. He reviewed and made additional comments on this manuscript on October 11, 2006.

25. I am grateful for permission to draw freely from "From Rubble to Redstarts," presented by Dusty Gedge at the Greening Rooftops for Sustainable Communities conference in Chicago, May, 2003. I subsequently interviewed him in London in September 2005, and have also referenced several other papers presented by him at subsequent Greening Rooftops conferences and the World Green Roof Congress, in Basel, Switzerland.

26. Frith, M., P. Sinnadurai, and D. Gedge. "Black Redstart—an Advice Note for its Conservation in London," *London Wildlife Trust,* 19 9.

27. Gedge, Dusty. "From Rubble to Redstarts."

28. See also the projects by Brenneisen cited earlier in this chapter.

29. Interview with Dusty Gedge, September 2005.

30. See the Web site http://www.canarywharf.com/mainfrm1.asp. Another source is an interview with Alex Butcher, September 2005.

31. Interview with Alex Butcher, September 2005.

32. Ibid.

33. Canary Wharf Web site, www.canarywharf.com/mainfrm1.asp.

34. Interview with Alex Butcher, September 2005.

35. Interview with Dusty Gedge, September 2005.

36. Ibid.

37. Ibid.

38. Ibid.

39. I was referred to this project by Dusty Gedge, and visited it in September, 2005. My sources include documents provided to me by him and written by design team members. This project is the result of a link established between ongoing research in Switzerland at the University of Wadensvil and at Royal Holloway, University of London in the UK. This research aims to provide design guidelines for green roofs and how best they can meet issues associated with urban biodiversity.

40. Gedge, "Additions to Komodo Dragon Green Roof," June 9, 2006. The author is grateful for comments received in August 2007 from Sven Seiffert, Team Leader Horticulture, ZSL.

41. Interview with Dusty Gedge, September 2005, and Chris Laidlaw, LIFFE, September 2005.

42. I am grateful for permission to draw freely from Jane Riddiford's and Charlie Green's "Living Roofs—A catalyst for building communities," a paper presented at the World Green Roof Congress, Basel, Switzerland, September 15-16, 2005. Other sources are separate interviews with Charlie Green and Dusty Gedge in September 2005.

43. Interview with Charlie Green, September 2005.

44. This garden was brought to my attention by Dusty Gedge. The text is based on an interview with Melissa Ronaldson, Anne Gilman, and Deborah Peacock in September 2005, and review comments by Ms. Ronaldson provided in September 2005.

45. Sources for this section are a pamphlet titled "Your parks. Our Natural Heritage." by the Royal Parks Foundation;. www.royalparksfoundation.org; and "Gourmet Gardens," in Royal Parks, the magazine of the Royal Parks Foundation, Spring-Summer, 2005, p. 16-17.

46. The author is grateful for comments received in September 2007 from Dr. Nigel Reeve, ecologist.

47. I am grateful for permission to draw freely from Linda Velazquez's and Benjamin Taube's "European Airport Greenroofs—a Potential Model for North America," a paper presented at Greening Rooftops for Sustainable Communites, Washington, DC, May 4–6, 2005.

48. Comments received from Linda Velazquez, September 14, 2006.

49. Ibid.

50. Ibid.

51. Comment received from Linda Velazquez, September 14, 2006. FraPort AG, the airport authority, was uncertain as to how many actual greenroofs there were, and so this figure is a minimum, not necessarily all of them.

52. Interview with Dusty Gedge, September 2005.

CHAPTER FIVE

1. See Appendix C for a list of green roof-related products and manufacturers. Depending on the specific project, the data about the exact green roof manufacturer and other specified products were not always available.

2. Although every effort has been made to be accurate and consistent with both the botanical and common names of plants, there are sometimes differences in the common names, which, by definition, should be expected.

3. I am grateful to Charlie Miller and his staff at Roofscapes Inc. for providing documentation on these three projects, including summaries, images, and comments. Some text was also part of the documentation for the Awards of Excellence given by Green Roofs for Healthy Cities. See www.greenroofs. org.

4. I am grateful for permission to draw freely from two papers: Tanya Garcia-Muller, "Evaluation of the First Green Roofs in the District of Xochimilco in Mexico City After 15 Months," presented at the World Green Roof Conference, Basel, Switzerland, September 15–16 2005, p. 331–333, and Ulrike Grau, Gilberto Navas Gomez, and Michael Seimsen, "Ten Years of Extensive Green Roof Experience in Mexico," presented at Greening Rooftops for Healthy Cities Conference, Washington, D.C., May 4–6 2005.

5. Based on an interview with Sarah Wayland Smith at the office of Balmori Associates in 2005, the text from the 2004 Award of Excellence for Green Roof Design from Green Roofs for Healthy Cities (see www.greenroofs.org), and correspondence with Balmori's office. I am grateful for their dedication and attention to detail.

6. Review comment by Diana Balmori, Spring 2006.

7. Based on an interview with L. Peter MacDonagh at the World Green Roof Congress, Basel, Switzerland, September 2005, materials about each project received from his office, and subsequent reviews and comments by MacDonagh and Elizabeth Ryan.

8. Interview with L. Peter MacDonagh at the World Green Roof Congress, Basel, Switzerland, September 2005.

9. Ibid.

10. Ibid.

11. Based on interviews with Cornelia Hahn Oberlander, New York City, April 2004, and with Elisabeth Whitelaw, Vancouver, June 2004. I am grateful for permission to draw freely from two papers: Cornelia Hahn Oberlander and Elisabeth Whitelaw, "Aesthetic Design and Green Roofs" presented at the Greening Rooftops for Sustainable Communities Conference, Washington, D.C. May 4-6, 2005, and Elisabeth Whitelaw, "Vancouver's Public Library and the Urban Oasis—Robson Square" presented at the Greening Rooftops for Sustainable Communities Conference, Chicago, May 29-30, 2003.

12. Oberlander and Whitelaw, "Aesthetic Design and Green Roofs."

13. Chris Johnston, Kathryn McCreary and Cheryl Nelms, "Vancouver Public Library Green Roof Monitoring Project," presented at the Greening Rooftops for Sustainable Communities Conference, Portland, Oregon, June 2–4, 2004.

14. The sources for this text include: a tour of the project with architect Robert Eastwood, of Number Ten, Winnipeg, in June 2004; a phone interview with Brent Wark of Ducks Unlimited Canada, Sept. 14, 2006, and subsequent review comments from him; review comments from Rick Wishart at the Interpretive Centre; and information from the Web sites of Ducks Unlimited Canada, Native Plant Solutions and the interpretive center itself. See also www.sedac.ciesin.columbia.edu /ramsardg/.

15. Phone interview with Brent Wark, September 14, 2006.

16. Ibid.

17. Ibid.

18. Ibid.

19. The sources for this text include: three documents provided by Gap, Inc. ("901 Cherry: Air, Light, Energy, Environment, Architecture," "901 Cherry—Frequently Asked Questions" and "901 Cherry Overview"); interviews with Paul Kephart in Portland, Oregon, June 3 to 4, 2004, and in Basel, Switzerland, September 2005; Kevin Burke, "Green Roofs and Regeneration Design Strategies—The GAP's 901 Cherry Project," presented at the Green Roofs for Sustainable Communities Conference, Chicago, May 29–30, 2003; review comments from Liz Muller and Melissa Swanson at Gap Inc.; and a

site visit with Paul Kephart and Aurora Mahassine on September 13, 2003.

20. Gap, Inc., "901 Cherry: Air, Light, Energy, Environment, Architecture."

21. Kevin Burke, "Green Roofs and Regeneration Design Strategies—The GAP's 901 Cherry Project."

22. Ibid.

23. Interviews with Paul Kephart.

24. Gap, Inc., "901 Cherry, Frequently Asked Questions."

25. Interviews and e-mails with Paul Kephart. See also p. 282–283.

26. Ibid.

27. The sources for this text include: an interview with Stephen Bell, director of the museum at that time, Portland, Oregon, June 2004; Bruce Dvorak, "The Greening of a Nature Museum—Demonstration Project," presented at the Greening Rooftops for Sustainable Communities, Chicago, May 29–30, 2003; Stephen Bell, "The Greening of the Peggy Notebaert Nature Museum," presented at the Greening Rooftops for Sustainable Communities, Chicago, May 29–30, 2003; project documents received from Mr. Dvorak, Marcus de la Fleur, and David Yocca; review comments from the museum staff, including Jill Riddell, Director of Conservation, and Joel Alpern, Museum Staff; phone interview with Christopher Dunn, Technical Operations Manager, on June 5, 2007: and www.naturemusuem.org.

28. Stephen Bell, "The Greening of the Peggy Notebaert Nature Museum."

29. The following plant lists are adopted from Bruce Dvorak, "The Greening of a Nature Museum—A Demonstration Project," presented at the Greening Rooftops for Sustainable Communities, Chicago, May 29–30, 2003.

30. Conservation Design Forum Green Roof Research, Elmhurst, Illinois, information sheet.

31. I am grateful for permission to draw freely from Donald Russell and Roger Schikendantz, "Ford Rouge Center Green Roof Project," paper presented at Greening Rooftops for Sustainable Communities Conference, Chicago, May 29–30, 2003.

32. Reid R.Coffman and Graham Davis, "Insect and Avian Fauna Presence on the Ford Assembly Plant Ecoroof," paper presented at the Greening Rooftops for Sustainable Communities Conference, Washington, D.C., May 2–4, 2005.

33. I am grateful for permission to draw freely from Eric Shriner,"Conservation Architecture: Endangered Plants on an Old Slaughterhouse Roof," paper presented at Greening Rooftops for Sustainable Communities, Chicago, May 29-30, 2003.

34. Interview with Eric Shriner, Portland, Oregon, June 2004.

35. Review comments from Eric Shriner, August 9, 2006.

36. Ibid.

37. Ibid.

38. I am grateful for permission to draw freely

from the following: a guided tour of the facility during the Green Roofs for Sustainable Communities Conference, Portland, Oregon, June 2004; Portland Ecoroof Tours by Environmental Services, Portland, Oregon, 2004; Chris Bowles, "Water Quality Friendly Field Operations Facility," Powerpoint presentation, August 2004, Beaverton, Oregon; Chris Bowles, "Water Quality Friendly Field Operations Yard," at the Metropolitan Washington Council of Governments Conference on Low Impact Development, August, 2004. There were also review comments from Mr. Bowles throughout the fall 2006, and Eric Gunderson, the architect, on October 4, 2006.

39. Review comments from Chris Bowles.

40. Ibid.

41. The sources for this section are the Awards of Excellence document for 2005 from Green Roofs for Healthy Cities, and extensive documents by Cathy Garrett. I am grateful for her focused attention on this project, and for comments from Chris Pattillo in November and December, 2007.

42. Review comments by Cathy Garrett, Sept. 10, 2006 and September 27, 2006.

43. Ibid.

44. Ibid.

45. Ibid.

46. The plant lists are based on those in the Planting Plans that were sent to me for review.

47. The sources for this section are: the Awards of Excellence document for 2005 from the Green Roofs for Healthy Cities website; phone interview with Terry Guen on August 27, 2006; subsequent e-mail comments of September 26, 2006 and others; and www.millenniumpark.org. I am grateful to Douglas Pettay of Terry Guen's office for his assistance in providing digital images.

48. Awards of Excellence document.

49. E-mail comment and document from Terry Guen, June 3–4, 2007.

50. Review comment by Terry Guen, September 26, 2006.

51. Awards of Excellence document.

52. Ibid.

53. The plant lists are taken from the Millennium Park Web site, www.millenniumpark.org.

54. Text based on the Awards of Excellence document.

55. Ibid.

56. Ibid.

57. Review comment by Terry Guen, September 26, 2007.

58. Phone interview with Terry Guen, August 27, 2006.

59. Ibid.

60. Ibid.

61. Ibid.

62. This text is based on the Awards of Excellence document.

63. The sources of this section are: an interview with Mr. Kula in June 2004; Richard Kula, "The Case of the Winnipeg Mountain Equipment Co-op," presented at Greening Rooftops for Sustainable Communities, Portland, Oregon, June 2–4, 2004;

Richard Kula, "Green Roofs and the LEED TM Green Building Rating System," presented at Greening Rooftops for Sustainable Communities, Washington, DC, June 4–6, 2005; subsequent review and comments by Mr. Kula; and general review and comments by John Morgan of Prairie Habitats, Argyle, Manitoba.

64. Richard Kula, "Green Roofs and the LEED TM Green Building Rating System" and subsequent comments in the fall of 2006 and the summer of 2007.

65. John Morgan, Prairie Habitats, planting invoices from October 5, 2004 and subsequent comments on re-planting, August 15, 2006.

66. Richard Kula, comment, summer 2007.

67. John Morgan, Prairie Habitats, planting invoices from October 5, 2004 and subsequent comments on re-planting, August 15, 2006.

68. The sources for this section are project materials provided by Polshek Partnership Architects (PPA) and Quennell Rothschild & Partners (QRP). I received many review comments from Mark Bunnell, landscape architect at QRP and Susan Rodriquez, architect at PPA.

69. The sources for this section are: are review comments from Olaf de Nooyer of the Renzo Piano Building Workshop in the fall of 2006 and the winter of 2007; interviews with Paul Kephart, Kyle Glenn, and Aurora Mahasine on September 13, 2003; subsequent interviews with Paul Kephart in Portland, Oregon, on June 4, 2004 and in Basel, Switzerland in September 2005.

70. Review comment from Olaf de Nooyer, Renzo Piano Building Workshop, November 2006.

71. Interview with Paul Kephart, Basel, Switzerland, September 2005.

72. www.calacademy.org

73. Interview with Paul Kephart, June 4, 2004.

74. Interview with Paul Kephart, Basel, Switzerland, September 2005.

CHAPTER SIX

1. Site visit, July, 2004; leaflet prepared by the Bridge of Flowers Committee; tourist map of the region. See also www.shelburnefalls.com.

2. Site visit, July 2005; on-site interview, Rose-Marie E. Goulet, artist.

3. See www.montreal.com.

4. Interview, Adam Distenfield at Rockwerks, July 17, 2004.

5. Site visit, July 2005, and comments from Johanne Senecal and Stephane Morin, September, 2006.

6. Site visit, November 7, 2004; Michael Winerip, "Up on the Roof, Harlem Gains Acres of Beauty," *The New York Times*, Section L, p. 29; e-mail correspondence with Pat Vitucci, park superintendent, October 2006 and August 2007.

7. Winerip, p. 29 and phone interview with Nicola Barber of Abel, Bainnson, Butz, LLP and subsequent comments in August 2007, and e-mail comments from Pat Vitucci in August 2007.

8. Ibid.

9. Phone interviews, Robert Martin of Robert Martin Designs, May 9 and 10, 2007, and subsequent email correspondence. I am grateful to Mr. Martin for sharing his library of images on this project.

10. Multiple site visits, 1997–2007, phone conversations with the client and design team members, e-mails with the client, and drawings prepared while employed as a landscape architect at Madison Cox Design from 1997–1998.

11. These were the existing conditions when work began, while the author was employed as a landscape architect at Madison Cox Design in the fall of 1997.

12. Mark Davies of Higher Ground continues to maintain the at-grade and roof gardens, and provide horticultural expertise when needed. Occasionally he has introduced new plantings.

13. Site visit, August 14, 2005, and correspondence (phone and e-mail) with the architect, Mr. Diehl.

14. The plant list is based on an inventory completed by Mr. Diehl in July, 2007.

15. Site visits, September 28, 2003, May 22, 2006, and August 7, 2006; and comments and review provided by Leeann Lavin, Director of Communications, and Patrick Cullina, Vice President, October 3–10, 2006 and August–September 2007.

16. Interviews with Cornelia Hahn Oberlander, New York, April 2004 and a guided tour by Elisabeth Whitelaw on June 5, 2004.

17. Clinton Presidential Center Museum Fact Sheet, William J. Clinton Presidential Center; Park TREES Fact Sheet, William J. Clinton Presidential Center Museum Guide; "Green Tour," November 26, 2005, Joe Ann Ray, docent; additional site visit, November 2004.

18. Phone interview, Deborah Strong of the Clinton Foundation and Jonathan Seaman, June 19, 2007, and subsequent e-mail correspondence.

19. Park TREES Fact Sheet; multiple site visits, 2004 and 2005.

20. "Building Green on the Arkansas River," "Ending World Hunger. Saving the Earth," and "Read to Feed, Children Changing the World," pamphlets published by Heifer International; "Education Programs, 2005–2006," and "2005 Project Profiles," booklets; *WORLD ARK*, May/June 2006; documents prepared by the architect and generously shared with the author; and e-mail correspondence with the architect's office and staff at Heifer International.

21. E-mail correspondence with architect Reese Rowland, autumn 2006 to summer 2007.

22. Email correspondence with Martin Smith of Larson Burns Smith, the landscape architectural consultant.

23. Ibid.

24. E-mail correspondence with Reese Smith, July 6, 2007.

25. Site visit and interview, September 19, 2004, and subsequent e-mail correspondence.

26. This text is based on a site visit and interview with Rob Crauderueff on April 28, 2006, and on the following materials published by Sustainable South Bronx: "South Bronx Environmental Health and

Policy Study" (a collaboration between the South Bronx community and New York University), "Block Party with the Trees!" "GREEN . . . it's the new Black," *GREEN THE GHETTO!* newsletter, Vol. 3, Issue 3, Winter, 2006, "The History of Hunts Point Walking Club!!" and subsequent comments from Mr. Crauderueff and Miquela Craytor, autumn 2007. See also www.ssbx.org.

27. *GREEN THE GHETTO!,* slogan on cover.

28. E-mail correspondence, Susanne Boyle, June 27 and 10, 2007.

29. Susanne Boyle's and Kathleen Bakewell's complete plant schedule.

30. Interview, Richard Heller, New York, November 18, 2005.

31. See www.landscapehouston.com, www.petfriendlyfertilizer.com, and www.landscapevitamins.com.

32. Interviews, Mr. Kephart, San Francisco September 13, 2003 and Basel, Switzerland, September 2005; Paul Kephart, "Soils Specifications and Guidelines, Garden Roof Assemblies," Garden Roof Product Information Series, American Hydrotech, September 24, 2003; e-mail correspondence, 2006; www.ranacreek.com.

33. Ibid. See also p. 183–186.

34. Paul Kephart, "Soils Specifications and Guidelines, Garden Roof Assemblies" Garden Roof Product Information Series, American Hydrotech, September 24, 2003.

35. E-mail correspondence, John Morgan at Prairie Habitats, autumn 2006; and www.prairiehabitats.com.

36. E-mail correspondence, Cooper Scollan, nursery manager, autumn 2006; and www.ranacreeknursery.com.

37. Phone interview, Brent Wark, Ducks Unlimited, September 14, 2006; e-mail correspondence, Brent Wark, autumn 2006; www.ducks.ca /CONSERVE/PROGRAMS/NATIVEPLANTS.

38. Midwest Trading Horticultural Supplies Co., www.midwest-trading.com.

39. Classic Groundcovers, www.classic-groundcovers.com.

40. Midwest Groundcovers, www.midwestgroundcovers.com.

41. Interview with Signe Nielsen in her office in New York City on November 17, 2005, and subsequent e-mail comments autumn 2005, and in 2006 and 2007. All quotations are from the interview or e-mail comments. All plants lists received via e-mail in June and July 2007. Dates of completion are as follows: Brookdale, 1997 (intensive roof); Felissimo Kobe, 1998 (intensive roof); Armory, 2000 (intensive and extensive roofs); Day care center, 2001 (intensive roofs); BPCA Site 19B, 2003 (extensive roof); BPCA Site 2A, 2007 (extensive roof); Cooper Union, 2008 (estimated), (extensive roof).

42. I am grateful for permission to draw freely from Randy Sharp, "Green Walls and Green Roof Gardens" presented at Greening Rooftops for Sustainable Communities, Minneapolis, Minnesota, April 29–May 1, 2007, and e-mail correspondence of July, 2007. See also www.g-sky.com.

43. Site visits, August 6, 2006 and September 30, 2006; "High Line Cell Phone Tour," published by Highline.org; Web site pamphlet from Museum of Modern Art exhibit, 2005; Phone and e-mail correspondence, Peter Mullin, Friends of the Highline, autumn 2006 and 2007; and www.thehighline.org/.

44. See thehighline.com and www.dillerscofidio.com.

45. Shaila Dewan, "The Greening of Downtown Atlanta," *New York Times,* September 6, 2006, pp. E1, E10; e-mail and phone correspondence with Tina Arbes, autumn 2007. See www.beltline.org.

46. Charlie Miller of Roofscapes., Inc. is among those who support this position, and provided this rationale.

47. Kaplan, Mordecai M., Eugene Kohn, and Ira Eisenstein, eds. "The Four Kinds of Children." *The New Haggadah for the Pesah Seder.* New York: Behrman House, 1941: pp. 23–27.

BIBLIOGRAPHY

Books

Amidon, Jane. *Radical Landscapes: Reinventing Outdoor Space*. New York: Thames & Hudson, 2001.

Cantor, Steven L. *Contemporary Trends in Landscape Architecture*. New York: John Wiley & Sons, 1997.

_____. *Innovative Design Solutions in Landscape Architecture*. New York: John Wiley & Sons, 1997.

Dunnett, Nigel and Kingsbury, Noel. *Planting Green Roofs and Living Walls*. Portland, Oregon: Timber Press, 2004.

Earth Pledge. *Green Roofs: Ecological Design and Construction*. Atglen, PA: Schiffen Publishing, 2005.

_____. *Sustainable Architecture White Papers*. New York: Earth Pledge, 2004.

Gilfoyle, Timothy J. *Millennium Park: Creating a Chicago Landmark*. Chicago: University of Chicago Press, 2006.

Giradet, Herbert. *Cities, People, Planet: Liveable Cities for a Sustainable World*. Chicester, U.K.: John Wiley & Sons, 2004.

Grant, Gary. *Green Roof and Facades*. UK: IHS BRE Press, 2006.

Johnston, L. and J. Newton. *Building Green: A Guide for Using Plants on Roof, Walls and Pavements*. London: London Ecology Unit, 1996.

Kouri, R. *Drip Irrigation for Every Landscape and All Climates*. Santa Rosa, Calif.: Metamophic Press, 1992.

Loken, S., W. Spurling, and C. Price. *GREBE—Guide to Resource Efficient Building Elements*. Missoula, Montana: Center for Resourceful Building Technology, 1994.

Lyall, Sutherland. *Designing the New Landscape*. Foreword by Sir Geoffrey Jellicoe. New York: Van Nostrand Reinhold, 1991.

Marsh, W.M. *Landscape Planning: Environmental Applications*. New York: John Wiley & Sons, 1991.

Melby, Pete. *Simplified Irrigation Design*. 2nd ed. New York: Van Nostrand Reinhold, 1995.

Osmundson, Theodore. *Roof Gardens: History, Design and Construction*, New York: W.W. Norton & Co., 1999.

Reed, Peter. *Groundswell, Constructing the Contemporary Landscape*. New York: The Museum of Modern Art, 2005.

Robinette, Gary. *Plants, People and Environmental Quality*. Prepared for the U.S. Department of the Interior, National Park Service, Washington, D.C.: U.S. Government Printing Office, No. 2405–0479.

Schiechtl, Hugo. *Bioengineering for Land Reclamation and Conservation*. Edmonton, Alberta: University of Alberta Press, 1980.

Snodgrass, Edward and Lucie L. Snodgrass. *Green Roof Plant: A Resource and Planting Guide*. Portland, Oregon: Timber Press, 2006.

Okamoto, Rai Y. and Frank E. Williams, with Klaus Huboi, and others. *Urban Design Manhattan, Regional Plan Association*. New York: Viking Press, 1969.

Wager, Erhard and Christoph Schubert-Weller. *Earth and Cave Architecture*. Switzerland: Verlag Niggli AG, 1994.

Wilson, Alex and Nadav Malin, eds. *GreenSpec Directory: Product Directory with Guideline Specifications*, Montpelier, Vermont: Capital City Press, 2002.

Magazines, Journals and Newspapers

Daphne Bramham, "Vision Creates a Park for the Century," *The Vancouver Sun*, June 21, 2002.

"The Business of Green," *The New York Times*, May 17, 2006.

Marty Carlock, "The Fleeting and the Steadfast," *Landscape Architecture Magazine*, 95, no. 4, April 2005, 108–113.

Eric D. Davis, "Water Conservation Strategies for LEED Points," *Landscape Architecture Magazine* 95, no. 6, June 2005, 64–71.

Theodore Eisenman, "Chicago's Green Crown," *Landscape Architecture Magazine*, 94, no. 11, November 2004, 106–113.

_____, "Sedums Over Baltimore," *Landscape Architecture Magazine*, 94, no. 8, August 2004, 52–61.

Kevin Flynn, "So You're LEED Accedited—Now What?" *Landscape Architecture Magazine*, 95, no. 8, August 2005, 54–65.

Dusty Gedge and Gyongyver Kadas, "Green Roofs and Biodiversity," *Biologist*, 52, no. 3, July 2005, 161–169.

"The Heat is On: A Survey of Climate Change," *The Economist*, 380, no. 8494, September 9–15, 2006, 20 page insert.

Susan Hines, "Shared Wisdom: All this Useless Beauty," *Landscape Architecture Magazine*, 95, no. 11, November 2005, 112–121.

_____, "Ulterior Exterior," *Landscape Architecture Magazine*, 95, no. 11, November 2005, 104–111.

Mark Hinshaw, "Expressing City Government, Seattle Gets a Civic Center it Can be Proud of," *Landscape Architecture Magazine*, 95, no. 10, October 2005, 75–83.

_____, "Mission Statement," *Landscape Architecture Magazine*, 94, no.1, January 2004, 76–83.

_____, "Office Park Oasis," *Landscape Architecture Magazine*, 94, no. 9, September 2004, 38–44.

Jane Jacobs, "The Greening of the City," *Landscape Architecture Magazine*, 95, no. 7, July 2005, 28–30.

Lorraine Johnson, "The Green Fields of Ford," *Landscape Architecture Magazine*, 94, no. 1, January 2004, 16–23.

John King, "Up on the Roof," *San Francisco Chronicle*, March 14, 2004.

———, "15 Seconds that Changed San Francisco, The Loma Prieta Earthquake . . . " *San Francisco Chronicle*, October 21, 2004.

Elias Landolt, "Orchideen–Wiesen in Wollishofen (AZuruch)–ein erstaunliches Relikt aus dem Anfang des 20, Jahrhunderts," *Vierteljahrsschrift der Natufforschenden Gesellschaft in Zurich*, 146, September 2001, 42–52.

Clare Cooper Marcus, "A Still Imperfect Union," *Landscape Architecture Magazine*, 93, no.12, September 2003, 66–77, with several smaller inset articles.

Linda McIntyre, "Green Roof Guru," *Landscape Architecture Magazine*, vol. 97, no. 1, January 2007, 64–71.

William Neuman, "It's Getting Easier to be Green," *The New York Times*, August 13, 2006, RE–1, 8.

Brian Preston, "An Affinity for Natural Beauty." *Imperial Oil Review*, 18, summer, 1994, pp. 18–21.

Ann Raver, "A Porch and Flowering Meadow, 6 Floors Up," *The New York Times*, July 20, 2006, F6.

Kim Sorvig, "Landscapes for Sustainable Energy," *Landscape Architecture Magazine*, 90, no. 6, June 2000, 48–56.

J. William Thompson, "Remembered Rain," *Landscape Architecture Magazine*, 94, no. 9, September 2004, 60–67.

Lisa Owens Viani, "Prairie from Ground to Sky," *Landscape Architecture Magazine*, 96, no. 12, December 2006, 28–33.

Other Publications: Pamphlets, Brochures, Booklets, Maps, etc.

American Hydrotech, Inc., *The Garden Roof Planning Guide*, www.hydrotechusa.com.

American Standards for Nursery Stock, www.anla.org /applications/Documents/ Docs/ANLAStandard2004. pdf.

Diane Balmori, Stuart Match Suna, Dan Miner, Leslie Hoffman, project partners, "Producing Green at Silvercup Studios." September 29, 2005.

Chris Bowles, "Water Quality Friendly Field Operations Facility," Powerpoint presentation, August, 2004, Beaverton, Oregon.

———, "Water Quality Friendly Field Operations Yard." at the Metropolitan Washington Council of Governments Conference on Low Impact Development, August, 2004.

"Building Green, Building Smart." Arlington County Department of Environmental Services, Arlington, Va. March 2005. www.arlingtonva.us.

Canary Wharf Shops, Restaurants & Estate Map, "Urban Style." Design by Paul Anthony, Ravenshaw Studios Limited, Group, 2004. www.canarywharf.com /mainfrm1.asp.

Center for Urban Ecology, "Green Roof Species" list, prepared by National Park Service, U.S. Department of the Interior, National Capital Region.

Center for Urban Ecology, "Green Roof," prepared by National Park Service, U.S. Department of the Interior, National Capital Region

"Chicago Public Sector Green Roof Projects, as of May, 2003." jointly prepared by the Department of Planning and Development, The Department of Environment, and the Mayor's Office.

Chicago Department of Environment and Richard M. Daley, Mayor. "A Guide to Rooftop Gardening," 2003.

Ducks Unlimited, Appendix A, "Cross-Reference of Canadian Names–Scientific Names of Plant Species" to "Revegetating with Native Grasses in the Northern Great Plains." from Ducks Unlimited website www.ducks.ca.

Eastwood, Robert, Number Ten Architects, Winnipeg, Manitoba, and Ducks Unlimited Canada, "Oak Hammock Marsh Conservation Centre," and "Prairie Green Roofs" two Powerpoint presentations.

English Nature and London Wildlife Trust, "London's Life-Force: How to Bring Natural Values to community Strategies," 2005. www.wildlondon.org.uk /resourcefiles/LondonsLife-Force1.pdf

"Green Roof Awards of Excellence," Greening Rooftops for Sustainable Communities, Chicago, 2003; Portland, Oregon, 2004 and Washington, D.C., 2005. www.greenroofs.org.

"Green Roof Design 101 Course Participant Manual," presented by Green Roofs for Healthy Cities, Inaugural Launch, Portland Oregon, June 2 and 5, 2004.

"Guide to Green Roofs in and around Washington, DC," co-produced by the Government of the District of Columbia and Green Roofs for Healthy Cities, May, 2005.

Heritage of London Trust, various pamphlets on historic properties. www.heritageoflondon.com.

London Development Agency, "Design for Biodiversity: a Guidance Document for Development in London," 2005. www.lda.gov.uk.

London Wildlife Trust, various pamphlets on London's wildlife and green spaces. www.wildlondon.org.uk.

Cornelia Hahn Oberlander, Elisabeth Whitelaw, and Eva Matsuzaki, *Introductory Manual for Greening Roofs*. Prepared for Public Works and Government Services Canada, 2002. www.pwgsc.gc.ca.

Steven Peck, Chris Callaghan, Monica E. Kuhn, and Brad Bass, *Greenbacks from Green Roofs: Forging a New Industry in Canada*. Status Report on Benefits, Barriers and Opportunities for Green Roof and Vertical Garden Technology Diffusion. Prepared for Canada Mortgage and Housing Corporation, March 1999.

Portland Ecoroof Tours, by Environmental Services, City of Portland, Oregon, 2004. www.cleanriverspdx.org.

The Premiere of Producing Green at Silvercup Studios, fold out brochure, Sept. 29, 2005. Prepared by the company at the grand opening of its green roof.

Katrin Scholz-Bath. *Green Roofs: Stormwater Management from the Top Down.* Environmental Design and Construction, 2001. www.edcumag.com.

United States Environmental Protection Agency. *Solid Waste Management and Greenhouse Gases. A life Cycle Analysis of Emissions and S inks.* May–June, 2002.

"Why Build Green? Frequently Asked Questions" by City of Portland Office of Sustainable Development, July 29, 2003. www.green-rated.org

ZinCo International. *Green Roofs Planning Guide,* 6th ed., *Recommended Standards for Designing and Installation on Roofs.* January 2000.

ZinCo International. *International Roofs in their Most Attractive Form.* March 1998.

Decades of research in Europe on green roof design have produced reams of data and numerous publications. The FLL guidelines, mentioned earlier, are just one example of the comprehensive contribution that Europeans have made. Most of these publications are in German, or occasionally other European languages, and only some have been translated into English. Clearly, one reason that research in North America at times duplicates what has already been achieved in Europe is that the wealth of previous data is not translated. It is fortunate that scholars are gradually addressing this deficiency. Still, since North America has a vast range of climate zones, vegetation possibilities, and sources and types of substrate, it is important to follow the European models and test them under careful scientific laboratory conditions in the United States, Canada and Mexico.

Two European scientists who have become increasingly involved in green roof research and design are Manfred Köhler at the University of Applied Sciences in Neubrandenburg, Germany and Stephan Brenneisen at the University of Applied Sciences in Wadenswil, Switzerland. Much of their work has been published in both English and German. Köhler's work has focused on measuring the ecological effects of green roofs. Much of Brenneisen's work is devoted to using green roof technology for indigenous habitat restoration (a few of his projects are described in Chapter Four).

In Canada, Dr. Brad Bass at the Centre for the Environment in Toronto and Dr. Karen Liu, in Montreal and Vancouver, have carried out considerable research, and both were involved with early efforts with Green Roofs for Healthy Cities in Toronto. Bass's major research is focused on studying the impact and potential of green roofs on the urban heat island in major cities. Liu has focused on the insulating and other properties of green roofs in relation to individual buildings.

In the United States, many universities have major research programs, including Michigan State (East Lansing), North Carolina State (Raleigh) and Penn State (College Station). Scientists at Michigan State were part of the design team at the River Rouge Ford Plant green roof, described in Chapter Five, and were involved in studying different substrates and methods of installation for that project. Universities are increasingly involved in demonstration projects and experiments with green roofs on their campuses, as well as providing expertise throughout their region to those seeking to install green roofs.

Mexico is the latest nation to participate in the development of green roofs in North America. Some Mexican projects and research efforts are described in Chapter Five.

There are several major resource publications in English on green building that have applications for green roof design. For example, Green Roofs for Healthy Cities publishes the semi–annual *Green Roof Monitor*, a summary of events in green roof design. It is also freely accessible online. EarthPledge has produced many publications. Many of the other trade organizations and non–profits have their own newsletters. *The Environmental Building News*, a newsletter on sustainable design, is a publication of BuildingGreen, Inc. which is based in Brattleboro, Vermont, and often includes articles on green roofs. The same publisher produces the *GreenSpec Directory*, an alphabetical compilation of more than 2000 green building products which are organized according to the CSI specification system. Most green roof systems are included in the category of thermal and moisture protection. There is also an index by both company name and product name.

In 2004 and 2005, various issues of *Royal Parks*, the Magazine of the Royal Parks Foundation, focused on specific projects in the park system. The May 16th, 2004 issue of the *New York Times Magazine* was a special issue on landscape architecture, including roof gardens. The January, 2007 issue of *Metropolis* magazine contained several articles on green roofs and sustainable design.

Listed below are papers delivered at conferences organized by Green Roofs for Healthy Cities. The reader may access all of these documents online by visiting the appropriate Web site of the sponsoring organizations (Web sites are provided in Appendix A.)

Greening Rooftops for Sustainable Communities, Chicago, Illinois, May 29–30, 2003

Bass, Brad, Drayenoft, E. Scott, Martilli, Alberto, Stull, Roland B., Auld, Heather. "The Impacts of Green Roofs on Toronto's Urban Heat Island."

Bell, Stephen V. "The Greening of the Peggy Notebaert Nature Museum."

Brenneisen, Stephan. "The Benefits of Biodiversity from Green Roofs—Key Design Consequences."

Burke, Kevin. "Green Roofs and Regeneration Design Strategies—The Gap's 901 Cherry Project."

David, Kim and Kim, Marian. "Vancouver's Green Roof Inventory and Next Steps."

Dvorak, Bruce. "The Greening of a Nature Museum— Demonstration Project."

Emilsson, Tobias. "The Influence of Substrate, Establishment Method and Species Mix on Plant Cover."

Hauth, Emily and Lipton, Tom. "Plant Survivor Findings in the Pacific Northwest."

Hutchinson, Doug, Abrams, Peter, Retzlaff, Ryan, Liptan, Tom. "Stormwater Monitoring Two Ecoroofs in Portland, Oregon, USA."

Laberge, Kevin M. "Urban Oasis: Chicago's City Hall Green Roof."

Lipton, Tom. "Planning, Zoning and Financial Incentives for Ecoroofs in Portland, Oregon."

Rowe, Bradley, Clayton, L. Rugh, VanWoert, Nicholas, Monterusso, Michael A., Russell, Don K. "Green Roof Slope, Substrate Depth and Vegetation Influence Runoff"

Russell, Donald K. and Schikendantz, Roger. "Ford Rouge Center Green Roof Project."

Shirley, Chris. "The Sustainability Value of the Green Roof as a Water Recycling System (GROW) in Urban Locations."

Shriner, Eric. "Conservation Architecture: Endangered Plants on an Old Slaughterhouse Roof."

Velasquez, Linda. "Modular Green Roof Technology: An Overview of Two Systems."

Wayland-Smith, Sarah. "Drawing Green in New York City: Aesthetic Design + Sustainable Development."

White, John W. and Snodgrass, Edmund. "Extensive Greenroof Plant Selection and Characteristics."

Whitelaw, Elisabeth. "Vancouver's Public Library and the Urban Oasis—Robson Square."

Greening Rooftops for Sustainable Communities, Portland, Oregon June 2–4, 2004

Brenneisen, Stephan. "From Biodiversity Strategies to Agricultural Productivity"

Eckert, Eckert. "MAG Gesilingen—A Public Park on a Private Shopping Mall in Germany."

Emilsson, Tobias. "Impact of Fertilization on Vegetation Development and Water Quality."

Gedge, Dusty and Kadas, Gyongyver. "Bugs, Bees and Spiders: Green Roof design for Rare Invertebrates."

Johnson, Chris, McCreary, Kathryn, Nelms, Cheryl. "Vancouver Public Library Green Roof Monitoring Project."

Johnson, Marie. "The Role of Land Use Tools in Portland's Toolbox for Promoting Eco-Roofs."

Kula, Richard. "The Case of the Winnipeg Mountain Equipment Co-op."

Mishra, Anand. "Canadian Public Policy and Green Roofs: Moving from Policy to Practice."

Peck, Steven W. and Loder, Angela. "Green Roofs' Contribution to Smart Growth Implementation."

Greening Rooftops for Sustainable Communities, Washington, D.C. May 4–6, 2005

Brenneisen, Stephan. "Green Roofs—Recapturing Urban Space for Wildlife—A Challenge for Urban Planning and Environmental Education."

Cantor, Steven L. "Traditional Rooftop Gardens and Green Roof Gardens: Benefits Versus Costs."

Carter, Timothy L. and Rasmussen, Todd C. "Use of Green Roofs for Ultra-Urban Stream Restoration in the Georgia Piedmont (USA)."

Coffman, Reid R. and Davis, Graham. "Insect and Avian Fauna Presence on the Ford Assembly Plant Ecoroof."

Edkert, Heidrun. "Lessons from Intensive Green Roof Projects Around the World."

Frith, Matthew and Gedge, Dusty. "An Eye for the Green Top: An Independent Voice for Green Roofs in the UK."

Grau, Ulrike, Gomez, Gilberto Navas, Seimsen, Michael. "Ten Years of Extensive Green Roof Experience in Mexico."

Köhler, Manfred. "Green Roof Technology – From a Fire–Protection System to a Central Instrument in Sustainable Urban Design."

Kruuse, Annika. "Sweden's Green Space Factor."

Kula, Richard. "Green Roofs and the LEED TM Green Building Rating System."

Miller, Terry and Lipton, Tom. "Update on Portland's Integrated Cost Analysis for Widespread Green Implementation—Executive Summary."

Oberlander, Cornelia Hahn and Whitelaw, Elisabeth. "Aesthetic Design and Green Roofs."

Peck, Steven W. and Goucher, Dayna. "Overview of North American Policy Development and the Policy Development Process."

Philippi, Peter M. "Introduction to the German FLL–Guideline for the Planning, Execution and Upkeep of Green Roof Sites."

Snodgrass, Edward. "100 Extensive Green Roofs: Lessons Learned."

Taylor, Brian L., Gangnes, Drew A., Ellison, Micaela. "Seattle Green Roof Evaluation Projects: An Introduction."

Velasquez, Linda and Taube, Benjamin. "European Airport Greenroofs—a Potential Model for North America."

Zoll, Corrie. "Being the First Kid on the Block: Installing a Green Roof in an Emerging Market."

Greening Rooftops for Sustainable Communities, Minneapolis, Minnesota, April 29– May 1, 2007

Sharp, Randy. "Green Walls and Green Roof Gardens."

Proceedings of the World Green Roof Congress, Basel, Switzerland, 2005

Bamfield, Brad. "Whole Life Cost Analysis of Green Roof Systems," 59–60.

Baumann, Nathalie. "Conservation on the Roof: Ground Nesting Birds on Green Roofs," 170–176. (In German).

Berghage, R.D., Beattie, D.J., Jarrett, A. R., Rezaei, F., and Nagase, A. "Quantifying Evaporation and Transpirational Water Losses from Green Roofs and Green Roof Media Capacity for Neutralizing Acid Rain," 200–207.

Brenneisen, Stephan. "Novartis Campus—Landscape Transformation onto the New City of Knowledge in Basel," 133–139. (in German)

Currie, Beth Anne and Bass, Brad. "Estimates of Air Pollution with Green Plans and Green Roofs Using the UFORE model," 265–275.

Doshi, Hitesh, Banting, Doug, Li, James, Missios, Paul, Au, Angela, Currie, Beth Anne, Verrati, Michael. "Environmental Benefits of Green Roof on a City Scale—An Example of (the) City of Toronto, 316–318.

Emilsson, Tobias. "Vegetated Roofs in Sweden: Green Revolution or Green Image?" 290–295.

Fassbinder, Dr. Helga. "Biotope City," 21–27.

Frith, Matthew. "Homes for Green Roofs—a Challenge for British Housing," p. 277–289.

Garcia, Tanya Muller. "Evaluation of the First Green Roofs in the District of Xochimilco in Mexico City after 15 Months," 31–333.

Gedge, Dusty. "Green Roofs and Urban Biodiversity—The UK + CH Science and Technology Transfer Project," 70–74.

Gedge, Dusty and Kada, Gyongyver. "Green Roofs for Biodiversity—Designing Green Roofs to Meet (the) Target of (BAP) Biodiversity Action Plan Species," 177–184.

Kephart, Paul. "Living Architecture: California Case Studies of Green roofs," 120.

Köhler, Manfred. "Urban Storm Water Management by Extensive Green Roofs," 150–156.

Lotsch, Bernd. Director, Museum of Natural History, Vienna, "The Conflict about Beauty—Aesthetics between Nature and Architecture," 37–46.

Lundberg, Louise. "Swedish Green Roof Research—an Overview," 320–323.

Riddiford, Jane and Green, Charlie. "Living Roofs—A Catalyst for Building Communities," 324–330.

Roehr, Daniel and Heubert, Susanne. "The Daimier Chyrsler Project at Potsdamer Platz, Berlin—Planning, Installation and Analysis of the Use of Trees," 104– 118.

Schmidt, Marco. "The Interaction between Water and Energy of Greened Roofs," 227–235.

Schmidt, Marco and Hauber, Gerhard. "Rooftop Greening at Posdamer Platz and the Effects on Urban Water," 157–168. (in German)

Setterblad, Marten and Kruuse, Annika. "Design and Biodiversity: A Brown Field Roof in Malmo, Sweden," 185–188.

Shirley-Smith, Chris. "Green Roof Water Recycling System 'Grow'," 208–213.

Velazquez, Linda S. "An International Call for the Green-roof Projects Database," 334–342.

Vetsch, Peter. Architect, "Earth Houses—Living Under the Ground," 53–57.

Although the green roof industry in North America is young, there are already a considerable number of well-established trade organizations and resource clearinghouses, including Web sites. The following is a history and description of some of these, with a focus on the United States and Canada. In some cases, the information that each organization provides overlaps with others; there is some healthy competition as well. The reader is encouraged to review the Web sites or contact representatives of these organizations for additional information.

AMENA

AMENA, Associación Mexicana para la Naturación de Azoteas, or the Mexican Green Roof Association, was founded in 2005. Its main objectives are to promote green roofs in Mexico and provide education about them. Some of the members received training in universities in Germany and Mexico, including the founder and president, Tanya Müller García. She reports, "AMENA strives to bring under one umbrella all those involved with roof greening in Mexico, including architects and landscape architects, universities and environmental organizations, contractors and green roof consultants. AMENA is also working with the local government of Mexico City to create public policies that will include incentives for those who decide to implement green roofs."

Building Councils

In the United States and Canada, green building councils often promote not only green roofs, but sustainable design in all its facets. The membership consists of representatives of all aspects of the building industry. The councils seek to form alliances with federal, state (or provincial, in Canada), and local agencies to encourage sustainable design, including green roofs. One major focus is to develop LEED-related products and resources. The United States Green Building Council (USGBC), and its equivalent in Canada, the Canada Green Building Council, are the source for LEED training, and the authorities that review, evaluate, and award LEED certification.

The Canada Green Building Council has two main offices in Ottawa, Ontario and Vancouver, British Columbia, and its bilingual Web site is www.cagbc.org. Its Web site includes a link to individual case studies of about 35 LEED-rated building projects throughout Canada. Both of these organizations have experienced enormous growth in recent decades.

The USGBC, headquartered in Washington, D.C., "is a community of more than 11,000 organizations from every sector of the building industry united by a common purpose: to transform the building marketplace to sustainability." The members of USGBC, including corporations, builders, universities, federal and local agencies, and nonprofit organizations, work "together to promote buildings that are environmentally responsible, profitable and healthy places to live and work." The USGBC also offers courses "to increase knowledge about green building and to help educate those interested in becoming a LEED Accredited Professional." Proceedings from the annual Greenbuild International Conference & Expo are available at www.greenbuildexpo.org. The USGBC provides programs for local and regional advocacy and education, including LEED workshops and accreditation training.

Centre for the Advancement of Green Roof Technology

The British Columbia Institute of Technology's Centre for the Advancement of Green Roof Technology (CAGRT) initiated its research program in 2002 with the construction of a dedicated green roof research facility. CAGRT was established to evaluate how extensive green roofs perform within Vancouver's temperate rainforest climate, conduct third party testing of green roof products in collaboration with industry partners, encourage innovation in the regional green roof and living wall industry, provide professional training, and broaden public awareness of the benefits of these sustainable construction methods through education and demonstration. CAGRT's inter-disciplinary team evaluates the performance of green roofs and living walls as integrated components of the building envelope for their beneficial functions of stormwater mitigation, thermal efficiency, acoustical improvement, and enhanced biodiversity. The organization delivers green roof courses, workshops, and monthly tours of the research facility, and its Web site offers publications, regional case studies, and industry and product information.

Earth Pledge

Based in New York City, Earth Pledge is a nonprofit organization which supports programs in sustainable design. Theodore W. Kheel, the founder and president, is a lawyer and arbitrator who founded the organization in 1992 to promote interest in the Rio Earth Summit. His first effort was to enlist the support of the artist Robert Rauschenberg, who created "Last Turn, Your Turn," which became the official artwork of the summit. Leslie Hoffman became the executive director of Earth Pledge in 1994, and her leadership has resulted in a host of major programs. There are four current initiatives, one of which is green roofs, which has its own Web site, www.GreeningGotham.org. It provides comprehensive information about green roof design and includes a "toolbox" with photographs and profiles of green roof projects in the New York City area. The organization provides lectures, courses, and technical expertise to individuals as well as government entities on green roof design, and it has funded or directed major research efforts and installations, primarily in New York City. Its research staff has installed monitoring equipment on several New York City green roofs in order to measure temperatures and monitor stormwater overflow. Currently, there are three other initiatives focusing on different aspects of sustainable design: efforts to use renewable energy; techniques to help farmers transition to sustainable agricultural practices; and the promotion of the use of non-polluting materials and methods in the fashion industry. The organization has pioneered work in urban agriculture and green roofs for affordable housing. The sustainable agriculture initiative has its own Web site, www.farmtotable.org.

Earth Pledge's building features a green roof. Consistent with their farm to table initiative, which encourages people to plan and develop small vegetable gardens, the plantings on the green roof include herbs and vegetables. No space is wasted; the parapets themselves are turned into planters that provide perimeter protection as per building code requirements.

The organization also publishes white papers on sustainable design on a range of topics including architecture, technology, and common materials. *Green Roofs: Ecological Design and Construction,* a book that gives brief case studies of green roof designs all over the world, was published in 2005.

Greenroofs.com

Greenroofs.com is an Internet-based news media organization and describes itself as "the international greenroof industry's resource and online information portal." Developed by the husband and wife team of Linda and Aramis Velazquez in 1999, it has expanded rapidly. Essentially, it is an information database and clearinghouse for the green roof community worldwide offering the interchange of ideas, projects, news, travel, research, organization and government updates, marketing opportunities, and exclusive features. Web site-wide access is always free and unrestricted; and since Greenroofs.com is not membership based, they are independent of any particular professional organization.

Greenroofs.com stresses the international flavor of the green roof industry by drawing information from Europe, North American and Asia. There are feature articles posted in a magazine-like format on various aspects of the green-roof industry, research links to government and university studies, as well as regular features by Linda Velazquez and guest editors. The interactive Forums page offers a variety of categories for posting and the Greenroofs.com blog, written by the editors, chronicles their musings of the green world at large. Greenroofs.com publishes the Greenroof Projects Database, a large repository of international projects searchable by multiple fields, and there is an online form for designers, contractors, and manufacturers to share

information on current and built projects (available in English, Spanish and German with more languages coming). They also publish the Greenroof Directory of Manufacturers, Suppliers, Professional Services, Organizations, Students & Green Resources. This database enables users to search for and connect with other individuals and Web sites in six different categories to find materials and practitioners. Finally, another asset is "Greenroofs101," which provides an array of background information on green roof technology, history, benefits, components, materials, industry support, applications, and more.

Green Roofs for Healthy Cities

Green Roofs for Healthy Cities, based in Toronto, Canada, is the major trade organization for North America. Its main mission is to increase awareness of the benefits of green roof infrastructure throughout North America and to help advance the development of a market for green roof designs, products, and services. The organization has sponsored annual meetings in Chicago (2003), Portland, Oregon (2004), Washington, DC (2005), Boston (2006) and Minneapolis (2007). Experts gather to share information on designs, research and policy developments, and there is a major trade exposition as well. Over 400 people attended the first meeting, in Chicago, while over 500 attended in Portland, 800 in Washington, and over 900 in Boston. The increasing turnout at each meeting, attracting manufacturers' representatives, designers and contractors, and people in related fields, demonstrates the growth in interest in this field throughout North America.

The history of Green Roofs for Healthy Cities is indicative of how quickly the industry has developed in North America. Its founder and current president, Steven Peck, recalls that Dr. Brad Bass, who works for Environment Canada, was the first to utter the words "green roof" to him, at a workshop in 1997 on municipal environmental infrastructure. At that time, Mr. Peck had done extensive work in public policy development for environmental technologies, focusing on constraints, opportunities, and the rules of government. In collaboration with a group of people including Dr. Bass, Monica Kuhn (who translated a lot of German texts into English), and Chris Callahan, they received a grant from the Canadian government to write a report on green roofs, "Greenbacks from Greenroofs: Forging a New Industry in Canada," which was published by Canada Mortgage and Housing Corporation in 1998. The report identified major barriers to market development and proposed various strategies to help overcome them. The group talked to ten companies in North America that had made initial steps in establishing a green roof industry. The following seven became the founders and funders of a new green roofs trade organization:

Garland, an American membrane manufacturing company, but with offices in Canada, was still developing a system.

Soprema, a membrane manufacturer (French based) with divisions in Canada and US, had a system.

Flynn (Canada), the largest roofing contractor in Canada, did fabrication and roofing.

IRC Building Sciences Group, a roofing consulting firm, did a lot of technical roofing analysis.

Sheridan Nurseries, a nursery which shipped all over North America

DeBoer Landscaping, a landscape contractor based in London, Ontario.

Sempler Gooder Roofing, a regional Canadian roofing contractor

These seven diverse groups provided about $60,000 in seed money, identified themselves as Green Roofs for Healthy Cities, and focused on initial projects in Toronto. With the $1.1 million that they raised, they built two green roofs with several of these entities providing crucial expertise, materials, and personnel, one on Toronto's City Hall (Fig. 1-8) and another one for scientific research on stormwater and energy at the Eastview Toronto Community Center. The 6000-square-foot (557.4 m^2) green roof at City Hall had eight different plots to demonstrate different types of green roof materials, sedum treatments, food production, and approaches to developing habitat for native plants and invertebrates. The 10,000-square-foot (929.0 m^2) green roof at the community center and the City Hall green roof were monitored by the National Research Council, an organization that does research on diverse topics such as aerodynamics and building materials. Dr. Karen Liu, who was head of the Council at the time, developed some of the first technical studies in North America in terms of water quality, thermal performance, and membrane longevity. Earlier studies at Berkeley demonstrated that if green roofs have cooling features, they outperform reflective roofs. Dr. Bass broke new ground by doing some of the first modeling studies that demonstrated that, if urban areas had as little as 5% extensive, irrigated green roof coverage, this would result in somewhere between a 1 to 2 degrees Centigrade (1.8 to 3.6°F) reduction in urban heat island effect. One predicted effect would be a 4% to 7% decrease in peak load energy demand, saving hundreds of millions of dollars.

Due to the interest in their efforts, the six member groups of GRHC decided to open to more members, in an effort to expand their knowledge base and generate more funding. Green Roofs for Healthy Cities is now a 501C6 fully incorporated non-profit organization, and has several membership categories, including individuals, students, small businesses, non-profits, governments, and corporations.

One major goal of the organization is to push for designs in which the green roof is "fully integrated into the utility systems of the building or as part of sustainable design." Mr. Peck notes that over "500,000 people are employed in building industries and in related disciplines," and he seeks to gain advocates for green roofs from all of them.

Green Roofs for Healthy Cities also conducts local market symposiums in partnership with local and county gov-ernments. These symposiums feature local projects, provide networking opportunities, and help identify research and policy opportunities to promote green roof development by reducing the costs to public and private building owners and developers. This has resulted in the development of various building specific and community-wide research projects and the adoption of supportive policies ranging from energy efficiency grants and stormwater rebates, to floor area ratio bonusing and fast tracking of permitting processes. In a study of market developments of its corporate members, GRHC found that the market for green roofs grew by over 80% between 2004 and 2005, with almost three million square feet (278,700 m^2)of green roof completed in 2005.

Green Roofs for Healthy Cities has also developed a series of courses and seminars on green roofs design. Green Roofs 101, 201, and 301 cover in great detail the entire process of green roof design; some of these materials have been resources for this book.

International Green Roof Association

The International Green Roof Association is a multi-national, non-profit organization that maintains a global network on green roof topics. It sponsors workshops and conferences (primarily in Europe), publishes a newsletter, and has a public relations arm which promotes green roof design.

International Green Roof Congress

The International Green Roof Congress has held two meetings, in Nertingen, Germany in 2004, and in Basel, Switzerland in 2005. The Website www.greenroofworld. com provides information about future conferences and access to papers presented at previous conferences. There are also links to the Web sites of other organizations throughout Europe. Many European countries have individual organizations that promote green roofs, act as clearinghouses for information, and provide contacts to professionals in different areas of design.

Livingroofs.org

One of the most prominent green roof organizations in Europe is Livingroofs.org, a non-profit founded by Dusty Gedge (who was profiled in Chapter Four). Based in London, the organization and its Web site highlight efforts to provide living roofs for habitat restoration, initially concentrated on the black redstart, a native bird. Now it has evolved into an independent Web site specifically for promoting green roofs and providing advice for their installation. Among its diverse goals, Livingroofs.org provides an online forum for discussion and presentation of green roof topics; offers advice to anyone seeking to implement a green roof; advocates the benefits of green roofs; identifies constraints and solutions; promotes and disseminates research; and develops policy and standards. The organization provides independent consultants on green roofs projects, online resources, tours of green roofs projects in London, seminars, conferences and speakers. Although Livingroofs.org was founded to provide information about applications in the United Kingdom, it also offers resources for many other geographic locations.

A related organization is the Green Roof Consultancy (GRC), which can provide expertise in green roofs for clients seeking an ecological approach to complex design problems. The consultancy has evolved as a partnership with Ecology Consultancy Limited (www.ecologyconsultancy.co.uk) and www.livingroofs.org. The organization draws on recognized professionals in ecology, biodiversity and stormwater drainage and the collective expertise acquired over the last decade developing of green roof systems to meet complex ecological considerations in the United Kingdom. As consultants they have worked closely with international colleagues, especially in Switzerland.

The Sustainable Building Industry Council

The Sustainable Buildings Industry Council (SBIC) was founded by the major building trade associations in 1980 as the Passive Solar Industries Council. The name was changed to more accurately reflect the full scope of its efforts in the allied fields of architecture, engineering, building systems and materials, product manufacturing, energy analysis, and "whole building" design. The council remains a strong supporter of passive solar strategies and technology-driven building solutions, but from the beginning, its work has touched on all aspects of sustainable design and construction: energy efficiency, renewable technologies, daylighting, healthy indoor environments, sustainable building materials and products, and resource conservation, in short, all the components that make integrated, better buildings possible.

Whole Building Design Guide (WBDG)

The WBDG is a web-based portal providing practitioners from the United States government and industry with access to information on a wide range of building-related guidance, criteria and technology from a 'whole building' perspective. The materials are organized into three major categories: design guidance, project management and operations & maintenance. "A Board of Direction and Advisory Committee, consisting of representatives from over 25 participating federal agencies, private companies and non-profit organization, guides the development" of the materials on the WBDG web site, www.wbdg.org. Funding for the Web site is provided by the Naval Facility Engineering Command's (NAVFAC) Engineering Innovation and Criteria Office, the United States General Services Administration (GSA), the Department of Energy (through its National Renewable Energy Laboratory). The Sustainable Building Industry Council assists with the Web site as well. The Federal Green Construction Guide for Specifiers, which includes several specifications for green roofs, is at www.wbdg.org/designs.greenspec.php. These specifications include many green green performance recommendations, including relevant LEED programs.

Appendix B:
NAMES AND ADDRESSES OF ORGANIZATIONS AND CONTRIBUTORS

The following is a list of addresses, e-mail addresses, Web sites, and phone numbers for the contributors to the book. They are organized by chapter, in the order they appear in the book. It is not possible to include every person or firm that played a major role in each project discussed or case study presented. However, you may wish to contact the organizations or individuals listed here to obtain additional information or a particular consultant or specialist.

CHAPTER THREE
Emory Knoll Farms, Inc.
Ed Snodgrass
3410 Ady Rd.
Street, MD 21154
T. 410-452-5880
F. 410-452-5319
ed.snodgrass@greenroofplants.com
john.shepley@greenroofplants.com

ASTM Specifications
ASTM International
100 Barr Harbor Drive
PO Box C700
West Conshohocken, PA 19428-2959
www.ASTM.org

CHAPTER FOUR
Utility Building: 1910 Water Pumping Station, Zurich, Switzerland
(see publication referenced in notes)

Train Station, Zurich
Dr. Regula Muller Boesch
Topos
Idastrasse 24
8003 Zurich
T. 01-451-52-55
F. 01-451-52-78
mueller@toposmm.ch

University Hospital, Basel
Stephan Brenneisen
T. +41 (0) 58 934 59 29
stephan.brenneisen@zhaw.ch

Organic Farm: Asphof Rosenfluh
stephan.brenneisen@zhaw.ch

Warehouse and Garden Center: Business
Alex Gemperle AG
Alte St. Wolfganstrasse 11
6331 Hunenberg
T. 041-780-13-76
F. 041-780-45-05
alex.gemperle@gemperle.ch

Research on endangered bird species
Nathalie Baumann
University of Applied Sciences, Wädenswil
Dept. Naturmanagement-Urban Greening
Grüntal, Postfach 335
CH-8820 Waedenswil
T: +41 (0)58 934 55 83
F: +41 (0)58 934 50 01
nathalie.baumann@zhaw.ch

Cave Architecture: Switzerland and Germany
Peter Vetsch
Luttenstrasse 23
CH-8953 Dietikon ZH
Switzerland
info@vetsch.ch
www.vetsch.ch

Town Center: Geislingen, Germany
Heidrun Eckert
Zinco
Grabenstrasse 33
72669 Unterensingen
Germany
heidrun.eckert@zinco.de

Adler Thermae Spa & Wellness Resort, Tuscany
Claudia Zancolli, Public Relations
I-50327 Strada di Bagno Vignoni 1
S. Quirico D'Orcia (Siena), Tuscany. Italy
T. +39.0577.88 90 00,
F. +39.0577.88 99 99
pr@adler-thermae.com www.adler-thermae.com

Hugo & Hanspeter Demetz
Demetz Hugo
Burgfriedenkapelle
I-39042 Brixen (BZ)
T. +39 0472 831523
F. +39 0472 207189
demetzarch@libero.it

Malmö, Sweden brown roof
Annika Kruuse
ISU Institutet för hållbar stadsutveckling
Anckargripsgatan 3
211 19 Malmö, Sweden
T. 0708 288 717
Annika.Kruuse@mah.se

Mårten Setterblad
Agnevägen 26, 182 64 Djursholm, Sweden
T. +46 (0) 704 035 802
T. +46 (0) 8 755 10 84
marten.setterblad@gmail.com

Scandinavia sedum roofs
Tobias Emilsson
Department of Landscape Management and
Horticultural Technology
Swedish University of Agricultural Sciences, Box 66
SE-23053 Alnarp, Sweden
T. 46-7023-04164
tobias.emilsson@lt.slu.se

Ulrik Reeh
Veg-Tech
Hayrups Alle 7, 3. tv.
DK-2900 Hellerup, Denmark
T. 45-3962-6869
F. 45-2835-6869
ulrik.reeh@vegtech.dk
www.vegtech.dk

Canary Wharf
Alec Butcher, Landscape Manager
alec.butcher@canarywharf.com
For Dusty Gedge, see end of Appendix.
www.blackredstarts.org.uk/

Cambridge Roof Garden, LIFFE Building
anton.beck@cannon-bridge.co.uk

Private/Public Partnership
Charlie Green
The Office Group
175-185 Gray's Inn Road
London WC1X 8UP, UK
charlie@theofficegroup.co.uk

Public School: London
Melissa Ronaldson
melissa@lcherbalists.co.uk

Inn the Park, St. James Park
Sara Lom and Dr. Nigel Reeve
Royal Parks Foundation
nreeve@royalparks.gsi.gov.uk
www.royalparks.org.uk

Zoological Park: Komodo Dragon House
See end of Appendix for Gedge and see University
Hospital, Basel, for Brenneisen. See www.zsl.org
Sven.seiffert@zsl.org

Airports
Lindasv@greenroofs.com
BTaube@atlantaGa.Gov

CHAPTER FIVE
Charles Miller: Heinz 57; Life Expression Center:
Oaklynn Library
Charlie Miller
Roofscapes Inc.
7114 McCallum Street
Philadelphia, PA 19119
T. 215-247-8784
F. 215-247-4659

CMILLER@ROOFMEADOW.COM
WWW.ROOFMEADOW.COM

Mexico: Autonomous University of Chapingo;
Public school facilities, Xochimilco
Dr. Gilberto A. Navas Gómez
Uxmal 117-402
Col. Narvarte
C.P. 03020, Mexico, D.F.
T. +52-55 54401679
navasg_chapingo_uni@mac.com

Michael Siemsen
Institut für Agrar- und Stadtökologische Projekte an der
Humboldt-Universität zu Berlin (IASP)
Invalidenstrasse 42
10115 Berlin, Germany
T. +49 (0)30 20939060
michael.siemsen@rz.hu-berlin.de
www.agrar.hu-berlin.de/ASP

Ulrike Grau
Universidad Autónoma Chapingo
Fitotecnia 7, Colonia de Profesores
Chapingo, Estado de México
C.P. 56230, Mexico
T. +52-55 10132877
uligrau@hotmail.com

Tanya Muller Garcia
tamuller@amenamex.org (see address p. 322)

Balmori Associates: The Solaire Building;
Silvercup Studios; Gratz Industries
Diana Balmori
Sarah Wayland Smith
820 Greenwich Street
New York, NY 10014
T. 212-431-9191
F. 212-431-8616
swayland@balmori.com

The Kestrel Design Group: Green Institute;
Central Library
L. Peter MacDonagh
Elizabeth Ryan
7101 Ohms Lane
Minneapolis, Minnesota 55439
T. 952-928-9600
F. 952-928-1939
pmacdonagh@kestreldesigngroup.com
www.kestreldesigngroup.com

Cornelia Hahn Oberlander, CSLA; Robson Square
& Vancouver Public Library
Elisabeth Whitelaw
1372 Arcadia Road
Vancouver, B.C. V6T lP6 Canada
T. 604-224-3967
F. 604-224-7347
coberlan@interchange.ubc.ca

Oak Hammock Marsh Conservation Center
Robert Eastwood
Number Ten Architects
310-115 Bannatyne Ave. East
Winnipeg, Manitoba, Canada R3B OR3
T. 204-942-0981
reastwood@numberten.com

DUC Corporate Headquarters
Rick Wishart
Ducks Unlimited Canada
P.O. Box 1160
Stonewall, Manitoba, Canada, R0C 2Z0
T. 204-467-3254
F. 204-467-9028
webfoot@ducks.ca
www.ducks.ca

The Gap
Gap Inc.
Two Folsom Street
San Francisco, CA 94115
www.gapinc.com

Paul Kephart
Rana Creek
35351 East Carmel Valley Road
Carmel Valley, CA 93924
T. 831-659-3820
paul@ranacreek.com

The Peggy Notebaert Nature Museum
Jill Riddell, Director of Conservation
Joel Alpern, Museum Staff
Christopher Dunn, Technical Operations Manager
2430 North Cannon Drive
Chicago, IL 60614
T. 773-755-5145
F. 773-549-5199
jriddell@naturemuseum.org
jalpern@naturemuseum.org
cdunn@naturemuseum.org
www.naturemuseum.org

Conservation Design Forum
David J. Yocca
375 W. First Street
Elmhurst, IL 60126
T: 630-559-2000
F. 630-559-2030
cdf@cdfinc.com
dyocca@cdfinc.com
www.cdfinc.com

Ford River Rouge Plant,
Ford Motor Company
Environmental Quality Office
Suite 1400 One Parklane Blvd.
Dearborn, MI 48126

Don Russell (formerly with Ford)
Xero Flor America, LLC
1923 Raymond Ave.
Dearborn, MI 48124
T. 313-655-1243
don@xeroflora.com
www.xeroflora.com

Reid R. Coffman
Division of Landscape Architecture
University of Oklahoma
T. 405.325.2548
rrcoffman@ou.edu

Neuhoff Meat Packing Plant
Pivot Design
Eric Shriner
Pivot Design
3127 SE 33rd Ave.
Portland, OR 97202
T. 503-235-5429
F. 503-235-5673
eshriner@mindspring.com

Water Quality Center,
Chris Bowles
Clean Water Services
2025 SW Merlo Court
Beaverton, OR 97006
T. 503-547-8102
F. 503-547-8101
bowlesc@cleanwaterservices.org

Eric Gunderson
PIVOT Architecture
72 West Broadway
Eugene, Oregon 97401
T. 541-342-7291
F. 541-342-1535
www.pivotarchitecture.com

North Beach Place
Cathy Garrett and Chris Pattillo
PGAdesign Inc. Landscape Architects
444 17th Street
Oakland, CA 94612
T. 510-465 1284
F. 510-465 1256
garrett@pgadesign.com
pattillo@pgadesign.com
www.PGAdesign.com

Barnhart Associates Architects
Paul Barnhart
T. 415-495 4890
F. 415-495 4998
paul@baasf.com

Full Circle Design Group
Serena Trachta
Full Circle Design Group
329 Bryant Street, Suite 3A
San Francisco, CA 94107
T. 415-357-0110
F. 415-357-0112
sgt@fullcirclearchitecture.com

Bridge Housing Corporation
Jesse Wu
Bridge Housing Corporation
345 Spear Street, Suite 700
San Francisco, CA 94105
T. 415-989 1111
F. 415-495-4898
jwu@bridgehousing.com

Millennium Park, Chicago
Marion Meers, Karen Ryan
www.millenniumpark.org

Terry Guen Design Associates, Incorporated
Terry Guen
521 West Superior, Suite 327
Chicago, IL 60610
T. 312-337-9245 or 46
F. 312-671-8295
tgda@tgda.net
www.tgda.net

Winnipeg Mountain Co-op Building
Richard Kula
Sustainable Solutions Inc.
6-502 Rue St. Baptiste
Winnipeg, Manitoba Canada R2X 2H9
T. 204-775-6886
F. 204-775-6886
rkula@sustainable-solutions.ca
www.sustainable-solutions.ca

Sarah Lawrence College
Mark Bunnell
Quennell Rothschild & Partners LLP
Landscape Architecture & Planning
118 West 22nd Street
New York, NY 10011
T. 212-929-3330 x 210
www.qrpartners.com

Aislinn Weidele
Polshek Partnership Architects
320 West 13th Street
New York, New York 10014
T. 212-792-5997
aweidele@polshek.com

California Academy of Sciences
875 Howard Street
San Francisco, CA 94013
T. 415-321-8000
www.calacademy.org
Renzo Piano Building Workshop
Olaf de Nooyer, architect
odenooyer@rpbw.com

Kang Kiang
Chong Partners Architects
405 Howard Street, 5th Floor
San Francisco, CA 94105
T. 415-433-0120
F. 415-433-4368
info@chongpartners.com
kkiang@chongpartners.com

Ove Arup & Partners, Engineers
901 Market Street
Suite 260
San Francisco, CA 94103
http://www.arup.com/

SWA Group, Landscape Architects
2200 Bridgeway
Sausalito, CA 94965
T. (415) 332-5100
www.swagroup.com

Rutherford & Chekene, Engineers
Oakland, CA
www.ruthchek.com

Paul Kephart
Rana Creek
35351 East Carmel Valley Road
Carmel Valley CA 93924
T. 831-659-3820
paul@ranacreek.com

CHAPTER SIX
Shelburne Falls bridge of flowers
Place Viger
Artist Rose-Marie E. Goulet
goulet.e.rm@videotron.ca

RockWerks
Adam Distenfield
129 Noll Street
Brooklyn, NY 11206
T. 718-628-5993
www.brooklynrockwerks.com

Montreal Hilton Hotel
Johanne Sénécal/Stéphane Morin
Hilton Montréal Bonaventure
T. 514-878-2332
www.hiltonmontreal.com

Riverbank State Park
679 Riverside Drive
New York, NY 10031
T. 212-694-3600
www.nysparks.state.ny.us/parks

Abel Bainnson Butz
80 8th Avenue, Suite 1105
New York, NY 10011
T. 212-206-0630
www.abbla.org

Chelsea, NY Roof Garden
Robert Martin Designs
Brooklyn Navy Yard
Building 280, Suite 223
Brooklyn, NY 11205
T. 718 797-1183
F. 718 797 4957
robertmartin@robertmartindesigns.com
www.robertmartindesigns.com

Dean Anderson, Super Square Corp.
545 Broadway
Newburgh, New York 12550
T. 845-565-3539
Supersquare2@aol.com

Sniffen Court
Madison Cox Design
127 West 26th Street, 9th floor
New York, NY 10001
T. 212-242-4631
www.madisoncox.com

Steven L. Cantor, landscape architect
scantorrla@aol.com

Mark Davies, Higher Ground Horticulture
Higher Ground Horticulture
470 W 24th St, Suite 14E
New York, NY 10011-1205
T. 212-691-3633
higherground@verizon.net

Alan Wanzenberg, architect
333 W. 52nd Street
New York, NY 10019
T. 212-489-7980
www.alanwanzenberg.com

Roof garden in rental property, New York City
Fox Diehl Architects, New York, New York

Entrance: Brooklyn Botanic Garden
Leeann Lavin
Brooklyn Botanic Garden
1000 Washington Avenue
Brooklyn, NY 11225
T. 718-623-7200
leeannlavin@bbg.org
www.bbg.org

Cathedral Place and the Portland Hotel
See Cornelia Oberlander, Chapter Five

William J. Clinton Presidential Center and Park
jsemans@semanspartnership.com
www.clintonfoundation.org

Heifer International Headquarters,
Heifer Project International
P.O. Box 8058
Little Rock, AR 72203
T. 800-422-0474
www.heifer.org

Polk Stanley Rowland Curzon Porter, Architects
Reese Rowland, Principal in Charge
Polk Stanley Rowland Curzon Porter, Architects
700 S. Schiller
Little Rock, AR 72201
T. 501-378-0878
rrowland@polkstanley.com

Larson Burns Smith, Landscape architects
Martin Smith, Design Principal, Landscape architect
Larson Burns Smith
120 S. Izard
Little Rock, AR 72202
T. 501-378-0200
martins@larsonburns.com

Apartment, Park Slope, Brooklyn
Jeff Heehs
jhbklyn@yahoo.com

Sustainable South Bronx
Rob Crauderueff, Program Coordinator for Sustainable
Alternatives
Miquela Craytor, Deputy Director
890 Garrison Avenue, 4th Floor
Bronx, NY 10474
T. 718-617-4668
F. 718-617-5228
robc@ssbx.org

The RBA Group, Inc.
Susanne Boyle
The RBA Group, Inc.
One Huntington Quadrangle, Suite 4C20
Melville, NY 11747
T. 631.694.3131 ext. 229
susanneboyle@gmail.com
www.rbagroup.com

Jennifer Appel
Landsculpture & Design. Inc.
PO Box 920622
Houston, TX 77292-0622
T. 713-263-1682
F. 713-263-0395
jappel@landscapevitamins.com
www.landscapehouston.com
www.petfriendlyfertilizer.com
www.landscapevitamins.com

Richard Heller
Greener by Design
POB 765, 87 Wolfs Lane
Pelham, NY 10803
T. 914-637-9870
F. 914-712-0416
RHeller@Greenerdesigns.com
www.greenerdesigns.com

Rana Creek Habitat Restoration
See Chapter Five, Paul Kephart, California Academy
of Sciences

Prairie Habitats
John Morgan
Prairie Habitats Inc.
Box 10
Argyle, Manitoba, Canada R0C 0B0
T. 204-467-9371
F. 204-467-5004
jpmorgan@mts.net
www.prairiehabitats.com

Rana Creek Nursery
Cooper Scollan
35351 East Carmel Valley Road
Carmel Valley, CA 93924
T. 831-659-2830
F. (831)659-1204
cscollan@ranacreek.com

Native Plant Solutions
Brent Wark
Ducks Unlimited Canada
1255 B Clarence Avenue
Winnipeg, Canada MB R3T 1T4
T. 204-953-8202
F. 204-953-8209
b_wark@ducks.ca

Midwest Trading Horticultural Supplies, Inc.
P.O. Box 398
Maple Park, IL 60151
T. 630-365-1990
F. 630-365-3818
mtinfo@midwest-trading.com

Classic Groundcovers
405 Belmont Rd
Athens, GA 30605
T. 706-543-0145
www.classic-groundcovers.com

Midwest Groundcovers
PO Box 748
St. Charles, IL 60174
T. 847-742-1790
F. 847-742-2655
www.midwestgroundcovers.com

Signe Nielsen
Mathews-Nielsen
120 Broadway, Suite 1040
New York, NY 10217
T. 212-431-3609 x11
F. 212-941-1513
snielsen@mnlandscape.com
www.mnlandscape.com

Vancouver Aquarium/living walls
Sharp & Diamond, Landscape Architecture, Inc.
602-1401 West Broadway
Vancouver, British Columbia, Canada V6H 1H6
www.sharpdiamond.com
Randy Sharp, landscape architect

The Highline
Friends of the High Line
430 West 14th Street, Suite 304
New York, NY 10014
T. 212-206-9922
www.thehighline.org
Peter Mullan, Director of Planning

Diller Scofidio + Renfro, Architects
601 W. 26th Street, Suite 1915;
New York, NY 10001
T. 212-260-7971
www.dillerscofidio.com

BeltLine
BeltLine Partnership
PO Box 93351
Atlanta, Georgia 30377
Info@BeltLinePartnership.org www.beltline.org
Tina Arbes, Chief Operating Officer

GREEN ROOF ORGANIZATIONS

AMENA, Mexican Green Roofs Association
Tanya Muller
Asociación Mexicana para la Naturación de Azoteas, A.C.
Calle Uxmal 117–402 Col.
Narvarte C.P. 03020 México D.F.
T. 56-76-26-19
tamuller@amenamex.org
www.amenamex.org

Canadian Green Building Councils
Head Office
325 Dalhousie Street, Suite 800
Ottawa, ON K1N 7G2
T. 613-241-1184
F. 613-241-4782
www.cagbc.org

Centre for the Advancement of Green Roof Technology
British Columbia Institute of Technology, Centre for the Advancement of Green Roof Technology
555 Great Northern Way
Great Northern Way Campus
Vancouver, B.C., Canada V5T 1E2
info_greenroof@bcit.ca
www.commons.bcit.ca/greenroof

Earth Pledge
122 East 38th Street
New York, NY 10016
T. 212-725-6611
F. 212-725-6774
www.earthpledge.org

Green Roofs for Healthy Cities,
Steven Peck
406 King Street East
Toronto, ON M5A 1L4 Canada
T. 416-971-4494
F. 416-971-9844
speck@greenroofs.org
www.greenroofs.org

GreenRoofs.com
Linda S. Velazquez,
GreenRoofs.com
3449 Lakewind Way
Alpharetta, GA 30005
T. 678-580-1965
lindasv@greenroofs.com

International Green Roof Congress
www.greenroofworld.com

International Green Roof Association
www.igra-world.com
Living roofs.org
Dusty Gedge
7 Dartmouth Grove
London SE10 8AR UK
T. 07977 202373
dusty.gedge@greenroofconsultancy.com
www.livingroofs.org

Paul Early
Bon Marche Centre
241-251 Ferndale Road
London SW9 8BJ UK
T. 020 7326 0007
paul.early@greenroofconsultancy.com

National Institute of Building Sciences
(also the home of the Whole Building Design Guide)
1090 Vermont Avenue, NW,
Suite 700
Washington, DC 20005-4905
T. 202-289-7800
F. 202-289-1092
www.nibs.org

Sustainable Buildings Industry Council
1112 16th Street NW, Suite 240
Washington, D.C. 20036
T. 202-393-5043 fax
sbic@sbicouncil.org
www.sbicouncil.org

US Green Building Councils
1015 18th Street, NW, Suite 508
Washington, DC 20036
T. 202-82-USGBC
www.USGBC.org

The following list cites companies whose products are discussed or referenced in the book. In some cases, more than one address is given for companies that have more than one major address in North America. Space does not permit including all of the major European manufacturers and suppliers, but some of the listings below are subsidiaries of firms first established in Europe. Many of the representatives of companies now based in North America have European-trained staff and specialists. In some cases, multiple phone numbers are provided.

GENERAL

AMERICAN HYDROTECH, INC.
303 East Ohio Street
Chicago, IL 60611
800-877-6125
312-337-4998
info@hydrotechusa.com

HYDROTECH MEMBRANE CORPORATION
10951 Parkway Blvd.
Ville D'Anjou; Quebec H1J 151 Canada
514-353-6000
800-361-8924
www.hydrotechmembrane.ca

AMERICAN PERMAQUIK INC.
5500 Main Street, Suite B-1
Williamsville, NY 14221
716-633-3124

PERMAQUICK CORPORATION
6178 Netherhart Rd.
Mississauga, Ontario, L5T 1B7 Canada
905-564-6100
www.permaquik.com

BARRETT COMPANY
800-647-0100
www.barrettroofs.com

BUILDING LOGICS
1033 Downshire Chase
Virginia Beach, VA 23452
757-340-4201
www.buildinglogics.com

CARLISLE COATINGS & WATERPROOFING INCORPORATED
900 Hensley Lane
Wylie, TX 75098
800-527-7092
www.carlisle-ccs-com

CARLISLE SYNTEC INCORPORATED
P.O. Box 7000
Carlisle, PA 17013
800-4-SYNTEC
www.carlisle-syntec.com

CARL STAHL DECORCABLE, INC.
660 W Randolph St
Chicago, IL 60661-2114
312-474-1100
800-444-6271
www.decorcable.com

ELEVATED LANDSCAPE TECHNOLOGIES INC.
245 King George Road Suite #319
Brantford ON N3R 7N7 Canada
866-306-7773,
519-449-9433
www.eltlivingwalls.com
info@elteasygreen.com
support@elteasygreen.com

THE GARLAND COMPANY, INC.
GreenShield green roof systems
3800 East 91st Street
Cleveland, OH 44105
800-321-9336

GARLAND CANADA INC.
1290 Martin Grove Road
Toronto, Ontario M9W 4X3 Canada
800-387-5991 (Canada Only)
www.garlandco.com

GRACE CONSTRUCTION PRODUCTS
www.graceconstruction.com

GREENGRID SYSTEM
Weston Solutions, Inc.
20 North Wacker Drive, Suite 1210
Chicago, IL 60606
312-424-3319
www.greengridroofs.com
www.westonsolutions.com

GREEN LIVING TECHNOLOGIES, LLC
Green Roofs and Green Walls.
800-631-8001
info@agreenroof.com
www.agreenroof.com

GREEN ROOF BLOCKS
Saint Louis Metalworks Company
11701 New Halls Ferry Road
Florissant, Missouri 63033-6900
314-972-8010
www.greenroofblocks.com

GREEN ROOF INNOVATIONS
P.O. Box 2775
San Carlos, Carmel, CA 93921
831-625-5625
www.grinnovations.com

GREENSCREEN
1743 S. La Cienega Blvd.
Los Angeles, CA 90035-4650
800-450-3494
sales@greenscreen.com
www.greenscreen.com

GREENTECH
8401 Mayland Drive, Suite F
Richmond, VA 23294
804-965-0026
www.greentechitm.com

G-SKY GREEN ROOFS AND WALLS
Green Wall panels and green roofs
669 Ridley Place, Unit 208
Delta, British Columbia, Canada (Annacis Island)
V3M 6Y9
604-708-0611
www.g-sky.com

HENRY BUILDING ENVELOPE SYSTEMS
www.henry-bes.com
866-848-4195

JAKOB, INC.
955 NW 17th Avenue, Unit B
Delray Beach, FL 33445
561-330-6502
866-215-1421
info@jakob-usa.com
www.jakobstainlesssteel.com

KEMPER SYSTEM
1182 Teaneck Road
Teaneck, NJ 07666
800-541-5455
www.kempersystems.net

LEXCAN LIMITED
52 Bramwin Court,
Brampton, Ontario L6T 5G2 Canada
North America Toll Free: 1-800-268-2889
www.lexcan.com

OPTIGRÜN GREEN ROOF SYSTEMS
Resource Conservation Technology Inc.
800-477-7724
www.conservationtechnology.com

PRAIRIE TECHNOLOGIES, INC.
6900 Bleck Dr.
Rockford, MN 55373
800-403-7747
www.prairie-tech.com

SARNAFIL INC.
100 Dan Road
Canton, MA 02021
800-576-2358
800-451-2504
www.sarnafilus.com

SARNAFIL LTD.
1260 Lakeshore Road East
Mississauga, Ontario
Canada L5E 3B8
800-268-0479

SIPLAST
1000 E. Rochell Blvd.
Irving, TX 75062-3940
800-922-8800
www.siplast.com

SOPREMA, INC.
310 Quadral Drive
Wadsworth, OH 44281
800-356-3521
www.soprema.us

SOPREMA, INC. (Canada)
1640 rue Haggerty
Drummondville, Québec J2C 5P8 Canada
819-478-8163
800-567-1492
www.soprema.ca

TECTA AMERICA, TECTAGREEN
5215 Old Orchard Road, Suite 880
Skokie, IL 60077
866-832-8259
www.tectaamerica.com

TREMCO SEALANTS (Canada)
torscs@tremcoinc.com
www.tremcosealants.com/

TREMCO SEALANTS (USA)
800-321-7906
tscs@tremcoinc.com
www.tremcosealants.com/

XERO FLOR AMERICA, LLC
P.O. Box 24066
Lansing, MI 48909
517-290-4177
greeroof@xeroflora.com
www.xeroflora.com;

XERO FLOR CANADA LTD.
30 Stephenfrank Road
Scarborough, Ontario
Canada M1P 3W3
49-4224-022774
www.xeroflor.com

ZINCO USA
P++49 7022 / 6003-540
heidrun.eckert@zinco.de

ZINCO CANADA INC.
P.O. Box 29
Carlisle, Ontario
Canada L0R 1H0
905-690-1661
greenroof@zinco.ca
www.zinco.ca

Drainage and Root Barriers

AMBE LIMITED
7201 Ohms Lane, Suite 150
Minneapolis, MN 55439
952-831-1233
www.ambeltd.com

AMERICAN WICK
1209 Airport Road
Monroe, NC 28110
800-242-WICK
www.americanwick.com

BIOBARRIER, BBA FIBERWEB
Reemay Inc.
70 Old Hickory Blvd.
Old Hickory, TN 37138
800-284-2780 x7137 or 7054
www.bbafiberweb.com

COLBOND
P.O. Box 1057
Enka, NC 28728
800-365-7391
enka-engineering@colbond.com
www.colbond-usa-com;

JDR ENTERPRISES, INC.
292 South Main Street, Suite 200
Alpharetta, GA 30004
800-843-7569
www.j-draincom

ELJEN CORPORATION
1215 McKee Street
East Hartford, CT 06108
800-444-1359
www.eljen.com

KORO DRAIN
Mansonville Plastics BC, Ltd.
19402 56 Avenue
Surrey, British Columbia
Canada V3S 6K4
800-663-8162
www.mansonvilleplastics.com

NILEX INC. (Canada)
800-667-4811
www.nilex.com

NILEX INC. (USA)
15171 East Fremont Drive
Centennial, CO 80112
800-537-4241
www.nilex.com

TENCATE MIRAFI
3655 Holland Drive
Pendergrass, GA 30567
708-693-2226
www.tcmirafi.com

TENSAR EARTH TECHNOLOGIES, INC.
5883 Glenridge Drive
Suite 200
Atlanta, GA 30328
888-828-5140
www.tensarcorp.com

BROCK WHITE CO.
1325 Ellice Ave.
Winnipeg, Manitoba R3GOG1 Canada
204-786-8426
www.brockwhite.com

Growing media, soil, mulch and equipment

ANSWER GARDEN PRODUCTS LTD.
27715 Huntingdon Road, RR 5
Abbotsford, British Columbia V4X 1B6 Canada
604-856-6221
info@envirowaste.ca
www.envirowaste.ca

NYC COMPOST PROJECT
Brooklyn Botanical Garden
Urban Composting Project

1000 Washington Ave.
Brooklyn, NY 11225
compost@bbg.org
www.nyc.gov/sanitation
www.nyccompost.org

EAGLEPICHER FILTRATION & MATERIALS, INC.
P.O. Box 12130
Reno, NV 89510
800-366-7607
www.eaglepicher.com

FAFARD
P.O. Box 790
Agawam, MA 01001
800-PEAT MOSS
www.fafard.com

FRASER RICHMOND BIO-CYCLE LTD.
12620 Wooldridge Road
Pitt Meadows, British Columbia V3Y 1Z1 Canada
604-465-3506
saujla@direct.ca

GREAT PACIFIC PUMICE INC.
Vancouver, Canada
604.250.2750
gpapum@telus.net

HYDROCKS SOIL ENHANCER
Garick Corporation
13600 Broadway Avenue
Cleveland, Ohio 44125
800-2-Garick
(800-242-7425)

LANDSOURCE ORGANIX
100 Britannia Road East
Hornby, Ontario L0P 1E0
877 548 8558
info@landsourceorganix.com
www.landsourceorganix.com

MIDWEST TRADING HORTICULTURAL SUPPLIES
P.O. Box 1005
St. Charles, IL 60174
847-742-1840
www.midwest-trading.com

NORTHEAST SOLITE CORPORATION
Northeast Office: Saugerties, New York
845-246-9571
800-474-4514
Midwest Office: Brooks, Kentucky
502-957-2103
800-272-0441
http://www.nesolite.com
http://www.nesolite.com/greenrf.htm

PETERSON PACIFIC CORPORATION
29408 Airport Road
Eugene, OR 97402
541-689-0804
www.petersonpacific.com

RED RIVER SOILS
(a division of Consolidated Envirowaste Industries Inc.)
2427 Waverly Street;
Winnipeg, Manitoba R3T 2E7 Canada
204-275-7980
info@envirowaste.ca

REXIUS SUSTAINABLE SOLUTIONS
1275 Bailey Hill Road
Eugene, OR 97402
888-4-REXIUS
www.rexius.com

ROOFLITE
www.rooflite.us

STALITE
Carolina Stalite Company
P.O. Box 1037
Salisbury, NC 28145-1037
800-898-3772
www.stalite.com

STANCILLS, INC.
877-536-9572
www.stancills.com

WHITE PREMIUM ORGANICS
2560 Foxfield Road
Suite 200
St. Charles, IL 60174
800-777-1108
866-586-1563
www.garveyintl.com

IRRIGATION

BERRY HILL IRRIGATION, INC.
3744 Highway 58
Buffalo Junction, VA 24529
800-345-DRIP
434-374-5555
www.berryhilldrip.com

NETAFIM USA
5470 East Home Avenue
Fresno, CA 93727
800-777-6541
www.netafimusa.com

KISSS USA
Sustainable Engineering Solutions
8667 NW Gales Creek Road
Forest Grove, OR 97116
800-376-7161
www.ses-ontheweb.com

RAINBIRD
1000 W. Sierra Madre Ave.
Azusa, CA 91702
626-963-9311
800-RAINBIRD
www.rainbird.com

THE TORO COMPANY: CONSUMER DIVISION
8111 Lyndale Avenue South
Bloomington, MN 55420
USA 888-384-9939
Canada 800-544-5364
www.toro.com

T-SYSTEMS INTERNATIONAL, INC.
7545 Carroll Road
San Diego, CA 92121
858-578-1860
800-765-1860
www.tsystemsinternational.com

LEAK DETECTION

INTERNATIONAL LEAK DETECTION
11 Partlett Drive
Ajax, Ontario L1S 4V2 Canada
866-282-5325
www.leak-detection.com

MID Systems
Moisture Intrusion Detection Systems, Inc.
1207-B Crews Road

Matthews, NC 18105
704-846-5150
(also marketed by www.buildinglogics.com)

NURSERIES

BLUESTEM NURSERY
P.O. Box 239

Laurier, WA 99146
1946 Fife Rd

Christina Lake, BC V0H 1E3 Canada
250-447-6363
www.bluestem.ca

CLASSIC GROUNDCOVERS
405 Belmont Rd
Athens, GA 30605
706-543-0145
www.classic-groundcovers.com

EMORY KNOLL FARMS, INC.
3410 Ady Road
Street, MD 21154
410-452-5880
www.greenroofplants.com

GROWILD, INC.
7190 Hill Hughes Road
Fairview, TN 37062
615.799.1910
www.growildnursery.com

HUMBER NURSERIES LTD.
8386 Highway 50
Brampton, Ontario, Canada L6T 0A5
905-794-0555
www.gardencentre.com

INTRINSIC PERENNIAL GARDENS, INC.
10702 Seaman Rod
Hebron, IL 60034
800-648-2788
www.intrinsicperennialgardens.com

LINNAEA NURSERIES LTD.
666-224th Street
Langley, British Columbia, Canada V2Z 2G7
888-327-7705
www.linnaeanurseries.com

MIDWEST GROUNDCOVERS
P.O. Box 748
St. Charles, IL 60174
847-742-1790
www.midwestgroundcovers.com

NATIVE PLANT SOLUTIONS
1255B Clarence Avenue
Winnipeg, MB R3T 1T4 Canada
204-953-8200
800-665-DUCK
nps@ducks.ca

N.A.T.S NURSERY LTD.
24555 32nd Avenue
Langley, British Columbia, Canada V2Z 2J5
604-530-9300
www.natsnursery.com

NORTH CREEK NURSERIES, INC.
388 North Creek Road
Landenberg, PA 19350
877-ECO-PLUG
www.northcreeknurseries.com

PRAIRIE HABITATS INC.
Box 1
Argyle, Manitoba, Canada R0C 0B0
204-467-9371
www.prairiehabitats.com
www.premiumplants.net

RANA CREEK NURSERY
35351 East Carmel Valley Road
Carmel Valley, CA 93924
831-659-2830
www.ranacreeknursery.com

ROOF GREENING SYSTEMS INC.
P.O. Box 24173
Pinebush Road RPO
Cambridge, Ontario, Canada N1R 8E7
877-951-3288
www.roofgreening.ca

PAVEMENTS

BIOPAVER
www.biopaver.com
info@biopaver.com

BISON DECK SUPPORT
a United Construction Products, Inc. Company
1975 W. 13th Ave. Denver, CO 80204
303-628-7950
www.bisonus.com
www.BisonDeckSupports.com

ENVIROSPEC PAVE-EL (Canada)
P.O. Box 519
Port Credit Postal,
Mississauga, Ontario, Canada L5G 4M2
905-271-3441
info@envirospecinc.com
www.envirospecinc.com

ENVIROSPEC PAVE-EL (USA)
Ellicott Station
P.O. Box 119
Buffalo, NY 14205
716-689-8548
info@envirospecinc.com

HANOVER ARCHITECTURAL PRODUCTS
240 Bender Road
Hanover, PA 17331
717-637-060
www.hanoverpavers.com

MUTUAL MATERIALS
601 119th
Bellevue, WA 98005
800-477-3008 (USA and eastern Canada)
604-888-0555 (western Canada)
www.mutualmaterials.com

TILE TECH
830 South Hill St.
Suite M102
Los Angeles, California 90014
213-489-2555
www.tiletechpavers.com

WAUSAU TILE
P.O. Box 1520
Wausau, WI 54402-1520
9001 Business Highway 51
Rothschild, WI 54474
715-359-3121
www.wausautile.com

SOLAR

ALTAIR ENERG
www.altairenergy.com

BIG APPLE SOLAR
37 West 28th St., 12th floor
New York, NY 10001
718-389-5357
www.basicsolar.org

SOLARGRID
The Garland Company, Inc. (see listing in General)
www.bpsolar.com

SOLAR INTEGRATED TECHNOLOGIES
1837 East Martin Luther King Jr. Blvd.
Los Angeles, CA 90058
323-231-0411
www.solarintegrated.com

UNITED SOLAR OVONIC
3800 Lapeer Road
Auburn Hills, MI 48326
800-843-3892
westerninfo@uni.solar.com
www.uni-solar.com

WATERPROOFING AND SEALING

CARLISLE SYNTEC INCORPORATED
P.O. Box 7000
Carlisle, PA 17013
800-4-SYNTEC
800-453-2554
www.carlisle-syntec.com

CEMENTAID, CANADA WATERPROOF
CONCRETE (CANADA) LTD.
8461 Keele Street, Unit 24
Concord Ontario L4K1Z6 Canada
905-761-7062
waterproof.concrete@rogers.co
www.waterproofconcrete.com

CEMENTAID, US
Glacier Northwest Inc.
5975 E Marginal Way, South
Seattle, Washington 98134
206-764-3000
www.glaciernw.com

SEALOFLEX WATERPROOFING SYSTEMS
2516 Oscar Johnson Drive
Charleston, SC 29405
800-770-6466
www.sealoflex.com

Appendix D: SAMPLE SPECIFICATION AND MEDIA SELECTION

SAMPLE PERFORMANCE SPECIFICATION, HEINZ PROJECT, CHAPTER FIVE
(COURTESY OF CHARLIE MILLER, WWW.ROOFMEADOW.COM.)

The following is representative of performance specifications for green roofs. It incorporates information about the overall expectations for performance (e.g., weight, moisture retention, durability). It also describes the critical physical or chemical properties required for each component of the assembly. Specific test methods to confirm compliance with the specification are provided. This type of specification facilitates the introduction of alternative components, while ensuring that the completed green roof will perform as designed.

TYPE III
EXTENSIVE VEGETATED ROOF COVER

SECTION 02931
VEGETATED ROOF COVERINGS
PART 1: GENERAL

1.01. SUMMARY

A. Section specifies all labor, materials, transportation, equipment and services necessary to assemble a complete vegetated roof cover as shown on the drawings and described herein. This system shall be installed in conjunction with a compatible roof waterproofing system.

B. Related requirements specified elsewhere include:
    1. Roof deck insulation–Section 07220.
    2. Roofing–Section 07530.

1.02. REFERENCES

A. Referenced standards and abbreviations
    1. System provider's specifications and recommendations.
    2. *American Standard Testing Method Standards* – abbreviated as "ASTM."
    3. *Guidelines for the Planning, Development and Maintenance of Green Roofs; Appendix – Determination of Apparent Density, Maximum Water Capacity, and Water Permeability* (English version): Richtlinien für die Planung, Ausführung und Pflege von Dachbegrünung, Forschungsgesellschaft Landschaftsentwicklung Lanschaftsbau e.V., 1995, abbreviated as "FLL."
    4. *Methods of Soil Analysis,* American Society of Agronomy (1996), abbreviated as "MSA."
    5. *Test Methods for the Examination of Composting and Compost* (latest), abbreviated as "TMECC."
    6. *Recommended Chemical Soil Testing Procedures, North Central Region Publication #221,* abbreviated as "RCSTP."

1.03. DEFINITIONS

A. Drain access chamber: Open-ended box or cylinder that covers drains and/or scuppers. The chamber must be designed to admit water freely at the base. It must also have a removable lid to prevent debris from entering the chamber. The choice of chamber type will depend on the type of deck drain or scupper in use. See 1.05 Submittals.

B. Drain conduit: Perforated conduit installed in the drainage layer that is used to intercept and drain away percolating rainfall during design storm events.

C. Drainage layer: A granular mineral material layer used to: 1) promote aerated conditions in the overlying growth media layer, and 2) manage rainfall runoff and convey it to the roof drains, and 3) augment the root volume for the plants.

D. Growth media layer: An engineered soil-like material designed to retain moisture, manage plant nutrients, and support vigorous growth of the foliage.

E. EFVM (Electric field vector mapping): A leak location technique that relies on the electrical conductivity of the cover material (moist media) and electrical insulating properties of the waterproofing membrane. The compatibility of EFVM with a specific waterproofing system must be established in advance by the EFVM service provider.

F. Manning formula for conveyance:
ft3/s (m^3/s): K = 1.49 x (A x R$^{(\frac{2}{3})}$)/n; A=area (ft^2), R=hydraulic radius (ft), n=Manning's roughness coefficient (dimensionless).

    K = (A x R$^{(\frac{2}{3})}$)/n; A = area (m^2), R = hydraulic radius (m), n = Manning's roughness coefficient (dimensionless).

G. Rootbarrier: A thermoplastic membrane designed to prevent root penetration of the underlying waterproofing and to retain moisture in the root zone.

H. System provider: Company that provides or certifies all materials required for installation of the vegetated roof cover, furnishes on-site coordination and inspection, and offers long-term support and warranty protections for the completed green roof assembly.

I. Waterproofing provider: Company that provides or certifies all materials required for installation of the building waterproofing, furnishes on-site coordination and inspection, and offers long-term support and warranty protections for the completed waterproofing, including flashings, counter-flashings, coping, and deck drains.

1.04. SYSTEM DESCRIPTION

A. Design requirements
    1. The vegetated cover shall be a two-media system, consisting of a 4-inch (10.2 cm) growth media layer installed over a 2-inch (5.1 cm) granular drainage media layer.
    2. The system is intended to be used without irrigation in temperate climates. However, the system is compatible with the base capillary irrigation system. The base capillary system is designed to distribute water uniformly at a slow rate to the bottom of the drainage layer.
    3. In cases where thermal insulation will be installed above the primary water-proofing membrane (i.e., inverted roof membrane assembly), the thickness of the insulation may not exceed 2/3 of the thickness of the vegetated cover unless the insulation is under-drained. The installer must show that the under-drain layer has sufficient capacity to prevent flotation of the insulation and overlying cover system during the design rainfall event.
This assembly is suitable for roofs with pitches ranging from *zero* to 7 degrees or 12.5 percent.

B. Performance requirements: The completed vegetated roof covering system shall:
    1. Support a perennial vegetated ground cover.
    2. Provide efficient drainage of moisture that is in excess of that required for the vigorous growth of the installed vegetation.
    3. Protect roof waterproofing materials from damage caused by exposure to ultraviolet radiation, physical abuse, and rapid temperature fluctuations.
    4. Retain 1.75 inches (4.44 cm) of moisture at maximum water capacity, in accordance with the referenced FLL or ASTM E-2399 standards.
    5. Not exceed 40 pounds per square foot (195.3 kg/m2) in wet dead weight (ASTM E-2397).
    6. Continue to perform as designed for the duration of the warranty period, without a requirement to amend or refresh the media.

1.05. SUBMITTALS

A. Product data (included with bid response):
    1. System provider's technical literature showing compliance with specified requirements.
    2. System provider's statement indicating that proposed use is appropriate for each product.

3. System provider's statement that it has reviewed and approved the details for the associated water-proofing system, including deck drains, flashings, penetrations, and coping.

B. Shop drawings (provided prior to contract initiation):
　　1. Details of installation, showing conditions at terminations, transitions, and penetrations.
　　2. Layout for the internal drain conduit.
　　3. A profile schematic, in half scale, showing thickness of all materials.
　　4. Fabrication detail or system provider's information for drain access chambers. (*Note:* Preparation of these details requires, as a pre-requisite, that the waterproofing provider give a detailed description to the system provider for all roof drains, scuppers, and overflows, including accurate dimensions and geometric configurations.)

C. Samples
　　1. 4-by-4-inch square (10.2 cm by 10.2 cm)of each for each of the following:
　　　　a. Root-barrier (if a suitable root-barrier is not included as a part of the waterproofing system).
　　　　b. Protection layer.
　　　　c. Synthetic sheet components, including fabrics, sheet drains, reinforcing materials, and wind protection materials.
　　2. 12-inch (30.5 cm) length of drainage conduit.
　　3. 6-ounce (0.17 kg)sample of both drainage and growth medias for initial approval of the architect.

D. Statement of existing conditions that must be both achieved and present to begin installation of the vegetated roof covering system.

E. Statement of method for protecting the surface from wind disturbances until the foliage layer is established.

1.06. CONTRACT CLOSEOUT

A. Signed warranty documents.

B. Maintenance program.

1.07. QUALITY ASSURANCE

A. System certification: Signed by the system provider, certifying that the submitted vegetated roof covering system:
　　1. Complies with the specified system requirements (see 1.04 System Description).
　　2. Is eligible for the specified warranty required of the system provider.

B. Certified laboratory results: Showing compliance of the media with the specifications

C. Waterproofing certification: Signed by the waterproofing provider, certifying that the proposed vegetated roof cover system is fully compatible with the waterproofing assembly

D. Warranty: A copy of the standard system warranty shall be attached as an exhibit to the contract agreement.

E. System provider's field supervision: The System Provider shall furnish a quality control specialist to observe critical aspects of the installation.

F. Laboratory: Tests shall be conducted by an independent laboratory with the experience and capability to conduct the tests indicated.

1.08. SEQUENCE

A. Description of work sequence with attention to preventing deterioration of installed roofing by minimizing the use of newly constructed roof deck for storage, walking surface, and equipment.

1.09. MAINTENANCE

A. A 2-year establishment period maintenance contract for plantings.

B. *For consideration by the owner:* a long-term inspection and maintenance contract that includes all of the system components, media, and plantings specified within this section.

PART 2: MATERIALS

2.01. ROOT-BARRIER SUBSYSTEM (required, if a suitable root barrier is not included as part of the waterproofing system)

A. Root-barrier subsystem shall be installed immediately above the completed waterproofing (or thermal insulation, if this is project incorporates an IRMA configuration).

B. The subsystem consists of a 30-mil (0.03 inches or .762 mm) EPDM, polyvinyl chloride, polypropylene, or polyethylene membrane.

C. The membrane shall be seamed, according to the recommendations of the system provider, in order to provide a watertight surface.

D. The completions at terminations shall be according to the recommendations of the system provider.

2.02. PROTECTION LAYER

Depending on whether or not irrigation is planned, this layer shall consist of:

A. Composite protection, at a minimum, of a 16 oz/sy non-woven polypropylene fabric. The waterproofing provider may specify an alternative protection layer. In this case, the protection layer must be approved for use by the System Provider.

2.03. DRAIN CONDUIT

Perforated low-profile conduit:

Height	$\leq$ 2.25 in (5.7 cm)
Open area (sides and top)	$\geq$ 7%
Slot or perforation size	$\geq$ $\frac{1}{16}$ in. (1.59 mm)
Hydraulic conveyance (K)	$\geq$ 0.09 ft^3/sec (.0025 m^3/s)

2.04. GRANULAR DRAINAGE MEDIA

This is a mineral product that satisfies the following specifications:

Density at maximum water capacity (FLL or ASTM-E2399-05)	$\leq$ 60 lb/ft^3 (961.1 kg/m^3)
Water permeability (ASTM E2396-05)	$\geq$ 25 in/min (63.5 cm/min)
Total organic matter, by loss onignition (MSA)	$\leq$ 1%
Abrasion resistance (ASTM-C131-96)	$\leq$ 25% loss
Soundness (ASTM-C88 or T103 or T103-91)	$\leq$ 5% loss
Porosity (ASTM-C29)	$\geq$ 25%
Alkalinity, CaCO$_3$ equivalents (MSA)	$\leq$ 1%
Grain-size distribution (ASTM-C136)	
Pct. Passing US#18 sieve	$\leq$ 1%
Pct. Passing -inch sieve	$\leq$ 30%
Pct. Passing ⅜-inch sieve	$\geq$ 80%

2.05. SEPARATION FABRIC

Root-permeable needled non-woven needled polypropylene geotextile fabric. The fabric may not be heat calendared. This component shall satisfy the following specifications:

Unit weight (ASTM-D3776)	$\leq$ 4.25 oz/yd^2 (144.1 g/m^2)
Grab tensile (ASTM-D4632)	$\leq$ 90 lb (40.8 kg)
Mullen burst strength (ASTM-D4632)	$\geq$ 135 lb/in^2 (39,506.4 kg/mm^2)
Permittivity (ASTM-D4491)	$\geq$ 2 sec^{-1}

2.06. GROWTH MEDIA LAYER

A. This material is a mixture of mineral and organic components that satisfies the following specifications:

Non-capillary pore space ratio at field capacity, 0.333 bar (TMECC 03.01, A)	≥ 10% (vol)
Moisture content at field capacity (TMECC 03.01, A	≥ 15% (vol)
Non-capillary Pore Space Ratio at Maximum Water Capacity (FLL or ASTM-E2399)	≥ 6%
Maximum water capacity (FLL or ASTM-E2399-05)	≥ 40% (vol)
Density at maximum water capacity (FLL or ASTM-E2399-05)	≤ 85 lb/ft^3 (1,361.5 kg/m^3)
Water permeability (FLL or ASTM-E2399-05)	≥ 0.05 in/min (1.3 mm/min)
Alkalinity, Ca CO$_3$ equivalents (MSA)	≤ 2.5%
Total Organic Matter (TOM), by loss on ignition (MSA)	≤ 3-8% (dry wt.)
pH (RCSTP)	6.5-8.0
Soluble salts (DTPA saturated media extraction)(RCSTP)	≤ 6 mm hos/cm
Organic supplements (compost, peat moss, etc.) combined respiration rate (TMECC 05.08, B)	≤ 1 mg CO$_2$/g TOM/d
Cation exchange capacity (MSA)	≥ 10 meq/100g
Grain-size distribution of the mineral fraction (ASTM-D422)	
Clay fraction (2 micron) ≤	≤ 3%
Pct. Passing US#200 sieve (i.e., silt fraction)	5–15%
Pct. Passing US#60 sieve	10–25%
Pct. Passing US#18 sieve	20–50%
Pct. Passing 1/8-inch sieve	55–95%
Pct. Passing 3/8-inch sieve	90–100%
Chemical analysis	
Nitrogen, NO$_3$ (RCSP)	25–100 ppm
Phosphorus, P$_2$O$_5$ (RCSP)	20-200 ppm
Potassium, K$_2$O (RCSP)	≥ 150 ppm

Other macro- and micro-nutrients shall be incorporated in the formulation in initial proportions suitable for supporting the specified planting.

2.07. BORDER UNITS

To allow free flow across edges, these units should be installed on top of strips of sheet drain.

A. Edge Elements
These are used to separate gravel margins from the green roof proper.
Cantilever (i.e., "L-shaped") border units (These are available in fiber-reinforced cement, stainless steel,
recycled polyethylene, or aluminum). These are typically non-perforated.

Height:	≥ 0.25 inch (6.35 mm) higher than the top of the growth media layer
Base Length:	greater of 6 inches (15.2 cm) or 1.5 times the height of the element

Note: Gravel margins are not necessary on many projects. Furthermore, on roofs with pitches of less than 1 inch per foot (8.33 percent, a separation fabric diaphragm may be used in lieu of rigid boundary units.

B. Eave baskets
These are used to contain gravel at the margin in eave areas. The units are designed to resist the downslope forces of green roof materials. They are required for roofs with pitches in excess of 1 inch per foot

(8.33 percent). Eave baskets are 'U-shaped' border units (These are available in perforated stainless steel or perforated aluminum).

2.09. DRAIN ACCESS CHAMBERS

A. These are designed to enclose roof drains and scuppers. They prevent intrusion of media and protect the drains from clogging by wind-blown paper, leaves, etc. Drain access chambers are typically 12 inches (30.5 cm) square (or 12 inches in diameter). In order to use these chambers, the drains must be finished in accordance with the Roofscapes, Inc. requirements (see 1.05 Submittals). Drain access chambers are available in a variety of forms and materials, including aluminum, stainless steel, plastic, and fiber-reinforced cement.

2.10. DRAINAGE SYSTEM

A. Polyethylene or polystyrene drain sheet. This sheet is used as an underlayment for border units to promote free flow. The sheet is a dimpled membrane sheet, satisfying the following specifications:

Membrane thickness (ASTM D-751)	≥ 20 mil (.02 in or 0.51 mm)
Height (ASTM D-1777)	≥ 0.40 in (1.0 cm)
Compressive strength	$\geq 5,200$ lb/ft^2 (25,388.6 kg/m^2)
Transmissivity @ i=1 (ASTM D-4716)	≥ 16 gal/min/ft
(confining pressure of 500 psf) (i=1)	
Fabric:	
Permittivity (ASTM-D4491)	≥ 1.8 sec^{-1}
Puncture resistance (ASTM-D4833)	≥ 50 lb (22.7 kg)
Mullen burst Strength (ASTM-D3786)	≥ 160 lb/in^2 (46,822.4 kg/mm^2)
Grab tensile (ASTM D-4632)	≥ 100 lb (45.4 kg)

PART 3. EXECUTION

3.01. EXAMINE WATERPROOFING

A. Examine the completed waterproofing system, with the roofing applicator present, for compliance with drawings, installation tolerances, and other conditions affecting performance.

    1. For the record, prepare a written report, endorsed by the roofing applicator and the vegetated cover installer. As appropriate, list conditions that may be detrimental to the performance of the work.

    2. Proceed only after unsatisfactory conditions have been corrected.

B. The owner shall delineate material and equipment laydown areas on the roof.
The owner shall also specify the maximum aggregate load permitted within each laydown area.

3.02. PREPARE SURFACE

A. The surface of the waterproofing system shall be swept and washed.

B. Until the drainage media course is installed, traffic over the working area shall be strictly controlled and limited to essential personnel only.

C. Heavily traveled areas (e.g., corridors for transporting media to the working areas) must be protected in a manner approved by the waterproofing installer.

D. Suitably protect laydown areas using ?-inch (12.7 mm)plywood or particle board over 1-inch (25.4 mm) sheets of expanded polystyrene (EPS), or similar sheathing material.

3.04. INSTALL ROOT-BARRIER SUBSYSTEM

For waterproofing systems that are not root resistant:
A. Roll out root-barrier membrane. The layout should minimize the aggregate seam length. Overlap adjoining sheets by a minimum of 2 inches (5.1 cm). Allow slack to accommodate contraction during cold weather.

B. Weld seams using hot-air welding equipment (Leister, or equivalent)

C. One-hundred percent of all seams shall be tested by one of the following methods:
    1. Electrical field vector mapping (available through Roofscapes, Inc.)
    2. Air lance
    3. Hand scribe

3.05. INSTALL PROTECTION LAYER

Roll out the protection fabric on top of the completed waterproofing system.
Overlap seams a minimum of 6 inches (15.2 cm).

3.06. INSTALL INTERNAL DRAINAGE CONDUIT

A. Assemble the internal drainage conduit according to the layout provided by the System Provider Roofscapes, Inc.

B. Cover the assembled conduit using separation fabric.

C. The conduit will be completely concealed below the top of the growth media when properly installed.

3.07. INSTALL DRAIN ACCESS CHAMBERS AND BORDER UNITS, ETC.

A. Assemble edge elements and eave baskets on top of 2-foot (0.6 m) wide strips of sheet drain. Cover the edge elements and sheet drain with separation fabric to prevent intrusion of media.

B. Immediately place granular media, stone, or course aggregate to stablize the border units.

C. Wrap drain access chambers with separation fabric to prevent intrusion of media.

3.08. INSTALL GRANULAR DRAINAGE MEDIA

A. Place the granular drain media layer. The media shall be dispensed at the roof level in a manner that will not suddenly increase the load to the roof. It shall be immediately spread to the specified thickness.

B. Immediately cover with separation fabric. As necessary, protect from wind using temporary ballast.

3.09. INSTALL GROWTH MEDIA

A. Place the growth media layer. The media shall be dispensed at the roof level in a manner that will not suddenly increase the load to the roof. It shall be immediately spread to the specified thickness, plus 10 percent, after moderate compaction. Unless otherwise approved, compaction shall be using a 4-foot (1.2 m) wide lawn roller with a total load of not less than 200 lbs and not more than 300 lbs.

B. Thoroughly soak with water using a sprinkler or hand sprayer. For a 4-inch (10.2 cm) growth media layer, expect to use about 25 gallons per 100 square foot (255 L/m^2).

3.10. PLANT VEGETATION

A. Direct Seeding Method
    1. The planting mixture should include species that will generate a continuous ground cover. Maximum mature plant heights shall be less than 24 inches. Large drifts of single species should be avoided.
    2. All extensive planting schemes in temperate climates must incorporate non-deciduous or semi-deciduous *Sedum* species. These should be established from fresh cuttings. The plant mixture should include a minimum of four species of *Sedum* in approximately equal quantities. Cuttings should be distributed over the surface of the media at a minimum rate of 30 lbs/1000 square feet (1.5 kg/ 10 m2). In most temperate climates, planting using *Sedum* cuttings can be undertaken from April 15 through May 15 and September 15 through October 31. When installed outside this window, frequent watering may be required until the plants are established.
    3. Seed mixtures (optional) should include a minimum of five perennial varieties. Turf forming grasses should be avoided. Consult with the system provider, Roofscapes, Inc. for recommendations concerning the incorporation of grasses in planting mixtures. For seeding rates and seasonal restrictions consult the seed provider. Prepared seed mixtures are available that are tailored to different climatic zones. In no case shall the seeding rates be less than 250 seed/square yard (300/square meter) (all species combined).
    4. If more than 24 hours have elapsed since installing and soaking the growth media, thoroughly resoak the growth media prior to commencing the broadcast distribution of seed or cuttings.

5. Immediately cover with the wind protection system.

6. As required, soak the prepared seed bed at the completion of planting operations.

7. Depending on the season that plants are established and the plants included, periodic watering may be required during the first growing season.

B. *Plug Installation*

1. All extensive planting schemes in temperate climates must incorporate non-deciduous or semi-deciduous *Sedum* species. *Sedum* should represent at least 25 percent of the all installed plants. Additionally, the plant mixture should include a minimum of four different species of *Sedum* in approximately equal quantities.

2. Non-*Sedum* varieties should be selected that are adapted to the specific growing conditions.

3. Plant installation may occur April-October.

4. Plants should be established from 72-cell 3-inch (7.6 cm)deep plugs propagated in sterile nursery medium, according to the plant provider's recommendations. Plugs larger than this can be used. However, the establishment rate is typically better with the smaller plants. The recommended minimum planting rate is one plant per square foot (11/square meter).

5. Thoroughly soak the growth media prior to commencing planting

6. As required. Make cuts in the wind blanket to insert the plugs. The plugs should be set into the media to their full depth and the media pressed firmly around the installed plug. At the end of each day, soak those areas that have been newly planted.

7. Depending on the season that plants are established and plants included, periodic watering may be required during the first growth season.

8. Do not mulch

C. Pre-vegetated Mats

Consult the system provider for information about type and availability of pre-vegetated mats.

3.11. PROVIDE 2-YEAR MAINTENANCE SERVICE

The green roof installer shall offer a two-year maintenance service. This service will include:

A. Hand weeding and/or chemical weeding and fertilization, as required to maintain the health and vigor of the plants.

B. The installer shall guarantee an 80 percent cover rate at the end of 24 months. As necessary, plants shall be replanted to achieve this requirement.

NOTICE

No warranty expressed or implied is offered for any work based on the information provided herein, unless:

> **1) Roofscapes, Inc. is provided a supervisory role in the construction of the vegetated roof cover, and**
>
> **2) Installation and maintenance of the vegetated cover is provided by a contractor that is trained and licensed by Roofscapes, Inc.**

Roofscapes, Inc. will not assume any responsibility for the inclusion of this material in specifications or documents published by others.

MEDIA SELECTION

The following is a guide provided by Charlie Miller, PE of Roofscapes, Inc. in which the criteria for the selection of different growing media are described. The choice of green roof planting media depends on many factors. This memorandum is concerned only with veneer landscapes, which can range in depth from a couple of inches ("extensive" vegetated covers) to several feet ("intensive" roof landscapes). However, the principals of design are the same, regardless of depth. Using veneer landscapes, it is generally possible to support larger plants using shallower depths of planting media than would otherwise be possible. This is due to three factors:

1. The roots of plants can extend horizontally over large areas. This increases access to moisture and nutrients.

2. Containerized plants often suffer from temperature shock (hot or cold) due to the large surface areas of the container, as compared to its volume. Veneer landscapes have a lower surface area.

3. Moisture conditions change more gradually, due to the lateral continuity of the media

The design of veneer landscapes incorporates multiple layers. With few exceptions the layers are arranged so that the particle size increases with depth. This mimics many natural systems, where surface layers of topsoil, rich in loam and organic matter, overlie sandy "subsoil," and eventually a foundation of fractured rock or shale. As in nature, we want the plants to send their roots into the deepest zone (i.e., the bedrock) where moisture and temperature conditions will be most stable. Therefore, irrigation, when required, is introduced in the deepest layer.

Few green roofs have more than three layers; most have two layers. The uppermost layer should be effective in absorbing and holding moisture derived from rainfall and dew. The underlying well-drained media will generally have a lower moisture storage capacity. However, its high surface area will help stabilize humidity in the system. To reduce weight it is also common to replace the granular drainage layer with a synthetic drain sheet (e.g., Meadowflor' by Roofscapes). However, it always advisable to use a granular drainage layer when possible.

Five types of media are most commonly encountered. These are:

1. Drainage media (i.e., base layer)   D   (e.g., Roofmeadow® A)
2. Single-layer extensive media   SE   (e.g., Roofmeadow® M2)
3. Two-layer extensive media   DE   (e.g., Roofmeadow® M3)
4. Intensive media for three layer installations I (e.g., Roofmeadow® M4)
5. Turf media   T   Turf

Key attributes of the various media include:
- Grain-size distribution (generally, clay is a negligible ingredient in all media formulations)
- Moisture content at maximum water capacity
- Moisture content at 'field capacity' (i.e., a measure of water retention capability during dry periods)
- Void ratio (air content) at maximum water capacity
- Volatile fraction (i.e., a measure of organic content)
- Maximum salinity
- Cation exchange capacity
- Total Nitrogen

There are many ways to prepare formulations that meet these criteria. However, depending on the ingredients used, the weight and appearance of the media may vary greatly. From a qualitative standpoint, the various media types are characterized in Table 1.

LIVING/GREEN WALLS

Table 1. GENERAL MEDIA CHARACTERISTICS				
	Typical Grain-Size Distribution	Maximum Water Content	Moisture at Field Capacity	Volatile Fraction
D	Coarse Gravel	Low	Low	NA
SE	Gravelly Texture	Moderate	Moderate	Less than 8%
DE	Course to Fine Mixture (silt less than 15%	Moderate to High	High	Less than 8%
I	Sandy Texture (silt less than 20%	High	High	Less than 12%
T	Sandy Texture (silt less than 10%)	Moderate to High	Moderate	Less than 3%

(courtesy of Randy Sharp, Sharp & Diamond Landscape Architecture Inc.)

"Green wall" is an all-encompassing term that refers to all forms of vegetated wall surfaces. Two major system categories fall under the umbrella term "green walls": living walls and green façades. Green walls have a great potential for positive environmental change in dense urban areas due to their ability to introduce much needed greenery over currently unused urban wall spaces. Based on current applications and available green roof data, there are considerable cost-savings to both the public and private sectors associated with green walls. For example, the reintroduction of vegetation into cities in all of its forms has been correlated with the reduction of the UHI (Urban Heat Island) effect, and therefore with reduced energy consumption.

Living wall systems are composed of pre-vegetated panels or integrated fabric systems that are affixed to a structural wall or frame. Modular panels can be comprised of polypropylene plastic containers, geotextiles and irrigation, growing medium and vegetation. The panels support a great diversity and density of plant species (e.g. a lush mixture of groundcovers, ferns, low shrubs, perennial flowers and edible plants).

Due to the vertical nature, diversity and density of plant life, living walls require more intensive maintenance (e.g. regular water and a supply of nutrients to fertilize the plants) than green façades or green roofs. Living wall installations can be found in both tropical and temperate locations. Living walls perform well in full sun, shade and also interior applications.

Many living walls are comprised of pre-vegetated panels that are grown in a greenhouse and are assembled 4 to 6 months later on a frame that is attached to a structural wall. A wide diversity of plants can be used in living wall applications. Species are usually selected based upon their tolerance of the vertical growing system, site-specific environmental conditions, color, texture, rate of propagation, and root system. The panels support groundcovers, ferns, low shrubs, perennial flowers and edible plants.

For living walls, a high density concrete wall may be watertight, however with metal or wood frame structures, a waterproof membrane may be required, installed in advance. At the start of the installation, a steel frame is secured to the wall by attaching anchor bolts. The panels are installed in horizontal rows starting at one end.

A drip irrigation system is installed for water distribution at the top of the wall, or for individual panels depending on the system. The excess water that flows through the panels drips on to a drainage bed comprised of river rock over a perforated drain line. For other living wall applications, water can be collected at the bottom of the wall in a tray or gutter and be re-circulated to the top of the wall or stored for reuse.

The growing medium in the living wall panels is fully saturated once a day during the first week after installation. Thereafter, water is applied to maintain enough moisture without over saturation. The living wall is monitored for plant performance during a variety of conditions including intensive rainfall, wind, snow and prolonged periods of freezing conditions. A modular system is designed for easy replacement of individual panels or groups of panels if required. The system allows for the flexibility over time if the client wants to try different plant species.

A living wall can be irrigated with potable water, collected rainwater, or water from an integrated grey water recycling system. Irrigation systems can take several forms including a channel system carrying water along each row of plants, drip irrigation with emitters located above each panel and continuous synthetic moisture fabric in which water is distributed at the top of the wall.

Green façades are systems in which climbing plants or cascading groundcovers are trained to cover specially designed supporting structures. Plants are rooted at the base of these structures, in intermediate planters or on rooftops. Green façades can be attached to existing walls or built as freestanding structures. Recent North American and European installations commonly rely on trellises, rigid panels or cable systems to support vines and keep them away from building surfaces.

The following two tables are provided with the permission of Forschungsgesellschaft Landschaftsentwicklung Landschafts-bau e.V. (www.fll.de). Table 1 is from the 1992 translation into English, reissued in 1995, of the *Guidelines for the Planning, Execution and Upkeep of Green-Roof Sites*. Table 2 is a new version of the table being prepared for use in an upcoming edition.

Table 1. STANDARD COURSE DEPTHS FOR DIFFERENT TYPES OF ROOF-GREENING			
Type of roof-greening	Depth of the vegetation support course in cm	Depth of the drainage course in cm	Total depth of the green-roof superstructure in cm
Intensive greening with high upkeep costs, regular watering Flat roofs only Grassed area Low-lying shrubs Medium-height shrubs Tall shrubs and bushes Large bushes and small trees Medium-size trees Large trees≥	 ≥ 10 ≥ 10 ≥ 15 ≥ 25 ≥ 45 ≥ 80 ≥ 125	 ≥ 2 ≥ 2 ≥ 2 ≥ 10 ≥ 15 * ≥ 20 * ≥ 25 *	 ≥ 15 ** ≥ 15 ** ≥ 20 ** ≥ 35 ≥ 60 ≥ 100 ≥ 150

Type of greening	Depth of the vegetation support course in cm	Over-all depth of the green-roof superstructure, in cm	
		Depth of the drainage course in cm	Total depth of the green-roof superstructure in cm
Simple intensive greening, moderate upkeep costs, periodic watering flat green-roof sites with: Grass / herbaceous plants (grass roof, rough-grassed area) Wild shrubs, coppices Coppices and shrubs Coppices sloping green-roof sites with: Grass / herbaceous plants (grass roof, rough-grassed area)	 ≥ 8 ≥ 8 ≥ 10 ≥ 15 ≥ 15	 ≥10 ≥ 10 ≥ 12 ≥ 17 ≥ 17	 ≥12 ≥12 ≥14 ≥ 19 ≥19
Extensive greening, low upkeep costs, without supplementary watering arrangements flat green-roof sites with: Moss-*sedum* *Sedum*-moss-herbaceous plants *Sedum*-grass-herbaceous plants Grass and herbaceous plants (dry lawn) sloping green-roof sites with: Moss-*sedum* *Sedum*-moss-herbaceous plants *Sedum*-grass-herbaceous plants	 2 - 5 5 - 8 8 - 12 ≥ 15 2 - 5 5 - 10 10 - 15	 4 - 7 7 - 10 10 - 14 ≥ 17 4 - 7 7 - 12 12 - 17	 6 - 9 9 - 12 12 - 16 ≥ 19 6 - 9 9 - 14 14 - 19

* The sizes selected for drainage courses are not determined solely by water drainage needs, but also by the additional space needed for root growth and by the need to ensure a good air supply.
** Overall depth is greater than the sum of the depths of the two courses. Depending on the types of materials used, the depths of the vegetation support or drainage course will need to be increased in order to achieve the quoted overall depth.

Table 2. STANDARD COURSE DEPTHS FOR DIFFERENT TYPES OF ROOF-GREENING

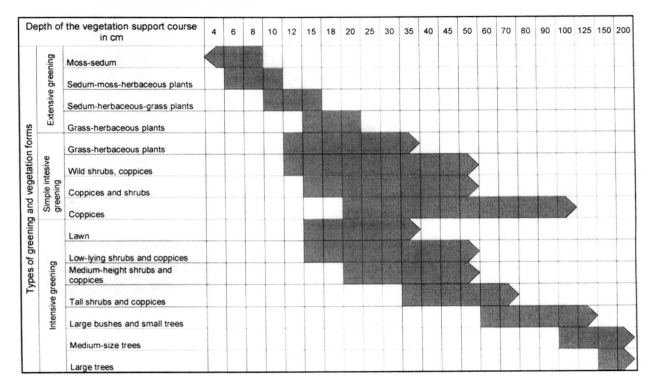

		Depth of the vegetation support course in cm	4	6	8	10	12	15	18	20	25	30	35	40	45	50	60	70	80	90	100	125	150	200

(Types of greening and vegetation forms)

Extensive greening: Moss-sedum; Sedum-moss-herbaceous plants; Sedum-herbaceous-grass plants; Grass-herbaceous plants

Simple intensive greening: Grass-herbaceous plants; Wild shrubs, coppices; Coppices and shrubs; Coppices

Intensive greening: Lawn; Low-lying shrubs and coppices; Medium-height shrubs and coppices; Tall shrubs and coppices; Large bushes and small trees; Medium-size trees; Large trees

WATER RETENTION

Effects of roof-greening include reduction of the water run-off caused by precipitation, the storage of retained rain water in order to meet water needs of the vegetation grown on the roof, and the slowing down of draining processes affecting excess water. From both ecological and economic perspectives as well as in terms of drainage techniques, these features are significant. The following reference values are used to identify the desired effects: maximum water capacity; water permeability; coefficient of discharge; slowing down of water run-off; and annual coefficient of discharge.

MAXIMUM WATER CAPACITY

Maximum water capacity serves to identify the water storage capability of materials used in the layered superstructure in compacted condition. The maximum water capacity indicates the water content of a substance upon previous saturation with water followed by a 2-hour dropping off period. This reference value is used to indicate vegetation-technical characteristics.

Appendix F: IMPERIAL TO METRIC MEASUREMENTS CONVERSION CHART

If you have	Multiply by	To calculate
LENGTH		
inches	25.4	millimeters
inches	2.54	centimeters
feet	.3048	meters
yards	.9144	meters
millimeters	0.0393	inches
centimeters	0.393	inches
meters	3.28	feet
meters	1.093	yards
miles	1.61	kilometers
kilometers	0.621	miles
AREA		
square feet	0.0929	square meters
square meters	10.763	square feet
square miles	2.59	square kilometers
square kilometers	0.386	square miles
acres	4,046.87	square meters
acres	0.40468	hectares
hectares	2.47	acres
VOLUME, WEIGHT and DENSITY		
cubic feet	0.0283	cubic meter
cubic yards	0.7645	cubic meter
cubic meters	35.314	cubic feet
cubic meters	1.31	cubic yards
lbs.	0.453592	kgs
kgs	2.2046	lbs.
kgs	0.001	metric tons
lbs/f^2	4.88243	kg/m^2
kg/m^2	0.2048	lbs/f^2
lbs/f^3	16.0185	kg/m^3
gallons	3.7854	liters
liters	0.2641	gallons
100 board feet	0.235974	cubic meters
TEMPERATURE		
degrees F	5/9 (degrees F – 32) or (degrees F – 32)/1.8	degrees C
degrees C	(degrees C x 1.8) + 32	degrees F
TEMPERATURE INTERVAL		
degrees F	0.555556	degrees C
degrees C	1.7999985	degrees F

THICKNESS

One mil is one one-thousands of an inch = .0254 mm; a weird metric/English hybrid when you think about it: as a result, 1mm equals 39.4 mil. Therefore,

mils	0.0254	millimeters
mils	0.001	inches
millimeters	39.4	mils
inches	1000	mils

INDEX